CW00555636

A HISTORY OF THE UNIVERSITY OF WALES
VOLUME 1

The University Movement
in Wales

J. GWYNN WILLIAMS

CARDIFF
UNIVERSITY OF WALES PRESS
1993

British Library Cataloguing in Publication Data

A catalogue record for this book is available from the British Library.

ISBN 0-7083-1239-X

Typeset by Action Typesetting, Gloucester
Printed in Great Britain by The Cromwell Press, Broughton Gifford, Wiltshire

I
goffáu
cadernid a doethineb
sylfaenwyr
Prifysgol Cymru

Contents

Illustrations

Acknowledgements

The illustrations in this volume are reproduced by kind permission of the following:

The National Library of Wales: 2, 13, 15, 16, 17.
The National Monuments Record at the Royal Commission on Ancient and Historical Monuments of Wales: 1.
The University College of Wales: Aberystwyth, 3.
The University College of North Wales, Bangor: 4, 5, 6, 7, 9, 12, 14, 16, 18, 19, 20.
The University College of Wales College of Cardiff: 8, 10.
The University of Wales Registry: 11.

Preface

Not long after I accepted the University of Wales's kind invitation to write part of its history I speedily discovered how little I knew of the university movement which led to the Charter of 1893 and which left an indelible imprint upon the University itself. Hence this preliminary volume which will, I hope, be a contribution to our knowledge of higher education in Wales. In a work of this kind it is not, of course, possible to give a detailed account of departmental developments; such information must be sought in the histories of individual colleges.

I am greatly obliged to the staff of various institutions: to Mr Huw Flynn Hughes of the University Registry who guided me through the University archives; to Mr R. Brinkley of the College Library, Aberystwyth and to Dr I. J. Salmon at Yr Hen Goleg; to Mr B. James and to Mrs Susan Bellamy, both formerly of the College Library, Cardiff; to Mr R. G. Pritchard, in charge of the Welsh Library, Bangor and to the Reverend D. T. W. Price of St David's College, Lampeter. At the National Library, justly celebrated for its expert service to readers, I received welcome assistance from Mr J. Graham Jones and Mr Richard Lewis.

I am most grateful to the following for discussing various matters with me: Dr W. P. Griffith, Professor Geraint H. Jenkins, Dr Gwilym Arthur Jones, Professor Ieuan Gwynedd Jones, Mr Donald Moore, Dr Prys Morgan, Mr Ned Thomas, Mr Alwyn Roberts, Professor Glanmor Williams and Dr Huw Glynn Williams.

Lord Cledwyn of Penrhos and Mr David Jones, Librarian of the House of Lords, helped me to understand parliamentary procedure when the Charter was under examination in both Houses of Parliament.

It is entirely fitting in a federal university that my greatest single debt is to a scholar in a sister college; Dr E. L. Ellis, the historian of the University College of Wales, was the first to undertake a systematic exploration of sources at the Public Record Office and at the National Library in order to understand the history of a Welsh college, especially in its social setting. Dr B. L. Davies generously lent me his valuable unpublished studies of Hugh Owen and Henry Richard; I also derived much profit from conversations with him. Mr Tomos Roberts has helped me in matters large and small and has allowed me to take advantage of his unrivalled knowledge of the rich manuscript collections at the Bangor Library, of which he is the genial guardian. I am also grateful to my own College for facilitating my studies in every possible way and I extend warm thanks to Principal Eric Sunderland. Mrs Moira Thornton, who typed this volume, deciphered my handwriting with exemplary skill.

The staff of the University of Wales Press have been characteristically helpful and I pay tribute in particular to Ms Liz Powell for her care and unfailing courtesy. My wife has shown remarkable forbearance when weighty materials relating to the University colonized many parts of our home. She also read the whole of the typescript to my considerable gain.

BANGOR, 1993   J. GWYNN WILLIAMS

I

Aspirations

In 1886 a professor at one of the Welsh colleges drew attention to the celebration of the eight hundredth anniversary of the University of Bologna.[1] Professors were there in long gowns and brilliant hoods and students in strange garb. The Germans had long scarves and swords; the French surrounded their tricolour flag; the Italians brought with them the products of their towns, a wine cask from Turin, a cheese from Pavia and an ox prepared for slaughter from Padua. Bismarck and Boulanger were for the nonce placed in perspective. The writer went on to speak of Norway, a country no larger in population than Wales, yet with its own university. Had he felt so inclined he could have told his readers of universities in small countries, such as Estonia, not a republic until 1918, forced to endure the supremacy of Danes and Swedes, Germans and Russians for several centuries but which had a university since 1632, and Scotland with her four universities before the end of the sixteenth century. Representatives at Bologna who came from beyond Europe included Americans and Indians and the writer reflected upon Sir William 'Oriental' Jones (born a Welshman) who, almost unaided, had unveiled the secrets of Indian literature. The land, however, which had produced the Mabinogion lacked a university 'and so could not be present to do honour to the first of Universities at its birthday gathering'.[2]

For a brief moment, salvation had appeared at hand. The first known attempt to found a university in Wales was in time of war. During the early fifteenth century Owain Glyn Dŵr assumed the title 'Prince of Wales' and led his countrymen to liberate Wales from English rule. He aroused widespread enthusiasm; there were reports of Welsh students at Oxford and of labourers from England returning home to fight under his banner; he enlisted the support of the squirearchy of Wales and also of ecclesiastics trained in universities and experienced in the papal court, and he sought alliances with the Scots, the Irish and the French. In 1406 he issued the 'Pennal Letter', proclaiming his support of the French anti-pope at Avignon and clearly proposing that there should be

an independent church as well as an autonomous state. St David's was
to be a metropolitan church and only Welsh-speakers were to be
appointed to benefices in Wales. One clause, aptly described as 'the
most innovative and forward-looking'[3] in the agreement, declared that
there should be two universities, or *studia generalia*, as they are also
called in the original statement,[4] one in north Wales and the other in
south Wales, evidently intended to prepare men for service in church
and state. Early in the second decade of the fifteenth century the
rebellion collapsed and long centuries passed before there were realistic
plans to create a university in Wales. The departmental committee
which reported in 1881 recommended a college in both north and south
Wales, a pallid version of Glyn Dŵr's programme in 1406. This much,
however, could be said. The Glyn Dŵr uprising was a popular revolt
and the struggle for a university in the nineteenth century was a
popular movement. At the root of both lay a profound sense of a
separate national identity.

There is no sign that the first of the royal Tudors ever contemplated
planting a university in Wales or that he was ever petitioned to do so.
It was sufficient to many of his countrymen that 'the strong deliverer'
had fulfilled bardic prophecies by restoring Britain to its ancient
dignity. In any case Henry was parsimonious to a degree and he sat
upon a precarious throne. During his grand-daughter's reign Jesus
College was founded, the only Oxford college established during her
reign. The 'first benefactor',[5] as he has been called, was Hugh Price of
Brecon and the charter was granted by the Queen in 1571. There was
nothing in the charter itself nor in the names of the original fellows and
scholars to suggest a formal association with Wales, but informal links
were so greatly strengthened during the principalships of Francis
Mansell, Eubule Thelwall (the second founder) and Leoline Jenkins,
the College's most generous benefactor, that Jesus became regarded as
primarily a college for Welshmen. Students from Wales were also
attracted to St John's College, Cambridge, because of the benefactions
of their countrymen. It was reported that when John Williams (later
Archbishop of York) entered the College in 1598 he was 'much
welcom'd to *Cambridge* by the old Britaines of North-Wales, who
praised him mightily in all places of the University'.[6] It was not until
1600 that Sir William Herbert, a Monmouthshire squire, gave thought
to housing a college in his own mansion at Tintern in the Wye Valley.
His purpose was to provide an income of £400 per annum out of lands

in Monmouthshire and the appropriated parsonage of Llanidan in Anglesey. Herbert hoped to counter 'backwardness in religion',[7] but his plan evaporated. The puritans in power employed their best endeavours to refashion society; educational experiments burgeoned. Manchester in 1640 petitioned Parliament to become the third university in the land, 'many ripe and hopeful wits being utterly lost for want of education';[8] Oxford and Cambridge were too far and the expense too great. Rich northerners, it was indicated, were prepared to dip deep into their pockets. York, too, had urgent claims: bright youths were clouded in ignorance; the distance and 'dearness of the southern academy [*sic*]' meant sending them to the universities of Scotland which had 'long gloried in that happiness as to enjoy the literature of four',[9] as Welshmen were not slow to proclaim in the nineteenth century. Neither Manchester nor York succeeded, but Durham, supported by Cromwell, began in 1657, though the expectation that it should grow into 'a Literary Workhouse'[10] faded. Oxford and Cambridge no more cared for competition in the seventeenth century than in the nineteenth. In any case, the Restoration put an end to such ventures. A similar fate awaited a scheme designed to advance higher education in Wales. The readiness of many Welshmen to support Charles I seemed convincing proof that the light of the Gospel had not penetrated into dark places. Richard Baxter, the Presbyterian divine, in 1647 consulted the governor of Shrewsbury as to the possibility of raising a college for Wales in the town. Ten years later he still pressed the claims of Shrewsbury, as opposed to Ludlow, the seat of the Council of Wales, where there were many corrupting distractions. Shrewsbury had plentiful accommodation and, as he told a Welsh correspondent, it was best to have a college 'a little within the verge of England . . . that your sons may learn English';[11] it had 'a gallant free schoole' and some of its funds could be used by 'the Academy' to teach a hundred students. Once it had got under way, contributions would flow from people who would not themselves have taken the first step. The two Welshmen prominent in the deliberations were John Lewis, Glasgrug, Cardiganshire and John Ellis, the scholarly Rector of Dolgellau. Lewis, sensing that Oxford and Cambridge would oppose the proposals, gave such signals of submission as would placate an oriental potentate. The college would be 'without the least entrenchment unto our two great universities; but as wholly derivative and subordinate to them both for Professors and Degrees, or thence confirmed'.[12] To John Ellis there was a compelling case for placing the college in 'some equidistant towne'[13] in mid-Wales, such as Machynlleth, but particularly Aberystwyth or Cardigan because both had castles. Since Aberystwyth Castle had been blown up during the Civil War it seems that he was thinking of 'an Auditorium', as on the continent, an arrangement more suitable for the Mediterranean than for the shores of Cardigan Bay. It is indeed remarkable that Wales's first university college should be at Aberystwyth, close to the castle and in the Castle Hotel. The use of Church revenues for educational purposes was taken for granted in 1657, but over two and a half centuries were to pass before the University and its colleges received the benefit of Church lands. The question did not now arise, for although Cromwell, because of his 'love to our nation'[14] (according to Ellis), might well have favoured a Welsh academy, such plans were swept away at the Restoration. That, too, was the fate of sixty-five schools (with one exception) set up by the state in Wales between 1650 and 1653, in some of which the classical languages were taught. Those who later deplored the absence of a satisfactory system of secondary schools in Wales before 1889 might cogently have argued that the Long Parliament had attended to the proper priorities.[15]

The Nonconformists, as they must be called after 1662, did not surrender all hope of higher education.[16] Charles Edwards, for instance, entertained expectations in 1677 that the leaders of the nation would establish one or two colleges where able young men would receive wholesome learning preparatory to careers in the ministry or the state.[17] However, this was but a wisp of aspiration. Nonconformists, to whom we shall presently return, certainly gave attention to higher education in their academies, but these were not degree-awarding bodies. The path to the older universities was stony and was only partially eased in 1687 when seven fellowships were assigned at Jesus College to north Wales and seven to south Wales, and by the endowments of Edmund Meyrick in 1712 to help poor Welsh students at the college. In such circumstances it was not surprising that some writers sought sustenance from a generous interpretation of a remote past. Theophilus Evans, drawing inspiration from such authors as Geoffrey of Monmouth, spoke with confidence of the gifted scholars of the University of Caerleon-on-Usk who had met Augustine on the borders of Worcestershire and Hereford, as conveniently close then, he tells us, as Oxford was to be later.[18] In fact, we are to gather that in the fifth century the universities of Bangor Monachorum (Bangor-on-Dee) and of Caerleon surpassed those of England, much disturbed by internecine wars. Bangor Monachorum engaged the attention of Gibbon himself who, following Camden, spoke of the massacre at the battle of Chester in the early seventh century of 'above two thousand brethren'[19] who had declined St Augustine's invitation to co-operate in the conversion of the heathen English. Iolo Morganwg, having fallen under the spell of the Romantic movement, devised a fable (entirely baseless as we have seen) that Henry VII had granted a charter to the Abbot of Neath, Leyshon Thomas, to found a university at Neath.[20] What is certain is that in Henry VIII's reign the poet Lewis Morgannwg wrote this tribute to the abbey of Neath: 'The convent of Neath, how much talked of in England! The lamp of France and Ireland! A school much resorted to by scholars . . . With its organs for the White Men, and the great praise of disputants, Arithmetic, Music, Grammar(?), Philosophy, Rhetoric, Civil and Canon (Law).'[21] The word 'convent' here ('unifersi' in the original) means a religious community and is not used in its later, restricted sense. The authors of the first history of the University of Wales were prudently hesitant, wondering how much should be attributed to 'poetic license and the exigencies of our inexorable metre'.[22] They were quite persuaded, however, of the reputation of the abbots of Neath for learning and piety, and Glanmor Williams has long established that Neath's last abbot, to whom the poem was addressed, 'enjoyed considerable standing in his own order'.[23]

Delectable myths − that of Madog is yet another − died hard. The chairman of Newport's school board in 1880 told the Aberdare Committee that the Welsh had 'cultivated learning from time immemorial',[24] the arts and sciences before the Christian era; during the early years of Christianity Wales was celebrated for its colleges at Llanilltud Fawr and at Bangor Iscoed, and 'our history gives us a claim to have a national existence again in connexion with learning'. In 1883 those who petitioned for a college in Bangor and in Rhyl did not hesitate to appeal to a distant past. Refugees had arrived at Bangor Fawr (as it was called) from Bangor Monachorum and the Rhyl appellants inflated the number of resident students at Bangor Monachorum to 2,400.[25] It was not long before necessary myths were exposed to necessary scholarship at national colleges. The consequences were not always welcomed.

The literary revival of the eighteenth century, however, prepared the way for the educational movements of the nineteenth. The principal figures were Goronwy Owen, the Lewis brothers of Anglesey and Evan Evans (Ieuan Brydydd Hir); Evans, we are told, advocated a college or university for Wales.[26] The collecting of manuscripts and books provided a rich legacy for later generations, whilst the scholarship of the Celtic polymath Edward Lhuyd at the beginning of the century heralded the achievements of notable Welsh scholars two centuries later. The Methodist awakening stirred many members of a nation, relaxed, even carefree in religious matters, to an awareness and to a conviction, often dramatic, of personal salvation. In the course of time, though certainly not at once, Methodism gave a powerful impetus to the university movement. The swift spread of an evangelical religion was a clear signal that all was not well with the Church of England in Wales, a matter of immediate concern to Thomas Burgess when he was raised to the see of St David's in 1803. Burgess was no ordinary bishop. According to Rowland Williams he was 'the best English Prelate the Principality ever saw',[27] thus giving him well-merited precedence over William Laud and Samuel Horsley. He changed his mind towards the Welsh language, to which he was initially inimical and which he found more difficult to master than Hebrew. His first visitation to 'this dilapidated part of the Church of England'[28] must have greatly dismayed him. In the first half of the eighteenth century, we are reliably informed, one-third of the ordinands were graduates; in the second half, only one in seventeen.[29] Burgess may not have known the statistics, but the results were everywhere apparent. Nor could he ignore the fact that the two dioceses of south Wales were decidedly less well endowed than those of north Wales. There was also the colossal task of reclaiming the souls 'lost' to Methodism which embarked upon the proud venture of independence not long after his arrival. Whilst it would of course be wrong to ignore the work of the grammar schools and of the *offeiriaid llengar* (the literary priests) the situation was manifestly bad. One clear answer was a college to educate the clergy. At first Llanddewibrefi was actively canvassed; perhaps Brecon or Carmarthen would have been more suitable, but at length Lampeter, the market town on the banks of the Teifi, was pitched upon. Burgess himself gave liberally; there were benefactors from far and wide, including George IV, who contributed £1,000, whilst from the government itself came £5,000, the income from six benefices and £400 per annum (until the income reached £950).[31] The buildings, possibly more impressive at a distance than at close quarters,[32] were completed by 1827 at a cost of £20,000. In that year, too, the college opened its doors; in 1828 it received its first Charter.

The principal characteristics of St David's College upon foundation were threefold. It was residential; it provided a course of general culture in which literature, history and philosophy were linked with the study of Christian theology, and it had a royal charter which showed that its status (even though it did not award degrees) was akin to that of a university, not a theological college.[33] It must be allowed that the College at first did not greatly prosper, in common with the majority of young, small colleges. The inability to award degrees undermined its position and in 1847, for reasons which are not wholly apparent, the College's Visitor, Bishop Thirwall of St David's, refused to support any attempt to secure for the College a degree-awarding power. However, in that year Oxford and Cambridge agreed to appoint external examiners, thus, ostensibly at least, safeguarding the academic status of the College. In 1849, Sir Thomas Phillips, much concerned by the Reports of the Commissioners in 1847, devoted in his impressive reply a section to advance the claims of Lampeter to award its own degrees, as had Burgess earlier.[33] The granting of university privileges to Durham created a sense of injustice in Lampeter men 'deprived, in after life, of advantages dependent on the possession of a university degree, which they would have enjoyed had they graduated at Durham, or a Scotch or Irish university'.[34] The fear that the granting of an equal privilege would encourage a 'cry for separation' he at once dismissed as fanciful, though not every Welsh patriot would warm to the remark that the creation of a university at Durham 'has occasioned no longings for the restoration of the ancient Kingdom of Bernicia'.[35] He was, however, clear in his own mind that if the sole advantage which Lampeter could offer over a college in England was that Welsh could be studied there, then it deserved proper consideration since Welsh clergy were to minister to the needs of a Welsh-speaking population. In fact he saw no reason why degrees in arts and divinity should not be granted 'when the means exist to teach those branches of knowledge efficiently'.[36] In reply to those who objected that Lampeter trained clergy only, there was nothing to prevent the creation of another college to teach arts, science and general literature for all professions (with the exception of law and especially of

medicine which could only be taught in large cities). There can be no
doubt that the representations of Phillips and of others paved the way
for the granting to St David's in 1852 of a Charter to award a bachelor's
degree in divinity. Phillips had a large hand, too, in influencing the
ecclesiastical commissioners to recommend the removal of the College
to Brecon and to unite it with Christ's College, founded by Henry VIII
and now sunk into 'a common day school'.[37] The enabling legislation
of the following year envisaged that the two could become 'separate
parts of one University'.[38] St David's evidently did not lack powerful
friends and one is tempted to speculate what the future might have
been had Burgess's two successors as Visitors served the College with
like conviction and determination.

It seems certain that the most sustained exertions to promote St
David's College were made by 'The Association of Welsh Clergy in the
West Riding of Yorkshire'.[39] The Association was formed in 1821 and
was composed of Welsh clergy who had left their native land dispirited
by the inefficiency of their Church and who could no longer stomach
a system which had for generations given preferment to strangers and
neglected native clergy. It was their custom to assemble together on St
David's Day to consider matters relating to Wales and to conclude their
proceedings with dinner and toasts at a festive board decorated with
leeks. There was scarcely any aspect of Welsh life which did not engage
their attention. They published many pamphlets and regularly
petitioned Parliament; they pressed for the use of Welsh in assize
courts, county courts and quarter sessions; they declared that it was 'an
imperative duty' that 'the Welsh peasantry should be instructed
through the medium of their own language';[40] they castigated the
'cruel treatment of meritorious Welsh clergymen by the Anglo-Welsh
bishops'[41] and mercilessly exposed the mishmash which purported to
pass for Welsh at the lectern or upon the altar steps. Their principal
concern, however, was the creation of a university for Wales. Not the
least of its glories would be a university press: 'How many excellent
works might then be edited and published.'[42] Nearly seventy years
later the dream was fulfilled (though not the recommendation to
publish Dic Aberdaron's lexicon). The Association firmly resisted
attempts to move the college at Lampeter to Brecon and it always urged
that St David's should be prominently placed in any future university
of Wales. That this appeal was not narrowly sectarian may be gathered
from the Association's petition to Parliament in 1853:

... your petitioners, taking into consideration the object for which the college was principally intended, viz. the admission and education of these young men, who were destined to take holy orders, and also the peculiar state of the Principality, where four-fifths of its inhabitants are estranged from the Established Church, feel more and more the conviction that nothing short of a university, founded on broad and liberal principles, can meet the present necessities of the country, or raise the moral and intellectual character of its people, be they Churchmen or Dissenters.[43]

Whereas it would not be correct to say that the Association occupies a central place in the university movement, yet one cannot fail to be strangely warmed by the high patriotism of these Welsh clergy in dispersion.

Lampeter was by no means the only college in Wales which taught theology, but the others did not have a degree-awarding status.[44] Nonconformists, needless to say, set great store upon the training of their ministers. Nonconformist academies in England had been celebrated in the eighteenth century, partly because they provided a wider curriculum, including the natural sciences, than Oxford and Cambridge. Two of the theological colleges in Wales in the nineteenth century were direct descendants of early academies. The Presbyterian College at Carmarthen stemmed from the late seventeenth century; in fact, it did not, despite its name, belong to any single denomination, for it now trained students from among Protestant Dissenters of whatever persuasion. The Congregational College at Brecon (1838), later the Memorial College there (1869), owed its origin to the academy at Abergavenny (1757); the denomination opened another college at Bala in 1841. The Baptist College at Abergavenny (1807) removed to Pontypool in 1836; another was opened at Haverfordwest in 1839 and yet another at Llangollen in 1862. The Calvinistic Methodists founded colleges at Bala in 1837 and at Trefeca in 1842. Students who wished to graduate could not proceed to Oxford and Cambridge because of religious tests not fully abolished until 1871. Conscientious Nonconformists were thus unable to enter Jesus College, Oxford, despite its clear Welsh associations. It was natural, therefore, that they should resort to the Scottish universities, chiefly Glasgow and Edinburgh, in order to study moral philosophy or medicine; a few studied in Germany. It was to be expected that there would be lively attention in Wales when the 'University of London', as it was misleadingly called, opened its doors in Gower Street in 1828. There were no religious tests for staff or students; theology was not taught in any of its myriad forms; there was no residential accommodation and it was possible to live far more cheaply than at Oxford and Cambridge. There were, however, at this stage serious drawbacks. The 'University of London' could grant certificates but not degrees. Moreover, this 'sty of infidelity',[45] as it was genially called in *John Bull* in 1828, had aroused powerful foes. Anglicans and Tories united to found a college where young men would be imbued with the doctrines of the Church of England, and George IV, who had already smiled upon Lampeter, allowed it to be called 'King's College', a college, not a university, so as not to annoy Oxford and Cambridge. Neither London institution could grant degrees, but when the Whigs were returned to power a new University of London was granted a charter in 1836. It was a strange body, 'a mere government department . . . to conduct examinations',[46] and for this purpose some financial provision was made. The establishment in Gower Street had now to call itself University College. Like King's College, it presented students for the degree of the University, which was virtually an external body; the staff of neither college had a share in its management, nor in any matter relating to examinations. The new University was clearly a practical solution to a situation which had become ungovernable. Both sides wisely decided to accept the *fait accompli*. The Anglican, Tory establishment, however, could not readily reconcile itself to the presence in the metropolis of a godless college where the teaching of theology was not merely discouraged but prohibited. It is within this background that we are to understand the Anglican demand for the creation of the University of Durham (1832), principally designed for the training of clergymen, and also, immediately germane to our purpose, the active encouragement given to Lampeter by the granting of three separate charters, the second of which allowed it to award degrees in theology in 1852, as we have seen, and the third, degrees in arts in 1865.

The tutors at Welsh denominational colleges were for years faced with the heavy task of teaching at an elementary level because students were grievously ill-prepared upon arrival. Sunday schools had made great headway in Wales but their aims were limited; not much could be expected from the private adventure schools, whilst the old endowed grammar schools were not only few in number and thoroughly English in atmosphere but were usually closed to Nonconformists and also to the poor, contrary to the intentions of their founders. For several decades the prime attention was given to elementary education. In England two societies sprang up in the early nineteenth century to promote the education of poor children. The schools of the British and Foreign Society (1808) were wholly undenominational whereas those of the National Society (1811) taught the principles of the Church of England. Not until 1833 was a grant provided by the state. From 1837 onwards the National Society made rapid progress, but not so the British Society because of the problem of persuading Nonconformists to act in concert. One major difficulty was that of 'voluntaryism', Congregationalists and Baptists being convinced that it was wrong to accept money from the state for education. This principle was also for some years a source of division amongst those who sought a university for Wales. The year 1843 was important in Wales on several counts. It saw, for instance, the defeat of James Graham's Bill which, it was feared, would have given the Church of England a controlling influence over the education of children working in factories, a defeat which generated enthusiasm for British Schools in north Wales. This year, too, saw the appearance of a 'Letter to the Welsh People' by Hugh Owen, who explained in clear, simple terms how British Schools might be set up and how applications might be made for state grants.

Owen's dominant place in the development of higher education (and of other branches as well) was so crucial that he must be introduced at the first opportunity.[47] Born at Y Foel, a farm in Llangeinwen, Anglesey, in 1804, he attended for nearly ten years a celebrated private school at Caernarfon kept by Evan Richardson. One of the very few leaders of the university movement not to have received university education, he spent nearly eleven years as a clerk in legal chambers before embarking upon a career lasting almost forty years as a civil servant in the Poor Law Commission at Somerset House. A Calvinistic Methodist by upbringing, he became a Congregationalist upon marriage. London Welshmen he knew exceedingly well and he never returned to Wales to live. Amongst the beneficiaries of his demonic energy were deaf mutes, the cabmen of King's Cross, the London Fever Hospital and societies for the encouragement of thrift and of total abstinence. He was chiefly responsible for setting up the Social Science Section of the National Eisteddfod in 1861 and he was a prime mover in resuscitating the Cymmrodorion Society. Apart from the university movement, his work in founding the Bangor Normal College in 1858 is especially remembered. The College, designed to meet the mounting need for properly trained teachers which the excellent Borough Road School could no longer satisfy, was an undoubted success. Fourteen years before the first university college in Wales was established the Normal College opened the doors of higher education to many who later distinguished themselves in the educational life of Wales.

Hugh Owen's chief preoccupation during the 1840s and 1850s was with elementary education. His letter of 1843, together with agitation against Graham's Bill, led to the establishment of forty-two schools in north Wales whilst the voluntaryists in south Wales set up a Normal School to train teachers in 1846. The National Society was also energetic and its published report in 1845 deploring the inadequacy of educational provision in Wales prompted William Williams, the member for Coventry, to raise the question in the House of Commons. Since Williams was a stalwart supporter of higher education in Wales he deserves more than a passing reference.[48] Born in Llanpumpsaint, Carmarthenshire, in 1788, he had done well in the cotton trade in London and had acquired a substantial fortune; unmarried, it was said of him that 'he takes care of his *brass* that he may have *gold* to contribute'.[49] A leading radical – he was buried next to Joseph Hume at Kensal Green – he abhorred the cruelty of the legal system, particularly the lash. Charles I he considered to be a tyrant and in the Commons he moved that a statue to Cromwell should be raised at public expense. In the next decade, *The Times*, presumably to distinguish him from lesser bearers of the name, called him '*the* Williams'.[50] It was he who pressed the government in 1846 to appoint a commission to inquire into 'the state of education in the Principality of Wales, especially into the means afforded to the labouring classes of acquiring a knowledge of the English language'. It is true that the Reports which ensued were but the most recent in a series (reaching back to 1816–18) which dealt with the education of the poor.[51] Yet they assumed a historic significance far greater than that of their predecessors.

The commissioners appointed in 1846 were able men, though limited by their class and outlook. They amassed an immense body of facts, a rich source for historians which is not yet fully digested. Some of their comments were shrewd and penetrating. Saunders Lewis, for example, in *Tynged yr Iaith* (1962) spoke with approval of R. W. Lingen's assessment of the linguistic position in the valleys of south

Wales.[52] Nevertheless, the Reports, when published in 1847, were fiercely denounced throughout Wales, not because they unveiled the primitive state of many schools, in any case readily apparent to the most cursory beholders, but because they laid the blame on the Welsh language and upon Nonconformity as the enemies of progress. Special offence was caused by intemperately accusing Welsh women of unchastity. The commissioners, in short, had displayed lack of understanding and of perspective, for they should have reminded themselves of the atrocious condition of education in the industrial and rural areas of England, indeed, within sight of Canterbury Cathedral itself. Sir Thomas Phillips, a Conservative Churchman whom we have already encountered, knighted for his defence of Newport against the Chartists, produced within a short time a magisterial rebuttal. Calvinistic Methodists, who had hitherto not been lively in political affairs, were led into protest by the forthright arguments of their intellectual leader, Lewis Edwards, who was incensed by the gross injustice of the Reports. Second to none in marshalling the forces of political Nonconformity was Henry Richard (1812–88), soon to retire from his Congregationalist pastorate in London. In fact the assault upon the Blue Books, pressed forward during 1848, the year of the revolutions in Europe, created a 'new climate of opinion . . . favourable for the planting of the seeds of a new kind of radicalism in Wales'.[53] One immediate consequence was a vigorous campaign to restore the reputation of the Welsh woman, soon to be somewhat idealized as the 'Angel in the House'.[54] The Welsh language, so ignominiously traduced, faced cross-currents. To some the Reports reinforced the conviction that Welsh, widely spoken and not in apparent peril, was a serious obstacle to advance, prohibiting access to the professions and to commerce in Wales as well as England. It was, therefore, to be consigned to an inferior position. Patriots, on the other hand, enraged by the slur upon their mother tongue, were determined to rescue it from the clutches of utilitarians and philistines and to restore its ancient dignity. These conflicting pressures were at work throughout the century and they have not ceased. At various times and in varying degrees they profoundly affected the university movement.

During the aftermath of the 1847 Reports attention was inevitably drawn to higher education. William Williams, partly because he had echoed some of the views of the commissioners themselves and partly because of his opposition to 'voluntaryism', was fiercely attacked by

Ieuan Gwynedd (Evan Jones). In 1848, Williams, temporarily out of Parliament, indicated in his 'Second Letter' that he had earlier struggled to win support for training colleges in Wales and also for a university. Many years later it was said that he had been promised government help for a university during Robert Peel's second administration and that these attempts had been foiled because of the lifelessness of Welsh members.[55] In his 'Second Letter' Williams contrasted the government's 'tender care and munificent liberality' towards the Irish, rewarding them for their 'turbulence and disaffection' whilst loyal Wales was given but 'a stingy pittance'[56] for education. A college, similar to the new Queen's Colleges in Ireland, with training colleges attached, should be launched in Wales to educate the middle classes. In 1849 E. G. R. Salisbury, closely linked to William Williams, wrote two letters on 'Education for Wales', one to Williams and the other to the Marquis of Lansdowne, President of the Council; in the latter he supported the founding of a university college in Wales.[57] Three and a half decades later the Principal of the Bangor Normal College wrote in *Y Traethodydd* that Salisbury had recently revealed that Williams and he had waited upon Lansdowne to urge him to set up two university colleges in Wales, Williams favouring one in south Wales and Salisbury one in north Wales.[58] Lansdowne was not to be prevailed upon and he thus administered the first of a succession of ministerial rebuffs to champions of the Welsh university movement.

We must now retrace our steps to consider the growth of opinion within Wales itself. In 1828 an anonymous writer was drawing attention to the Low Countries (for Belgium was not an independent country until 1830) and to the six universities there, the earliest having been founded in 1426, and to the educational system extending to the smallest village.[59] The days of greatest achievement were past but the Low Countries, small though they were, enjoyed a marvellous legacy. Two years later, *Seren Gomer* published a letter by 'Dyfnaint', principally addressed to the secretary of the London Gwyneddigion Society, in which he pressed for a university, upon the London plan, where 'all the Sciences known to man shall be taught in the Welsh language'. Churchmen and Dissenters were to join in 'the National Institution'. Every Welshman had a role in the great endeavour, 'one of the most glorious achievements that GWALIA ever knew'.[60] The scheme was to be laid before societies in England and Wales and at the next meeting of the Eisteddfod; a member of the royal family was to become patron, William Owen Pughe was to be chairman of the managers and the site of the university should be in the most central part of Wales. The secretary of the Gwyneddigion replied enthusiastically.[61] It was shameful that there was no university in Wales and it was wholly necessary to have one. No single society could deal with such a question which must be addressed to all the inhabitants of the Principality. Early in 1831, another correspondent, 'Einion Môn', deplored the fact that Wales was the only European nation without a university.[62] He disagreed, however, with Dyfnaint as to the best method of achieving this most laudable aim. The first duty of the Welshman was to dispatch petition after petition to Parliament from every town and parish, couched in firm, respectful language, to ensure that the law of the land should be administered in the Welsh language and that all important offices in Church and state within Wales should be held by those who understood Welsh. If these ends were attained, a fine university would soon follow, to which the leading gentry would send their offspring and where they would master Welsh. Many Hindus knew as much English as Welshmen, yet neither lawyer nor Churchman was allowed to serve in India without a proven knowledge of the native language. Englishmen generally would not object to similar arrangements in Wales. All Welshmen, high and low, Churchmen and Dissenters, must unite to further this great cause.

In 1841 William Jones, at first a Baptist, but priested in 1836, embarked, whilst Vicar of Nefyn, upon a challenging, perilous theme, *The Character of the Welsh as a Nation* (1841). He had good things to say. He was much attracted by the Scottish experience, the excellent parochial schools and the four universities. Lampeter could not possible supply the deficiency within Wales and he spoke with feeling of 'the indifference and ungenerous disposition of the wealthier classes'.[63] Forty years later not many of his clerical brethren appeared to recognize the force of his arguments against sending Welshmen across the border to master English and to broaden their horizons. There are signs that he may have been considered unwise,[64] a judgement some Anglicans are inclined to pronounce upon those who have newly joined their ranks. His remarks upon the plight of young Welshmen, however, could not be ignored:

> ... is it not plain that a large number of the youths of the Principality are obliged to renounce the idea of a collegiate education, in consequence

of the enormous expense attending it, who would have to see that privilege placed within their reach by the establishment of similar institutions in their own country, conducted on a judicious plan, and holding out encouragement to talent and attainments. The Scotch Universities offered a sound education, year after year, to some hundreds of the natives of Scotland, who reside in their vicinities, and who are not possessed of sufficient means to procure instruction at a distance. A poor man, whose earnings exceed not twenty shillings a week, living in or near one of the four towns in which the Colleges are situated, is able to secure a collegiate education for his child. The scarlet cloak which the students wear has frequently covered a cloak all in tatters.[65]

It has been argued that the delay of a quarter of a century in founding the first university college at Aberystwyth may in part be attributed to disagreements concerning the 'voluntaryist' principle. Strong voluntaryists included David Rees, Llanelli, and Samuel Roberts, Llanbrynmair, both notable Congregationalists. A co-religionist opposed to them upon this issue was Hugh Jones, for many years pastor of Lammas Street Chapel, Carmarthen. In 1849 under the ambitious pseudonym of 'Cromwell o Went' – it was an age of pseudonyms – he warmly supported a 'General College'[66] for Wales, with which would be associated a Normal College for the training of teachers (though not in competition with the Swansea college for teachers). It was to be for members of all sects or of none, and like London University it was to award degrees. It was to ensure fair play to all the children of Wales (presumably those who measured up to the required standard). He added that William Williams of Coventry and Kilsby Jones would willingly respond to invitations to explain the basic principles of the enterprise. Another strong supporter of a 'National University' in 1849 was Henry Griffiths,[67] Principal of the Congregationalist College at Brecon. He was also opposed to the voluntaryist principle. If prejudice and impetuosity were cast aside, the people of Wales would achieve an honourable position among the nations of Europe. Griffiths was one of the earliest theologians in Wales to espouse Darwin's theories of evolution; his son, a distinguished physicist, became Cardiff's second principal. In the same year, William Davies,[68] Ffrwd-y-fâl, Llansawel, Carmarthenshire, was allowed to publish his views in *Yr Haul*, though the editor did not agree with them. London University was to be the pattern. If Churchmen and Nonconformists were educated together,

proceeding thereafter to their own theological colleges, there would be
a greater sense of unity in the community. Davies wanted two
institutions, one in north and the other in south Wales, and he hoped
that the government would contribute £20,000 to found each college
and £3,000 per annum for each thereafter. In his assessment of actual
needs he was realistic enough; in another sense he was hopelessly
optimistic, as the next decades were to show. To his plea Davies
attached twenty-four quatrains stimulated by a public meeting at
Brecon which had urged the dispatch of hosts of petitions to Parliament
to secure the desired end.

The most systematic attempt at this stage to devise a university of
Wales was by Benjamin Thomas Williams, then only twenty years of
age. Born at Narberth, the son of a Congregationalist minister, he was
first educated at the Presbyterian College, Carmarthen, where he
became a Unitarian. It is of more than passing interest that during his
period there the College Board recommended that 'there is a growing
desire amongst intelligent men of various denominations to coalesce for
the establishment of an Academical Institution on a large scale . . . It
would be a vast step in the cause of unsectarian education in Wales.'[69]
Geraint Dyfnallt Owen's suggestion that this was the first sign of an
impulse to establish a university in Wales cannot, however, be
sustained in the light of earlier proposals.[70] Deterred by religious
scruples from entering Oxford and Cambridge, B. T. Williams
proceeded, as so many Welshmen did, to Glasgow where he excelled at
logic and metaphysics. He thereafter became a member of Parliament,
a county court judge and a useful member of Aberystwyth's College
Council. In his pamphlet, *The Desirableness of a University for Wales*
(1853),[71] he contrasted the state of education in Scotland with the
plight of his native land, where a liberally based university would be an
inestimable blessing. He especially deplored the absence of a medical
school because he believed that Welshmen had a natural aptitude for
this branch of study. The University of Wales should consist of 'but
one good and extensive College'; it was, therefore, to be a unitary
university. Moreover it would be wholly unsectarian because a
sectarian college could never embrace the whole nation. So much for
Lampeter, then, and any other theological college in Wales.
Nevertheless, a scheme based on the godless institution at London
would not do at all; permission must be made for 'the religious
element', as he dubbed it with some detachment. Each sect, and the

Anglican Church, was to have a divinity hall, as in Scotland, superintended by a distinguished minister, and each sect would provide theological instruction; otherwise, students would be taught together. Williams was prepared to give a certain precedence to the Anglican Church, surprisingly so in view of the 1851 Census and of his own religious antecedents and beliefs. His readiness to make concessions we must attribute to his desire to ensure the 'patronage of liberal and enlightened bishops and clergy', without whom the project would collapse. Division and animosity could only perpetuate the 'predominance and sway of the Saxon race'. As an act of elementary justice a professorship of Welsh should be instituted. Hugh Owen was to say that he was entirely ignorant of Williams's pamphlet for sixteen years and had been 'deprived of the valuable cooperation of its learned author'.[72] Indeed, it is a curious reflection upon the capricious nature of posthumous reputation that Williams is now more remembered for this juvenile venture than for his more demanding labours as politician and judge.

Thus it was that in the years preceding 1854, especially in the aftermath of the 1847 Reports, the fundamental issues relating to higher education had generated public concern and informed discussion. B. T. Williams, influenced by the Scottish experience, favoured one unitary university in Wales; a substantial body of opinion would later have agreed with him. The presence, however, of four universities in Scotland meant, as William Jones had noted, that students were able to live 'in their vicinities'.[73] This consideration became increasingly important and the early pleas of William Williams and of E. R. G. Salisbury for a college in south and north Wales were to be vigorously reinforced. To avoid religious dissension, many recommended the system which prevailed at London where there was no religious teaching (except, of course, at the Anglican King's College). B. T. Williams, whilst recognizing that his unitary university would have to be wholly unsectarian, provided for 'the religious element' in closely associated divinity halls. Others believed that students should be educated together and proceed thereafter to theological colleges. This question aroused sustained debate. Further anticipation of future developments included proposals for a Medical School and for a Normal College (or Day Training Department, as it was to be known) for the training of teachers. The call in 1828 that all subjects should be taught in Welsh did not make headway, but it was to be seized upon by R. J. Derfel who argued that Wales urgently needed a university in which Welsh should be the principal language.[74] Two matters of particular importance had been raised by William Davies of Ffrwd-y-fâl. First, in order to promote educational advance, men of all religious persuasions should act together. The Yorkshire clergy would have agreed for they wanted a university 'founded on broad and liberal principles'.[75] Second, the state should provide the means. The voluntaryists disagreed, and so did the state. These two issues were to preoccupy the leaders of the university movement for several decades.

II

Seed-Time

There are sound reasons for believing that the movement to establish a University of Wales, as opposed to the uncoordinated efforts of individuals, really began in April 1854. It was at a private meeting in the London home of Thomas Charles, kinsman and namesake of the founder of the Welsh Sunday Schools, that Hugh Owen submitted a motion to provide Wales with one or more Queen's Colleges similar to those launched in Ireland. Amongst those present were ministers renowned in the history of Welsh Nonconformity: Lewis Edwards, David Charles, Henry Rees and Samuel Roberts. Those engaged in active politics included George Osborne Morgan, Richard Davies, Treborth and E. R. G. Salisbury. So favourable was the response that Owen, Morgan and Salisbury were deputed to proceed as they saw fit. Frequent meetings were apparently held and the accounts of charities in Wales inspected; a constitution and prospectus were drawn up, and though not issued, they were subsequently printed in an appendix to the Aberdare Report.[1]

Before considering these plans, it is as well to speak briefly concerning developments in Ireland.[2] In 1845 three Queen's Colleges, Belfast, Galway and Cork, were incorporated; they were undenominational, teaching was entirely conducted within the colleges and substantial sums made available by the government for buildings and annual grants. In 1850 the scheme was completed by the creation of a new university, the Queen's University. The government resolved that it would not admit students to the degrees of the University other than those educated at the Queen's Colleges. The Queen's University was thus a teaching, federal university. It also exercised firm control over the colleges, it maintained high standards and its degrees were of good repute.

In following this scheme, Owen and his colleagues rejected the model of the unitary university which had flourished in Scotland. At one time Lord John Russell would have preferred each of the three Queen's Colleges to award degrees as did each of the four Scottish universities, but this proposal was wisely rejected for the renown of the Scottish universities was based on centuries of development. Nor was Owen disposed at this stage to follow the example of Owens College, Manchester, which was affiliated to London University for whose degrees it prepared its students. By a supplemental charter of 1850 the University of London was empowered to recognize institutions throughout the British Empire which were now permitted to present candidates for London degrees. By 1853 as many as sixty-eight medical schools and twenty-three non-medical institutions were affiliated to London University.[3]

Why was it, then, that Hugh Owen was attracted to the Irish precedent? It was at once evident to him that Wales and Ireland had problems in common. In the passage which follows Owen was speaking primarily of Wales, but the circumstances of Ireland were also in the forefront of his mind: 'Excluded from the English Universities by the great expense of a University education, by the inconvenience attendant upon a long absence from their homes in a distant part of the country, and, above all, by religious scruples, a class daily increasing in numbers, in wealth, and in importance have long been left unprovided by any better means of instruction than those which were accessible to the children of the poor.'[4] Plans to remedy 'so great an evil' had proved abortive in Wales because 'an object so truly national' could only be achieved by the co-operation of religious denominations reluctant to compromise. In Ireland there had been similar differences and he quoted with great satisfaction the words of the President of the Belfast College that they had 'solved the problem of combining various denominations for mental culture, without interfering with religious convictions'.[5] Further, provision for the distinctive characteristics of the people, as in Ireland, could only be made by recognizing a separate identity: 'experience has shown that education to be effective must be National' and 'it is impossible to force one class of minds into a mould adapted for those of others',[6] a reminder to Owen's critics that he could recognize the force of nationhood. In a central part of Wales, he urged, one or more Queen's Colleges should be planted on the Irish model. A financial basis could in the first instance be secured by employing the many charitable endowments of Wales which lay idle and were not fulfilling the intentions of testators. But it is evident, too, that in addition to personal contributions he hoped for parliamentary grants, as in Ireland. On purely empirical grounds alone it was safer to seek comparison with the Queen's Colleges, from the first enjoying state aid, than with Owens College dependent wholly on private benevolence for its survival and which had made an unsuccessful and premature appeal to the government for help within a year or two of its foundation.[7] In an outline of a constitution prepared by Hugh Owen and his colleagues it was said that a Queen's College was to be founded in Wales 'to afford the Middle Classes of Wales the advantage of a Collegiate Education, based on unsectarian principles'.[8] The courses, to be pursued within the college, were to be those which 'usually form part of a liberal education, with the addition of practical instruction in civil engineering, agriculture, and other branches of useful and experimental knowledge'. At this stage there is no mention of degrees, only of 'collegiate education'. Owen clearly had in mind the initial steps in the development of the Queen's Colleges, from 1845 to 1850. In his scheme there is no counterpart to the degree-awarding Queen's University established in 1850. In different times these plans might have matured, but circumstances were not advantageous. First, the outbreak of the Crimean War, followed by the Indian Mutiny, did not encourage a direct appeal for government aid. Second, the prime mover became immersed in plans to establish at Bangor a Normal College for the training of teachers which opened its doors in 1858. Third, it was indisputable that popular opinion in favour of a university had not been ignited and that the movement was languishing. In 1872, looking back upon these years at a dinner to celebrate the opening of the University College at Aberystwyth, Osborne Morgan had this to say: 'We did not immediately obtain the response we expected, and under the circumstances we did what, perhaps, was the only thing we could have done, but what is often a very difficult thing to do. We waited. And at last the answer came.'[9]

They waited until 1863. The intervening years were not wholly fallow. In 1858 London University received a new charter (Mark 11B,[10] as it is known to connoisseurs of London charters). Its effects were momentous. Henceforth a candidate presenting himself for examination for a London degree need no longer be a member of an 'affiliated' institution or indeed of any college; he could reside in any part of the world provided he fulfilled certain academic requirements. Provincial colleges were now free to concentrate upon teaching and London would examine. Inevitably these new arrangements were to affect the thinking of advocates of higher education in Wales as elsewhere. In 1861 Hugh Owen, at the Aberdare Eisteddfod, successfully submitted a plan for the formation of a Social Science Section of the Eisteddfod which provided a forum to discuss varied matters relating to Wales.[11] From the standpoint of higher education in Wales the meeting of 1863 was especially significant. But we must not anticipate events. The year 1862 was the bicentenary of the Act of Uniformity which had obliged about two thousand dissenting clergy to become Nonconformists for conscience' sake. It was an occasion worthy of commemoration and Dr David Thomas, a Congregational minister of Stockwell, London, reflected upon the best manner of doing so. Musing at the Mermaid in Mumbles, where he had retreated for health reasons, it struck him that the finest way would be to establish a college or university in Wales. He accordingly wrote a letter to the *Cambria Daily Leader*, a newspaper owned by his son. Within a week he had met Thomas Nicholas, then tutor at the Carmarthen Presbyterian College. He tells us that he 'sought to put him ablaze with my fire. I succeeded. He became an enthusiast'.[12] Nicholas was a man of parts. Raised in Pembrokeshire, he was educated at the Lancashire College, Manchester, and at Göttingen, where he gained a doctorate. Convinced, and rightly convinced, that he had a significant contribution to make to educational discussion and fortified by his experience at the least sectarian of the Welsh theological colleges, he wrote stirring letters to the *Cambria Daily Leader* and to the *Carnarvon Herald* which were subsequently published as a pamphlet through the liberality of William Williams, MP for Coventry, the zestful promoter of the interests of Wales as he saw them. Nicholas had no doubt of the talents of his countrymen, 'sufficient to march abreast of any province of the empire'.[13] They were also a reverent people well fitted to exercise earthly power. Nevertheless, they were 'too much like globules of mercury — bright, nimble and fugitive',[14] needing to be coalesced and solidified. Wales had not hitherto 'vindicated'[15] her place among the nations because of inadequate mental training; she did not have 'even a heresy worth mentioning',[16] a wounding rebuke from a theologian. Ignorance of English was a major impediment. 'Shut in by the barriers of a different speech — a speech which can never be naturalized in the regions of experimental science and commerce — and held in check by an infatuated worship of the past, it [Wales] is now sadly in the rear of her nearest neighbour.' The answer was a proper system of education. The lower classes did not greatly concern him for they were better educated in a relative sense than those above them. Writing as he was eight years before Forster's Education Act (1870), he was taking an unduly optimistic view of existing arrangements. His principal purpose, clearly, was to remedy the defective provision for the 'better-conditioned and most gifted sons'[17] of the middle classes. His 'Middle Schools' were designed for the farmer, the shopkeeper and the trader, and in industrial areas they should specialize in mechanics, mineralogy and metallurgy. Some pupils, but only some, should proceed to 'High Schools', organized on a collegiate basis and leading to university education, one in north Wales and one in south Wales. The university as such would only be 'the ornamental capital crowning the Corinthian column'.[18] Nevertheless, it was his recommendation concerning university education which attracted the liveliest attention. In defining a university Nicholas had a tendency to stress unduly the 'comprehensiveness'[19] of instruction and in pointing to two models, Queen's University and London University, he did not at this stage sufficiently indicate the fundamental difference between the two institutions, namely that the former was a teaching university and the other an examining university. It seems that he found the London model the more attractive, partly because of the principle of 'affiliation',[20] which had in fact enabled his own college at Carmarthen to be linked with London University. Higher education could not be seriously contemplated without state aid and he did not think that voluntaryists would object in this instance. Government grants, together with the high honour of royal patronage, would stimulate the 'generous sons'[21] of Wales. A university in Wales would help Welshmen rid themselves of a 'crestfallen spirit . . . the sure mark of a subjugated enervated race'.[22] Undue fears, on the other hand, of a 'distinctively *Welsh*'[23] institution were to be allayed, though he did not rule out a professorship of Welsh. Bilingualism had many advantages; the chief purpose was for all to 'join hands for the propagation of English – for commerce and science the richest and noblest language of earth'.[24]

Hugh Owen was so impressed by Nicholas's 'very able letters'[25] that he invited him to prepare a lecture for the Social Science Section of the Swansea Eisteddfod of 1863, where both men met for the first time. In October Nicholas visited London and was introduced to George Osborne Morgan and Morgan Lloyd, of whom we shall presently say more. William Williams announced his willingness to contribute a thousand pounds to what we may now more realistically call 'the university movement', and Nicholas was asked to prepare a draft address to the leading friends of education in Wales and to invite them to the Freemasons' Tavern on 1 December. At this meeting William Williams was elected chairman and it was resolved to seek 'the immediate establishment of a University', which should be 'a truly national institution' located in Wales; in order to secure government aid the people of Wales should demonstrate their commitment by creating 'a National Fund'.[26] A committee of eleven persons was formed and on 9 December Nicholas was appointed secretary, Morgan Lloyd sub-treasurer, Osborne Morgan and Hugh Owen honorary secretaries.

That the movement should be centred upon London and directed from London need not occasion surprise. In the capital were the springs of power, the two houses of Parliament, the central law courts and the large commercial and financial houses at the heart of a great and growing empire. Since the early eighteenth century, at least, there had been a conviction amongst London Welshmen that they should not merely represent their compatriots; they should also lead them within Wales itself.[27] The London Welsh societies were much more than convivial gatherings of nostalgic expatriates; they were the only possible forum of national leadership. In 1885 Thomas Charles Edwards said that but for Liverpool, Manchester and London there would not have been a university in Wales.[28] Had he not been fund-raising on St David's Day in Manchester he would certainly have given the primacy to London and not to the northern cities, important though they became at critical periods. Within a year of the foundation of Aberystwyth, three societies were established in the capital, the Welsh Antiquarian Society, Urdd Y Ford Gron (to uphold the prestige of the Eisteddfod) and the third Cymmrodorion Society[29] (as it is known) which was to be intimately linked with the early history of the University of Wales.

It is fitting that attention should be drawn to the principal figures amongst London Welshmen (with the exception of Hugh Owen whose outstanding services we have already noted). Morgan Lloyd[30] (1822–93), believed to be a descendant of the Llwyd family of Cynfal, was a farmer's son from Trawsfynydd; educated at the Calvinistic Methodist College, Bala, and at Edinburgh, he became a barrister much favoured by monoglot Welshmen; a Liberal MP for Beaumaris from

1874 to 1885, he fell out with Gladstone on Home Rule for Ireland and never returned to politics; contemporaries ranked him high amongst those who founded the Aberystwyth College and the London committee was often chaired by him in his chambers in King's Bench Walk, the Temple. George Osborne Morgan[31] (1826–97) was born at Gothenburg, Sweden, where his father was chaplain; for a time fellow of University College, Oxford, his victory as Liberal in Denbighshire in the election of 1868 caused great excitement; he consistently supported Welsh educational aspirations in the House and outside; it was he who abolished flogging in the army. Robert Jones[32] (1810–79), born in Llanfyllin and educated at Oxford, was Vicar of All Saints, Rotherhithe, a for thirty-seven years; he was a remarkable scholar (it was said that if all the Welsh books in the British Museum were destroyed he could reproduce them); he prided himself on being a Tory, not a Conservative, and was described as 'a host in himself, in anecdote, speech or address';[33] of unusual eloquence he supported all Welsh movements, especially the Aberystwyth College which he believed would be a blessing to the Church of England in Wales by raising clergy from amongst the common people. David Thomas[34] (1813–94), whom we have already encountered, was, like Nicholas, a Pembrokeshire man; for thirty-three years he was Congregational minister at Stockwell; he gave good service to the university movement despite a settled aversion to committee meetings where members 'reach their conclusions by creeping processes which exhaust my patience'.[35] Stephen Evans[36] (1818–1905) was a Cardiganshire man who prospered for a time as a warehouseman in London until he suffered a reversal of fortunes; though of an impetuous nature, he was one of the chosen few who got on well with Hugh Owen, partly because he deferred to 'the calmer judgement of his revered leader';[37] a Vice-President of Aberystwyth College, he gave it sterling service for many years. John Griffith[38] (1821–77), popularly known as 'Y Gohebydd' (the Correspondent), was born and bred at Barmouth; he went to London as assistant to Hugh Owen, whom he served for two years, and came into close contact with prominent Liberals in the capital; when he was appointed London correspondent of the *Baner* there could have been no better choice and the horizons of monoglot Welshmen were widened by his racy reports not only from London but also from France, Austria and the United States; a political agitator, he eloquently championed the Cardiganshire tenants evicted after the

1868 election and zealously supported Henry Richard's efforts to secure the secret ballot; he constantly drew the fortunes of the Aberystwyth College to the attention of his readers and he was a member of the London committee and later of the College Council.

By February 1864 the committee was sufficiently emboldened to issue a lengthier address than the initial one drawn up in the previous October. Once again it was prepared by Nicholas.[39] As to the government of the proposed university, there were two excellent models, the University of London and the Queen's University. Both were recent creations, both had recognized the 'ecclesiastical peculiarities'[40] of each country and both acted impartially. Nicholas had earlier tended to favour the former, but now he recommended a combination of the two. Queen's University had its own machinery in the three colleges but although London now examined all candidates irrespective of their place of origin he was attracted by the system which enabled institutions of proper standing to be affiliated to the University. He was not recommending that the degree of a university in Wales should be thrown open to all (as in London after 1858) but that the two new colleges and all existing colleges deemed to be of due standard should be united in an 'Educational Confederacy'[41] with the university as its crown. In this respect his model differed from that of Ireland, where the three Queen's Colleges were bound together and governed by the Queen's University and where the affiliation of other colleges had been firmly rejected by the English government. The University of Wales, like the University of London, would be governed by a 'Corporation of Noblemen and other Gentlemen of education';[42] management should be entrusted to a Senate of men of 'high standing' appointed by the Crown, though he imagined that they would in time be selected from amongst distinguished graduates of the University.

The scope of the education to be provided was extensive.

> While in times past the ministry seemed to be the only outlet to native talent, the increase of trade, the introduction of Railways, the immense development of mining and manufacturing operations, the openings offered by competitive examination for the higher posts in the Civil and Indian services... invite the young man of education in our day to a thousand lines of honourable employment and promotion. The varied and comprehensive course of education which the University would supply would fit our young men for such openings.[43]

If Wales were to emulate Scotland in success, two thousand students would be under regular collegiate instruction. It would be as absurd to send all legal cases to Westminster Hall or all invalids to England as to send all Welshmen for education to another land. 'Those who have laboured for the education of the poor will not stand aloof when the education of the middle and higher classes is sought to be advanced in proportionate ratio.'[44] These classes were to Nicholas 'the bone and marrow of the nation'.[45] London University, the Queen's University and the Scottish Universities had received the bounty of the state. 'Wales, alone, though contributing towards the outlay, remains unvisited by this generosity.'[46]

Nicholas's views, fully in tune with those of Hugh Owen, have appeared to later generations narrow and restricted. The stress on education as the highway to material advance, often to the detriment of cultural values, has occasioned strenuous strictures. Ieuan Gwynedd Jones speaks of 'educational technocrats' and their 'repellent philosophy': 'The hard, calculating utilitarianism of these prophets of higher education is everywhere evident, involving the sacrifice of language and tradition and history on the altar of utilitarianism.'[47] He is surely right in rejoicing that the Aberystwyth College was an expression of more humane principles, certainly as it developed and acquired confidence. Hywel Teifi Edwards[48] further illumines the discussion, roundly castigating Owen and Nicholas. Yet he justly recognizes that Nicholas, in particular, was expounding views widely held by prominent Welshmen of the 1860s, who would have agreed with Nicholas that 'the establishment of a University which should have the effect of fostering a merely Welsh nationality, and promoting in any degree the separation of the inhabitants of the Principality from the great English community, would prove a great evil'.[49] To Nicholas it was axiomatic that Wales should be fused into the United Kingdom, not only politically but in a deeper sense. 'As to language, what is required is not the extinction of the Welsh, but the diffusion of English. Let the perpetuation of the vernacular, and other peculiarities of the nation, be left to the free choice and sympathies of the people when fully enlightened as to their own interests; but meantime, let the light enter, and let all the barriers which divert the influences of modern civilization from Wales be removed.'[50] The Welsh language, as he saw it, was exceedingly flourishing and beyond peril. The baleful shadow of the Blue Books, however, lay heavily upon him and it seemed incontestable that ignorance of English prevented most Welshmen from participating in the unending benefits of the Industrial Revolution. In Britain and in Germany he had seen at first hand that burnished talents could deliver men from the age-long bondage of poverty. Although, as we have seen, he did in his pamphlet consider the possibility of a professorship of Welsh, he was in the enlarged Address more circumspect for it would be imprudent to alarm a wide audience by appearing to encourage 'peculiarities' and 'separation'.[51] We cannot doubt that many mid-Victorian Welshmen applauded his deft, persuasive advocacy of the virtues of social engineering.

At first the promoters of a college yet unborn were ineluctably drawn into conversations with St David's College, Lampeter, whose champions urged its claims to become the University of Wales. In December 1863 (when the London committee had been formed) a former scholar of St David's, the Reverend Owen D. Thomas, wrote that 'it would be the most advisable plan for all Wales to unite at once and support Lampeter as a "University" to the utmost of their power.'[52] Eight years earlier an anonymous pamphleteer declared that the College should become the core of a university of Wales.[53] At the time the College's location was under scrutiny and there was, as we have seen, a serious intention to move it to Brecon and to unite it with Christ's College, a proposal firmly supported by Lampeter's Principal and Vice-President. The unknown writer, much opposed to the scheme, won the day. One of his potent weapons was a threat, realistically described as 'spine-chilling',[54] that it might be bought by Cardinal Wiseman as a Jesuit seminary, a Demetian counterpart, one supposes, to St Beuno overlooking the Vale of Clwyd. St David's remained secure on the banks of the Teifi and, armed in 1852 with its second charter empowering it to grant degrees in divinity, the College was ready by 1864 to negotiate with Hugh Owen and his colleagues to act jointly to obtain a government grant and to establish a University of Wales. By April it was agreed by both parties that there should be erected in Wales a new college, 'open and unsectarian';[55] St David's would retain its distinctive character as an Anglican college and the two colleges would constitute one university, with its own chancellor, vice-chancellor and senate, and would be authorized to grant degrees and to nominate its own board of examiners. Candidates were to be examined only upon proof of having attended their own colleges for at least three years, a positive renunciation in this instance of the London system; the right of affiliation was asserted in respect of any college which measured up to the required standard. By May difficulties were apparent. The immediate cause of discord was that whilst Lampeter was prepared for the committees representing each body to co-operate in the creation of a new university and in winning a government grant, it also wished each committee to act independently in other matters. By June it was all over. The London committee deemed it expedient to defer further discussions in the hope that future negotiations might succeed, Lampeter being assured of the committee's 'unabated cordiality of feeling'.[56]

Failure was not surprising. The bishops had not much cared for the initial harmony and there was to be no miraculous blending of oil and water. The Welsh public at large would not have supported a national university unless it were demonstrably unsectarian; upon this rock negotiations foundered. Lampeter was not cast down. The ecclesiastical commissioners had agreed to augment the College's endowments and in January 1865 a third charter permitted the conferment of the BA degree. The future seemed bright. There the matter rested until 1868. Why was it resurrected? Early in that year the *Welshman* announced that 'no one doubts that in the long run St David's will become a University'.[57] After the election of 1868, however, the signs were less propitious. Lampeter could by no means count upon government or parliamentary support. Overtures to the 'so-called University Committee in London' were courteously received. David Charles, the new secretary,[58] thought that Lampeter and other theological colleges might well be affiliated to a university of Wales. Since little could be expected of the Lampeter principal, Llewelyn Lewellin, in office since 1827 and daily becoming 'duller and duller',[59] the initiative lay with Joshua Hughes, shortly to be Bishop of St Asaph, the first Welshman to be raised to the episcopacy since the reign of Queen Anne and only now, so it seems, because an entry in Crockford had erroneously led Gladstone to suppose he was 'a university man'.[60] Hughes wanted one university for Wales, composed of Lampeter and Aberystwyth and excluding the Nonconformist colleges, in the hope that the Anglican Church might recover the sheep which had wandered into other folds. Lampeter may have been prompted to action by well-founded fears that the government would cease to pay the four hundred pounds granted annually since 1826 and also because of the increasing number of competing theological colleges in England. Formal approaches to the government were not made until late December 1871, and then by Stewart Perowne, the Vice-Principal, who affably declared that the unhappy differences which had shipwrecked negotiations in 1864 were 'in no way of importance to our common object'.[61] He enclosed a list of 'suggestions',[62] and amongst those not modified by the university committee were recommendations that the government should establish fellowships, open to all graduates of the university, to promote postgraduate research and to strengthen the teaching powers of the colleges, and that the university should include schools of mines, engineering, medicine and surgery. The one fatal proposal concerned examinations in theology which would have undermined the unsectarian university. After June 1873 there was no further exchange of messages. As the historian of the College rightly observes, employing D. Emrys Evans's metaphor, this was yet another instance of the Lampeter moth darting towards the university flame and withdrawing when its wings were threatened with singeing.[63]

Co-operation had failed because the fundamental conditions of united action were missing, thus gravely injuring the university movement. The repeated collapse of conversations reflected views not always openly expressed but which were held, and genuinely held, by a large proportion of the clergy. W. Basil Jones's letter in October 1869 to Joshua Hughes is revealing. Jones was then Archdeacon of York and in 1874 became Bishop of St David's, and thus Lampeter's Visitor. A university in Wales, he said, must needs compete with existing universities, there was a danger of lowering standards, much of the population of Wales was nearer to Oxford than to Aberystwyth or Lampeter, and 'a sensible parent would *caeteris paribus* prefer sending his son to some English place of education, to keeping him always within hearing of his native tongue'.[64] He went on: 'Wales is not a distinct portion of the United Kingdom in the sense in which Scotland and Ireland are. It has no political existence; it is barely a "geographical expression", and unpalateable [*sic*] as it may be to some of our countrymen, it is nevertheless true that Welsh nationality is little more than an exaggerated provincialism. Wales differs from England as the Highlands differ from the Lowlands of Scotland and in no other way.'[65] When Aberystwyth held its opening ceremony the Principal of Lampeter said that he was unable to be present because he was meeting his brother magistrates at Aberaeron. He added that 'no one of our

professors can make it convenient to attend'.[66] Religion exalts; it also
divides and diminishes.

If it had been impossible to reach an accommodation with the
Anglicans of Wales, it was at times difficult to mobilize the forces of
Nonconformity on behalf of the university movement. It is instructive
to turn to the writings of Lewis Edwards, Principal of the Calvinistic
Methodist College at Bala, one of the ablest and most influential
Welshmen of the nineteenth century. He had, it will be recalled,
attended the London meeting in 1854.[67] Five years earlier in *Y
Traethodydd* (which he had helped to found in 1845) he urged the
establishment of good schools in Wales to teach Latin and Greek
thoroughly. He did not propose to call them 'colleges'; Rugby, Harrow
and Eton were content to be called schools, whereas the
Nonconformists of Wales elevated the smallest institution at once into
a college. In 1865 he wrote again in the same journal concerning higher
education in Wales.[68] It would, he thought, be idle for a University of
Wales to hope to compete with the older universities; the best Welsh
students would proceed to places of excellence in England and
Scotland. If poor men of ability were rewarded with scholarships – a
course much favoured by him – they could manage reasonably at
Oxford and Cambridge. On the other hand, he acknowledged the
importance of proximity. A lad brought up by the sea tended to think
of seamanship, local papers flourished because readers wanted to hear
local news and a Welsh institution would attract attention. Most
important of all, learning would become more respected. Edwards was
convinced that true learning was not properly respected in Wales where
denominational colleges set the greatest store upon homiletics, the art
of making sermons. Would a university in Wales succeed? It would
need to recruit the nations's best men and, if possible, the best men of
other nations. But he suspected that the most talented, were forty
scholarships available, would prefer to pay more, if they could, in order
to study in England or Scotland and to see the world, even though the
education might not be superior. Edwards then touched upon a matter
of first importance. It would be necessary to create fellowships within
the institution itself for those who had excelled in their final
examinations. Most of his countrymen, he did not doubt, would hoot
at such an idea[69] ('Ni wnant ond hwtio y meddylddrych ar unwaith').
The well-informed, however, knew that fellowships were the principal
strength of the ancient universities, and Edinburgh now proposed to

make similar arrangements. The fellows should have a say in the government of the university and be given additional emoluments for assisting members of staff. 'It is but foolishness to speak of a Welsh university without fellowships.'[70] ('Nid yw ond ffolineb son am brifysgol Gymreig heb *fellowships*.') What were the prospects, then, of establishing such a university in Wales? The government had certainly created a strong corporation under the name of the University of London, largely for the benefit of English and Welsh Nonconformists, and it was improbable that it would form a similar body for Wales alone. Moreover, although distinguished men were members of the corporation they had been unable to persuade the government to provide a suitable building in which to hold their meetings; they were now reduced to hiring rooms at Burlington House. Since the government dealt so meanly towards a substantial, influential institution it was unlikely to do much for 'the small world of Wales'.[71] The London pattern was thus summarily dismissed. He was not optimistic, either, for a university modelled on the Queen's University and its Colleges, designed as part of a plan to civilize the Irish, for their performance hitherto was insufficient to warrant emulation. In short, Wales should not expect the government to finance a new corporation. Edwards himself would not oppose energetic exertions on behalf of a university – a name, after all, counted with some people – as part of a campaign to win justice for Wales. But, faced with failure, they should not be downcast as if 'naught availeth'.[72] A total refusal to help should prompt Wales to consider what could be done without state aid. Wales needed two good schools or colleges, one in the north and one in the south. At this point, we may briefly pause to note that here Edwards equates schools and colleges; earlier when he spoke of continental 'schools' he evidently meant universities, and it is perhaps unfortunate for our present purpose that 'school' ('ysgol') means 'high school' in one context, 'college' in another and 'university' in yet another. Indeed, his diction in this instance is curiously similar to American usage. The central argument, however, is unimpaired. He was not concerned with the person endowed with one talent, for whom there was ample opportunity throughout Wales. The imperative need was to provide training for students intending to become scholars of the front rank in institutions which taught not merely homiletics (as in denominational colleges) or the science of medicine, but chiefly those things which lie unseen at the root of all learning.[73]

In the *Traethodydd* article of 1865 a discerning mind presents tough truths. D. Emrys Evans said that he held 'a somewhat similar view'[74] to Thomas Nicholas. However, there are differences. Nicholas had canvassed the needs of the middle classes, largely in materialistic terms. Edwards does not mention class in any structured sense. He does speak of the poor, from whom able men would emerge, and in essence he is concerned with the man of many talents wherever he might be found. He is in fact an élitist, representing the traditional values of European civilization. His purpose was not to decry the educational entrepreneur — at Bala or elsewhere — but to discourage enthusiasts from talking glibly about universities and to state plainly that scholarship concerned an 'audience fit, though few'.[75] In tracing the course of the university movement it is proper to record that such a voice was heard, even though it was imperfectly understood and was not regarded as a clarion call by those engaged upon a large enterprise.

Edwards's sophisticated note of reservation reinforced in some measure the doubts of Nonconformists concerning the proposed university. The denominations had a natural affection for their own colleges, in no wise weakened by the prospect of an 'unsectarian' university. Edwards for his own part would not have been at all displeased to see his two schools, or colleges, emerging out of denominational colleges. In 1863 Morgan Lloyd wrote from the Temple to assure him that the university would 'not interfere with any existing institution, but it appears to me that some scheme may hereafter be devised to affiliate the Bala College with the new University Corporation'.[76] The large sum of money collected for the Bala College had aroused expectations and in 1864 Edwards said that he hoped to make Bala 'something like a University for Wales'.[77] In the following year he told Richard Davies of Treborth in categorical terms that the Calvinistic Methodists should have a college where their students might prepare for 'the very highest examinations'.[78] His message was plain: 'they should graduate from our own College... and if Bala is not at present equal to University College, *it ought be made so...*'[79] Only a few months after the opening of the College at Aberystwyth he wrote to Richard Davies of Treborth: 'I cannot say that I have much faith in this University for Wales... I feel it very difficult to forgive the Welsh Calvinistic Methodists for their stupidity in preventing this College at Bala to be made a National Institution, the very thing they are aiming at in founding this

University for Wales.'[80] Instead, Bala had been crippled and was
getting weaker by the day.

Rifts within a denomination, however, were as nothing compared
with dissensions between denominations. We need not enlarge upon
them here. Suffice it to say that they impeded united action and that the
atmosphere of the time was more denominational than national. It is
therefore all the more surprising to hear that David Rees, Llanelli,
should have written to Lewis Edwards in 1863 advocating the closure
of all theological colleges at once and the creation of one university for
all.[81] Edwards replied courteously, but made no reference whatsoever
to a university, thus further discouraging discussions. Nor was it easy
at first to persuade Nonconformists that natural attachment to their
own theological colleges, which they had sacrificed to establish and to
maintain, need not prevent wholehearted participation in a university
movement at once national and undenominational. It may well be true,
too, that the stress laid by Hugh Owen and his colleagues upon worldly
success, exclusively so at times, may not have appealed to those who
thought more in terms of consecrated service. A further obstacle
springing from genuine religious conviction was the principle of
'voluntaryism', which at first certainly deterred Henry Richard and
Samuel Morley.[82] Invited at an early stage to become a member of the
London Committee, Richard declined because 'I had always
maintained and had formerly taken a rather prominent part in
proclaiming the principle that Education is the work of the people and
not of the Government.'[83] He added that even if this principle had not
stood in the way 'the project so far as I understand it did not commend
itself as desirable or practical.' This remarkable statement is a clear
indication that the champions of the university movement had not yet
succeeded in awakening an influential body of opinion to the need for
a university. Then again the constant reiteration that the university was
designed to provide for the middle class would scarcely appeal to the
sons of toil. As late as 1879 *Y Cronicl* printed verses asserting that since
the purpose of a university was to give access to rich appointments, the
beneficiaries should pay for their fat endowments. 'It is not just to tax
the poor to apprentice gentlefolk. They should pay for their education
as do others for their apprenticeship.'[84] Alas, there was little evidence
that the well-shod were contributing according to their capacity. For
the most part, the squirearchy, minor and major, remained disdainfully
aloof. Sir John Hanmer, of that ilk, thought that a college at

Aberystwyth would be 'a little provincial South Wales concern' and 'of no advantage to Wales'.[85] In 1869 'Gohebydd' berated the gentry of Wales for standing aside from the struggle when they extracted so much from 'the brains and marrow bones'[86] of their countrymen. Only two members of the gentry, he thought, could be mentioned with honour, Bulkeley Hughes of Plas Coch and Sir Richard Bulkeley, both of Anglesey and both of whom had made a modest contribution. One industrial magnate, David Davies of Llandinam, subscribed handsomely: it was he who cried out in near despair at the opening of Aberystwyth: 'Where are our rich men of Wales?'[87] If there was antipathy, there was also apathy. In 1868 'Gohebydd' noted that some were asking rather dryly whether a university was needed at all, and to what end.[88] Others wondered whether north and south would ever combine in a common undertaking and agree upon a site.[89]

There were further concerns. Many had sincere misgivings that in the absence of a satisfactory system of secondary schools higher education could not prosper. Until the provision of the 'missing link', as it was described in Darwinian terms, was it wise to build a castle on a beanstalk? The Principal of Jesus College, who never encouraged the creation of university institutions in Wales, told the Church Congress at Swansea in 1879 that 'until the whole system of secondary education was reorganised, it was premature to think of a national university',[90] in itself a perfectly legitimate point, though it must be conceded that it was disingenuous of him to inform the assembled clergy that 'no one could fail to sympathise with the feeling which prompted the demand'. A further uneasiness was that before 1868 Welsh issues were not adequately represented at Westminster. In the words of *Y Beirniad* in 1865 'the voice of Wales has never been heard in Parliament. Wales has never sent men to Parliament who can represent her nor who cared a whit for her advancement.'[91]

In these unpromising circumstances there began a sustained campaign on behalf of the university movement, further injured by a severe, unheralded commercial crisis. Overend and Gurney, hitherto a discounting and bill-banking house of the highest repute, had undertaken such dangerous risks that in May 1866 it was unable to meet liabilities. Prosperous, prudent men became alarmed; there was a run on the banks and many speculative ventures tumbled. Thomas Nicholas was later to recall these disturbing events, to which we must shortly return. Again, even in good times it was difficult to emulate the

success of the denominations in building new colleges. The Calvinistic
Methodists contributed £26,000 towards the fine college at Bala, the
foundation stone being laid in 1865, whilst the new Memorial College
at Brecon was raised by the Independents for £12,000 in 1869 on four
acres of land in one of the most beautiful parts of Brecon.[92] Chapels
were being built or enlarged at a remarkable rate and the smallest of
congregations were open-handed in acutely difficult circumstances.
Thomas Nicholas and his successor as secretary drew attention to these
conflicting claims.[93] Moreover, it took time to organize chapel
collections on behalf of the university movement on a systematic basis.
In fact, to committed chapel members an unsectarian approach – and
there could be no other – appeared tame and colourless. Others
suspected that the Calvinistic Methodists were using the movement to
advance their own interests. Nor does it seem that public meetings were
as effective as had been hoped in the early years. A secretary of the
movement in Liverpool recalled the thin audiences; at Chester, where
a joint meeting was held, he reported that only twenty came to hear
Hugh Owen, despite the attractions of a brass band, and at Holywell
the next day only five were present, one of whom had to be put in the
chair.[94] Indeed, one has the distinct impression that more members of
the press were often present than of the public. The abortive
negotiations with Lampeter wasted six months, Nicholas thought.[95]

By November 1864 the committee felt, and with good cause, that the
time had come 'to agitate Wales on the question'[96] and to this end it
was resolved, in a curiously worded minute, to enlist the services of
'respectable clergymen'[97] throughout Wales. In January 1866 it was
noted that 'the tardiness with which the movement has proceeded
threatens its destruction'.[98] There was even talk of 'an earnest
endeavour' to 'obtain the Prince of Wales as President'.[99] Thirty years
were to pass before he was finally captured, and then as Chancellor. In
relation to financial arrangements, it is not altogether impious to
wonder whether expense accounts and a ten per cent commission on
the first annual subscription (and five per cent thereafter) did not give
an impression that too much seed corn was being consumed. Of actual
malversation there is no sign, but there were occasional suggestions of
incompetence, so much so that *Seren Cymru* advised its readers in late
1869 not to contribute to the proposed college.[100] High expenses had
eaten into capital for six years and not a single Welshman had yet learnt
his *hic, haec, hoc* at a university college in Wales. It is certain that there

was never enough capital to create an efficient organization. Nicholas, quite properly, wanted four canvassing agents, two in the north and two in the south, to be in regular employment, apart from the summer months.[101] It was a vain hope.

Few movements are free from tensions. Unhappily, disagreements between Hugh Owen and two successive secretaries reached undue proportions. The letters of both Nicholas and David Charles indicate, upon an impartial reading, that Owen had the sinister power of raising devils in the hearts of men more than nominally Christian. To Nicholas he was 'the saintly Hugh Owen'[102] and to Charles 'the most unpleasant man I ever tried to work with'.[103] Both became paranoid on the subject and it is not edifying to dwell upon such intemperate animosities. David Thomas of Stockwell wrote of Nicholas and of Owen: 'Both good men in their way, they seemed to have a mutual repugnance.'[104] Needless to say, mutual repugnance between two principal officers of the university movement was injurious at a critical stage. It is sad to reflect that Nicholas, whose papers had so impressed Owen in 1862, felt impelled to resign in November 1867. Thereafter he delivered several unhelpful broadsides in the press, justifying his role and attacking his transgressors.[105] We do better to remember the scholarly works he later published, and which are still useful, such as *The Annals and Antiquities of the Counties and County Families of Wales* in two volumes in 1872. David Thomas suggests that his death was hastened by the frequent annoyances he suffered at the London Committee meetings and he adds that he was spared a pauper's burial at Hammersmith cemetery only because his friends purchased a grave.[106]

The search for a site was less urgent than the collection of subscriptions. Nevertheless any unequivocal offer of a site had to be carefully considered. We should perhaps refer in passing to an ambitious scheme in 1857 to establish a College at the Gnoll, Neath, to provide scientific education of the highest order in response to the mounting needs of industry.[107] Had this grandiose commercial venture succeeded, the centre of higher education in south-west Wales would have been at Neath, not Swansea. The progenitor of the scheme, however, was less than reliable and was some years later rewarded with a spell in gaol. The fundamental unsuitability of such a college in Wales may be gauged from the proposed annual fees of two hundred pounds which would have caused havoc to the private economies of

many students at Oxford and Cambridge. Seven years later the London
Committee was generously offered six acres of land at Llanilltud Fawr
(Llantwit Major) by Dr Nicholl Carne of St Donat's Castle,
Glamorgan.[108] Had money been available to build a college it would
have been a remarkable deliverance; during the whole of the succeeding
year, alas, only seven hundred pounds were collected. Early in 1867
Dr Carne made a further offer, that of St Donat's Castle as 'a
temporary hospice'[109] in case it was decided to build upon the site he
was ready to donate. The committee was naturally moved by his 'great
liberality' and thanked him warmly for such evidence of 'patriotic
zeal'.[110] It did not, however, feel 'as yet quite justified in finally
deciding upon the permanent site of the South Wales College'. The
committee even thought of establishing a temporary college outside
Wales, at Chester;[111] had it done so it would have angered well-
wishers of the movement. For a time hopes centred upon
Caernarfonshire.[112] The prodigious railway building of the 1840s had
offered tempting prospects to developers; in 1846 the Chester and
Holyhead Railway Company decided that the ninety acres it had
bought near the Straits between the bridges of Telford and Stephenson
were ripe for exploitation. Heedless of expense and hungry for large
returns the Company proposed to build an enormous hotel and a new
station at the junction of the lines to Caernarfon and Holyhead and to
create also a residential area to be known as Britannia Park. The designs
were entrusted to Joseph Paxton, celebrated for the Crystal Palace and
much admired for his parks, such as that at Birkenhead. Optimism was
unrestrained. Although the Great Western Hotel at Paddington
managed with 150 beds, no fewer than 500 were judged necessary for
the Britannia Hotel, to be linked to the station by a glass avenue
resembling the Crystal Palace and decorated with plants and flowers.
In 1852 the grounds were completed, but the fizz and bubble had gone;
when the Menai Bridge station was opened in 1858 there was no grand
hotel. Late in 1865 Hugh Owen was negotiating with the Britannia
Park Company to seek a site and was told that seven acres would be
given free 'to erect the University of Wales in Britannia Park' and that
there was not in the whole Principality 'a more desirable site, so easily
approached from all parts of England and Wales and Ireland'.[113] The
committee was also mulling over an offer from a Captain John Jones of
Liverpool who was prepared to give his 'interesting and valuable'
museum to the college, provided it was built near Bangor and provided

that 'the teaching is equally favourable to all classes, Church of England and sectarians'.[114] Soon the committee was assailed by doubts, for unforeseen conditions began to emerge; there was a serious danger of falling prey to speculators and the scheme fell through. Thus it was that the prospect of having a college in north or south Wales in the 1860s came to naught. It is piquant to reflect that the sites considered were close to the seats of the two colleges founded two decades later. Had either of these proposals succeeded, it is almost certain that a college would not at any stage have been placed at Aberystwyth. The first university college in Wales was founded there, not because of deliberate choice, as in the case of Cardiff and Bangor, but because it was there that the wheel of fortune had spun to a standstill.

We have seen that the university committee had in its struggle for subscriptions been obliged to face the bitter consequences of a financial crisis. Yet it was the ill wind which gave Aberystwyth its opportunity. One of the bold adventurers laid low by insolvency was Thomas Savin[115] of Llwyn-y-maen, Oswestry. A man of phenomenal energy, he was also a child of impulse who could brook no delay. It is reported that in his early days he came to sell his wares in a Welsh border town where it was customary for farmers not to engage in other business until all the livestock had been sold. Overwhelmed with impatience, Savin immediately bought a thousand sheep so that he could at once start selling his goods. In the same spirit he embarked upon the building of railways, at first with David Davies, Llandinam, until they fell out, and then upon the erection of the colossal Castle Hotel at Aberystwyth and of another at Borth. His grand plan was to develop the seaside towns of Cardigan Bay, bringing to them in his own trains visitors from densely populated areas. At this stage, then, it was intended that Aberystwyth should become the Brighton, not the Athens of Wales. The manner in which the hotel was built was astonishing. A London architect, J. P. Seddon,[116] already working for Savin at Towyn, Merioneth, was brought at speed to Aberystwyth in 1864 and commissioned to build a hotel around the existing Castle House. It was so called because of its proximity to the remains of the castle, a house built for Sir Uvedale Price by John Nash, architect of Regent Street and Buckingham Palace. Savin was prone to change instructions at a moment's notice, and Seddon had to make do with a wooden model and rough sketches for detailed drawings. He succeeded beyond all reasonable expectation and despite subsequent repairs and fire, the building, almost all by now Seddon's work, earned this tribute from an authority on architectural history: 'certain aspects of the building, the bowed section on the sea-front – originally the hotel bar, later the college chapel! – and the entrance and stair tower on the rear are amongst the grandest and most boldly plastic fragments produced in this period. Neither Oxford nor Cambridge have anything of comparable quality!'[117] Savin spent £80,000 upon the building and seriously over-reached himself. When the tempest broke in 1866 he was mercilessly buffeted. There was no succour. It was in these circumstances that the hotel was offered to the university committee, for £15,000 in the first instance, and at length for £10,000, a remarkable bargain by any standard. In March 1867 the matter was settled. Savin accepted his fate with a cheerful, endearing fortitude; he became a lime merchant at Llanymynech and an alderman at Oswestry.

It called for boldness and tenacity of purpose to take this decisive step. No one could foresee the discouragements which yet lay ahead. Whether Aberystwyth was the best site would be vigorously contested for years. What was incontestable was the committee's determination to seize an opportunity and to act resolutely when resolution was most needed. Action was in itself invigorating. Nicholas felt that the public at large, hitherto a shade sceptical of the whole venture, now experienced a surge of confidence.[118] Many words and many labours had taken a tangible form. Half a century later the Haldane Commission saw this clearly. It had been difficult to sustain 'popular faith'[119] whilst the design remained 'an unembodied idea'; thereafter there was 'a marked advance'. The decision to purchase, however, had a further consequence. The committee had unanimously resolved that 'the securing of the Castle Hotel for a Central and sole College for Wales was most desirable.'[120] Gone, as it seemed, was the high ambition to plant a college in north Wales and another in south Wales, both part of a federal university. There was uneasiness, too, in the event baseless, that subscribers might object because of the understanding that there were to be two colleges. To Hugh Owen the new arrangement was but a temporary accommodation to meet the realities of the moment. Four years later he stated plainly that the committee had never departed from its original intention to obtain a university.[121]

During the year following the purchase of the hotel was fought the

'Great Election', as it was popularly called. The election of 1868 may not have been a spectacular triumph as was at one time supposed. Twenty-four of the thirty-three Welsh members were landowners, thirty were Anglicans, many of the Liberals were more than tinged with Whiggery and most of the electorate was still unrepresented. The return, however, of Henry Richard for Merthyr Tudful and of Osborne Morgan for Denbighshire was a sign that the old order was shaken. One of the immediate results, as K. O. Morgan has noted, was 'the growth of a new cohesion among the Welsh members at Westminster'.[122] At the end of December 1868 Thomas Gee said in a leading article in the *Baner* that a happy augury of improved relations with the government was the presence of men in Parliament who could understand and represent the Nonconformists of Wales. In February 1869 a large number of Welshmen converged upon the capital to celebrate the Liberal victory and advantage was taken to invite supporters of the university movement to the Westminster Palace Hotel.[123]

The meeting had a two-fold significance. First, there was an awakening realization that the movement could not succeed without actively enlisting the full support of the ordinary people of Wales. Thomas Gee, it is true, still spoke in the accents of Thomas Nicholas in 1862. The working classes, he said, were being provided with educational opportunities 'in every direction', but if attention were given to them alone 'the middle classes would be deprived of advantages' and the consequences made manifest within a few years. He then remarked that he was 'sorry to find that there was apathy among the middle-classes to support the movement'. David Charles, Nicholas's successor, was certain that they would have to depend for financial help, not upon the aristocracy and the wealthy but upon 'the people in general'. Hitherto the poorer classes had given little, largely because of considerable ignorance; henceforth they would be the movement's 'great strength', for he had evidence that when once the issue was placed before them 'they saw the value of the institution . . . and personally felt a great desire for its success and readily came forward with their mites'. This, too, was the message of Osborne Morgan. The boat, he had to confess, had 'struck a little reef', but he had been immensely impressed by the quarrymen of Caernarfonshire and Merioneth who had set an example to the gentlemen. A new plan must be adopted 'to set the people to work themselves'; they must be taught that it was 'a people's question', as they had taught them during the election in which they had

played 'a glorious part'. In drawing attention to these green shoots −
and in 1869 they were few and frail − Morgan and Charles were
pointing to the ultimate salvation of the university movement.

The second matter of significance at the meeting was the decision to
form a deputation to wait upon the Prime Minister to seek a
parliamentary grant. An attempt was apparently made to elicit the
support of the former Lord John Russell who sent a cordial letter to the
committee in January 1868 but who was soon thereafter relieved of the
burden of office.[124] In March Disraeli agreed to receive a deputation
from Owens College, before whom he waved to great effect a large
cambric handkerchief laced with black; otherwise, there was not much
else to remember.[125] In June he firmly refused even to meet
representatives of the Welsh committee. The entry into office of
Gladstone naturally caused expectations to run high. It was not until
May 1870, however, that he was able to meet Osborne Morgan and
Henry Richard who no longer espoused the 'voluntaryist' principle
which had prevented his early participation in the movement. Both
Morgan and Richard derived enormous satisfaction from the
encounter. Richard reported that Gladstone had agreed that 'the Scotch
and Irish colleges were quite in point and [that] he did not see how
Wales could fairly be excluded'.[126] He further conceded that there was
a distinction between Wales 'and other parts of England' on grounds of
nationality which it would be 'foolish and impossible to ignore'. He
'confessed that he thought Wales had been badly used', and
recommended that as much representative power as possible should be
brought to bear upon the government and also upon Churchmen to
induce them to join the movement. Morgan reported to the committee
on similar lines, adding that Gladstone had admitted that Wales,
because of its 'clearly marked nationality'[127] could not be placed on the
same footing as an English town or district 'however popular or
important'. Both had gathered that in response to sufficient pressure
the government was 'not indisposed to yield', but the committee agreed
that the premier's frank, unofficial utterances should be 'used with
reserve'. Gladstone had, however, introduced a note of caution. He had
'feared' that he would need to bring the matter to the attention of the
Chancellor of the Exchequer, an ominous addendum. He said, too, that
aid had been refused to Owens College; indeed, he was accused of
having shown 'no enthusiasm and was apparently ill-informed'[128]
when a deputation from Owens waited upon him.

In accord with Gladstone's recommendation a memorial was presented to the government in March 1871.[129] Its fourteen clauses in the main rehearsed familiar arguments. Once again 'all fanciful ideas of nationality' were disclaimed – Nicholas's words in 1864 – and attention drawn to the liberal subventions to the Scottish and Irish universities. The merits of Aberystwyth were extolled as 'the central town of Wales' and the detailed needs for £50,000 presented. The strictly undenominational institution was to have the status of the Queen's Colleges or of the two London colleges and was eventually to 'assume a *University* character'. All religious sections of the community had contributed and a parliamentary grant would be a powerful stimulus to voluntary gifts. There was a concluding reference to Wales's loyalty and its comparative freedom from crime. Gladstone replied that he was now prepared to recognize the Queen's Colleges as an acceptable precedent.[130] However, the fact that the proposed college at Aberystwyth was undenominational was not a sufficient reason for distributing state grants. In fact 'I do not see how the Government could assist any particular college without raising great difficulties.'[131] If aid were now given to Aberystwyth, Owens College, which had been refused a grant, and other colleges would be bound to make representations to the government, an unmistakable retreat from his words to Richard and Morgan almost a year earlier that 'though they had refused to aid Owens College at Manchester, he considered Wales might be excepted from the principle on which they had then acted'.[132] A further interview in June with Gladstone, then accompanied by Robert Lowe, the Chancellor of the Exchequer, proved fruitless.[133] The Treasury had won. Gladstone's reply was profoundly dispiriting; he cannot be exonerated from the charge of encouraging false hopes, indeed, in Gladstonian parlance, of tergiversation.

The financial position was of course parlous before the first appeal was made to the government, as Nicholas was not slow to show in the press.[134] After the early enthusiasm following the purchase of the Castle Hotel in 1867, the response had been disappointing. The interest on the £6,000 borrowed for the down-payment was a steady drain upon exiguous resources. Several subscribers had died and the zeal of others had waned. Enemies of the cause, said Nicholas, were proclaiming that the University of Wales was consumptive at birth and that the only comparable deceit was that 'arch-sham of the age, the

National Eisteddfod'.[135] During his successor's tenure, it was noted that promises to Nicholas had been withdrawn, that there was a reluctance to move at Llanberis and Bethesda until Lord Penrhyn had given consent, that as late as autumn 1870 no systematic canvass of the county as a whole had been made, that the secretary's failure to give reports was having a debilitating effect on the movement and that there was no inclination to send him to America to collect a putative £2,000.[136] In fact during the first six months of 1870 the secretary's salary of £300 per annum, plus expenses, made heavy inroads into the total subscriptions of £883. Seddon had to be paid for his improvements and attempts to secure a mortgage on the building foundered totally. By September 1871 the situation was desperate. The request of the British and Foreign School Society to rent the building for temporary occupation in order to train women teachers had to be turned down on the ground that 'it would not be expedient in view of the College building being offered for sale'.[137] It seemed that the whole enterprise was collapsing in ruins.

In such circumstances scapegoats are speedily sought and found. Members of the London Committee who had dominated the movement from its inception had not, it was thought, measured up to the needs of the hour. They were splashing about ineffectually in shallow water. The London Welshman has sometimes been unworthily traduced by the few who resented his capacity for taking charge and for his supposed omniscience during brief visits to the land of his fathers. As early as 1757, Lewis Morris, who had a comprehensive set of ungovernable prejudices, told his brother that he 'would rather deal with a Turk or Jew than with a London Welshman'.[138] Something of that spirit now erupted. London Welshmen had indeed played a crucial role in the movement for higher education in Wales. It remains true, however, that by the late 1860s several of them were demoralized and were unable to pierce the encircling gloom. Welshmen outside London resolved to take the initiative. There was already a portent in May 1868 when a Representative General Committee of one hundred subscribers was formed at the Freemasons' Tavern in London, twenty-seven from south Wales, seventeen from north Wales, thirteen from Merseyside and fifteen, apart from MPs, who came from London. More than half the executive committee of thirty members may be described as provincial members. Henceforth, subscribers were to meet alternately in London and in Aberystwyth; efficient committees were at length formed at Manchester, Liverpool and at Aberystwyth. In September 1871, fourteen members of the executive committee, 'resident in the country',[139] wrote a critical letter to all other members to say that 'immediate measures' should be taken to open the College and to request that a meeting be convened. In October, at a special committee meeting, a warm welcome was given to proposals from Manchester. A 'pull altogether'[140] was urged and a scheme adopted to form a guarantee fund by establishing five centres, London, Liverpool, Manchester, north Wales and south Wales, each responsible for raising £400 per annum towards current expenses. On 2 November, at a further meeting, Jonathan Pell of the Belle Vue and his Aberystwyth colleagues moved in the strongest terms that the College be opened in January 1872. At length it was resolved 'that the College be opened for Educational Work not later than 1st October, 1872'.[141] Earlier in the year Hugh Owen had characteristically proposed by circular that there should be an early opening. The real impetus, however, came in consequence of the 'Provincial Revolt', as it has been aptly called. At a dark hour, the courage and resolution of the provincial members were decisive.

III

The First College, 1872–1880

The brave, poverty-stricken College opened its gates on 16 October 1872.[1] The day before had been a public holiday. The shops were closed and the buildings, including the new pier, gaily decorated. In the College Hall there was a celebration breakfast supplied by the Belle Vue Hotel. It was of Dickensian amplitude, the tables heavy with hams and fowls, pies and jellies of all kinds, enough sustenance, perhaps, to face the day's proceedings which included twenty-five speeches of varying length in English and an unspecified number in Welsh in the Temperance Hall (unreported by Gohebydd). The one which drew most attention was delivered by David Davies, Llandinam. The wealthy men of Wales had not played their part and it was idle to plead poverty when Wales had one-third of the United Kingdom's coal. In any case 'this young child of ours cannot live on speeches'[2] – a timely reminder – and his promise of £1,000 and of yet another of £2,000 for scholarships led to 'volleys of hurrahs'. Others followed suit and by the end of the day £5,000 had been received in cash or promises.

The self-styled 'The University College of Wales' did not for some time have a satisfactory constitution. The 'Tentative Scheme', as it was appropriately called, entrusted the executive committee with ill-defined duties of management. In practice real power lay in the hands of Hugh Owen, so much so that the *Cambrian News*, not always the College's best friend, once remarked that 'the danger is of there being an Owen's College, Wales as well as an Owen's [sic] College, Manchester'.[3] By October 1874 control of the College buildings was vested in twenty-one trustees and a new constitution adopted.[4] There was to be a Court (not exceeding one hundred members), a Council and a Senate. It was natural, especially in view of the origins of the College, that laymen should have ultimate control. In turn, it was reasonable to expect them to exercise a wise forbearance when difficult issues arose concerning academic affairs. They did not always do so.

Almost inevitably, Hugh Owen became honorary secretary and David Davies honorary treasurer. Henry Austin Bruce, first baron

Aberdare, was elected president; it was probably the best choice. He had not been to university, but he had lived abroad and had mastered Latin (which he quoted frequently in correspondence), French and Italian. After a spell as a stipendiary magistrate, he was Liberal member for Merthyr Tudful from 1852 until his defeat in 1868. A seat in Renfrewshire enabled him to enter the cabinet as a 'Heaven-born Home Secretary',[5] according to Gladstone. This initial qualification, however, was insufficient to preserve his licensing legislation from the fury of the brewers, on the one hand, and of the temperance movement, on the other, and he was despatched to the House of Lords as Lord President of the Council. After Gladstone's defeat in 1874 he did not return to active politics and henceforth he devoted himself largely to the promotion of education. In a hierarchical society it was considered advantageous to have a peer of the realm as president. There was about him something of the patrician and at times even of the grandee. In private correspondence he was prone to speak of his countrymen as 'Taffies', which suggests a measure of detachment, but not many knew that he understood Welsh sufficiently well to translate poems into English, including one by a seventeenth-century weaver of Llanystumdwy.[6] Entirely lacking in originality, as he himself readily confessed, he was a stabilizing, moderating influence; it was generally allowed that his tact, courtesy and charm helped to make him unusually proficient in the arts of conciliation. A pre-eminent quality was his readiness as an Anglican to understand the aspirations of Nonconformists. To one of his co-religionists he wrote in 1875 of 'the unfortunate alienation of the great majority of the Welsh people from the Church of England', adding that

> I should be far better pleased if, recognizing the errors of the past, for which the present generation of the clergy is not responsible, they [the Welsh clergy] sometimes joined in promoting objects of general Welsh interest, outside the immediate interest of the Church. Middle class education in Wales, if conducted on a large scale, must be unsectarian. In my opinion, clergymen would act wisely and patriotically in admitting the inevitable truth, and in uniting their efforts with those of their fellow countrymen of all denominations in promoting the general good.[7]

It was an important, revealing affirmation. From the standpoint of Aberystwyth, however, there was one cause for uneasiness, though it was not widely known. From the outset he did not believe that the College was wisely sited. As early as 1863, he had enquired of his political agent at Merthyr: 'What say you to the University for Wales? I do not think it would do for Wales what the Scotch and Irish colleges have done for their countries, unless it were attached to some considerable town, such as Swansea or Cardiff. It *might* then become a common intellectual centre, and do much for us. But would the north and south ever unite in a common scheme, and agree upon the site?'[8] His early anticipation of later controversies was perspicacious. Equally, it was unlikely that he would be Aberystwyth's daring pilot in extremity.

The appointment of the first principal had been given urgent attention. None of the nine applicants was deemed suitable and soon exploratory approaches were made to Thomas Charles Edwards, now in his mid-thirties, a Calvinistic Methodist minister of a flourishing English chapel at Liverpool.[9] Educated at his father's college at Bala and at Oxford, where he distinguished himself in classical studies, he was highly esteemed by such outstanding men as Benjamin Jowett and Mark Pattison, whose advice he frequently sought and usually took. He did not find it easy to contemplate leaving his Liverpool pastorate. The fact that his uncle, David Charles, hoped to be invited to become principal was but a minor embarrassment, for few were persuaded of his claims. More weighty were his father's pronounced reservations. In June 1872, Lewis Edwards wrote that 'I am not sure whether it would not be better to put an end to it at once. The name, University College, sounds very well at a distance, but it is very doubtful whether any thing will come of it, besides failure and disgrace.'[10] He added that he was increasingly doubtful of the venture but that he would appeal for guidance to 'One who knows'.[11] At a down-to-earth level he advised his son to act warily in his dealings with Hugh Owen, who was conducting the negotiations: 'you must have all the conditions on paper *in H.O.'s handwriting.*'[12] Thus emboldened, and having travelled to Oxford to consult Jowett and Pattison, Thomas Charles presented Owen with twelve conditions, which included an annual salary of £500 with residence and the right to preach. Owen doubtless welcomed plain speaking and the matter was soon settled.[13]

Thus there began for Edwards a tempestuous period of nearly twenty years. We need not be surprised that in the circumstances he was occasionally choleric and impatient or that 'he gave the impression that he found himself in an unkind world'.[14] In essence he was a courageous man of broad sympathies; regarded by many as a warm-hearted patriot, he discouraged narrow provincialism; a powerful preacher in both Welsh and English (indeed, one of the few who excelled in both languages) and in time a theologian of repute, he disliked the disfiguring denominational feuding which often paralysed constructive, united action; manifestly committed to the welfare of his students, he earned their respect and affection; not for nothing was he called 'the Prince'. In retrospect, as in 1872, it is difficult to think of a person better qualified at the time to become principal of Wales's first university college.

During the first session a storm blew up which powerfully demonstrated that in religious matters the College should proceed with the utmost circumspection. Care had been taken from the outset to ensure that the College was entirely unsectarian, but it soon faced severe criticism on two fronts. On the one hand, it was charged by the uncharitable as being a godless college, akin to the abominable institution in Gower Street. On the other hand, it had seemed reasonable to ask the Principal to organize a religious service for students on a purely voluntary basis. When he readily acquiesced, there was a tintinnabulation, for he was accused of having taken an unwise course. He was a man of liberal views; indeed, one of his earliest pupils suggested that had he not been chained to the Bala rock he might have become an Anglican.[15] Not for a moment did he suppose that any man could be defiled by exposure to the majestic beauty of *The Book of Common Prayer*, portions of which he read at the morning service. Robust Nonconformists, led by Thomas Gee, thought otherwise; the Anglican liturgy was more than a branch of literature. Even when the College had produced its own *Manual of Prayer and Praise*,[16] endorsed by a prominent Anglican and by representatives of the main Nonconformist bodies, there was further hubbub. Attention was drawn to page five where 'more especially we pray for the good estate of the Catholic Church'; this was considered to carry the misconceived spirit of ecumenicism a prayer too far. These departures from grace were compounded by the proposal to call College terms by such names as Lent and Michaelmas, relics of a Romish past which should have been expunged at the Reformation and certainly not perpetuated at Aberystwyth. Rejoinders that the names of days of the week were of pagan origin carried little weight, for these were a common, not a divisive, inheritance. From Aberdyfi came a call urging 'the noble ship',[17] now on the rocks, to 'helm about', and from Denbigh's *Baner* a succession of salvoes across her bows.[18] The College's executive committee blamed the senate, clear evidence that the responsibilities of the two bodies were not precisely defined. Renewed talk of accommodation with Lampeter in 1873 exacerbated a painful situation, though in fairness to Gee he did not object to the ultimate inclusion of Lampeter within a University of Wales. He conscientiously believed that Aberystwyth should be a secular institution and that the authorities were in manifest breach of the original undertaking to establish a wholly unsectarian college. However, he did not carry the majority of Nonconformists with him on this issue (not even the quarrymen of Caernarfonshire), for they were not attracted by a cold secularism and in fact favoured religious worship in the College provided it was genuinely unsectarian. It is to Gee's credit that he allowed Gohebydd to defend the College in the columns of his own paper. For the Principal this was an unsettling induction. In August 1873 there was a hint – though it was nothing more – that he contemplated leaving the College. Instead, he seems to have hearkened to his father's advice to take 'no notice of howling dogs'.[19] By October 1874 Gee proclaimed himself satisfied with the state of the College. Within the College anxious fears subsided, but they were not forgotten.

A further potential problem confronting a new institution, especially a small one, was that of dealing with a member of staff prone by temperament to infringe the ordinary conventions of academic life. That Aberystwyth should have a department of music was widely welcomed as was the decision to invite Joseph Parry to return from America where he had given ample testimony of his outstanding gifts. 'Pencerdd America' became 'Pencerdd Gwalia'. At the College and beyond he generated unabated enthusiasm. Women, hitherto not part of the student body, were now allowed into the department as members of Parry's choir, a development which dismayed Hugh Owen, who urged the Principal to impose strict residential segregation by means of partitions, locks and bolts.[20] In College Parry was a poor disciplinarian and he was often impulsive and unorthodox; he held classes in the town, his choral duties involved many absences and there was talk of irregularities at Zion Chapel, Oswestry.[21] At length the College decided that it could not yoke a reindeer to a plough and his appointment was terminated. To extinguish a department of music at

Aberystwyth was no small matter, as the College was to rediscover more than a century later. It was during his period at Aberystwyth that Parry had written Wales's first opera, *Blodwen*, and taken his doctorate at Cambridge; it was here that he composed the hymn-tune 'Aberystwyth', which in time made the name familiar in many parts of the globe. Doubtless Parry's fate was in some measure determined by the severe economies imposed upon the College and it is not easy for those who do not bear direct responsibility to assess justly the precise arithmetic of difficult decisions. However, men of ripe judgement were later critical. Writing in 1927, J. E. Lloyd, who as a student well remembered Parry, said that he 'imparted. . . an infectious enthusiasm and a genuine love of the art', and concluded that 'a serious mistake was made by the authorities for lack of vision and sympathy'.[22]

The College opened its doors to twenty-five students, augmented to sixty-two during the course of the session. The first registered student, obliged to relinquish his studies because of ill-health in 1873, remembered that 'we had merely the bare rooms, with the necessary chairs and tables. We were like a family going into a partly furnished house, with all the rest of the furniture to buy as they became able to afford it.'[23] Many were ill-prepared to follow their course and stayed for comparatively brief periods; several led a threadbare existence. It is, of course, a dismal truth that not every scholar is able to communicate effectively: of one of the early professors at Aberystwyth it was said that 'no one knew more or could teach less'.[24] Those who remained for an appreciable time often spoke with gratitude of their professors. The Principal himself, for example, taught a wide range of subjects; his lectures were said to be 'splendid', and in the Greek New Testament class he was 'a true master of exegesis and a pure fount of theological learning'.[25] M. W. MacCullum, the English professor, left a lasting impress on Owen M. Edwards.[26] The greatest scholar was Hermann Ethé, who taught German, French and Italian, as well as Hebrew, Aramaic and Sanskrit; a note in the College Calendar said that 'Dr Ethé will be happy to read with students in the other Oriental languages'. A radical *émigré*, a hater of absolutism in all its forms, and no lover of puritanism, he remained a refreshingly incongruous figure at Aberystwyth until his scandalous expulsion in 1914. He was probably the only scholar of international repute in any of the Welsh colleges until the end of the century. A welcome addition was the Welsh professor, D. Silvan Evans, the lexicographer, who encouraged others to enter unexplored territories.

Increased residential facilities within the College helped to create a lively social life. A college *Magazine* (the forerunner of the Dragon) first appeared in 1878 and the debating society was particularly popular. Athletics were encouraged, partly in response to the advice of Jowett who thought that 'Dissenting students were too bookish, which tends to enfeeble the mind'.[27] Others thought that the presence of ministerial students, often of mature years, brought to their academic work 'a wide outlook, a philosophy of life and a power of criticism which made for real university culture'.[28] Amongst the early generation of students were men of exceptional ability: Tom Ellis, later as member of Parliament destined to influence the formation of the University of Wales; T. F. Roberts, a prodigy from Aberdyfi, who became the College's second Principal; E. J. Ellis-Griffith, a silver-tongued advocate and politician; S. T. Evans, a future president of the Probate, Divorce, and Admiralty Division of the High Court and an outstanding international jurist; J. E. Lloyd, the historian of Wales, and Owen M. Edwards, man of letters and administrator. Apart from S. T. Evans, all proceeded to Oxford or Cambridge, but, significantly, not one went to Jesus College, Oxford. 'If you can enter a college, do not go to Jesus,' T. C. Edwards had told O. M. Edwards; 'go to a thoroughly English college.'[29] Of special significance was the mingling of students from various parts of Wales. As one of them wrote subsequently, for the first time in history, north and south Wales had 'met unarmed'.[30] Far from encouraging a crabbed provincialism, as some had petulantly predicted, there developed in the College a healthy, vigorous sense of national consciousness. The young Tom Ellis, as he wandered along the paths surrounding the ruined castle, drew inspiration from the coastline extending from Pembrokeshire to Bardsey Island which seemed to represent the unity of a new Wales, far from the conformist influences to the east; westward was a bright horizon of fresh hopes.[31] Ellis, in time, was to feel the force of conformist pressures to the east, but we cannot doubt his sincerity. When he died, J. E. Lloyd recalled those student days: 'Never before had young Welshmen of all classes from North, South, East and West Wales, Churchmen and Nonconformists, grammar school boys and preachers, been gathered together in one place of study. Little wonder that, small as was the company and boyish as were many of the scholars, the air was full of new ideas; and, above all, that the idea of Wales, one despite her divisions, and demanding the service of her sons, then became clear and definite.'[32] This chapter inevitably records a series of lamentable conflicts and rebuffs. It also tells of courage and of endurance, and on no account should we lose sight of the aspirations of a generation of gifted young men whose tenacity later helped to preserve Aberystwyth in critical days and whose idealism was transmitted to the University which they helped to create.

By June 1879 it was evident that relations between council and senate had rapidly deteriorated. The council decided that it proposed to have an impartial test of the work of the College conducted by experienced external examiners. The Senate objected fiercely to a direct intrusion into academic affairs without proper prior consultation and presented a formal protest to the council. The students, led by Ellis Jones-Griffith, not unexpectedly supported the senate; when the examiner arrived they courteously, but firmly, refused to be examined. Aberdare wrote to the Principal to say that 'I am deeply disappointed by the course you yourself have taken in this matter.'[33] Edwards replied that 'it is evident that this policy of managing the College from London has failed... Let the Senate now at length try their inexperienced hands.'[34] Mark Pattison, Rector of Lincoln College, Oxford, said that the council provided the funds out of which senate members were paid: 'The paymaster naturally expects to have the management – equally the Principal and Professors, who work the institution, know far better than the Council can possibly know, what ought to be done.'[35] The academic issue was fundamental, for it was clearly wrong that an honorary secretary in London should arrange examination papers and appoint the examiners, and only two, to judge a wide range of subjects. The matter was patched up after a fashion, but the *Western Mail*, seldom averse to a little mischief-making, ran a headline to say that the senate and principal had caved in.[36] Henry Richard thought it unnecessary to wash dirty linen in public. Gladstone, he reported, had referred at Mill Hill to the contretemps and said that it was as natural for young institutions to proceed through such a stage 'as it was that dogs should have the distemper and children the measles'.[37] The most damaging aspect, perhaps, was that relations between president and principal were impaired by this unhappy dispute, which served also to confirm serious misgivings concerning undue lay, London control.

The financial position of the College during these years was acute and at times desperate. If not for the unwavering support of David Davies, Llandinam, bankruptcy would have been certain. The sum raised at the opening breakfast was but a tithe part of the £50,000 Davies thought necessary for an endowment fund. The debt on the College building was £7,000. True, notes of encouragement were heard from local committees, especially from Manchester, but promises were more readily made than fulfilled. True, too, that there were savings upon the termination of David Charles's appointment as secretary, for no successor was to be appointed.[38] The daunting task of organizing and co-ordinating collections remained. It was at this point that Hugh Owen stepped forward. Like 'an ancient Roman', as Henry Richard said of him, 'he had never despaired of the Republic'.[39] That a man of sixty-eight should upon retirement offer his services was in itself remarkable. That he should have performed these self-imposed tasks with relentless determination and without concern for his own comfort or welfare was soon seen to be heroic.[40] The mountainous clerical work could for the most part be tackled at his London home, but after consultation with Gohebydd he concluded that a systematic house-to-house canvass, together with organized chapel collections, was to be the basis of his mission, and it was nothing less, to arouse the enthusiasm and elicit the support of many for whom higher education remained at best a benign abstraction. Thus it was that the trim figure of Hugh Owen, with his small black travelling bag, alighting from a cab or waiting patiently on solitary railway platforms, became familiar throughout Wales. His usual procedure was to attend pre-arranged meetings, discuss operations, see that all was in order and leave for the next appointment. In Anglesey, for example, he held three meetings, involving much travelling, in different places in one day. Circulars were dispatched to ministers and clergymen to seek congregational collections; the principal Nonconformist denominations at their general assemblies recommended their respective chapels to co-operate. The last Sunday in October for the years 1875, 1876 and 1877 was designated *Sul y Brifysgol* (University Sunday). Now at last an existing, efficient machinery was employed to reach ordinary people who had hitherto been passed by. Owen calculated that during these years nearly £7,000, mostly in very small sums, had been received by house-to-house canvass and chapel collections.[41] Owen knew well the measure of the sacrifice; he himself had no expense account and it is little wonder that he was impatient with even a suspicion of prodigality. Long afterwards he remembered with horror that 12s. 9½d. per head had been paid for the opening breakfast. Henceforth, council members would have to make do with a piece of boiled beef, potatoes and bread and cheese. The registrar was called to account for the price of gum and paper-fasteners and upbraided for buying quill-pens of the kind 'used in the House of Lords, and by persons to whom the cost was no object'.[42] Writing to the principal, he said that 'I fear that the difficulty of getting in money is making me somewhat *hard*, and leading me to grudge to part with a shilling more than I am obliged to.'[43]

It was not all unrelieved gloom. In June 1874 Owen was able to tell subscribers that the debt had been cleared on the College building now valued at £50,000. There was an occasional windfall such as the capital endowment of £2,500 for a chair of natural science by a London businessman, Henry Parnall, who also left the College a legacy of £5,000 in 1878. The National Eisteddfod regularly gave small sums from its annual profits, the North Wales Commercial Travellers' Association, the South Wales Commercial Travellers' Association and the district of Ffestiniog had each given a scholarship of £20 per annum, and the quarry district of Dinorwig and Deiniolen two scholarships of £25 per annum.[44] In 1877 Gladstone delivered at Nottingham one of his encouraging out-of-office speeches, frequently quoted thereafter in the College's Calendars.[45] Such streaks of light, however, were not messengers of dawn and even to hope for an endowment fund of £50,000 seemed like crying for the moon. A further attempt would have to be made for state aid, this time to a government more likely to give a straightforward refusal than its predecessor. In the event Disraeli's President of the Council, the Duke of Richmond, temporized beyond reason. An initial approach was made in June 1875 by a weighty deputation led by Aberdare who argued that England's 'fostering care'[46] had not been extended to Wales, whereas Scotland and Ireland had richly benefited from political union. Marked differences in language and religion presupposed that a separate people should not be treated as if they inhabited a collection of English counties. Anticipating the hoary argument against creating a precedent, he stressed that Owens College lay at the heart of a densely populated area, in clear contrast to Aberystwyth now requesting £2,500 per annum and a capital grant of £5,000. The duke was in jocund mood. He observed in his spry fashion that David Davies, who had supported Aberdare, had done very well for himself without formal education. 'If I had been Lord Aberdare', he bantered, 'I should have kept that gentleman in the background.'[47] He himself had to think of other colleges, he was not empowered to grant any money but the Cabinet would give the College's Memorial its 'best attention'. Aberdare was later to say that he regarded Richmond's response as 'guarded'.[48] In fact it was a thinly veiled rebuff, for there was no reply. In July 1877 the College tried again. Richmond, still in office, was confronted with evidence of support from 256 bodies representing 76 per cent of the population. Henry Richard whimsically remarked that he almost envied the Conservatives the chance of winning general popularity 'at so cheap a rate'.[49] Apart from a kindly reference to Hugh Owen, 'his old friend' (from Whitehall days) who had gone over the Memorial with him beforehand, Richmond was no longer blandly emollient, insinuating, quite without warrant, that some members of the deputation had wanted 'the power of granting cheap degrees'.[50] Nearly a twelvemonth elapsed before Richmond, in a briskly dismissive letter, announced that he and his Cabinet colleagues 'do not see our way to making any such grants as you suggest'.[51]

It now seemed that there was no hope and good men were hard pushed to discern the finger of providence. The council was obliged to make severe cuts; not even the Registrar was spared. The Principal was asked to economize; he reduced his own salary substantially and got rid of three members of staff, replacing them at a lower cost. Even so, Archdeacon Griffiths of Neath thought the staff too large and too expensive, a view supported in part by Aberdare. 'I think too that eight Professors ought to suffice for 58 students and even for a larger number. It seems to me that the somewhat ambiguous designation of the College is misleading – we are a College not an University – and we cannot expect to have at our disposal those Professors who belong to a University, the mother of many Colleges.'[52] Wearied, though not even now in despair, Hugh Owen, in a letter to Henry Richard, reflected upon the manner in which 'turbulent Ireland'[53] had been 'petted' by the government and recalled a conversation with R. W. Lingen, one of the commissioners of 1847, who had told him that a government department could not help Owen's cause: 'you should go to the House of Commons'. Wales, however, had then no voice in Parliament 'and was consequently obliged to submit to be wronged. Happily it is otherwise now; and I am hopeful if the Welsh members were to act unitedly in reference to a grant to this College they would succeed in getting it.'[54] He added that the College Council had argued that Welsh members be asked to consider the best way of bringing the

College's case before Parliament. It was a highly significant letter. Neither government ministers nor government departments were to resist the united voice of the true representatives of the people.

The campaign for university education was part of a larger movement embracing also primary and secondary education. Hugh Owen's mighty exertions were directed to remedy defects and promote advance at each level. By the late 1870s secondary education increasingly engaged his attention, as indeed that of others. Speeches, letters and pamphlets proliferated. In 1876 Lewis Lloyd, headmaster of Friars School, Bangor, later bishop of Bangor, wrote a pamphlet, *The Missing Link*, to which T. Marchant Williams replied in trenchant terms in *The Educational Wants of Wales* (1877). The old Welsh endowed schools, for long incompetently governed, were much improved by 1880, but were wholly inadequate to meet the lowest estimate of the required accommodation. The answer, according to some, was the creation of higher elementary schools linked to the existing grammar schools by means of scholarships. Others favoured a new kind of secondary, or intermediate, school, the solution at length adopted. In the mean time, in 1879, at a meeting at Rhianva, near Menai Bridge, the home of the Verneys, Hugh Owen had successfully proposed the establishment of the North Wales Scholarship Association to bridge 'the chasm',[55] as he called it, separating the elementary school and the higher grade school, and to help talented pupils to compete for awards to colleges and universities. When the Association was wound up in 1889 over £3,000 had been contributed by individuals; although it had been but a temporary palliative, two future professors were amongst the Association's beneficiaries.[56]

The question of scholarships also arose, and in lively fashion, in connection with Jesus College, Oxford. The principal, H. D. Harper, was determined to throw to open competition the closed Meyrick scholarships, hitherto restricted to pupils of certain Welsh grammar schools. He at once precipitated a fierce controversy. Harper's supporters became known as the 'classical party' and his opponents, led by the bellicose Dean H. T. Edwards of Bangor, as the 'national party'. The former included Aberdare and also the Aberystwyth principal, who did not in any case favour closed scholarships in his own college. The conflict further soured relations between principal and dean, whose opposition to Aberystwyth became marked and even unbalanced during the succeeding years. Of more immediate concern was that in

March 1879 the dean wrote to Henry Richard urging him to use his best endeavours to frustrate Harper's proposals and to raise the matter in the House of Commons.[57]

It was against this background that Hussey Vivian, the Swansea industrialist and Liberal member for Glamorgan, moved in the Commons that it was 'the duty of the Government to consider the best means of assisting any local effort which may be made for supplying the deficiency of Higher Education in Wales'.[58] He delivered an impressive speech, well-argued and wide-ranging, indeed from post-Lyell pre-history onwards. We may surmise that the impressive statistics were supplied by Hugh Owen. It was calculated that one out of 840 of the population in Scotland was a university student, in Ireland one in 3,121, and in Wales (including St David's and Jesus College) only one in 8,000.[59] Concerning Jesus College's scholarships he cautioned the government to resist change until it had 'fully considered the whole question of University education in Wales'.[60] His central argument was that 'it is upon the question of nationality that the claim of Wales must mainly rest'.[61] He acknowledged that Welsh members should have pressed the matter more vigorously heretofore but the government should take note that they could assert themselves as forcefully as Irish or Scottish members. He was seconded by J. H. Puleston, the Welsh-speaking Tory member for Devonport (for this was a bipartisan occasion) who believed that he had 'some knowledge of the inner life of the Welsh people'.[62] The first government spokesman, Lord George Hamilton, Vice-President of the Committee of Council on Education resorted to ridicule: '... suppose that Cornwall could establish a separate nationality and that she set up a similar plea – what would be said in that case? The question was, where were they to stop?'[63] Gladstone's brief remarks, perhaps even his very presence, may have 'consolidated his hold on the devoted affection of the Welsh people'.[64] His ventures into Tudor and Stuart periods were not altogether happy: Wales had received 'not only an equitable, but a liberal treatment from the English sovereigns',[65] and 'the old Puritanism of England took no root whatever in Wales'. The real damage had been done after 1688, and here he was on firmer ground. Thereafter 'nothing Welsh had received Parliamentary encouragement' and Wales 'was most cruelly injured through its anglicized religious institutions'. Jesus College, in turn, had 'done nothing for Wales as Wales'.[66] The Principality had distinctive claims to which some recognition should be afforded by the government 'without giving any pledge which should fetter their own liberty'.[67] B. T. Williams (Carmarthen), a member of the Aberystwyth council, asked that the College be 'placed upon a safe and sure footing'[68] by the grant of a subsidy. Morgan Lloyd (Beaumaris) declared that they were not presenting on behalf of the Welsh people a petition *in forma pauperis* but a demand 'as of right'.[69] Osborne Morgan (Denbighshire), in a stirring contribution, then said that they were asking very little of the government, 'not more than they were in the habit of shooting away in a single morning over the heads of a couple of hundred Zulus'.[70] The Chancellor of the Exchequer, Sir Stafford Northcote, as had Lord Hamilton, provocatively referred to the dispute at the College,[71] and gave no promise whatsoever of aid. Lyon Playfair, member for Edinburgh and St Andrews Universities, made a welcome intervention in support of Welsh members.[72] The motion failed by 54 votes to 105. Nevertheless it was 'an important landmark; it made Welsh higher education a political issue for the first time.'[73] It was to be widely discussed during the ensuing months. In the debate Viscount Emlyn, Conservative member for Carmarthenshire, came near the mark when he said that it would be 'impossible to draw up a scheme that would be acceptable to all concerned without holding a full inquiry'.[74] That, as we shall shortly see, was the outcome.

IV

The Aberdare Report

Whatever effect the Midlothian campaign may have had elsewhere in the return of a Liberal government, Joshua Hughes, Bishop of St Asaph, was convinced from his conversations with the 'lower and lower middle classes'[1] that the desire for higher education had much to do with the result of the election in Wales. Here Liberals had won twenty-nine out of the thirty-three seats and in May 1880 Lord Aberdare felt free to remind Gladstone that his exertions in Midlothian ('non tibi sed patria') would not have obscured from him the fact that in every Welsh contest 'one subject was everywhere prominent, and that every candidate, whether successful or not, pledged himself to press upon Government the consideration of the defective condition of Intermediate and Higher Education in Wales'.[2] Hugh Owen had a large share in drafting this letter in the study of Aberdare's London home; it has been suggested that it should rank in equal importance with Hugh Owen's letter to the Welsh people in 1843. Formally, the letter of May 1880 was sent in the name of Aberdare, who, shortly after Owen's death, recalled the occasion with gratitude.[3] Apart from the theological colleges in Wales, which were numerous, the letter ran, but which scarcely needed to be taken into account, there were only two colleges, Lampeter and Aberystwyth. Under Jayne, the present Principal, Lampeter had enjoyed some infusion of vigour, but it was doubtful whether any Nonconformist would wend his way there. On the other hand, though strictly speaking 'nonsectarian', Aberystwyth attracted Nonconformists in the main; it was doing 'fair work', it was satisfying an urgent need, 'but its situation is unfortunate'. Had the college been placed in a large town such as Swansea, the numbers would have trebled. In order to secure 'moral and material support' from north Wales it had been necessary to seek a central site, but the choice of Aberystwyth, determined by chance, 'will I fear forever prevent this College from attracting Endowments and Students in sufficient number to enable it to fulfil adequately the purpose for which it was designed'. Concerning the complicated question of intermediate education, exact information was essential to determine the degree of deficiency. In sum, he requested the appointment of a Royal Commission to deal with both intermediate and higher education. Proposed 'Heads of Enquiry', enclosed in the letter, were almost certainly drawn up by Owen; they bear a striking similarity to the letter of instruction sent to members of the Departmental Committee, and not to a royal commission, as suggested by Aberdare, which, it was considered by some, would take longer to deliberate.

Within three weeks, Owen had written to Hussey Vivian that it would be of the utmost benefit if an inquiry were conducted by 'a few gentlemen acquainted with the people and their national peculiarities, denominational differences, and sectional jealousies'.[4] It is remarkable that of the six names submitted by him, four were eventually appointed. Owen also further outlined the scope of the investigation. It is much to Vivian's credit that although he did not agree with Owen's views he forwarded the letter to Earl Spencer, President of the Council in Gladstone's administration. Meanwhile the government itself was engaged in informal consultations. C. G. Edmondes, later Principal of Lampeter, described as 'certainly one of the ablest and nicest men in Wales',[5] said in a letter which eventually reached Spencer that 'all the Welsh University talk' needed 'a thorough shaking and sifting by capable men'. A balanced commission composed of men generally respected would 'bring the diverse and centrifugal Celt into something like accord'. Self-interest, personal feeling, religious jealousy and misrepresentation might be largely eliminated by allowing evidence to be taken before 'proper men'.[6] In late July 1880 the government decided to appoint a Departmental Committee. Aberdare accepted the chairmanship. Great care was taken to appoint 'proper men'; not one woman's name flitted across the scene. It was not all plain sailing. Aberdare wanted James Bryce, later viscount, a distinguished scholar and administrator, in preference to John Rhys who was chosen by Earl Spencer. Viscount Emlyn, the Conservative member for Carmarthenshire and later Earl of Cawdor was also nominated by Spencer. In the 1879 debate he had not displayed much enthusiasm and Aberdare doubted whether he had enough knowledge of educational organization. A Churchman and landlord, he was said to be 'pledged' to Lampeter and Aberdare believed that he would be serviceable in 'checking nonconformist ambition',[7] a somewhat quaint remark since there was only one Nonconformist on the committee,

Henry Richard. The other two members were Lewis Morris, a poet and a vigorous controversialist, whom Aberdare evidently admired, and Canon H. G. Robinson, Prebendary of York, who had a universal grasp of the intricacies of educational endowments. The presence of only one Englishman was unlikely to cause alarm. Nevertheless, the inadequate representation of Nonconformists and also of north Wales prompted Richard and others to seek to remedy these twin defects. Amongst the persons suggested were Lewis Edwards (scarcely suitable since his own son's college was under scrutiny) and Owen Thomas of Liverpool, another Calvinistic Methodist and also intellectually of the front rank.[8] The government, however, stood firm.

That there was some dismay in Wales at the composition of the committee cannot be doubted. The *Baner* probably reflected accurately the standpoint of many Nonconformists.[9] Henry Richard and Lewis Morris, it believed, enjoyed general confidence; Canon Robinson, relatively unknown, was considered to have liberal inclinations but was English; Viscount Emlyn had many good qualities but was unlikely to understand the feelings and mental attitudes of Welshmen; John Rhys was as familiar as any with the Welsh scene, but his links with Oxford and with Harper, Principal of Jesus College, caused disquiet. The person in whom the *Baner* had least confidence was the chairman, who had not, it was asserted, hitherto given adequate indication that he understood the Welsh people or Welsh Nonconformity. The claims of Hugh Owen were pressed, but Owen seems to have declined in the reasonable belief that he would render more valuable service by giving evidence to the committee. The terms of reference of the committee, appointed on 25 August, were to inquire into the condition of intermediate and higher education in Wales, and to recommend measures for improving and supplementing existing provision. Of special significance for our purpose was the instruction to consider 'whether a University for Wales, with power to grant degrees (in arts) is necessary, or would tend to confer a real benefit on higher education in the Principality'.[10]

An inquiry into higher education in Wales inevitably involved a close examination of the College at Aberystwyth, now in its ninth year. It was recognized that it was a unique institution in Wales and that it was 'the outcome of what may properly be called a national movement, the fruit of patriotic enterprise and voluntary effort'.[11] According to Hugh Owen – and no one was better placed to present such an authoritative analysis of the financial contributions – the total amount received between December 1863 and June 1880 was £65,398, of which £51,131 consisted of voluntary subscriptions.[12] The largest single sum seems to have been £4,000, from David Davies, Llandinam; six others contributed sums of £1,000 and upwards; 4,034 persons gave over half a crown each, 4,938 exactly half-a-crown and at least 100,000 miscellaneous sums below that amount. The unsectarian nature of the movement appeared to be demonstrated by Owen's well-informed estimate of the contributions of members of the various religious denominations, and it as well to be reminded that Anglicans (including, admittedly, a number who were in comfortable circumstances) gave 33 per cent of the total, Calvinistic Methodists 29 per cent, the Independents 24 per cent and other denominations 14 per cent.[13] Since the opening of the college, 313 students had been in attendance. Their places of origin occasioned much discussion and are therefore tabulated as follows.[14]

Anglesey	8	Flintshire	12
Brecknockshire	8	Glamorgan	22
Caernarfonshire	22	Merioneth	23
Cardiganshire	117	Montgomeryshire	12
Carmarthenshire	34	Monmouthshire	6
Denbighshire	9	Pembrokeshire	3
England	35	Radnorshire	–

The highest number to have attended the College at one time was 93 and the number in attendance at the time of the inquiry was 57. The yearly cost of education to the student was £10 in fees and between £30 and £40 for board and lodging. The cost to the College of educating each student was more than five times the amount received in fees, namely £53. Since 1872 only ten students had graduated, four at Cambridge, three at Oxford, and three at London.[15] Confronted with these bare facts alone the committee announced that the College had 'disappointed the hopes of its promoters' and that it had 'failed to attract students in sufficient numbers to entitle it to be regarded as a successful institution'.[16] One of the committee's main duties was to cast light upon this sombre scene.

First, the creation of Aberystwyth was said by many witnesses to have been unfortunate. Hugh Owen told the committee that the founders of the College believed that 'Aberystwyth was a remarkably eligible position'.[17] He was obliged now to conclude that 'their opinion was not well grounded'. In the course of his evidence he also said that 'it was thought that the college would be resorted to by persons, certainly, from all parts of North Wales, and it was hoped too that the people of South Wales would also avail themselves of it.'[18] Clearly he was thinking more in terms of north Wales than of south Wales. North Wales witnesses, however, did not think they had been especially blessed. The Dean of Bangor argued that a youth could travel as speedily and as cheaply from Bangor to Oxford as from Bangor to Aberystwyth.[19] W. Cadwaladr Davies who had eagerly collected money for the College, spoke in the same vein, adding that to have to run the gauntlet of the Afonwen Junction was grievous and that before he knew where he was a traveller to Barmouth had to stay the night at Porthmadog.[20] South Wales witnesses were no less adamant. To the Mayor of Swansea, Aberystwyth was 'out of the way'[21] and to the Principal of the Baptist College, Pontypool, 'not at all a suitable place'.[22] Few would agree with the Bishop of St Asaph who claimed that 'now distance is destroyed by railways',[23] though he added 'to a certain extent', by way of qualified tribute, one imagines, to the drowsy Cambrian line.

Then there was the issue of denominationalism. The College was to all purposes an unsectarian institution, no lectures or tutorials were given on divinity and no pressure whatsoever was exerted to encourage students to attend a particular place of worship. Yet it was not easy to dispose entirely of insinuations in the press and elsewhere that the College bore the stamp of Calvinistic Methodism. The Dean of Bangor was fierce on such matters in public, though less 'sweeping' and 'impulsive' before the committee, as Aberdare told Gladstone, 'when he knew that what he said would be sifted'.[24] A Merthyr Tudful witness, however, was not to be muzzled. 'The College', he announced, 'is practically a Calvinistic Methodist institution.'[25] This was certainly not broadly true of the College staff, and the principal was thinking of students when he said that there had 'always been a preponderating number of Calvinistic Methodists'[26] in the College. He himself was in a vulnerable position particularly when the committee frequently asked witnesses whether they favoured a layman as principal. Their affirmative replies were duly noted in the Report.

The small staff at Aberystwyth could not fairly be accused of inadequacy. Some criticism was levelled at second hand, but Hugh Owen's estimate was that 'the teaching at the college is very good'.[27] It was undoubtedly dispiriting for able men to be confronted with minds so often 'a blank' that 'it was necessary to begin with them at the very beginning'.[28] T. S. Humpidge, professor of natural science, observed that his new students had come to him 'without any knowledge of Chemistry whatsoever' and were 'perfectly ignorant of science'.[29] A poor grasp of English was a serious impediment and W. J. Craig, a former professor of English, used to take a special class for those who scarcely knew any English.[30] The real disability, however, lay in the absence of satisfactory provision beyond the elementary school, a disability, it may be added, which had afflicted Irish students entering the Queen's Colleges before the Irish Intermediate Act of 1879 came into operation; from Belfast College came the testimony of the principal that intermediate education had given a powerful stimulus to higher education amongst males and females. It was noted too that Scottish students who proceeded to university from the admirable parochial schools, established initially by John Knox, had perforce to tackle work more appropriate to secondary schools.[31] In Wales the headmasters of the old endowed grammar schools which prepared men for Oxford and Cambridge did not wish to send their pupils to Aberystwyth. Indeed, according to Stephen Evans, a vice-president of Aberystwyth, the staff of the endowed schools were not merely uncooperative; they were actually hostile, and it not infrequently happened that when a pupil proposed to go to Aberystwyth pressure was exerted upon him not to go. A 'very considerable' number of boys aged fifteen or sixteen had been expected from the old grammar schools but 'we have been completely disappointed from the very first'.[32] Humpidge was in full agreement with Canon Robinson that the gymnasium and the lyceum in Germany and Switzerland educated those who were 'not wealthy, but very much in the position of the middle class population in Wales'.[33] When asked from what class Aberystwyth students were usually drawn, Hugh Owen answered *tout court*, 'the middle class'. Whilst it was reassuring to hear that students were 'anxious to get education for the love of it', it was also clear, not only that they were ill-prepared upon entry, but that there was an imperfect understanding of the object and purpose of the College and that 'a large number of Welsh people confound a university and colleges with higher and lower schools'. The ages of the 313 students who had attended the College since 1872 ranged from fifteen to twenty-nine; 12 per cent were under seventeen. As to length of study, 81 had attended for less than one session and 202 for less than two sessions.[34]

This leads us naturally to consider the views of witnesses concerning the establishment of 'provincial colleges', as the Report called them, and of a university for Wales. Not unexpectedly, the headmasters persisted in their opposition. W. Glynn Williams, of Friars School, Bangor, said that both Lampeter and Aberystwyth were 'misfortunes'[35] and that similar institutions would diminish the number of youths entering English universities. A. G. Edwards, warden of Llandovery College and later to be Wales's first archbishop, thought that apart from training students for the ministry, colleges of advanced education were not needed in Wales. From schools of the first grade (so-called by the Taunton Commission) pupils would proceed amply prepared to the older universities at nineteen; indeed, it was thought that a boy half way up the sixth form would already have reached the standard of the pass degree at Oxford and Cambridge. The new colleges sprouting up throughout the land which were following the Scottish practice of entry at sixteen undermined a hallowed English tradition. In Wales, isolation and provincialism would be perpetuated.[36] The Principal of Jesus College did not want Aberystwyth destroyed but he thought that the liberal, patriotic men who had founded the College would have done more good had they provided bursaries to send Welshmen to Liverpool and Bristol.[37] Another witness opposed to additional colleges in Wales was the Principal of Bristol, Alfred Marshall, thereafter an illustrious economist.[38] Bristol, he informed the committee, had been founded as a college for the 'West of England and for south Wales'; among the governors of the college were the mayors of the principal towns and the heads of two educational establishments in south Wales. The prime need in Wales was 'trade schools' and scholarships to enable pupils to proceed to existing colleges. If another college were to be founded in Wales it should be near a large centre of population; from Bristol's standpoint Swansea would be the best choice.

In the main, however, irrespective of Aberystwyth's ultimate fate, there was general agreement that colleges were needed in Wales. 'It cannot be said that the evidence received by us on this point was absolutely unanimous', observed the Report, 'but it certainly made a considerable approach to unanimity.'[39] Many believed that local colleges both awakened and fulfilled a desire for higher education. The large proportion of Cardiganshire men at Aberystwyth seemed proof enough, although it should not be forgotten that the county had an educational tradition, centred primarily on Ystrad Meurig in its flourishing days and was called 'the Levitical county'[40] before St David's College was even bruited. Had Glamorgan provided students in the same proportion as Cardiganshire it would have sent 600 to Aberystwyth, instead of a trivial twenty-two. At Merthyr Tudful the committee was told by a minister of religion: 'Too much stress cannot be put on the importance of bringing the means of education as near as possible to the people. The love of home and country is so strong that with difficulty will the Welshman depart even for the sake of a college education.'[41] At Cardiff the Reverend J. Cynddylan Jones, who had an intimate knowledge of the seven counties of south Wales, said that he had not detected 'a vehement desire and readiness to make great sacrifices for education in the bulk of the people', adding that 'the love of knowledge grows in the tasting' and that 'they have not tasted the sweetness of knowledge'.[42] Seen from the south, Aberystwyth was a north Wales college, and it is significant that almost all the exhibitions and scholarships had been given by the people of north Wales. The Victoria University had given an opportunity to men who would never otherwise have graduated. It was incontestable, too, that Galway, the most successful of the Queen's Colleges, had opened doors to the professions to its best students, doors which had hitherto been closed. Colleges and schools were interdependent and schools needed 'an opening upwards'[43] in the words of the Bishop of St Asaph, if they were to flourish. It followed that no college planted amongst poor people should ever charge more than they could afford, and he recalled that Lampeter's comparatively high charges had at one time a harmful effect on grammar schools in the diocese of St David's. Some witnesses, perhaps wiser than their brethren, believed that the interests of education in Wales would be best served by attending first to intermediate education. W. B. Rowlands, a barrister and chairman of Haverfordwest grammar school, thought it much better to begin at the basement of a building, not at the top storey.[44] The Rector of North Benfleet in Essex held that if there was a general sentiment to establish a complete system of education in Wales (contrary to his own personal preference) it would be best to perfect the elementary and secondary schools, pause for ten years before considering the creation of a university and 'wait till the national sentiment has had time to inform itself',[45] in the event a searchingly shrewd remark.

To return to the question of colleges, with which we are immediately concerned, Thomas Gee of Denbigh did not command widespread support in proposing that there should be two colleges for young men in north Wales (at Bangor and Rhuthun) and three in south Wales (unspecified, apart from Aberystwyth); in addition he wanted two colleges for women in north Wales (Denbigh and Dolgellau) and three in south Wales (also unspecified). He was, however, realistic enough to recognize that they could not be established at once.[46] Most witnesses considered two colleges would suffice, one in north Wales and one in south Wales. The case for a college in Glamorgan was overwhelming and the Aberystwyth Principal envisaged a college there rather like Bristol in which science was the core of the teaching, Aberystwyth being left as it was but with a strengthened classical or literary side. A former Aberystwyth professor, impressed by the development of Owens College, Manchester, foresaw a prosperous future for a science college (though not exclusively so) in Glamorgan, 'a splendid collecting ground for just the right sort of men'.[47] Swansea was an obvious candidate, but Lewis Williams of Cardiff, and upon his own admission *parti pris*, sought to weigh impartially the claims of Swansea and of Cardiff, allowing the facts to speak for themselves: within a 25-mile radius of Swansea there was a population of 269,000, and within a similar radius of Cardiff a population of 483,000.[48] If a college were situated in Caernarfonshire, in addition to the Aberystwyth college, Thomas Charles Edwards was convinced that one or other would be bound to fail; two such colleges could not prosper. Hugh Owen was of the same mind; a college in north Wales would 'necessarily cripple the Aberystwyth College'.[49]

As to the establishing of a university in Wales, the Report did not doubt that 'amongst the people of Wales generally there is a desire for the creation of a university with the power of conferring degrees'.[50] Resolutions passed at public meetings and at the assemblies of religious bodies appeared to convey unanimous assent. Thus the moderator-elect of the Calvinistic Methodist General Assembly, representing 1,200 churches and nearly 120,000 communicants, confidently proclaimed that 'the feeling of our connexion is altogether in favour of a university for Wales'.[51] Yet it became evident that when individual witnesses were questioned there were pronounced differences of opinion. Once again, there was the predictable antagonism of headmasters who appeared to think that the choice lay between graduating at Oxford and Cambridge and at a Welsh university, whereas in practice the latter offered to most the only opportunity of graduating at all. Other opponents not so likely to be affected by 'professional bias',[52] as the Report put it, included the Earl of Powis, Richard Davies, member for Anglesey, and the Dean of Bangor. The Earl of Powis believed it would be beneficial for Welshmen to be brought into contact with 'the great centres of English literary life and thought',[53] though he did not object to assisting colleges in Wales which prepared students for the degree of the University of London; this he later did most honourably as President of the Bangor College. Richard Davies, whilst recognizing that there was great enthusiasm for a university in Wales, did not think it advantageous to create such a body; rather, he would affiliate the Welsh colleges to 'some of the older universities'.[54] The Dean of Bangor conceded that if Wales were an island and 'absolutely isolated' the solution would be to place the university in 'the best centre', where denominational halls would be grouped. In fact he was certain that 'the terminus of Welsh higher education ought to be in the English universities and not in Wales'.[55] The value of future degrees was, naturally, a matter of legitimate concern and was given the closest attention before and after 1893. Uneasiness on this score was expressed by a fellow of Jesus College in the course of remarks not lacking in presumption, and it did no harm for the committee to be told later by Alfred Marshall that 'the BA of Oxford and Cambridge means that the man has had some opportunities for learning the amenities of social life and is not an absolute fool, but nothing more'.[56] He had in mind the pass degree; the honours degree was an entirely different matter. The Reverend Abel Jones Parry of Swansea spoke sound sense: 'It is urged as an objection to a university for Wales that its degrees would be of little value. We cannot see why they should be so. The value of such degrees would depend on the examinations. This objection was urged against the London University at one time, but it has now lost its force and is never mentioned.'[57] Such was certainly Hugh Owen's opinion. There was, however, widespread apprehension concerning the proliferation of universities. Alfred Marshall's objection was partly based upon the inevitable multiplication of examiners. He wanted one examination for several places on the ground that examining injured the examiner, for it was 'simply destructive of his intellectual power',[58] a potent point not likely to be dismissed by reluctant practitioners. The received wisdom of the age was that new universities should not be too readily created. At Bristol, Marshall informed the committee, they had firmly decided not to become a university and they did not consider it expedient for Wales to have one. Multiplication, it was feared, would lead to depreciation. As Lord Ashby once observed, 'more means worse' was not an invention of the 1960s.[59] By the end of the century, however, Bristol was beginning to change its mind and in 1904 received its charter.

Those who desired a degree-awarding university in Wales spoke with various voices. There was no widespread desire for a unitary university, which would be out of the question if there were to be two colleges widely separated. B.T. Williams, it will be recalled, had in 1853 urged with the full assurance of untried youth that there should be one centre. Now a Queen's Counsel and a member for Carmarthen boroughs, he appeared to be making conflicting recommendations. At one stage in his evidence he supported the establishment of colleges similar to the Queen's Colleges in Ireland, one of which should be in a great centre of population. He then proceeded to say that 'my own view is that the fewer colleges the better, because I should like to see one large and national institution . . . say at Cardiff' which, he imagined, 'would drain all the students from any other institutions we might establish'.[60] T. McKenny Hughes, professor of geology at Cambridge and son of the Bishop of St Asaph, with some bravura wanted to 'throw all the colleges together into one locality', but speedily recognized that it 'cannot be carried out'.[61] The Principal of the Carmarthen Presbyterian College offered a novel objection to a concentration of resources. If Nonconformist students were brought to one centre in order to pursue the non-theological part of their studies, they would be unable to preach in the neighbourhood of their own colleges which would thus be denuded of the financial support of local chapels.[62] One of the most significant contributions came from Thomas Charles Edwards. In conceding that there should be a college in south Wales he was in effect looking ahead to a federal solution, for he was evidently attracted by the precedent of Owens College, Manchester, which was the first, and for a time, the sole constituent college of the Victoria University whose charter in April 1880 provided for the addition of other colleges 'not [to] be situated, like those of Oxford and Cambridge, in one town, but wherever a college of adequate efficiency and stability shall have arisen'.[63] Edwards clearly had in mind that the headquarters of the University of Wales should be at Aberystwyth, just as Manchester was the headquarters of Victoria, but he quite properly added that the college at Aberystwyth 'would not be any more a university than so many other colleges would be'.[64] In short, Aberystwyth was to be the local habitation of a federal university. This remained Edwards's hope.

There was conflict of opinion, later to be resurrected with some virulence, between the advocates of a teaching and of an examining university. The Bishop of St Asaph was adamant that 'a teaching university is the very thing that Welshmen stand in need of'.[65] Students should attend some courses at colleges not their own; there should be peripatetic professors, and also university professorships, as at Oxford and Cambridge, to supplement the teaching of the colleges, which should not become preparatory schools for English universities. The school boards of south-east Wales wanted a university, to be called 'the Cambrian University'[66] similar to the Queen's University in Ireland, comprising one college in south-east Wales and one in north Wales, in addition to Aberystwyth. Their ambitions relating to colleges were wholly fulfilled, but they could not then have known that Gladstone, newly returned to office, deemed it unwise to annul Disraeli's act of 1879 establishing the Royal University of Ireland.[67] The new creation, incorporated in 1880, was in effect an examining, not a teaching, university and degrees (except in medicine) could be granted to those who had passed prescribed examinations irrespective of whether they had followed courses in a university college. In 1882 the Queen's University was dissolved and the three Queen's Colleges were no longer constituent colleges of a teaching university. Hugh Owen was wholly unrepentant. For years his constant wish for Wales was a system patterned on London. The power of granting degrees was to be vested in an examining board appointed by the crown and constituted by royal charter. The university, to be called 'The Prince of Wales' University',[68] would comprise colleges on exactly the same footing and of the same name: 'one would be the Prince of Wales' College at Aberystwyth or elsewhere, and the other would be the Prince of Wales' College at Swansea or elsewhere'. The university would not have a special link with any college and would examine any candidate who presented himself, as in London, his metropolitan model. The great English universities would still remain open to Welshmen but he was persuaded that the opportunity to prepare for and to receive a degree within Wales would greatly augment the number of Welsh students.

Even amongst those who wished to see a university in Wales there was, then, a pronounced disparity of views. Was it to be a unitary or a federal university, a teaching or an examining university? If one witness is to be allowed to speak for an appreciable number of his countrymen, we may reasonably choose Abel Jones Parry, a Baptist minister from Swansea. We have already had cause to note his comments concerning the value to be attached to a Welsh degree. On the same occasion – he was representing the Swansea School Board – he maintained that objections to a university in Wales came from two groups: the wealthy, who could afford to send their sons to Oxford and Cambridge, and the clergy, who had a college in Wales – who were 'remarkably careful to restrict its benefits to themselves and their flocks'.[69] The presence of a degree-conferring college in Lampeter was a precedent for founding another, particularly since the benefits of Lampeter were restricted to a small portion of the community; it was time now to provide for the larger portion. A Welsh university would not discourage students from attending English universities and within Wales he thought that 'it would give completeness to the whole system of education; that it would act as a stimulus to the youth of the country in the direction of higher culture – that its accessibility would certainly enlarge the number of those who would seek its benefits – and that its very existence would raise the intellectual tone of the whole nation'.[70] Here was the authentic voice of a sane idealism.

In any inquiry into higher education in Wales close attention would need to be given to St David's College, Lampeter, which had the unique privilege in Wales of conferring degrees. It had more students in 1880 than Aberystwyth, seventy-eight as opposed to fifty-three; since 1865, 192 students had taken the BA degree, whereas only eleven Aberystwyth students had graduated at English colleges. Aberdare was later to tell Gladstone that the most impressive testimony given to the Departmental Committee was that of the Lampeter Principal, F. J. Jayne: 'his evidence was the best and weightiest we received and delivered with the greatest clearness, force and ability; as well as with the utmost candour and breadth of view.' Henry Richard, the sole Nonconformist on the committee, 'was as much impressed by him as any of us'. These expressions of approval he repeated to Mundella in 1884, adding, unexpectedly, that 'doctrinal differences sit very lightly on the consciences of Welsh laymen and that it is notorious that Nonconformist farmers and tradesmen often bring a son to the Ministry of the Church as a matter of business'.[71] How many Welsh clergy, he pondered, were the sons of Nonconformist parents, but he did not develop this enduringly beguiling theme. For our present purpose it is sufficient to note that Jayne wished to encourage Nonconformists to enter Lampeter, stressing that there were no religious tests. His attempts later to enrol them, however, caused sharp resentment and very few Nonconformists studied at Lampeter, being deterred, it seems, by the atmosphere of religious dissension.[72] One or two witnesses spoke approvingly of the college[73] but others were tepid. Bishop Ollivant of Llandaff recalled the low standard upon entry when he was Vice-Principal and the Bishop of St Asaph upon the considerable number of failures; the latter was especially critical of the practice of giving certificates to those who had failed the degree.[74] The sternest criticism came from an unexpected quarter, from a former Vice-Principal, Stewart Perowne, now Dean of Peterborough, who had been mainly responsible for the charter of 1865. He announced that it was a fundamental error to have placed the college at Lampeter far from 'all humanizing and socializing influences'.[75] Degrees awarded by a university in Wales would be of little value and he would much prefer to see Lampeter and Aberystwyth affiliated, if possible, to the older universities.

What future role was there, then, for Lampeter in any development of higher education? Jayne thought it possible to have a university 'of a modest kind'[76] in Wales which should act as feeder to the older universities. The bishops of St David's and of Bangor thought that a 'local university' would not succeed, but the Bishop of St Asaph, who strongly favoured a teaching university in Wales, envisaged a special role for St David's, not simply as a constituent college, like Aberystwyth, but as the local habitation of the University, precisely the role which T. C. Edwards had in mind for Aberystwyth.[77] A. G. Edwards of Llandovery wanted to extend the Lampeter degree to Nonconformists, reserving for St David's the exclusive right of conferring degrees in Wales.[78] The Dean of St Asaph touched upon a vital matter: 'It seems to me that as long as St David's College... grants degrees in arts, the Nonconformists in Wales have some right to complain that they are unable to obtain the same advantage in their own country without residence in what has been virtually a denominational college.'[79] A Baptist minister spoke for most Nonconformists when he declared that the presence of a degree-conferring college in Wales restricted to a small section of the community was a sound reason for establishing a second college to meet the needs of the largest portion of the same community.[80] In the course of the years Lewis Edwards had changed his mind. At one time he had thought the question of a university in Wales to be 'very unimportant', but he would now support the creation of a university, provided it was an examining, not a teaching body and based upon the governing principles at London University. Theological colleges would thus be able to present students for examination upon the same basis as any other college. The fact that Lampeter was able to confer degrees 'places all other colleges under great disadvantage'.[81]

It was natural that the Report, therefore, should include a brief section on the eight Nonconformist colleges primarily engaged upon preparing candidates for the ministry.[82] Most of their students, it noted, had come from the 'humble classes' and had after daily labour equipped themselves as far as possible by thrift and self-denial for a course lasting three to four years. The safe assumption was made that 'idleness and dissipation were not prevalent faults among students of this class';[83] doubtless the same might confidently be claimed for the vast majority at Aberystwyth and Lampeter. It was estimated that seventy Nonconformist ministers were now graduates, mainly of the Scottish universities, and that the number was increasing annually.

The Report then proceeded to consider the number of Welsh students of all kinds who were receiving university education.[84] It was by no means easy to form a reliable estimate. Upon the basis of university provision in Prussia, Wales should have 600 students under instruction, but it was improbable that there were more than 300 in all the universities together. Not many were achieving high honours: of these there were fewer in classical studies, because of the language difficulty, than in mathematics and science. Inadequate preparation at secondary level was the besetting problem. Preferential rights for Welshmen were reserved only at Jesus College, Oxford, where, out of forty students in residence, most derived financial help out of college funds. In the opinion of some they received scant benefit from the *genius loci*, thus retaining in isolation these angularities thought to be the mark of a provincial born and bred.[85]

The conclusions of the Report concerning higher education at once dealt with the almost unanimous view of witnesses that provincial colleges should be established in Wales. Colleges similar to those founded in several of the larger English towns were much to be desired in Wales. True, the Welsh people might suffer from inadequate formal training, but they had 'a natural turn for some forms of literary culture and self-improvement'[86] which would be further encouraged by more advanced education. There followed the dire observation that 'the experience of the University College at Aberystwyth, where various adverse causes have operated, must not be taken to be conclusive against the success of such colleges in Wales.'[87] Until intermediate education had paved the way, the time would not be ripe to create a 'considerable number' of colleges in Wales. For the time being there should be one additional college only in Wales, the overwhelming opinion being that it should be placed in Glamorgan, either at Cardiff, where there was the largest population, or at Swansea, where the industries were more varied. Then came a recommendation which was to be mulled over carefully throughout the land: 'The Glamorganshire college may be expected for some time, at all events, to meet the requirements of South Wales, and the college at Aberystwyth, whether retained on its present site or removed to Carnarvon or Bangor, must be accepted as the college for North Wales.'[88] Even in the best of times such colleges could not be self-supporting. Without government aid the Aberystwyth college would collapse, and there must therefore be a parliamentary grant of £4,000 per annum to each college, which, together with students' fees, would 'amply suffice' to pay the professional staff and effectively maintain the college. Attention was inevitably drawn to Scottish and Irish precedents. For the year 1881–2, £18,992 had been voted for the Scottish universities and £22,801 for the Irish universities.[89] Apart from the annual grant, there was the matter of capital expenditure. For building its new colleges, Glasgow had received £140,000 and the Queen's Colleges in Ireland £100,000. The question arose as to the capital needs of the Welsh colleges. The Report does not mention the requirements of a college established at Caernarfon or Bangor, presumably because the sale of the Aberystwyth building (if that became necessary) would provide sufficient capital for the purpose. Consideration, however, was given to the new college in Glamorgan. Provision for the Queen's Colleges pointed the way to a substantial state subvention, but there was no reason, according to the Report, why local contributions should not relieve the 'once for all' expense, as it was unrealistically called, particularly since south Wales had large resources. The colleges should respond to the social needs of the country, and in words which would have gladdened the hearts of

Hugh Owen and of Thomas Nicholas, 'the more practical the education, the more it takes account of the requirements of commercial and professional life, the more will it be in demand amongst a people who, in all efforts they make and the sacrifices they undergo, have very definitely before them the importance of fitting themselves for a career'. Applied science was to have a prominent position in the curriculum, classical studies were not to be disregarded, and a 'leading position' should be given to English literature and to modern languages which in large towns were 'most conducive to commercial success'. Care was to be given to the constitution of the colleges, which if in receipt of public funds, should have crown nominees upon their governing boards. The colleges were to be wholly unsectarian, no theological instruction was to be provided and the principal was always to be a layman. Opportunities were to be extended to women, and it was assumed that students would proceed from their second-grade schools, at sixteen or thereabouts, much earlier than pupils of first-grade schools *en route* to Oxford and Cambridge, that they would complete their studies before they were twenty and that they would enter into 'active business life'.[90]

The Report then dealt with a degree-conferring university in Wales.[91] It was not to be expected that such a body would at once be the equal of the London and Victoria Universities or of the Queen's University. Its work would be much more restricted and very few students would come from outside Wales. Welshmen able to go elsewhere would continue to do so and doubts had been raised as to the numbers who would attend a Welsh university. Nevertheless, the Report believed that a university in Wales would exercise 'a beneficial influence':

> It would bring such education more closely home to the daily life and thoughts of the people. It would gratify the national sentiment and furnish new motives for the pursuit of learning. It might, under favourable circumstances, tend to develop new forms of culture in affinity with some of the distinctive characteristics of the Welsh people. A lesser luminary in close proximity will shed more light than a far greater orb shining from a distant sphere, and so a Welsh university crowning the educational edifice might help to diffuse the light of knowledge more generally through the Principality than has been or can be done by Oxford or Cambridge with all their prestige.[92]

Hesitation concerning the success of the proposed university if immediately summoned into being was qualified by the presence of St David's College, which, though not a university in the proper sense of the word, nevertheless had the privilege of conferring degrees. True, only a small portion of the people derived benefit from the arrangement and Nonconformists could scarcely view with equanimity a monopoly enjoyed by a minority church. The Report recommended that St David's Charter for conferring degrees in arts subjects should be withdrawn and a new charter granted permitting degrees to be awarded by a syndicate or board to consist of an equal number of representatives of the colleges of St David's, Aberystwyth and any other college 'being a place of advanced secular instruction, which may be affiliated for the purpose'. Degrees would be awarded by examiners chosen partly by the syndicate and partly by Oxford and Cambridge. Candidates for a degree would be required to study for three years at one of the affiliated colleges, a condition of central importance because it was a clear renunciation of the systems pertaining in London and, after 1882, in the Royal University of Ireland. It would be necessary to consider to what extent students in theological colleges providing systematic secular education and also women students might be included in these arrangements. The powers hitherto granted by charter to St David's were reported to have had a beneficial effect upon the college; if it were possible to include other colleges the increase in numbers and 'a spirit of wholesome emulation' would tend in time to raise the existing standard at St David's, now believed to be 'quite equal to that of a respectable pass degree' at the older universities. St David's was to continue to enjoy an untrammelled right to confer degrees in divinity. These proposals here outlined were 'to prepare the way for the establishment of a Welsh University in a more complete form whenever the country is found ripe for it'. Concerning Jesus College, Oxford, and its relation to higher education in Wales, the committee was unwilling to make any recommendation.

One of the most striking features of the Report, and of the evidence submitted, is the dominant concern for the needs of the so-called middle classes. The chairman of the school board at Newport, a Calvinistic Methodist minister, spoke in terms familiar enough to the leaders of the university movement. The lower middle class, he argued, were under a special disadvantage, because of the operation of the Education Acts – he was thinking primarily of the Forster Act of

1870 – because both nationally and locally they were required to contribute to the education of 'the very poorest, without having an opportunity given them to afford to their own children a better education'. They were obliged to resort to elementary schools and to elementary schools only, 'and then the children of the very poor compete with their children for stations in commercial life'. Canon Robinson's question to a Rhondda colliery proprietor was equally revealing: '. . . is it not the fact that the education of the working classes as a body has been provided for by the Elementary Education Act, and as they have the education which they require amply provided, the question of their comparative poverty hardly arises in an inquiry with regard to higher education?'[93] Hugh Owen, though constantly speaking of middle-class education, anticipated that 'the exceptionally clever boy' would proceed with scholarships to a secondary school and then to one of the colleges.[94] The Aberdare Report is preoccupied with the shopkeeper and the farmer, the commercial traveller and the small industrialist, together with a sprinkling of artisans. It was generally agreed, and it could scarcely be otherwise, that the middle and lower middle classes in Wales were poorer than the corresponding classes in England. Statistics were presented to demonstrate that the average agricultural holding in Wales was 46 acres, in England 56 acres, that only 6.6 per cent of houses were assessed for duty in Wales, as opposed to 18 or 19 per cent in England.[95] The Report added that amongst the artisan 'classes' there was 'an exceptional appreciation' of education and 'in many cases a just readiness to make sacrifices in order to obtain it'.[96] The pervasive term is 'middle class'.

What was the reaction to the Report? In Aberystwyth it was understandably not much liked. At the outset, upon a superficial view, it had seemed that the auguries were propitious. The membership of the committee encouraged expectation that the problems of the College would be understood and fairly weighed in the balance. Aberdare was President of the College, Henry Richard Vice-President, Lewis Morris Honorary Secretary and John Rhys a governor of some years standing. The historian of the college, whose judgement is weighty, has no hesitation, however, in concluding that the committee had 'decided beforehand that the institution was moribund' and that there was 'little point in delaying the post-mortem'.[97] Whilst absolving the committee of wilful malevolence, he believes that the Report in relation to

Aberystwyth is 'open to serious challenge'. He supports his charges
with a formidable body of evidence. We have earlier noted that
Aberdare in his letter to Gladstone in May 1880 had spoken of
Aberystwyth's 'unfortunate' situation which would discourage both
contributions and students in sufficient numbers to ensure the success
of the College.[98] A. J. Mundella was informed that Aberdare had from
the first given his opinion that 'the College was no better than a school,
and that his own district in South Wales was the proper site for the
College'.[99] As chairman of the Committee he may also reasonably be
criticized for not having encouraged Thomas Charles Edwards to be
more forthcoming in his replies. There cannot have been a witness
better informed concerning the tribulations of the College but at times
he appeared strangely inhibited, perhaps because of a natural pride
when cast in the role of a defendant under examination. The Lampeter
Principal, however, was allowed to roam at large and was not called
upon to explain what he meant when he loftily remarked that 'accuracy
is not a characteristic of the Welsh mind'.[100] A crusty former student,
T. Marchant Williams (whose impeccable English accent much
impressed Aberdare) was not asked to say why he was so curtly
dismissive of his old college. Nor were two professors, representing arts
and science, closely questioned when they insisted that it was grossly
wrong to stigmatize the College as no better than a grammar school and
that the number of ill-prepared students had of late declined. As to the
other members of the committee, Lewis Morris seemed infatuated with
the idea of turning the College into a high school or into a college for
girls, Henry Richard has been accused of transferring his allegiance
from Aberystwyth to Cardiff and of not assisting the College after
1881, whilst Viscount Emlyn was considered 'pledged'[101] to
Lampeter, as we have seen, and of not being favourable at any time to
Aberystwyth.

The Report certainly damaged Aberystwyth's reputation and
prospects. The recommendation that the College at Aberystwyth,
whether it remained where it was or whether it was removed to
Caernarfon or Bangor, should be accepted as the North Wales College
was clearly interpreted by the northern counties of Wales as an
invitation to act with some dispatch. The proposal that only a layman
should be the principal of an 'unsectarian' college was, in the
circumstances of the day, reasonable. But the opportunity was lost, and
in a hurtful fashion, to pay a just, graceful tribute to Edwards for his

services as administrator and teacher and also as a tireless collector of funds for his struggling college. Indeed, as we have observed elsewhere, the fact that he was not a layman may in the early days have been a positive advantage;[102] henceforth, and for his remaining days at Aberystwyth, it was to be a disadvantage, bordering upon a stigma.

One of the criticisms levelled against the Report is that it tended to see the educational problems of Wales through English eyes, more especially those relating to intermediate education.[103] Paradoxically, it did not give sufficient attention to illuminating parallels in England, one of the manifold defects of the Blue Book Reports of 1847. This is particularly true of higher education, where a sense of proportion might have given a better perspective. In mid-century, for example, University College, London, suffered 'a period of stagnation';[104] at King's College, we are told, 'a general air of poverty and depression brooded over the dingy scene',[105] and in 1864–6 Bedford College was close to bankruptcy.[106] Owens College, Manchester, had begun life with a handsome legacy, but between 1851 and 1857 the number of day students had fallen from sixty-three to thirty-four; in 1857 the *Manchester Examiner* described the college as 'going thro' its diurnal martyrdom of bootless enthusiasm and empty benches',[107] and the *Manchester Guardian* castigated it as 'a mortifying failure'.[108] By the 1870s, it is true, the newer colleges were beginning to pick up, but Owens College in 1880, as Alfred Marshall told the Aberdare Committee, was overspending itself by £10,000 per annum.[109] He could also have added that Bristol was plagued with debts and that he wanted to resign in 1879, partly because he found the burden of begging for money highly distasteful. In fact he did resign in 1881, and in 1887 his successor became Dean of the Faculty for economy's sake.[110] Nor were the early days of Sheffield or of Reading wholly happy. A deeper awareness of the early history of English colleges would perhaps have led to a more generous appraisal of Aberystwyth's first eight years. It is curious that the report of a committee almost entirely composed of Welshmen was in some ways less positive and encouraging in tone than the Report in 1917 of the Haldane Commission of which only three of the nine members were Welsh. Again, the Haldane Report is well written, and is clear, spritely and constructive. Lucidity is not a marked characteristic of the Aberdare Report.

There is also in the Report an air of fuzziness concerning Lampeter's future, which may have led Emrys Evans into a rare error. It is necessary here to repeat that Lampeter had two charters, that of 1852 conferring a degree in divinity and that of 1865 conferring a degree in ·arts. In a sense Lampeter was a 'quasi-University',[111] as T. C. Edwards called it, for it was a degree-awarding college. Emrys Evans believed that the Aberdare Report intended that both charters be withdrawn, whereas the first was to remain, thus allowing the College to continue to offer degrees in divinity,[112] a monopolistic arrangement which would further incense Nonconformists. The intention was that the 1865 charter alone should be withdrawn and a new one granted to a 'syndicate', consisting of an equal number of representatives of Lampeter, Aberystwyth and any other suitable college to be later affiliated.[113] The terms of reference of the committee, as we have seen, asked it to enquire 'whether a University for Wales with power to grant degrees (in arts) is necessary'. In view of the committee's recommendation that science should be given a prominent place in a new college in south Wales it is difficult to believe that degrees in science were not being seriously contemplated. If this was the case it was necessary to deal directly and clearly with the terms of reference. On matters of this kind the committee was diffuse. It is evident that it proposed 'to prepare the way for the establishment of a Welsh University in a more complete form whenever the country is found ripe for it'.[114] The problem of creating a fully fledged university at this stage must in fairness be recognized, but the syndicate, 'neither fish nor fowl',[115] as it has been aptly described, pleased no one. The recommendation was not put into effect and at Lampeter it was never even referred to in the minute book of the College Board.[116] Offence was given to Nonconformists because not one theological college was included in the syndicate. Some years later T. C. Edwards wrote that 'one of the blots of the Departmental Committee was their tacit sanction of the exclusion of the Nonconformist Colleges from any share in the privileges of a Charter granting Degrees in Theology to a Church Institution.'[117]

Such reflections must not blind us to the Report's considerable merits. The committee had performed its work diligently and speedily; in less than a year after appointment it had reported. In thirty-two days it had heard 257 witnesses whose testimony was printed in 863 large, double-column pages. Occasionally one is tempted to think that it would have been better if some witnesses had not appeared at all. Yet, one of the committee's primary purposes was to act as a sounding-board for all manner of opinions, much as the Royal Commission on Land in the 1890s was to provide a safety-valve for the simmering discontent of the countryside. The committee was at times obliged to hearken to dark prejudices. The Reverend Clough Williams-Ellis thought it would be a misfortune for Wales to have a university; if it were established at Aberystwyth 'provincialisms and narrownesses would become inveterate'.[118] The Reverend Rupert H. Morris believed that a Welshman kept in his own country had no chance of ridding himself of narrow bigotries unless he came into contact with 'a freer air'[119] of English universities. The Reverend Hawker Hughes averred that 'no university in Wales under the most favourable circumstances would be able to gain for itself any prestige for nearly 100 years'.[120] The contrast is startling between the views of these Anglicans in dispersion and those of the exiled Yorkshire clergy in the early part of the century. Owen Roberts, a barrister and clerk to the Clothmakers' Association, who claimed to think in Welsh when in Wales, upon being asked what limit he would give to the Welsh language, replied: 'For the interests of my countrymen, I hope it will be the shortest possible. I think it is one of the greatest drawbacks they have to contend with.'[121] The committee usually dealt deftly with witnesses and Socratic questioning caused not a few to fumble and to flounder. There was a further factor of significance. The appointment of the committee and the opportunities to express opinion at preliminary meetings and at the hearings themselves acted as a catalyst to constructive thought. Ideas which had not been properly formulated were revealed as inadequate and to hear the views of others was itself an educative process. Daniel Rowlands, Principal of the Bangor Normal College, in his testimony saw no reason why colleges in Wales should not be affiliated for the purpose of degrees with Victoria University, as was intended in the case of Liverpool and Leeds.[122] When he enthusiastically surveyed the Report itself in *Y Traethodydd* in 1881 there was a perceptible change in tone.[123] William Edwards, an inspector of schools, told the committee that he wanted large public schools in Wales giving education up to the age of nineteen and that he would have nothing between them and universities outside Wales.[124] In 1883 he was a powerful candidate for the principalship of Bangor College.[125] A Cardiff doctor confessed at one of the hearings that he had for many years opposed the establishment of a university for Wales but declared himself a convert, having heard 'the sentiments expressed at different places of meeting, and the resolutions that have been passed'.[126] For many years after 1881 the Report was frequently thumbed and quoted as a document of high authority, based on a vast amount of information to which historians of the period will always turn with gratitude. The accounts, too, of the struggles of young Welshmen to receive the benefits of higher education, in some cases graphically described, had a share in convincing men of goodwill that timely assistance should be given both by the state and the individual without injury to the prevailing ethos of self-help.[127]

A refreshing feature of the Report was its readiness to devote a section to consider 'the particular circumstances and distinctive character-istics' of Wales.[128] It asserts at once that Wales 'has a distinct nationality of its own', no less a reality if somewhat obscured by a loyalty to government, by a readiness to live under the same laws as the English and by a refusal to agitate for 'a separate political existence'. Welsh nationality was to be neither ignored nor discouraged; its best features should be preserved and elevated by an educational system in tune with 'the distinctive peculiarities of the country'. Second, for a long time to come the language would be of prime importance in the social and educational life of Wales. Statistics, derived from Hussey Vivian's speech in Parliament in 1879, illustrated the vigour of the language. No less than 70 per cent, it was held, habitually spoke Welsh and in religious services the number was much higher; twelve Welsh newspapers had in turn a weekly circulation of 74,500 and one witness estimated that £100,000 was spent on Welsh literature in 1875. The profound attachment of the people to their language rendered impractical all speculation as to its future. The disadvantages of an inadequate grasp of English were underlined and they were unlikely to diminish greatly with the passage of time. Third, there was religion. Nonconformists were in 'a very great majority' and they maintained 'an almost universal interest in education'. Mistrust of the endowed schools and of Church influence had injured the progress of education. Fourth, whilst it was evident that parents had an imperfect awareness of the preparation necessary before their children were sent to college, the 'ardent desire' for education in young people and their readiness to struggle had deeply affected the committee. Fifth, illustrations were presented of the comparative poverty of the country, and finally, the accumulated disparities in Welsh and English educational endowments were in the ratio of one to three.

The significance of the recommendations themselves may be briefly summarized. The proposals concerning intermediate schools were of first importance and were naturally bound in the long run to affect the fortunes of university education in Wales. The Report speaks of securing a 'system of intermediate and higher education in harmony with the distinctive peculiarities of the country'.[129] It has, however, been shrewdly remarked that the committee did not really intend to create a 'system'; its purpose was to overcome defects in the existing provision.[130] In the forefront of its mind was the Irish precedent of 1879 when the state provided £30,000 for intermediate education and a similar sum for higher education. Hugh Owen, who had studied these arrangements carefully, told the committee that Wales, like Ireland, was 'a distinct nationality' and should be 'similarly favoured'.[131] The Aberdare Report responded in two important ways. It urged that the building of new schools was to be a charge upon the county rate and that the schools should be maintained by the product of a half-penny rate and a parliamentary grant, pound for pound. In England and Wales this was a revolutionary proposal and was subsequently incorporated in the long-delayed Intermediate Act of 1889, which gave Wales a network of secondary schools well in advance of England. Second, the Report recognized that higher education in Wales could not survive without assistance from the state. The £2,500 granted to Aberystwyth in 1884 was the first instance of government aid for university education in England and Wales.[132]

As to the nature of a future university, the Aberdare Report also pointed the way. Portions of its conclusions were, as we have observed, flaccid, to an extent because the committee had been confronted with conflicting arguments. However, it gave a clear indication in favour of a federal, not a unitary, university in accord, in this respect, with the views of T. C. Edwards. Moreover, by insisting that degrees should be awarded only to those who had pursued a formal course of instruction at one of the affiliated colleges, it firmly rejected the London University model persistently canvassed by Hugh Owen. The University of Wales was to be a teaching, not an examining, university.

The recommendations of the Report in relation to higher education were not welcomed by the supporters of Aberystwyth and understandably so; Anglicans were in the main hostile or tepid, and the *Western Mail* gave a snarl or two.[133] But Nonconformists, the great majority of the articulate, thinking people of Wales, were generally jubilant, for this year too saw the passing of the Sunday Closing Act. Their response may be fairly gauged from an article in *Y Traethodydd*, to which we have already referred.[134] Some of the author's sweetest notes were employed in praise of Gladstone, who had authorized the inquiry, and of Hugh Owen, recently knighted in the twilight of his days. The writer recalled the arrogant young Englishmen who in living memory had descended on Wales and produced their Report in 1847, ever afterwards 'a curse and an oath'. The Report of 1881, on the other hand, was informed by a spirit at once independent and just, generous and wise; and he quoted with approval the words of a correspondent that it was 'the best piece of work that has been done for Wales at any period'.[135]

We are not required to accept such an extravagant verdict, but modern historians, whilst allowing that the Report is not without spot or wrinkle, agree in broad measure that it is 'the educational charter of modern Wales'.[136]

V

The Three Colleges

One of the principal recommendations of the Aberdare Report was that a new college should be established in Glamorgan, either in Cardiff or Swansea. The former was the centre of the largest population, the latter the seat of more varied industries. It may be thought that the committee had been unduly hesitant because the claims of Cardiff appeared incontestable. In relation to other Welsh towns Swansea could, of course, present a strong case, but this was not the issue. Cardiff, unwilling to countenance competition, acted with commendable dispatch. The mayor, Alfred Thomas, later Lord Pontypridd, and the able town clerk, J. L. Wheatley, at once organized an 'education committee' and opened a list of subscriptions. Throughout January 1882 there was intense activity and Cardiff was said to have 'surprised itself'.[1] By early February a 'Statement of Facts' was produced, designed to demonstrate Cardiff's superlative merits and its unquestioned superiority in every conceivable respect over the venturesome contestant in west Glamorgan. There was to be much froth and bubble in the press, but sober readers of the 'Statement' (which ran into 10,000 copies distributed throughout Wales) could hardly fail to be impressed. The eastern half of south Wales had a population of 788,398, the western half of 302,927. In four years Cardiff's export trade had increased ten times more than that of Swansea and further telling statistics were presented relating to coal, shipping and transport, together with the favourable opinions of other towns. It is true that the Privy Council received messages adverse to Cardiff. The member for Bristol informed A. J. Mundella that Cardiff and its environs was 'an important part of the field we were established to occupy' and asked that Bristol's 'existence'[2] be taken into account. It has been demonstrated that the Welsh language and Nonconformity were stronger at Cardiff than many had supposed,[3] but one anonymous writer informed the Privy Council that Welsh Nonconformity was 'feeble' at Cardiff and that 'Popery and extreme High Churchism are paramount there'.[4] Lewis Morris, in an undated memorandum, told the government that Swansea was 'far more *Welsh*' than Cardiff, 'which is practically as much an English seaport as Liverpool'.[5] Pembrokeshire, Carmarthenshire and Cardiganshire would be 'shut out by distance, by national feeling and by language' from Cardiff. As to distance and accessibility 'it would be a case of Aberystwyth over again'. The only answer was one college in south Wales with branches at Cardiff and Swansea; many of the professors could live half way; buildings should be reduced to a minimum, 'costly Facades and Quadrangles' being described as 'mischievous'. There is no need to pursue Morris's novel, unrealistic views. To what extent they carried weight with Mundella we cannot tell but he would scarcely have forgotten that Morris was a member of the Aberdare Committee. Despite the fact that Cardiff's submission and its deputation of seventy-eight representatives (led by Henry Richard) was far more impressive than Swansea's deputation of only thirteen members, Mundella was not prepared to decide between Cardiff and Swansea. Three arbitrators were at length chosen: Lord Bramwell, a former Lord Justice of Appeal; Lord Carlingford, soon to be Lord President of the Council; and Mundella himself. Both parties appeared before them in early March; within a week Cardiff was unanimously chosen[6]. On 14 March 1883 a telegram communicating the information, dispatched at 5.30 p.m. was to be seen at 6 p.m. in the window of the *South Wales Daily News* office in St Mary Street. People in the street were jubilant; that evening public announcements were made from pulpit and platform, including one by the manager of a circus in the town. 'The new college', said a local paper, 'will from this day forward be either the glory or the shame and reproach of Cardiff.'[7] The College opened in the Old Infirmary buildings in Newport Road on 24 October amidst demonstrations of public joy and thanksgiving. Despite relentless rain there were large gatherings; many had come from the valleys and hillsides. Amongst the speakers of the day were Lord Aberdare, the new President, Henry Richard, the Vice-President, Sir Hussey Vivian, the Treasurer, William Abraham (popularly known as 'Mabon'), representing the miners of the Rhondda, and the Principal, John Viriamu Jones.

Swansea was naturally disappointed and had to wait until 1920 before justice was done. The resentments caused in west Glamorgan, however, were as nothing compared with the animosities generated by the choice of a college in north Wales. It is as well to be reminded of the recommendation of the Aberdare Committee: 'the college at Aberystwyth, whether retained on its present site or removed to Caernarvon or Bangor, must be accepted as the college for north Wales.'[8] It was not surprising that many in north Wales interpreted these words as a signal to establish a college in one of the six northern counties. Aberystwyth was manifestly not in north Wales, as the inhabitants of Cardiganshire would have fully concurred. In James I's reign some had objected to paying taxes, not merely because they were a thrifty people, but because the collector was 'a North Wales man'[9] and could not therefore be expected to know anything of local conditions. It was clear, in turn, from evidence submitted to the Aberdare Committee that north Wales witnesses considered Aberystwyth to be inaccessible.[10] By February 1882, Bangor's claim to be the site of the new college was in active preparation; in March a large representative meeting urged the government to give effect to the recommendations of the Aberdare Report, as promised in the Queen's Speech. Mundella, after a visit to Anglesey in May, told Gladstone that 'the eagerness of the Welsh people for the educational measures promised in the Queen's speech exceeded anything that I could have believed'.[11] In June the government appeared to be temporizing, but in response to an appeal in July Mundella announced in the House that 'in accordance with the wishes of the Departmental Committee a sum of £2,000, the first half-yearly payment of £4,000, would be placed in the Estimate for the Aberystwyth College that session, and the sum of £4,000 a year the next year for each of two colleges, one in North and the other in South Wales'.[12] Mundella was later to say that although he was well supported in his endeavours to extract £8,000 from state funds 'the Cerebus of the Treasury stood watchfully on guard'.[13] In the end it was Gladstone's 'thorough affection for the Welsh people' which was the principal determinant, so much so that a high Treasury official had said, 'Upon my word, I believe he is half a Welshman'.[14] Judging from Mundella's statement in July, it is evident that the government proposed at this stage to follow the Aberdare Committee's recommendation to provide for two colleges, and two colleges only. For Aberystwyth the announcement brought only partial relief. After years of struggle there was at last a government grant, but was it to be sustained succour or simply a stimulant at sunset? The Cymmrodorion Section of the Denbigh National Eisteddfod in August pressed for concerted action, and at its behest a meeting was held in November at

Aberdare's London home.[15] Aberdare ruled out any discussion of intermediate education because Mundella was preparing the necessary legislation, but he readily agreed to summon representatives of the six north Wales counties to Chester. The champions of Aberystwyth were thus placed at a heavy disadvantage which was much resented. Public and private accounts of the conference held on 23 January 1883 at Chester Town Hall indicate that it was a heated, jumbled affair. Some, led by W. Cornwallis West, wanted to give precedence to intermediate education, but Henry Richard's motion to accept the government grant of £4,000 for the north Wales college passed easily. Aberdare, as chairman, was in a difficult position. It is apparent that he wished, quite properly, that Aberystwyth should be given careful consideration, that he had prepared draft resolutions inviting the conference to accept Aberystwyth as the college for North Wales but that he desisted because justice was improbable in an assembly of 350 dominated by inhabitants of the northern counties. It seems, too, that he regarded himself, the chairman of the Departmental Committee, as a disinterested observer, or *amicus curiae*, as he put it. His preferred choice was to remit the problem to a committee of inquiry. A wild, unwise speech by the Dean of Bangor raised the temperature by several degrees. With quivering lips — a portent of the cruel malady soon to overwhelm him — he fiercely rejected the claims of Aberystwyth. More students from Cardiganshire had gone there than from the whole of north Wales; if the college was not moved, students from north Wales would go to Liverpool or Manchester; it was virtually a Methodist, not an undenominational, college. With the support of Thomas Gee he succeeded in ruling Aberystwyth out of court. In such circumstances it was idle for David Davies and Lewis Edwards to ask for Cardiganshire to be included in the list of counties to be considered. The question of a site was finally resolved by appointing a committee composed entirely of north Wales representatives. The conference left a bitter aftermath. That there was some antipathy to Aberystwyth cannot be doubted, but it had been given undue exposure by the Dean of Bangor. The fundamental reason for the exclusion of Aberystwyth was that it did not meet the needs of north Wales. In the words of Mundella, 'Wales requires local colleges which will afford education as cheaply and be as accessible to the people of the Principality as the Scotch colleges are to Scotsmen.'[16] When Rendel wrote that at Chester it had been resolved to raise a college '*in* — not *for* — North Wales'[17] he had grasped but half the truth.

There followed 'the battle of the sites', which soon showed that there were powerful divisions within north Wales itself. At one time there were thirteen aspirants and promises of subscriptions from all six counties. In the event, only six contestants appeared on 17 August before the same arbitrators who had determined the fortunes of Cardiff. The most realistic claims were presented by Bangor, Caernarfon and Wrexham. Wrexham had not been mentioned in the Aberdare Report, but it was the largest town in north Wales; three thousand colliers had promised to pay one halfpenny to one penny a week for three years and a school of mining would flourish at the heart of a thriving industrial community. Caernarfon was the ancient *caput* of Gwynedd: the courts of assize and of great sessions met here; the harbour had been much improved and the Welsh press in the town was in its heyday. Bangor's rivals made much of an alarming outbreak of typhoid in the city in 1882, producing analysts' reports testifying to the purity of their own water supply. One of the arbitrators thought that such pollution 'might happen anywhere',[18] but neither he nor his colleagues ventured to indicate on 24 August 1883 why they had chosen Bangor. However, we may reasonably surmise that they judged that a town on the north-eastern boundary of Wales was not suitable particularly since it was close to the colleges at Liverpool and Manchester. Caernarfon was not on the main railway line and may have been considered too 'Welshy'. It is possible that the arbitrators may have concluded that a college in a cathedral city, small though it was, might achieve a better balance between Churchmen and Nonconformists, Liberals and Tories, English and Welsh than had hitherto been possible at Aberystwyth. Weight would also have been given to the presence of educational institutions such as an old endowed grammar school and a Normal College. The readiness of ordinary people of the neighbourhood to contribute had commanded admiration. Indeed, during the hearing of Bangor's case, Mundella had commented upon the 'wonderful generosity on the part of some of the poor Welsh farmers, which we can only look upon as very remarkable'.[19] It was said that servant girls at the end of campaign meetings came forward to put down their names for a sovereign. The Dean of Bangor remembered with intense joy his visit to a humble Anglesey farmer who rose from his modest dinner and brought to him a £100 note from an earthenware pot, saying: 'Give this subscription to the North Wales College.'[20] In proportion to his resources, was

Carnegie, that most generous of benefactors, ever more bountiful? Quarrymen, who worked only four days at slack periods and who were often urged to finance the emigration of whole families, not a college, responded magnificently; in each gallery or 'ponc' a committee was appointed, each with a secretary and treasurer, to whom an agreed sum was handed each monthly pay-day; in the Penrhyn quarry there were thirty-four districts, bearing such names as Sebastopol, Jolly Fawr and Jolly Bach. The sum of £1,258 finally raised by Penrhyn and Dinorwig quarrymen was small in relation to the money required to found a college, but some rich men were inspired by their example. It is no wonder that the spectacle of three thousand of their number marching four abreast on opening day, 18 October 1883, should have attracted attention far and wide. Aberdare thoroughly approved of the arbitrators' decision. Privately he told Mundella that it was 'decidedly the best place in North Wales'.[21]

For a time Aberdare entertained the slim possibility that the government would reverse the decision of the arbitrators and declare that Aberystwyth might best serve the interests of north Wales. Since the government had accepted the recommendations of his Report, both he and Henry Richard were not well placed to campaign on Aberystwyth's behalf. Mundella in turn was bound to be wary concerning appeals to recognize Aberystwyth as a third college, for he could scarcely forget the terms of Gladstone's invitation to him in 1880 to become Vice-President of the Committee of Council on Education. He was to eschew all wasteful measures and employ the 'utmost . . . vigilance to secure the highest educational results at the lowest possible charge to the country'.[22] As late as March 1884 Mundella said in the Commons that having provided for two colleges he would be going 'very far'[23] if he were to ask for a third grant for Aberystwyth.

Cast down by the Chester Conference, T. C. Edwards thought that the College, designed as the nucleus of a future university, would now languish and decline. Indeed, more than two years before he had told his father that 'I am a good deal exercised in my mind about the question of one, two, or three Colleges. I cannot see we have room in Wales for *three*. On the other hand I feel the force of the objection to having two in S. Wales and not one in the North, and the difficulty of removing this College to N. Wales.'[24] In the spring of 1883, Henry Jones, the professor of philosophy, had undertaken to work for the north Wales sites committee, to the understandable displeasure of

Aberystwyth; in June, Silvan Evans resigned as part-time professor of Welsh; in October ten Aberystwyth students left for Cardiff and the College Council resolved to continue for one further year fearing, however, that it might then hear the dread toll of the passing bell. There were also feverish anxieties that the College would become a college for women or, the ultimate trauma, that the Jesuits would move in.[25] It seemed, too, that old friends of the College were deserting the standard. Osborne Morgan, associated, as we have seen, with Aberystwyth from the beginning, had told the Chester Conference that 'its geographical position renders it unfit to be adopted as the college for North Wales.'[26] By the summer of 1884 fissures amongst supporters of the College became more apparent because of successive failures to receive a full grant of £4,000; the local committee became strident and Aberdare talked of resigning as president, though in fact he held on to the Cardiff and Aberystwyth presidencies until his death.

Yet it was evident that after the Chester Conference there was a groundswell of opinion which favoured the continuance of Aberystwyth. Had Aberystwyth's case been fairly presented at Chester the outcome would almost certainly have been the same, but to have refused a hearing at all was in the eyes of many indefensible. T. C. Edwards was later to say that when 'the clever men of the Chester meeting refused to Aberystwyth its fair share of a chance' they must have been visited by 'a heaven-sent infatuation'.[27] A sense of fair play asserted itself, for it seemed an affront to snuff out a college which had struggled tenaciously since its inception against intolerable odds. Even those who had resisted Aberystwyth's claims began to feel uncomfortable. Lewis Morris and the Dean of Bangor aired a dangerous compromise that Aberystwyth should share part of the £4,000 allocated to the north Wales college.[28] Many Nonconformists thought it a peculiar twist of fortune that one college would be close to Llandaff Cathedral and the other in a cathedral city. Some considered it strange that the Dean of Bangor who had so furiously raged against Aberystwyth had ardently espoused the cause of Bangor. One writer welcomed the proposal to transfer Aberystwyth's staff to Bangor, for once the serpent was scotched the cathedral would be as toothless as Caernarfon Castle.[29] The Penrhyn influence was also viewed with alarm. To Herber Evans, Bangor was 'the only Conservative town and the only church city in North Wales'.[30] According to William

Rathbone, the member for Arfon and a firm supporter of the Bangor college, 'the dreaded shade of the Palace and the Castle and the personality of the Dean seem to have deprived of judgement some of my best friends'.[31] Thomas Gee was not one of them, but his powerful influence was now cast against Bangor. In 1880 he had wanted two colleges in north Wales, one at Bangor and the other at Rhuthun, but in the interval he had vigorously supported Denbigh in opposition to Aberystwyth. Once Bangor was chosen, he transferred his allegiance to Aberystwyth.[32] Aberdare, writing to Viriamu Jones in January 1884, deplored the public outcry: 'I wonder the Welsh are not ashamed of their contemptible opposition to Cardiff and Bangor . . . because there is a cathedral in one of them, and near the other.'[33] Yet in August 1883 he had shrewdly divined that 'no sooner will the announcement of the Arbitrators be made known than a large part of North Wales will declare against it and in favour of Aberystwyth. Such a cause may not be very creditable, but it would undoubtedly strengthen the case for Aberystwyth.'[34] The appointment of an Anglican principal with Tory leanings at Bangor in preference to Henry Jones further fuelled Nonconformist displeasure.

It was not long before messages supporting Aberystwyth began to arrive at the Privy Council Office. They came not only from Bala, Dolgellau and Newtown (directly within Aberystwyth's sphere of influence), but from further afield. Flintshire's English Congregationalists informed the Lord President that since Cardiff and Bangor were 'at the extreme ends'[35] of the Principality the needs of central Wales were thus entirely neglected. The Anglesey Calvinistic Methodists at their monthly meeting at Armenia Chapel, Holyhead, thought that Aberystwyth, which was doing 'such excellent work' and which had been supported by the people of Wales, should not be extinguished, 'as a matter of justice to Central Wales'.[36] There were reports, too, of encouraging meetings at Liverpool and Wrexham. The burgesses of Swansea, however, still smarting at their defeat, argued that in order to avoid a serious clash with Cardiff the college at Aberystwyth should be moved to Swansea, and they proceeded to list remarks hostile to Aberystwyth culled from the Aberdare Report.[37] Far more in tune with the prevailing spirit were the words of a Denbighshire rector, joint collector with Henry Jones for the college at Bangor. In his view Aberystwyth had 'done work of incalculable importance in stimulating the national mind towards higher education'; he greatly doubted 'whether we should ever have had the Government enquiry and provision of assistance' but for the college at Aberystwyth which had 'brought to the surface the latent desires of the Welsh people'.[38] At the opening of the Bangor College, Principal Reichel declared that Bangor owed its existence to the two south Wales colleges. Bangor had not injured Aberystwyth; indeed, Bangor and Cardiff were Aberystwyth's best friends, for how else could one account for the 'magnificent leap'[39] in the College's students in October 1884, from eighty to 104. At the same meeting Aberdare said that the college at Aberystwyth was really 'the mother of the movement'.[40] In dark days, the University College of Wales was not friendless.

There are signs that Aberdare was readier to support Aberystwyth in its battle for survival than was immediately apparent, and indeed to intervene directly with government on its behalf even after the Chester Conference. In private it was said of him that 'he quite eats his own declarations about a third college.'[41] Otherwise, he could hardly have compared Aberystwyth, in an intriguing simile in 1884, to the Roman Catholic Church: 'Though oft doomed to die, yet fated still to live.'[42] Such remarks, however, did little to please local champions at Aberystwyth, notably the peppery, pugnacious John Gibson, editor of the *Cambrian News*, who sensed a conspiracy with each passing breeze. The virulence of Gibson, R. D. Roberts and others aroused a Bootle benefactor of the College to fury: 'The inaccessibility of Aberystwyth to the outside world', he told the principal, 'must be accepted as a dispensation of Providence. Such a town deserves to be isolated.'[43] In justice it had to be conceded that Gibson made palpable hits. The Aberdare Report reflected the circumstances of the mid-1870s, not of 1880, and the 'people's college' could have been saved by a word (from Aberdare): the real battle, however, was to be fought, not in the columns of the *Cambrian News*, but in the offices of Whitehall and, above all, on the floor of the House of Commons. In 1883 the *South Wales Daily News* said that until 1867 Wales had but a sham representation; from 1874 Welshmen had to sit with the minority, 'but now all the conditions are altered'.[44]

To persuade Gladstone's government to grant more than the £8,000 already promised was no small matter. In June 1883 there was a stony statement by ministers that a third college could not be recognized. A temporary grant to wind up the College was the most that could be expected 'under any circumstances',[45] words which wary politicians are prone to avoid. An attempt to see Gladstone failed and in August there was another bleak response. A group of men were determined to fight: B. T. Williams, a former MP and now a county court judge; Humphreys Owen, a Montgomeryshire landlord who contributed richly to Welsh educational development; David Davies of Llandinam, member for Cardiganshire, and Stuart Rendel. Of these the leader was Rendel.[46] An Englishman, a managing director of the armaments firm Armstrong Whitworth, he had in the Liberal interest unexpectedly broken the hold of the Wynnstay family upon Montgomeryshire in 1880; a man of charm, acumen and probity, he was much esteemed by Gladstone. He had, however, to contend with Mundella, more skilled than most of his fellows in the arts of dissimulation and who had written thus to Viriamu Jones in December 1883: 'What do you say to the outcry about Aberystwyth? Would not a third college be mischievous?'[47] Undismayed by opposition, public or private, and fortified by enthusiastic meetings throughout Wales in support of a parliamentary campaign, Rendel in March 1884 presented a memorial at Westminster, signed by most Welsh members, to seek state aid.[48] He was supported by some English members such as James Bryce and a sprinkling of Tory members, one or two of whom doubtless hoped to fish in troubled waters. There is no need to repeat familiar arguments, but it is worth noting that the supporters of the University College of Wales were now obliged to consider a more limited constituency. They referred to the entrenched custom of Welshmen 'to speak and think of Central Wales also since the counties of which Aberystwyth is the national centre, whether technically in North or South Wales, are divided from both North and South Wales by bars of distance'.[49] Henry Richard, who had Mundella's ear, hoped that the government would not allow the College 'to be left without succour'.[50] At one stage Mundella told Richard that the Tories would not give money to a third college – a hapless remark, as we shall see – and to Rendel he made it known that he himself would not concede.[51] Before the debate, however, an intervention by Gladstone obliged him to offer £2,000 upon conditions, later increased to £2,500 upon promise of raising private subscriptions.[51] The full grant seemed as elusive as ever. In June 1885 the Liberal government was succeeded by the Marquess of Salisbury's first administration. It seemed as if the College would have to wait until the Greek Kalends. Yet it was soon evident that Edward

Stanhope, Mundella's successor, displayed considerable understanding; he indicated, for instance, that a deputation to the
government would not be necessary and that he would consider a
memorial signed by Welsh members. Suspicions were not easily
dispelled. Richard warned Rendel to beware of the Tories when they
bore gifts, for the apostle of peace could not forget the heat of many
battles. If a grant were made it would only be a tactic to attempt to
'corrupt the Welsh constituencies'. It might have that effect upon
'certain weak kneed people. . . However let us try them.'[52] Try them
they did and the Tory government to its great credit informed Rendel
on 22 August 1885 that 'they have come to the conclusion that
Aberystwyth may reasonably claim to be treated in the same manner as
Cardiff or Bangor.'[53] Stanhope, who communicated the information,
made a special point of saying that Aberdare and Lord Emlyn, and all
surviving members of the Aberdare Committee, had supported the
memorial. In doing so, we may add, they had moved more than a few
leagues from their original position.

When it reached its decision the Tory administration could hardly
fail to be influenced by a disaster which had befallen the College on the
night of 8 July 1885. A fierce fire destroyed the whole of the north
wing, where teaching and laboratory work were conducted; three
workmen were killed and Laura Place filled with salvaged remnants. It
is said that T. C. Edwards, returning in his carriage from New Quay
saw the devouring flames across the bay;[54] if so, they must have
seemed to him a portent of the last fire which consumeth all things.
Even in this calamity the *Western Mail* was unable to meet the needs of
the hour. The end of Aberystwyth was nigh and the people of Swansea
were urged that 'a long pull, a strong pull, and a pull together and the
College is theirs. Aberystwyth's difficulty is their opportunity.'[55] The
College's historian has fittingly observed that 'not for the first time or
last time, the Cardiff newspaper completely misjudged the temper of
the people of the Principality.'[56] The response of the College was its
salvation. In the words of T. C. Edwards, 'the College has at length had
its baptism of fire. It will arise from its ashes with a new life. Wales will
never now let it die.'[57] His role was crucial. In 1872, before his
appointment, he had asked, not unreasonably, that he should not be
obliged to collect funds for the College. That condition he had long cast
aside and during the next two years he addressed 520 meetings with
passionate eloquence. In 1922 Lloyd George was to speak of an old

woman in a Cardiganshire upland cottage who still had in a glass on the mantelpiece the half-crown she had kept for T. C. Edwards to collect.[58] Within Wales those who had contributed to the College in the 1870s felt a sense of personal responsibility, finely expressed by H. B. Jones ('Garmonydd') who proposed to raise funds in the Mold area:

> I know hundreds of quarrymen, colliers, lead miners and agricultural labourers who have contributed out of their scanty earnings, towards the funds of Aberystwyth College... They, like all true-hearted and loyal Welshmen, sincerely rejoice at the good start made by the sister, or rather daughter, colleges at Bangor and Cardiff. But you shall find they cherish for Aberystwyth a kind of personal and proprietary attachment. When they heard the news of the fire, they went back in memory to those Sunday evenings ten or twelve years ago when in their little Bethels they contributed their crowns, half-crowns and shillings towards the *first* Welsh university college, and felt as if some dire calamity had befallen themselves.[59]

One of the most remarkable achievements was that of a Calvinistic Methodist minister of Rhianfa, Pwllheli, D. E. Davies, who organized a campaign in the northern counties of Wales on behalf of Aberystwyth. It is idle to pretend that he was not often rebuffed. In April 1889 he listed the leading men in north Wales who had not subscribed. In Caernarfonshire they included Lord Penrhyn, Ellis Nanney, Assheton Smith, Colonel Platt and Lord Newborough. All the clergymen he saw had refused except the Vicar of Caernarfon.[60] He had also failed by then to melt the hearts of Richard Davies, Treborth, and of Robert Davies, Bodlondeb. He found that he succeeded with Liberal Methodists, but not with Tory Methodists. There was a further obstacle. The fact that both he and T. C. Edwards were Calvinistic Methodists did not please the Congregationalists and there was no improvement when they enlisted the services of that good Congregationalist 'Professor J. E. Lloyd, BA'.[61] Again, Davies was campaigning at a time when the Bangor College was straining every sinew in its own interests; those who had promised help to Bangor did not see why they should give precedence to Aberystwyth.[62] Nevertheless despite such discouragements Davies was able to report that he had promises of £1,600. Some were for minute sums; at Waunfawr three persons (including Mrs E. Williams, Gardd Eden) had promised twopence each. Naturally there were defaulters, or 'sinners', as Davies called them. In him there was something of the spirit of Hugh Owen: 'I am determined that I must get the amounts promised in this year. I feel so much for the "Mother College"... that I shall not be discouraged by what people say or do.'[63] Nearer Aberystwyth there were encouraging signals. A farmer in the Vale of Aeron had hitherto, with the caution of his tribe, regularly declined to contribute to the College; he was now ready to give a fiver.[64] If the fire had destroyed part of the College, it had also destroyed much prejudice. At penny readings 'Y Coleg ar Dân'[65] ('The College on Fire') was recited hundreds of times. The cause of higher education had reached the 'ordinary' people of Wales in ways which the 'middle-class' appeals of Thomas Nicholas could never have done.

Even before the fire there had been an increase in numbers, as we have seen. A new spirit could be discerned, not wholly unconnected with the arrival of the first official contingent of women students, as opposed to the part-time students who became members of Joseph Parry's choir. They were to be well cared for by a much respected shepherdess, E. A. Carpenter. After the fire it was feared that many students would leave, but the Principal's personal appeal to each student to remain succeeded beyond all expectation.[66] Aberystwyth's policy of throwing scholarships to open competition brought in an increasing number of English students who seem to have fitted in easily. This was part of T. C. Edwards's aim to break down 'provincialism'. Bangor viewed the matter in a different light; until there was a satisfactory system of intermediate schools, scholarships should generally be restricted to Welsh students so that they would not initially be at a disadvantage in their own land.[67] There was, of course, something to be said on both sides of an argument which occasionally bubbled up briskly. One thing was certain. The *esprit de corps* amongst Aberystwyth students was high; by 1892 it found expression in the creation of the Old Students' Association under the presidency of Tom Ellis. Similar associations have flourished in the other colleges, but it would be ungracious to question the claim of the College historian that 'from the beginning Aberystwyth has been remarkably, perhaps uniquely, successful in attracting and retaining the loyalty and affection of its old students'.[68] Chief among the reasons for such exceptional devotion was that students of the 1870s and 1880s identified themselves directly with the struggle to survive of Wales's first university college when forces, seen and unseen, seemed bent upon its destruction.

Rebuilding took place on the original site, a much cheaper solution than building afresh elsewhere. T. C. Edwards's rousing appeals to Welshmen during his American tour in 1890 helped to equip a new library, and a Melbourne man provided an ornamental roof for the highly unusual indoor quad, the centre of ambulatory diversions known as 'quadding' which enabled the sexes between lectures and at close quarters to observe one another, at the very least, without breaching strict rules.[69] The principal academic changes related to the establishment of a Day Training or Normal Department and of a Department of Agriculture. In the first case Aberystwyth was in advance of Bangor, though not of Cardiff, which was the first college to found a department for the training of teachers.[70] Apart from the Church college at Carmarthen, there was no training college in any of the seven counties for which Aberystwyth assumed a special responsibility. The government agreed and in 1892 a Day Training Department, initially for elementary school teachers, began its work. The development of agricultural studies was of prime importance to both Aberystwyth and Bangor. Almost inevitably there were demarcation disputes concerning Merioneth and Montgomeryshire where Bangor had already begun classes. At length the former came under Aberystwyth's wing and the latter was shared between the two.[71] Agriculture started at Aberystwyth in 1891.

The question of territorial division caused further controversy in discussions leading to the granting of Aberystwyth's long-delayed charter. Bangor was called 'The University College of North Wales', Cardiff 'The University College of South Wales and Monmouthshire'. What was there, then, left to divide? In the Memorial to Parliament in 1884 for which he was largely responsible, Rendel, it will be recalled, had pursued the claims of mid-Wales.[72] His nationalism, as has been well said, was decidedly limited for 'he thought less in terms of "Wales" as a coherent entity than of "mid-Wales", a vague, amorphous region'.[73] If patriotism was not enough, what was to be made of mid-Wales? Aberystwyth had at the outset called itself 'The University College of Wales' and T. C. Edwards cannot have been pleased when Viriamu Jones, in commiserating with the College upon its ordeal by fire in 1885, spoke of 'the College of Mid-Wales'.[74] The oldest college in Wales was the last to receive its charter and before it did so in 1889 there were rumbling sounds from Cardiff and Bangor. In March of that year the Bangor Council, 'whilst fully recognising the seniority in point of foundation of the University College at Aberystwyth and sympathising with the desire to commemorate that fact', declared 'the proposed title of "University College of Wales" to be inconsistent with the titles of other state-aided Colleges in Wales, and likely to produce an erroneous impression of the relation in which the three Colleges stand to each other'.[75] Bangor's objection was communicated to Aberdare as President of Aberystwyth and to the Privy Council. Cardiff acted in like fashion. Aberystwyth's Principal not unnaturally protested (though somewhat injuring his case by writing on paper headed 'University College, Aberystwyth').[76] In seeking the support of Thomas Gee he observed that when Cardiff and Bangor were founded it was generally believed that Aberystwyth was under sentence and that therefore the former were given territorial assignations embracing the whole of Wales. Aberystwyth, however, had 'the audacity to live on'[77] and understandably challenged Bangor's petition that it should be called 'the University College of Mid-Wales' on the following grounds: there was no such territory as mid-Wales, whereas north and south Wales meant a certain number of counties, the names being legally recognized; counties which might be included in mid-Wales had already been assigned to Bangor or Cardiff so that the government could not give 'an inch of territory' to the old college which would be assuming what did not belong to it by accepting the 'Mid-Wales' title; had Aberystwyth been suddenly brought into existence, an objection might reasonably be made to the claim that it was the University College of Wales, but the title was now seventeen years old. Edwards spoke of Bangor, especially, as 'the enemy' and of 'childish jealousy'. In the event the matter was settled by the Privy Council's cool impartiality, Aberystwyth's seniority of foundation being properly recognized in its charter. Strangely enough, when Reichel wrote in 1902 to the Aberystwyth Principal concerning the possible choice of Cardiff as the seat of the University Registry, he said that 'the fact that the title of Aberystwyth is so much closer to that of the University than the title of Cardiff would prevent any tendency arising to confuse the University College Cardiff with the University'.[78]

In 1891 T. C. Edwards resolved to leave Aberystwyth for Bala, where the principalship had been vacant since his father's death in 1887. That he should have done so was, in the perceptive words of David Williams, 'an indication of the ethos of the time and a measure of the change in values between his days and ours'.[79] The Aberdare Report's recommendation that the principal of a Welsh university college should be a layman must have caused him great hurt. In early October 1884 Lewis Morris wrote to complain to the Privy Council of the Principal's absences on preaching tours in the north of England.[80] There was another side to the question. Edwards was a link between the old Wales and the new. W. J. Gruffydd understood this well.[81] Aberystwyth's Principal, in his person, convinced ordinary people that a 'secular'[82] college at Aberystwyth was part of the Almighty's 'Grand Plan' and that it was safe for them to send their sons there for they would not be seduced from their faith by too much learning. Lloyd George in 1922 declared that T. C. Edwards 'erected a bridge over the chasm between the Wales of one Book and of many books'.[83] In the same year Thomas Jones ('T. J.') was moved to quote Emerson: 'An institution is the lengthened shadow of one man.'[84]

The lengthened shadow may not always have helped his successor, Thomas Francis Roberts.[85] Born at Towyn, Merioneth, the son of a Baptist policeman, Roberts at the age of fourteen entered Aberystwyth, where he remained for the best part of five years without following any set course and without sitting the London degree. At St John's College, Oxford, he took a double first and shortly afterwards became Cardiff's first professor of Greek at the age of twenty-three. Unusually solemn and taut for his years − he gave the impression that he had just seen a ghost − he worked so unsparingly that his less austere colleagues formed a 'Roberts Protection Society'. Those who knew him best detected shoots of saintliness which sustained him during his twenty-eight years as principal, years frequently punctuated by ill health. The College janitor believed him to be a good man, adding that he was 'not addicted to the Principalship'.[86] A superb teacher of Greek prose, it has been suggested that 'his study of the Classics saved him from exaggerated views of Welsh accomplishments'.[87] A sincere, noble patriot, one of his favourite phrases was: 'Not Wales for the Welsh but Wales for the world.'

Cardiff, which opened its doors in October 1883, was exceedingly fortunate in its first Principal. John Viriamu Jones was born in 1856 at Pentre-poeth, near Swansea.[88] The name Viriamu, uniquely strange in Wales, was the nearest approach South Sea Islanders could make to the pronouncing of Williams when they spoke of John Williams, the martyr-missionary of Erromanga, deeply admired by Viriamu's father, a Congregationalist minister, who may have hoped that his son would become a great preacher or missionary. Viriamu's career lay in other directions but a high moral purpose (wholly free from cant or priggishness) always governed his actions. Academic distinctions came easily to him: he was first out of 500 candidates in the London Matriculation examination; at University College, London, medals in gold and silver were showered upon him and in 1875 he took firsts in chemistry and physics; a Brackenbury Scholarship at Balliol College, Oxford, led in 1880 to his being placed in the first class in the mathematical and natural science (physics) final schools; he became a fellow of the Royal Society in 1894 and never discontinued serious research, so much so that his Sunday visits to the laboratory (which were remarked upon) were in part responsible for the fact that Cardiff did not acquire the odour of sanctity long associated, not always justly, with Aberystwyth.

Profoundly influenced by his period at Oxford, Viriamu was increasingly attracted by the movement to establish provincial colleges much favoured by such prominent Oxford figures as T. H. Green and Benjamin Jowett. In 1881 he was appointed Principal of Firth College, Sheffield, the forerunner of Sheffield University, at the age of twenty-five. Two years later he did not hesitate to return to Wales. He described his motives thus: 'I left Sheffield because I thought that this was the dawning of a remarkable era in the educational and intellectual history of Wales, and that no nobler task could fall to the lot of any Welshman today than that of instituting this College wisely, and attempting to guide it aright in infancy, so that it may become a great and lasting benefit to the Welsh people.'[89] It is difficult to dissent from the provisional assessment of David Williams in 1950 that 'he is the one educationalist of undoubted genius that the Welsh national movement has produced'.[90] He was a born leader and in accounting for his magnetic appeal H. R. Reichel employed William Pitt's words to the Frenchman who could not appreciate the secret of Charles James Fox's influence: 'You have never been under the wand of the enchanter.'[91] Happily, in the case of John Viriamu Jones, something of that spell remains.

The new principal had gathered able staff around him. Andrew Seth (Pringle-Pattison being later added), the professor of philosophy, was succeeded by W. R. Sorley in 1887. The former at Edinburgh and the latter at Cambridge were amongst the most influential teachers of philosophy of their generation. W. P. Ker, an outstanding English scholar, was followed in 1889 by C. E. Vaughan, an authority on Rousseau. Viriamu had from the outset recognized that it was imperative to link the College with the industrial interests of south Wales. The Technical Instruction Act of 1889, enpowering the levy of a half penny rate, encouraged the County Borough of Cardiff to establish a Technical Instruction Committe which reached agreement with the College to set up a technical school within the College. The need to provide regular instruction in several local centres was seized upon by the counties of Glamorgan and Monmouth which speedily joined the scheme. An earlier attempt to found a chair of engineering had failed for lack of funds, but in 1890 the College was able to appoint a professor, thanks largely to the generosity of the Drapers' Company and to the funds raised under the Technical Instruction Act; the department was sited in Newport Road. A chair of mining was established in 1891, but its first occupant (Sir) William Galloway made little headway. In 1886 Cardiff strenuously endeavoured to persuade the government to found a medical school upon which Viriamu had set the greatest store. It was argued that of all faculties in the Scottish and Irish universities, the medical faculties were the most successful; the same would be the case in Wales. Aberystwyth and Bangor were not contenders and without a complete medical school the 'university element' would be 'sadly incomplete'.[92] The appeal failed, partly because of the government's parsimony and partly because of resistance to establishing provincial schools of medicine. Cast down but undeterred, the College raised £4,000 to add a storey to the buildings in Newport Road to accommodate departments of anatomy and physiology, opened in 1894 by Sir Richard Quain.

Greater success attended the College's efforts to promote the training of teachers. Here again, Viriamu was in the van, but due praise should be given to Lewis Williams, appropriately called 'an unsung hero of Welsh educational history'.[93] When the Cross Committee inquired in 1886 into the working of the Education Acts evidence was given by Williams, for many years chairman of the Cardiff School Board and vice-president of the College Council. Viriamu and Williams both recognized the importance of training elementary teachers following the Forster Act of 1870 (and compulsory education ten years later) and of secondary teachers after the passing of the Intermediate Act in 1889. Williams's main emphasis before the Cross Committee had been upon the training of women teachers. These aims, it was held, could best be achieved within university institutions.[94] With the approval of the government a Day Training Department was opened in 1890 for elementary teachers. In 1892 it was reconstituted with a separate Women's Department to train women teachers for secondary schools. Cardiff was in the forefront of these developments in Wales and it is certain that the new departments in the Welsh colleges contributed much to the raising of teaching standards. It is also true that government grants for the purpose gave the colleges a measure of financial stability. The needs of women students had been long recognized at Cardiff – the first mixed university college in Wales – by the opening of Aberdare Hall in 1885. Viriamu and his wife were perturbed that women in lodgings tended to neglect themselves by living, for instance, on tea and macaroons for long periods.[95] Under the Hall's first principal, Isabel Bruce (Aberdare's daughter), and her successors they were in good hands. Another venture was the creation in 1891 of the Training School of Cooking and Domestic Arts. No longer would it be necessary for Welsh women to acquire their teacher's diploma in a Liverpool or a London school.[96]

The financial resources of the College were often insufficient to meet elementary wants. Much encouragement was derived from a scheme of industrial scholarships launched in 1883 by the College Registrar, Ivor James.[97] There were signs that workmen in the seven counties of south Wales and Monmouthshire were prepared to contribute a farthing a week for ten years. This 'admirable scheme',[98] in Mabon's words on opening day, was later described as 'perhaps... Utopian',[99] but it was in part successful. By 1894 scholarship funds had been set up in various collieries. In the College Calendar for 1894–5 it was reported that Maerdy Colliery and District had contributed £225, Cwmaman £110, Naval £100 and Albion £120. Cardiff Football Club was not far behind with £90. After 1889 (and much fracas) the College received £800 from the Cradock Wells Charity, £300 of which was for scholarships for students from elementary schools. In purely financial terms the 'founding fathers' were 147 persons, mostly living in or near Cardiff, who promised to contribute £37,000; they included the Marquess of Bute and the Corporation of Cardiff, each agreeing to give £10,000. Ten years later less than half the promised sums had been paid.[100] In 1888 the College Treasurer made it known that the ship 'must shorten sail'[101] to avoid shipwreck. After 1891 there was a small surplus, mainly due to the voluntary tightening of belts by staff and to an increase in student numbers.

In view of financial circumstances in the early years it was remarkable that the College in 1886 acquired the magnificent library of E. R. G. Salisbury of Glanaber, near Chester, whose exertions, forty years earlier, on behalf of higher education in Wales we have already noticed.[102] His career as businessman, lawyer and politician had ended in bankruptcy, but during his prosperous days he had endeavoured to collect a copy of every book relating to Wales and the border counties. Bangor was anxious to buy the 14,000 volumes but money was scarce. The Cardiff Council could not help its own college and Ivor James and the professor of Celtic, Thomas Powell, prevailed upon Bute, Aberdare and others to provide funds enabling them to make an offer of £1,100, immediately accepted by the official receiver and anxious creditors, who had no inkling of the value of the collection. Upon purchase it was at once insured for £10,000 and brought down by a special train proudly flying the Red Dragon. Chester's city fathers were disconsolate when the purchasers declined an offer for the portion relating to Cheshire alone, a sum equal to that paid for the whole collection. Of its kind it was the finest library in existence; in different circumstances it might have developed into a national library for Wales. The College's servants had made a spectacular coup; they amply merit the gratitude of a distant posterity.

When the College at Bangor opened in October 1884, the principal officers were securely in place. In its search for a president the College had turned, as it was to do almost without exception, to north-east Wales. A Tory and a high steward of Cambridge University, a generous landlord in dismal days and a high Anglican, the Earl of Powis represented many of the best traditions of British life. Dignified and scholarly, he was sometimes pressed by College officials to wear his scarlet gown of a doctor of civil laws to impress the unbending, uncooperative minor gentry who tended to appear on ceremonious collegiate occasions. He remained in office, and was greatly honoured, until his death in 1891.[103]

Bangor's first principal, Harry Rudolf Reichel,[104] was born in 1856. His father, descended from a long line of German Moravians whose doctrines he found oppressive, had entered the Anglican Church and was raised to the bishopric of Meath in Ireland. At Oxford his son took four firsts, in Classical Moderations, Mathematical Moderations, Greats and Modern History. Benjamin Jowett said that he had gained higher schools than perhaps any living person. He was one of only two principals in the history of the Welsh colleges to have been a fellow of All Souls; the other was Goronwy Rees who, upon return to Wales, found it more difficult to identify himself with the Welsh people than did the Irish Anglican upon arrival. In 1883 the doors of Church and state and the groves of academe were open before Reichel yet he chose to be head of a college at Bangor which he had only whisked through by train. It seems certain that he was influenced by an Oxford friend, Viriamu Jones, whose advice he sought on his way to the interview. Unlike Viriamu, however, and like T. F. Roberts, he was not committed to research; nor was he much inclined to question hallowed beliefs, but his crisp, incisive speeches and papers on educational matters commanded respect and repay reading today. A few, Thomas Gee and Lloyd George amongst them, never forgave the College for passing over the young, charismatic Welshman, Henry Jones. Reichel, by contrast, was reserved – in youth his shyness amounted to an affliction – and he tended on occasion to subside into unnerving bouts of silence. His shortcomings, however, were mere specks of dust; those who found him disconcertingly straightforward soon discovered, not a stiff rectitude, but a shining integrity which profoundly affected the conduct of affairs both public and private.

Bangor, like Aberystwyth, found its first home in a hotel designed for more prosperous days. It had not been obliged, however, to purchase a building and to repair extensive damage as was the case at Aberystwyth. It paid an annual rental to Lord Penrhyn of £200 (half the rental paid by Cardiff for the Old Infirmary). At first most provincial colleges in Britain had to make *ad hoc* arrangements. The Yorkshire College of Science (later Leeds) began in a disused bankruptcy court, both Liverpool and Leicester in lunatic asylums. At Bangor changes were, of course, necessary, the kitchen and scullery being transformed into a library; here, it was said, 'students now swat where fat cooks once sweated before roasting fires'.[105] The Penrhyn Arms itself, built by Benjamin Wyatt at the end of the eighteenth century as a coaching house, had been much admired by visitors. Overlooking Beaumaris Bay towards the sea it commanded 'an uncommonly beautiful prospect of land and water'.[106] It was to be the College's only home until 1911.

At first there were six professors, equally divided between arts and science. Apart from Reichel himself (responsible for English and history) two were distinguished products of Cambridge and three of Glasgow. In a sense, as D. Emrys Evans remarked in like circumstances,[107] it is somewhat arbitrary to select names. Two, however, deserve special mention. Of Henry Jones, professor of philosophy, logic and political economy, it was said by his teacher at Glasgow, John Nichol, that, with one exception he 'gave me a more distinct impression of genius than any other student I have had in my long career'.[108] According to a Bangor student, observing him only at a distance, he 'shot out rays of energy and light'.[109] In 1891 he succeeded Edward Caird as professor of moral philosophy at Glasgow. He remained entirely loyal to Reichel, against whom he had competed for the principalship, and from his vantage ground in Scotland he was to survey the development of higher education in Wales with a lively, affectionate concern. James Johnstone Dobbie, the first holder of the chair of chemistry, was also responsible for the teaching of geology in the natural expectation, alas unfulfilled, that the quarry owners of the area would in an enlightened spirit of self-interest promote the study of mining and of quarrying. Dobbie's main contribution at Bangor was in the application of chemistry to the agricultural problems of north Wales, thus laying the foundations of the Department of Agriculture at the College. In 1888 he received from the government the largest sum yet awarded to any institution to further agricultural education and dairy farming. He won the confidence of farmers initially suspicious of academic advice, particularly in English, and in 1891 the Board of Agriculture reported that work at Bangor was a basis for organizing 'systematic agricultural development throughout the Kingdom'.[110] Everything considered, it would be safe to accept Mundella's tribute on opening day: 'I have heard but one opinion. . . and from men who are well able to form an opinion. . . that the North Wales University College starts with a staff of exceptional power and brilliancy.'[111] No great progess was made in the teaching of Welsh because the subject could not be studied for the BA degree, but the appointment of (Sir) John Morris-Jones as lecturer in 1889 was a landmark in the history of Welsh scholarship. When the College's first Registrar, W. Cadwaladr Davies, resigned in 1892 after service prodigal in its intensity (and which undermined his health), he was succeeded by John Edward Lloyd whose calm, authoritative investigations in time transformed the study of medieval Welsh history.

During the years 1892–4 the College was thrown badly off course.[112] A dispute relating to the University Hall for Women attracted extensive attention, some of it prurient. Prominent members of court and council resigned; there was a bruising correspondence in the columns of *The Times*, various newspapers and educational journals; a libel writ was heard at the Chester Assizes and spiteful references made on the floor of both Houses of Parliament. One issue concerned the authority of the head of the Women's Hall, unfortunately called the Lady Principal, a title which suggested, especially to her, a rival bailiwick; another involved her authority over an adult woman student. The staff were comparatively young, the students comparatively mature; in a hothouse Victorian atmosphere loose tongues magnified a minor indiscretion into a steamy indulgence at a time when the higher education of women was at a sensitive, experimental stage. The protracted dispute caused a damaging expenditure of time and of nervous energy. However, a sturdy institution is able to withstand many assaults, and so it was at Bangor.

As in the other colleges, state aid, though inadequate, was the bedrock of Bangor's finances. Six prominent men had contributed £1,000 each at the Chester Conference and there was great satisfaction that 8,000 people had undertaken to contribute £30,000 in the 1880s. Good intentions were sometimes blighted by contraction in the building industry, which affected slate production, and by the depressed state of agriculture in the mid-1880s and especially during the 1890s. There was great jubilation when news came in 1890 of the 'Manchester Bequest' of £47,000 which placed Bangor in a far more favourable position than the other colleges.[113] It was the posthumous gift of Evan Thomas, the son of a Pwllheli joiner, who had settled down in Manchester. A surgeon by training, he had offended the medical authorities and thenceforth devoted himself to the preparation of an elixir which he sold for half-a-crown a bottle. Quite possibly it was as harmless a placebo as the pills (which have been analysed) of Thomas Holloway whose vast wealth enabled him to build the spectacular college for women at Egham.[114] That this bounty should have come from a Manchester Welshman (much cultivated by the College's first registrar) was singularly appropriate for it was the son of a Flintshire man who had given twice this sum to found Owens College. Such a windfall was unique in the early history of the Welsh colleges. It took the Marquess of Bute several years to fulfil his promise to Cardiff of £10,000.

The three colleges, as might be expected, had much in common.[115] Their charters were similar and each college had a court, council and senate. Courts tended to be large, 238 at Aberystwyth, 284 at Cardiff and 191 at Bangor, in order to reflect all educational aspects of Welsh life; the practice of giving representation to contributors of certain sums long persisted, thus further inflating the size of courts. The council at Aberystwyth had a membership of fifty-six, at Cardiff forty-one and at Bangor thirty-one. Bangor's wish to have as large a council as Cardiff's was frowned upon by the Privy Council, which would have preferred twenty-five (perhaps wisely) but which conceded a further six members. Aberystwyth and Bangor thought it advantageous to have representatives of Oxford, Cambridge and London on their councils, but Cardiff in 1883 resisted such pressure on the grounds that it 'would be unworthy treatment if the people of Wales could not be trusted with the care of their own College'.[116] Following the lead of the newer institutions in England, no one was to be required to make any declaration concerning religious opinions or to submit to any religious tests. However, the spectre of an avowed atheist, Charles Bradlaugh, hovered in the wings. At Bangor the Earl of Powis was invited to aver that such a person could not become a principal or a professor at the College. At Cardiff, Lloyd Tanner, the professor of mathematics and astronomy, once associated with the National Secular Society but who disclaimed any links with the secular side of the Bradlaugh movement, survived a motion by Dean Vaughan to terminate his appointment in 1883 by thirteen votes to eight (of which six were cast by Anglicans). Theology was firmly excluded by charter from the curriculum of each college, a sure recipe for the growth of scepticism and infidelity according to a zealous Churchman who found that insufficient recognition was given to 'the Divine Being as the source of all blessing'.[117]

The equality of women with men was plainly enunciated and in practice fully upheld. Every attempt was made to keep the fees of students as low as possible, at about ten pounds per session (with modest extras for science students because of practical work). The number of students at Aberystwyth had increased from 58 in 1881 (the year of the Aberdare Report) to 230 in 1892, at Cardiff from 151 in 1883 to 312 in 1892, and at Bangor from fifty-eight in 1884 to 135 in 1892. Students from England were less than a tenth of the total at Cardiff, a fifth at Bangor and two-fifths at Aberystwyth. A report during the 1892–3 session said that the standard of education in each college was 'undoubtedly of university standard'.[118] Viriamu Jones was quoted as saying that 'our best men are refusing to take the London course'[119] because an examining university did not adequately reflect the true worth of their training and attainments. Independence from the London system, however, was not to be lightly won.

VI

The Struggle for the Charter

Although the three colleges were primarily concerned with their own survival and development during the 1880s, the prospect of creating a University of Wales was never far from the minds of the leaders of higher education. In his inaugural address at Cardiff in 1883, Viriamu Jones proclaimed that the College on a day not too distant must be affiliated to the University of Wales. 'The various Colleges of Wales will be isolated units till the University of Wales exists, not in name, but in fact. The inauguration of the new Colleges is the first step towards it. When the University is founded it will, I believe, bring about a harmony of sentiment and interest between the Colleges affiliated to it that cannot be attained in any other way.'[1] The University had four duties: to teach; to examine and to confer degrees and diplomas; to stimulate research; and to control intermediate education. As to teaching, both the University and the Colleges taught at Oxford and Cambridge, whereas in Scotland and Germany the Colleges 'do not exist as distinct from the Universities'. In England and Wales, however, there was a new dispensation. Colleges were being established in towns far apart from one another and they should not be left without the power to confer degrees upon their students. At the same time it was not prudent to proliferate degree-awarding bodies. A University of Wales, with affiliated colleges widely separated, would not be able to provide the main part of the teaching as one body corporate; only the colleges could discharge this function. The examining board of the University when constituted should consist of internal examiners to 'afford scope for development in accordance with the characteristics of Wales' and of external examiners to 'ensure an interchange of sentiment with the outside educational world'. In the mean time the University of London would undertake examining duties.

Extended attention has been given to this address because it conveys the essence of Viriamu Jones's views at an early stage. He developed his ideas in subsequent speeches – to the Cambrian Society, for instance, in April 1887 — but it would be as well to hasten to the August of that year when, we are told, 'the iron was ready for the anvil'.[2] The National Eisteddfod was being held at the Albert Hall and the Cymmrodorion Section had determined to devote three days to discuss the future of the Welsh educational system. One sitting was set aside to consider the question of a university charter and the proceedings were opened by Viriamu. Several years after his death it was said that 'his speech still lives in the memory of those who heard it. Its lucidity, cogency and conciseness were as conspicuous as the zeal and conviction of the speaker.'[3] It is no slight to H. R. Reichel and other speakers to dwell upon Viriamu's contribution.[4] The main message was the unity of the Welsh educational system, elementary, intermediate and higher; only the university could provide the necessary organization to co-ordinate the whole. Future elementary teachers should be enabled to pursue a scheme of study in the non-technical part of their work within the training departments of the university colleges, thus giving them a breadth of outlook not easily acquired in the traditional training colleges. It was evident, however, that the examinations of a government department were not best suited for prospective teachers trained at university colleges and that an appropriate substitute would be a certificate of the college or 'better still, the certificate of the three colleges combined for the purposes of examination. But what was this combination of colleges: what but University organisation? This naturally implies the formation of the Welsh University.'[5] Later Viriamu was to stress that the need for the University of Wales sprang directly from the desire that teachers in elementary schools should be trained at the university colleges.[6] As to an efficient system of intermediate education, long in gestation and by no means settled in 1887, Viriamu was convinced that an Intermediate Education Board should be an integral part of the university organization. Again, the University of Wales was to be a teaching university for this was fundamental to the fulfilment of Welsh educational aspirations. In 1895 Viriamu looked back upon the scene in 1887. He did not then much care for the architectural metaphor that the purpose of the University was 'to crown the educational edifice'.[7] Its aim, rather, was to bring symmetry and good order to disparate groups and he employed a more appropriate comparison derived from his study of physics, 'a department of science to which I have given some attention'. It has been quoted more than once, but it will bear repetition. 'Scatter iron filings on a sheet of cardboard, and they will arrange themselves in curves so harmonious and beautiful and mysterious that no one wearies of watching... The iron filings are the educational institutions of Wales; and the University, if it plays its part aright, is the magnet that shall link them in an orderly system.'[8] At the Cymmrodorion meeting of 1887 Viriamu gave a resounding peroration calculated to strike a responsive chord in an audience of Victorian Welshmen:

> May Wales judge wisely of the things she ought to desire, and work joyfully until they are attained. May she put far from her all narrowness and exclusiveness of spirit, believe profoundly that God has given to her a mission and a part of her own to perform in the high destiny of man, and may she gird herself to this task with simple earnestness and eager faith, thankfully recognising that it is to be accomplished not by force of arms nor in political isolation, but by intellectual and moral eminence in closest contact and heartiest sympathy with all portions of the great empire of which she may well be thankful and proud that Providence has willed she should form a part.[9]

There was more than rhetoric. The Cymmrodorion Section resolved that definite action be taken to impress upon the government the desire of the Welsh people for the establishment of a Welsh university and that a conference be convened of representatives of colleges and of intermediate and elementary schools. At this conference, held at Shrewsbury in January 1888, Viriamu again spoke to great effect. Apart from rehearsing previous arguments, he declared that the educational system in Wales was vitiated because the old Welsh grammar schools trained their pupils for Oxford and Cambridge whilst the Welsh colleges had to prepare their students for the examinations of the University of London. It was unreasonable to expect these schools to adapt to a dual system; so long as the Welsh colleges were tied to London University rather than to the University of Wales (more akin to Oxford and Cambridge than London) there would continue to be a lack of sympathy and co-operation between the best schools in Wales and the colleges. The old endowed schools, then, as well as the elementary schools, were to be closely associated with the new university. Three resolutions were passed by the January conference.[10] First, it was expedient that intermediate and collegiate education in Wales should be completed by a university organization; second, the Welsh university should inspect state-aided intermediate schools, and third, arrangements should be made for members of the conference to meet Welsh peers and members of Parliament.

At this stage the hand of Isambard Owen is increasingly to be observed. His services to the University were so considerable that we must introduce him briefly.[11] Born in 1850 at Chepstow, the son of a pupil of Isambard Brunel, and hence his name, he was educated at Cambridge and at St George's Hospital, London, where he became Dean in 1883. Tall, genial and dignified, he had a Roman nose, a well chiselled chin, bright blue sapphire eyes and long, cool tapering fingers. An immensely practical man who always travelled with a small bag of tools, he remained the master, not the victim, of inanimate objects, such as locks, bolts and windows. He brought many gifts to the service of university administration of which the University of Wales was a substantial beneficiary. Considered by some to be incurably bland, he was certainly *suaviter in modo* but he was also *fortiter in re* and Reichel spoke of his 'unique authority'.[12] Later in his career he was Principal of Armstrong College, Newcastle, and Vice-Chancellor of Bristol University. In 1925 the President of the General Medical Council said of him that 'few men of our profession in this generation have done so much constructive work of an abiding kind in settling the framework and directing the policy of modern universities'.[13]

In February, Isambard Owen wrote to Viriamu to say that he and John Rhys were agreed that Viriamu should not only take the lead in discussions relating to the proposed university but that he and Reichel should prepare a draft charter.[14] At the meeting with peers and members of Parliament in March 1888 the Earl of Powis had somewhat tamely suggested that a royal commission to look into the question of universities might be the best answer; Wales could then present a good case. Viriamu firmly deprecated the proposal, indefinite delay was out of the question and the university, which could be created by royal charter without any call for legislative action, would give unity to 'a disorganised conglomeration'.[15] It does not seem that Reichel at this stage shared Viriamu's dauntless optimism. Only a little earlier Reichel had said that years were certain to elapse between the opening shots of the campaign and final victory: 'immediate action will certainly not give us a university in 1887, but it may make the date 1897, not 2007.'[16] Indeed, Reichel's remarks to the parliamentarians were cautious to a degree. Viriamu, on the other hand, was buoyant, even believing that Wales might fairly hope to have a charter before an

Intermediate Act, a prognostication shortly to be proved wrong. In some ways the most interesting contribution to Westminster discussion came from Lord Aberdare who spoke with an unwonted enthusiasm. There are signs that he had become a little defensive concerning his Report. He was now able to speak more clearly and strongly, he said, after the experience of the last eight years. If another Departmental Committee were appointed, and he was clearly not recommending one, 'what an immense improvement they would find in the feelings and thoughts which would be expressed'.[17]

Isambard Owen was most anxious to proceed. Two days after the conference he told Viriamu that he wanted a draft charter adopted and completed in Wales 'before English politicians have time to get a finger in the pie'.[18] In response to a communication from Cardiff, Bangor's Court of Governors took the initiative in April to invite each of the other two colleges to appoint representatives to meet an equal number from Bangor to prepare a draft charter. In July the conference of representatives resolved that the time had come to apply jointly to the government for a charter 'to constitute a University for Wales on the same general lines as the charter already granted to the Victoria University, with such modifications as may be required by the peculiar conditions and circumstances of Wales'.[19] Nevertheless, at this meeting, presided over by Aberdare and of which R. A. Jones of the Bangor Council was secretary, it emerged that there was 'a great tug-of-war' concerning the nature of the university. Viriamu and Reichel were adamant that attendance at one of the colleges should be a fundamental requirement. They were supported by the professors on the committee but strenuously opposed by powerful Aberystwyth representatives, namely, Thomas Charles Edwards, Stuart Rendel (a future president), Humphreys-Owen and Henry Richard. The nature and extent of the controversy will need to be considered at a later stage. Suffice it to say here that it could scarcely have been unknown to the President of the Council, Lord Cranbrook, when an ostensibly powerful delegation led by Aberdare waited upon him to request two charters, one for the University and one for Aberystwyth College, and also a permanent grant of £4,000 per annum for Aberystwyth. Whether it was wise to request two charters on the same occasion may well be questioned. The Conservative President seems to have enjoyed the encounter. He affected to 'admire the ambition of the principality of Wales that they, before one of their eggs was completely hatched, should wish to develop into the full-grown bird'.[20] Eloquent tributes by Aberdare to the 'fine, noble qualities of the Welsh' and by William Rathbone to the people's thirst for education left him, to all outward appearances, largely unmoved. The delegates were told that the question could not be determined 'off-hand' and that in any case a royal commission was at that very moment inquiring into the University of London and had before it a petition requesting a teaching university. The consultations now in train were most germane and precluded a decision 'at so early a stage in the development of the Welsh Colleges'. Before Cranbrook courteously closed the door there was a parting suggestion that a draft charter, soundly based upon detailed investigation, could be presented to the government in due course. The ensuing period of 'hybernation',[21] as Isambard Owen called it, was to last three long winters. Why was this so?

A major reason undoubtedly was that the debate concerning an examining versus a teaching university had not been resolved. So long as a substantial body of opinion remained unconvinced of the need for attendance, progress was not possible. Moreover, as Aberystwyth's new Principal, T. F. Roberts, observed in April 1891, the question of a university had not 'evoked general enthusiasm on the part of the people at large'[22] for they were unable to appreciate the difference between a university and a university college. This may appear to be a startling admission to those nurtured on the conventional view of Welsh educational aspirations. Reichel had gone further. Two years after his arrival in Wales he announced to a Liverpool audience that it was fortunate that the Welsh colleges had not been incorporated immediately on their foundation into a university, otherwise academic standards might have been lowered in response to the clamour of an 'ill-informed and enthusiastic constituency'.[23] In 1888 he told Welsh peers and MPs that the standard of education in Wales was low, that there was 'a very widespread ignorance as to the true nature of University teaching'[24] and that 'possibly pressure would be brought on University authorities to lower the standard of the Welsh degree'. Such tendencies might be guarded against by temporary, if not permanent, association with representatives of the older universities. It was wholly characteristic of Reichel fearlessly to speak the plain truth as he saw it, and he would have agreed that the discussions and debates between 1888 and 1893, sometimes ferocious, were part of a necessary educative process. Another factor contributing to delay was that of deferred expectation. In an age when the political pendulum tended to swing with a wholesome regularity it was reasonable for Nonconformists and Liberals to nourish the hope that a Tory government would not last for ever. In fact they had good reason to be grateful to the Tories for passing in 1888 the Local Government Act, thus creating the machinery which rendered possible the long-awaited Welsh Intermediate Act of 1889. Indeed the implementation of this notable Act by joint education committees was bound to engage the attention and in part to divert the energies of Welsh educationists from the immediate need to found a Welsh university. From the outset, nevertheless, there was close co-operation between county education authorities and leaders of the university movement, the same personnel often serving on the different bodies. By the end of 1891 Aberdare rejoiced that people who had been flying at one another's throats a short time ago had worked together to establish good intermediate schools.[25] To the public at large, however, it seemed that the protagonists of university education had been unduly riven by dissension.

By the spring of 1891 it appeared that a more harmonious spirit had emerged. In April the Bangor Court again took the initiative, the prime movers being Ellis Edwards, Vice-Principal of the Bala College, and A. G. Edwards, Bishop of St Asaph. Representatives of the three colleges met members of the joint education committees of north and south Wales on three separate occasions and at the Bangor Court in October it was reported that thirteen members of each college together with twenty-two members of the joint education committees were to assemble at Shrewsbury.[26] This representative body, which held its first meeting on 11 November became known as the Welsh University Conference.[27] Aberdare wanted the comparatively young Marquess of Bute, a Tory and a Roman Catholic, to take the chair, but after some ungainly exchanges Bute declined the honour and Aberdare, with some show of reluctance, assumed his customary role. Once again, there were those who favoured a royal commission to ventilate the whole question and in reply to those who feared the risk of indefinitely postponing the issue the Bishop of St Asaph observed that the two state-aided colleges of Bangor and Cardiff had been established within three years of the publication of the Report of the Aberdare Committee which had itself acted with the utmost expedition. Others were less sanguine. Lewis Morris thought they would not be granted a royal commission by the present administration and that a succeeding Liberal government would take several years to appoint one: 'If you postpone the question now you postpone it for seven or ten years. The condition of Welsh education will not stand it.'[28] Delay would weaken the whole structure unless there were 'an opening upwards',[29] and here he was cunningly quoting the words of a former Bishop of St Asaph to the Aberdare Committee. Lewis Williams held that the conference would be in an anomalous position before Wales were they to seek a royal commission: 'If a Commission were appointed, we should have to defer to a number of gentlemen not more competent than ourselves.'[30] Such arguments wisely prevailed.

The conference formulated guiding principles.[31] They are best quoted *in extenso* rather than paraphrased.

> 1. That the University of Wales shall be a teaching university – that is, that no candidate shall be admitted to a degree unless he shall have pursued such a course of study at one of the colleges of the University as the University Governing Body may prescribe.

During the ensuing debates, this is what was meant by 'residence'. It did not mean that all students were required to live within college buildings. William Rathbone and others wished to qualify the rule in the interests of those who could not attend for three years and even Isambard Owen had at this stage intended that older students should take their degrees without attending the colleges. This resolution was passed unanimously, but was strenuously opposed thereafter as we shall see. Ellis Edwards moved that university extension lectures should be accepted in lieu of attendance; he was not supported. There was in addition a rider to this resolution:

> That the teachers or some of them in each faculty in each college shall have a substantial share in the original framing, and subsequent modification, of the curriculum of education.

The rider, unanimously passed, was later fiercely contested in public.

> 2. That the colleges in the University shall be the three University Colleges of Bangor, Aberystwyth, and Cardiff, and such other colleges as may hereafter be recognised by the University Governing Body.

This resolution aroused the greatest controversy. The Dean of St

Asaph, John Owen, objected because it excluded Lampeter and other theological colleges, such as Bala, from forming part of the basis of the University. He and Ellis Edwards asked that the resolution be postponed. John Rhys believed that by excluding Lampeter 'this open sore will rankle for years to come'.[32] It was a prophetic utterance. Lampeter's constitution made inclusion impossible and by a proportion of three to two the amendment seeking postponement of the issue was defeated.

> 3. That powers be sought enabling the University to give degrees in arts and science, and subsequently in such other faculties, including theology, medicine, law and music, as may be sanctioned from time to time by the Crown at the request of the University Governing Body.

Defenders of theology were active, but an amendment to place theology before arts failed. Lewis Morris favoured a school of law because his countrymen were 'a litigious people'.[33] The resolution was carried without difficulty.

> 4. That it is desirable that provision be made in the charter for the encouragement of extension lectures carried on by the colleges of the University.

This fourth proposition, in part a palliative to the first, was passed without opposition.

> 5. That it is desirable that the University should have power to undertake the inspection and examination of intermediate schools and other educational institutions and to grant certificates of proficiency in connection therewith.

Here we may discern the influence of Viriamu Jones.

> 6. That in order to secure the speedy establishment of a University on these lines, a committee be appointed to prepare a draft charter, and submit the same to a subsequent meeting of this Conference.[34]

These six resolutions constituted the brief to be followed by the draft charter committee of thirty-two members. The committee met several times in 1892 under the expert guidance of Isambard Owen, who had already prepared a preliminary draft for the benefit of the conference. He was later to say that although the earlier meetings demonstrated 'almost irreconcilable antagonisms of opinion on essential points', the scheme which eventually emerged had won the cordial agreement of practically every member of the draft charter committee. The essential features may be simply stated. The authorities of the University were to be the Visitor, the Chancellor, the Court, the Vice-Chancellor, the University Senate and the Guild of Graduates; there were to be no religious tests and women were to have complete equality with men. Since the royal Charter itself is examined in detail in a succeeding chapter it is sufficient here to consider only those matters of controversy which arose before, during and after the University Conference at the old Raven Hotel, Shrewsbury, on 6 January 1893. The proposed charter received general acceptance, largely because a decisive majority clearly favoured the recommendations and not because, as the *Western Mail* suggested, members feared they might be blockaded by the onset of snow[35] (which, it must be allowed, later tended to disrupt January meetings of the University at Shrewsbury). A powerful dissolvent of one cause of dissension had undoubtedly been the action of the draft committee in exceeding its brief. As we have seen, the University Conference in 1891 resolved not to establish a faculty of theology at first, though its inclusion at a later stage was firmly envisaged. The background to this change of policy must now be considered.

H. R. Reichel, for instance, a man of deep personal piety, had from his early days at Bangor been convinced that it would be wise to exclude theology as a subject of study until *odium theologicum* had perceptibly waned and until the secular faculties were in working order. Such a view was shared by R. A. Jones, active both in the educational and religious life of Wales and later described by Reichel as 'the most able, single-minded and modest of Welsh patriots'.[36] Both had resisted at the Bangor Court in April 1892 a motion by Ellis Edwards that theology should be given its rightful place in the new university. Edwards argued that religion counted for more than politics in Wales; when Sir William Harcourt and others addressed political meetings, the pavilion at Caernarfon was not crowded as it was for great religious gatherings.[37] The ensuing discussion drew forth a welter of metaphors. One speaker said that theology was 'mother's milk'[38] in Wales, another that it would be 'a millstone'[39] round the neck of the young University, whilst Reichel feared that they would have 'a hornet's nest ... about their ears'[40] if they began to distinguish between one theological college and another, which they would be bound to do since the university colleges were forbidden to teach theology. However, when the vote was taken, Edwards won handsomely, Reichel, with his usual candour, later recognizing that he had misjudged the situation and that denominational rivalry, though not stilled, had lost much of its vengeful spite.[41] The outcome of the debate at Bangor could not fail to influence the draft charter committee. Isambard Owen had from the beginning thought that a national university should not exclude a discipline which, beyond all others, had sharpened the minds of Welshmen; he and his colleagues on the charter committee far exceeded their instructions by providing for the study of theology, in the first instance at postgraduate level, as in Scotland.[42] Their initiative was widely acclaimed, not least by the conference in January 1893, as timely and conciliatory.

The advocates of non-attendance were not so readily appeased. The first resolution in November 1891 had stated plainly that the university was to be a teaching university and that candidates could not be admitted to a degree unless they had studied at one of the constituent colleges; graduation without attendance, as under the London system, was not to be countenanced. Indeed, it was upon this rock that negotiations in 1888 had foundered. Men of weight and authority at Aberystwyth, including the Principal, as we have seen, had then disagreed with Viriamu Jones and Reichel. In their view it would be wrong to make attendance a fundamental condition; 'to insist on it at present would make the university so unpopular', wrote Humphreys-Owen to his wife, 'that we should lose the support we should have'.[43] It was natural for Aberystwyth to give special attention to the views of the public which had sustained them in dark days. Nevertheless, by 1891 there had been a marked shift in sentiment and many honest doubters were at length convinced that the London model would not do for Wales. It was, of course, fitting to recognize that London had performed a unique service in setting and maintaining standards during the fledgling years of young colleges. The examiners were eminent, impartial men; in the workaday world the external degree had an undisputed value and in distant parts of the globe even a 'failed London BA' stood a-tiptoe amongst his fellows. But for this 'academical midwife',[44] Reichel once said, the new provincial colleges would never have seen the light of day. The role of the midwife was often vital, but once she had performed her task there was no cause to delay her departure. Both teachers and students suffered under a treadmill system. The former were obliged to follow a set syllabus at a time when the whole realm of learning was ever extending; they had no opportunity to teach aspects of a subject which had especially appealed to them and fertile, imaginative forays were regarded as an unprofitable indulgence. There was no à la carte, only table d'hôte.[45] One of the several thundering disputes between Thomas Charles Edwards and Henry Jones concerned this very matter. Edwards did not think the work at Aberystwyth suited Jones, so much so that he told O. M. Edwards, then a student, that 'it was not to teach a grand philosophy but to train men for London that I asked him here.'[46] One teacher recalled in 1927 that he was often faced with the question: '. . . is this in the syllabus? What right have I to save a student's soul at the risk of lowering his marks in the examinations?'[47] In brief, there was none of that rational liberty, so much prized in German universities. From the students' standpoint there were serious defects. Some subjects, such as history, were scarcely taught at all, whilst philosophy was restricted to the philosophy of one school. In Wales there was a particular grievance, for Welsh had no place in the initial degree scheme. Too many subjects were required at the matriculation and intermediate stages, thereby encouraging superficial, discursive minds. To Reichel the London degree was 'oftener the badge of information than of education'.[48] Viriamu Jones had swept triumphantly through the London examinations and knew at first hand the evils of cramming, presuming early, as he was to do later, 'on Nature's mercy'.[49] Perhaps the sturdiest onslaught on the London system came in the Report of the Royal Commission on University Education in London in 1913, which bears the firm imprint of its chairman, R. B. Haldane, in time to be intimately acquainted with the fortunes of the University of Wales:

> We are convinced that both a detailed syllabus and an external examination are inconsistent with the true interests of university education, injurious to the students, degrading to the teachers, and ineffective for the attainment of the ends they are supposed to promote. . . The effect upon the students and the teachers is disastrous. The students have the ordeal of the examination hanging over them and must prepare themselves for it or fail to get the degree. Thus the degree

comes first and education a bad second... However conducted, such examinations are an insufficient and inconclusive test of the attainment of a university education... [and]... it appears to us only fair that due weight should be given to the whole record of the students' work in the University. If the academic freedom of the professors and the students is to be maintained... it is absolutely necessary that, subject to proper safeguards, the degrees of the University should practically be the certificates given by the professors themselves, and that the students should have entire confidence that they may trust their academic fate to honest work under their instruction and direction.[50]

The justification for treating this aspect at some length is two-fold. First, the passionate desire to be liberated from the London system was a powerful motive force in establishing the University of Wales. Staff and students alike were to rejoice in their new-found freedom. Second, it was disturbing to the advocates of a teaching university to be confronted as late as 1893 with a systematic campaign to provide graduating opportunities for those unable to fulfil essential attendance requirements. Such a campaign is mainly associated with R. D. Roberts[51] (1851–1911) who found a resourceful, combative ally in John Gibson, editor of the *Cambrian News*. Born at Aberystwyth and brought up in the sternest traditions of puritanism – he was a church elder at twenty-one – Roberts lost his early certitudes after scientific training at London and Cambridge, being influenced perhaps by the perplexing perspectives of geology, his principal specialism. He was soon, however, to find satisfaction in an optimistic view of man which led him to espouse a variety of causes, mainly the University Extension Movement, of which he became the chief interpreter from 1886 to 1902, a period of challenge following the early rapture. Roberts later gave valuable service to the University as Deputy-Chancellor, but the claim that he was one of its founders should be qualified because many regarded him as a disruptive influence during the protracted period of *accouchement*.

Roberts had already made his standpoint known to Welshmen in *Y Traethodydd* in 1887 and it occasioned no surprise when in September 1891, shortly before the meeting of the Welsh University Conference, he produced a 'Memorandum on the Proposed University of Wales' which attracted much attention. In the memorandum he outlined the provisions at the older universities for those unable attend regularly for three years: the full, careful syllabus, weekly written work, followed by discussion in class with the tutor, and an examination at the end of each term. Students who satisfied the authorities were then excused the first university examination, the 'little go', and allowed to sit the honour examination after residence of two rather than three years. This arrangement was far superior to that of London and had Roberts gone no further he would have been widely supported. It was a different matter when he urged that the period of non-attendance should be extended to nine years. 'The Welsh University', he said, 'should. . . have power to recognise for degree purposes, not merely the work done at certain specified colleges of University rank, *but all teaching of University rank given by its accredited teachers whether within the walls of a College or not.*'[52] (My italic.) Once the principle had been accepted, he added rather blithely, the details could easily be settled. The principle, however, was by no means acceptable to the university colleges and we need not pause to consider the details save to say that Roberts wished all university college teachers to become *ipso facto* university teachers, that suitably qualified lecturers at theological colleges should also be recognized as university teachers and that the university itself should have a staff of itinerant lecturers 'placed wherever suitable local arrangements were made for undertaking continuous University work'.[53] Roberts fought tenaciously and in December 1892 he had prepared a rival draft charter[54] which aroused the ire of Isambard Owen. Some of his recommendations were worthy of attention, if not of adoption. All professors and lecturers should become 'University teachers' but some professors were to be more equal than others for he would empower the University Court to elevate a few college professors to the dignity of 'University Professors' receiving a handsome salary well beyond the ordinary, more leisure than was usual to pursue original work and more funds to develop the higher reaches of their subjects. Honours students, he anticipated, would be attracted from each college to a department set aside for 'the very highest teaching'.[55] This early attempt to deal with the problem of scarce resources by creating centres of excellence was unlikely to succeed in the circumstances of the day.

Roberts was evidently disposed to recognize suitable teachers in the theological colleges for the purpose of his scheme. Walter Evans, Principal of Carmarthen Theological College, had more grandiose plans. The degrees of the university should be open − the term 'open university' was not uncommon at the time − to students of the eight

Nonconformist colleges, Lampeter, the four teachers' training colleges, and to private students, elementary school teachers and ministers of religion in every communion.[56] Indeed, he wished the thirteen colleges to become constituent colleges of the University. In his enthusiasm he sent a copy of his plan to Gladstone who called it 'gallant'[57] in a characteristically guarded reply. Evans was, of course, fully entitled to say that the theological colleges of Wales had an honourable ancestry and had in an important sense paved the way for the new university colleges which should hold them in dutiful regard. Realists, however, recognized that having successfully pressed the case for state aid to the three university colleges because existing institutions were defective, it was now perverse to lavish immoderate praise upon theological and training colleges. The best riposte to Walter Evans fortunately came from Ellis Edwards of Bala who could speak with an authority, almost unequalled, upon the changing role of the theological colleges. The new university colleges, he declared, needed to be strengthened, not undermined, and it was injurious to the proper study of theology itself to expect the staff of theological colleges to be burdened by teaching secular subjects in addition: 'he who defends the retention of mixed arts and theology really advocates the lowering of both and simply retards the day when the theologian will be properly equipped.'[58] In fact, the most promising student would be deterred from attending colleges which still continued to offer a mixed curriculum. The advantages of separation had been amply recognized when the denominational colleges sought new homes close to the national colleges where secular subjects could most profitably be studied. Thus, the academy founded for the Congregationalists of north Wales at Bala in 1841, being thereafter known as the Bala–Bangor College, had been transferred to Bangor in 1888–90; the Baptist College for north Wales (established at Llangollen in 1842) moved to Bangor in 1892 and the Baptist College, removed from Abergavenny to Pontypool in 1836, came to Cardiff in 1893.[59] Thomas Charles Edwards, in turn, wanted theological colleges to concentrate upon their prime duty and he hoped that the Bala Theological College, whose head he had become after leaving Aberystwyth, would be open to members of other denominations and also to women.[60] A new spirit was abroad. As to teacher training colleges, Ellis Edwards noted that prospective teachers evidently welcomed the opportunity of enrolling in the Day Training Departments at Cardiff and Aberystwyth.

Roberts's plan was soundly defeated at the University Conference in January 1893. He believed that he was often misinterpreted. He had not, it is true, advocated the adoption of the London system, for he made provision for direct contact between teacher and taught by his itinerant scheme which, at a different level, had been remarkably successful in the eighteenth century. He did not accept defeat; he urged his views relentlessly in the press and at length petitioned the Privy Council itself.[61] His scheme clearly contravened the fundamental principle of attendance and in throwing his net so widely as to include the 'private' student he was in effect urging that there should be two types of degree within the same university, the one bearing a marked resemblance to the London external degree and the other to that of the orthodox teaching university.

The task of attacking Roberts's scheme was mainly undertaken by Isambard Owen who had first-hand knowledge of London University. He freely acknowledged that it had served the Empire well in difficult days, but he was convinced that only 'minds of exceptional power'[62] could devour knowledge wholesale like a boa-constrictor and digest it later. The average man was not much improved by the mere acquisition of factual information without being trained to use it as material for thought. The University of London itself had declined to award a medical degree on an examination test alone and had insisted upon personal supervision in a recognized professional school. The 'private' student would be likely to mean in Wales what it usually meant under the London system, the pupil of a professional crammer. What conceivable advantage would it be to a man from Blaenau Ffestiniog or from Aberdare to be examined by a person he had never seen, from Bangor or Cardiff? In any case, an industrious external student who performed well under such conditions would most likely have won a scholarship to one of the university colleges. The only acceptable answer was to assist the able by means of scholarships and bursaries, and Owen was inclined to allow special privileges in the colleges to comfortably placed students rather than hard cash, which should be reserved for the truly indigent. Again, from the standpoint of the state it was highly improbable that any government of whatever complexion would permit the creation of a second examining body on mainland Britain, partly because it would inevitably lack initial prestige and strength of numbers. A charter for an examining university would not be given unless it met a clear need; gratuitous competition was out of the question. If one included the Royal University of Ireland, which did not require attendance, there were already two 'open universities' in Britain. In fact, it should be added that at Trinity College, Dublin the practice had grown, contrary to statutes, of allowing students to qualify for degrees without attending lectures.[63] To establish an examining university in Wales was not simply an internal affair; it involved England and Scotland who would oppose it vigorously. In essence it was an imperial matter. Moreover, neither London University nor the Royal University of Ireland could be considered 'national' in the sense of being representatively governed, as was Wales's firm intent, for they were mainly ruled by crown nominees, and Wales could not expect different treatment. Further, it would be foolish to ignore the experience of London teachers who were profoundly dissatisfied with an open, cramming university. As Isambard remarked, 'Good as the work of the London University has been in its Imperial capacity, there is no doubt that its higher education in the Metropolis has been disastrous. It is difficult to develop good higher education in the face of a premium placed on mere coaching.'[64] The question of standards was crucial. If the new university was to provide for students not in attendance it would in effect be attaching two values to the same degree, a perilous course for an institution anxious as soon as possible to establish its reputation. Talented students might well be tempted to go elsewhere, for 'university credit is as delicate a matter as commercial credit'.[65] A good name was not achieved overnight and it was recognized that the bearers of the new university degree would in a sense be shorn lambs. From time to time, too, there was sharp comment concerning the practice in some small American colleges of selling higher degrees – for as little as a fiver according to Lewis Morris.[66] Whilst only a few Welshmen were caught up in this nefarious traffic, the spectacle of an occasional minister returning home 'doctored' after visits to the States was viewed by the upholders of university values with a mixture of amusement and disdain.

Throughout their proceedings the architects of the University resolutely refused to compromise with standards. Problems sometimes arose in unexpected ways. In one or two quarters there was an almost instinctive urge to misunderstand, to misinterpret and to misinform. For example, it was put out that the draft charter had been so 'cunningly devised'[67] as in effect to create three universities, not one.

Sections of two clauses were pitched upon as proof positive of cynical betrayal. Clause 65 stated that 'each Constituent College of the University shall be entitled to propose plans of study and examination for its own students for the several degrees of the University', but no heed was paid to the substantial qualifications which followed relating to the powers of the University Senate and to the decisive authority of the Court. The intention of the clause was to give as much freedom in the choice of subjects and in the manner of treatment as was reasonable. Reichel drew attention to the wide choice available in the older universities, where in the subject of history there were six or more periods from which to select;[68] valuable lessons might also be learnt from the experience of the Victoria University but with modifications to meet the particular needs of Wales. Manchester was at the heart of the Victoria University, Liverpool and Leeds but an hour away. Even so, in order to maintain a uniform curriculum professors at Liverpool and Leeds had to travel to Manchester, sometimes once a month and even once a week. The colleges in Wales were one day's journey apart and regular consultations after the Manchester pattern were manifestly unsuitable. The answer in Wales was guarded 'local option', in the familiar language of the day. The enemies of the draft charter had fallen upon clause 65 with a 'vulpine vigour',[69] thought Tom Ellis, but had wilfully ignored the fundamental requirements that schemes of study were to be sanctioned by the University Senate and by the University Court.

A sinister interpretation was also placed upon clause 54 which ordained that all degree examinations should be conducted by external examiners jointly with an equal number of examiners from the candidates' own college. A Border newspaper proclaimed that 'a new University should be in every way above suspicion';[70] it had to struggle against public prejudice and 'the imperious necessity' of 'starting on high ground' required that for a time no examiners should be appointed by the colleges. Others feared that senseless rivalries would seduce colleges to lower standards in order to achieve the best results. Such persistent mistrust was not easy to deal with, but the defenders of the University were well prepared. The double system of 'external' and 'internal' examiners was of Scottish origin and had been adopted by the Victoria University. Indeed, Isambard Owen could fairly say that the wording of the clause gave the external examiner a rather more effectual control over standards than under the Victoria

Charter. The Aberystwyth Senate, for instance, was firmly of the view that in cases of disagreement the ultimate responsibility should rest with external examiners whose role was in fact marginally strengthened in the Charter itself. There was an additional consideration of no small importance. It was vital to attract the best external examiners and there are indications that the Victoria University was unable to do so because of the low fees offered. London, on the other hand, had no difficulty because it was able, through the government, to remunerate them well. Isambard insisted that payment to the external examiners of the University of Wales must necessarily be greater than to those of Victoria because greater responsibility was cast upon them.[71]

At the Shrewsbury Conference in January, W. Cadwaladr Davies had stressed that delay would be highly inadvisable lest there be a change of government and a succession of short parliaments; Aberdare agreed that by the second reading of the Irish Home Rule Bill Parliament would be in 'a tolerable ferment'.[72] When the Principal of Lampeter asked that the draft charter be circulated in Welsh, Aberdare thought it unnecessary since all the recipients might be presumed to understand English. A Denbighshire member countered on the ground that 'there are thousands of people in Wales taking a great interest in education, to whom a Welsh copy would be better than an English copy.'[73] He added that it would be strange to ask for a Welsh copy of an Act of Parliament if they themselves did not prepare a Welsh translation of the draft charter. Indeed, one of John Morris-Jones's earliest tasks had been to translate the Local Government Act into Welsh. Cadwaladr Davies's offer to prepare a Welsh version was accepted and it duly appeared prefaced by a caveat that it was not an official translation and that his aim had been to present in Welsh the spirit of the original whilst attempting to keep as close as possible to the form and letter.[74] It is also worth noting, in passing, that Isambard's brother Maynard, a member of a first-rate firm of London solicitors, agreed to act as solicitor in drafting the Charter, that Viriamu's brother Brynmor acted as counsel and Cadwaladr Davies as his junior. The three gave their services *gratis* and there was thus no legal expense in carrying through the Charter.

The Shrewsbury Conference was followed by a period of intense consultation. The draft charter was submitted for comment by 1 March to the senates, councils and courts of colleges, to the Conference of the Joint Education Committees and to the county and county borough councils of Wales and Monmouthshire. In all probability the most searching discussion was at the February meeting of the Joint Education Committees which Isambard Owen was invited to attend. Upon him, too, fell the main burden of answering successive queries in the Welsh and English press; it was he also who spoke at each of the college courts displaying at their best his incomparable gifts of elucidation. A valuable guide to the issues to be determined, prepared initially for the University Charter Conference, was a slim volume, *British Universities: Notes and Summaries contributed to the Welsh University discussion by members of the Senate of the University College of North Wales*, edited and prepared by Bangor's professor of Greek, W. Rhys Roberts, when he was staying at an upland farm in the Nant Ffrancon Pass in April 1892. Roberts himself wrote a percipient general account of universities and there followed a summary of the constitution of English, Scottish and Irish universities by various members of staff. At the end of his introduction, Roberts wrote:

> It will be the duty of every Welshman who takes an interest in the future of his country to scan closely the draft charter, when it appears, and to ask himself: What does this new machinery give us? Simply degrees, titles, labels? Or does it − we will not say 'give', for that no machinery can do; does it permit, under favourable conditions, of the growth of a School of Learning in our midst? Does the proposed university add anything to the appliances of learning and the incentives to learning? Does it raise our ideals of learning? Does it mark a definite step forward now, and promise further progress in the future; or does it mean no advance, but the risk of retrogression?
>
> These questions should be asked by all, but especially by those who indulge the hope that the stream of national feeling which runs high in Wales today may prove not simply a force with which the politician has to reckon, and which the manager of men must turn to account, but one which can compel the respect of the best minds of the day.[75]

Various criticisms of the draft charter were made. Viriamu Jones himself was uneasy that there was insufficient right of appeal to the Visitor. Cardiff would have faculties not at Aberystwyth or Bangor and if an occasion arose when the University Court declined to act because of the preponderance of representatives from these two colleges Cardiff should have the right of appeal to the Privy Council.[76] The representative character of the Court was altogether disapproved of by some. The *Church Times* did not think much of popular representation: 'neither Balliol nor Magdalen, Trinity nor Queen's, know of it; Edinburgh and Aberdeen are ignorant of popular control; Durham and Dublin care little for county councils; but no matter, Wales must have everything of the latest pattern.'[77] R. D. Roberts in his alternative charter would have reduced local government representatives from 27 per cent to 17 per cent and increased the number of crown nominees from 13 per cent to 34 per cent, scarcely a rousing cheer for democracy. Glamorgan County Council petitioned the Privy Council to say that the densely populated county was not adequately represented. The framers of the draft charter replied that a compromise had been attempted whereby in addition to the single representative for each county there would be one other for each 100,000 of the population. From Caernarfonshire County Council and the inhabitants of Aberystwyth (led by John Gibson) came a call to reduce the academic element on the Court on the strange ground that academics would be more assiduous in their attendance and be better prepared, thus dominating the proceedings of the Court. Defenders of the draft charter were able to demonstrate that college representatives constituted no more than 36 per cent of the membership, whereas in the Victoria Court the proportion was as high as 65 per cent.[78] Indeed, a writer in the *Manchester Guardian* thought that the proposed court had 'a terribly non-academic appearance'.[79] It was certainly appreciably smaller than the college courts, but since it was expected to deal with academic affairs, Reichel was right to call it 'unwieldy'.[80] Tom Ellis had resisted having a University Council because he had the utmost confidence in the hundred 'best men' entrusted with the fortunes of the University. The Court, he thought, might well elect executive committees, as did London and Glamorgan County Council (both substantial bodies) but retaining, as they did, real power and real control in their own hands. In short, the University Court should not be like college courts which devolved important executive functions upon their councils. It was to be 'the supreme educational Parliament for Wales'.[81] This was the most democratic body ever envisaged for the government of a university; it should also be a thoroughly powerful, efficient body. If the government acted, as Ellis expected it to act, Wales would in this matter have 'effective Home Rule'.[82]

There were differences of opinion at all stages concerning the Guild of Graduates, corresponding to a convocation of graduates in most

British universities, in Cambridge to a Senate and in Scotland to a general council. It is true that Viriamu Jones had spoken of a convocation when he had addressed the Cambrian Society in 1887.[83] Isambard, however, had in mind an august, venerable body; in a document entitled 'Proposals for completing the organisation of the University of Wales', which bears his authentic stamp, he had this to say: 'The name "Guild of Graduates" is advisedly employed instead of "Convocation", in order to emphasize the point that the graduates in these proposals are not a mere assembly, but a corporate guild in actual fact, with a special educational duty of its own, and power of holding property to devote to it.'[84] Any person upon whom a degree had been conferred by the 'University Chamber' would be received into the Guild upon production of a diploma and of satisfactory evidence of having attained the age of twenty-one (for discretion, apparently, could not be expected earlier). A president and four censors were to meet the day before the Guild assembled to consider questions of discipline and were themselves to be fined for non-attendance. At all meetings of the Guild members were to wear the 'Academical Costume', carefully specified, proper to their degree, and on ceremonial occasions there was to be strict order of procedure. If a member was found guilty of grave offence the Guild was to request the 'University Chamber' to revoke his degree. For a lesser offence the president and censors were 'publicly to reprimand the offender in speech, writing or print, and to require amendment of his manners'.[85] D. Emrys Evans remarked that 'the more circumspect academic statesmen'[86] (of whom he assuredly was one) would have shuddered at these proposals. Indeed, it is probable that an antique pantomime of this kind – Isambard was also a freemason – would not have done. He was certainly captivated by the long ancestry of the ancient universities of Europe, of which the University of Wales was a lineal descendant; the savour of medievalism appealed to him and his constitutional plans were coloured by gothic romanticism. Not surprisingly, terms such as 'University Chamber', 'Cabinets' and 'Delegacies' were blown away long before the draft charter was in shape. 'The Guild of Graduates', however, was retained because the body Isambard visualized was to promote a sense of fraternity which was still preserved amongst graduates of the older universities but which the 'convocations' of recent creation had failed to imbue. The draft charter allowed the Guild to hold property, but, as we shall see, this provision finds no place in the Charter itself.[87] There was objection, too, in some quarters to a Guild of any kind. Lewis Morris was harshly dismissive of 'this foolish limbo';[88] such an anomalous body would have nothing to do save 'chafe at its own impotence'; it would be a fifth wheel to the University Court, and the proper place for University graduates was on the University Court and Senate. The inhabitants of Aberystwyth believed that the Guild would be dominated by members of the teaching staff, resident in Wales, whilst the majority of graduates, widely scattered through the world, would concern themselves but little with its fortunes.[89]

It was natural that uneasiness was felt in many quarters that the draft charter did not confer powers on the Court to admit to any degree in medicine or surgery. The case for developing medical education in Wales under the wing of the Cardiff College seemed unanswerable. In England there were nine provincial medical schools, in Scotland seven and in Ireland five, and whereas Wales had been unable to establish one such school from the thirteenth century onwards, in terms of population and of hospital accommodation Cardiff had great advantages over Oxford and Cambridge, Aberdeen or Belfast.[90] Indeed, anatomical work at Oxford was still being conducted in a small corrugated iron building and it was confidently hoped that the large employers of south Wales would not stand aside if opportunity beckoned. Forty years earlier B. T. Williams had urged the creation of a medical school in Wales.[91] Yet, to seek to confer medical degrees by charter was at this stage dangerous. Isambard Owen, whose authority on the practice and teaching of medicine could hardly be questioned, was convinced that one 'might just as well seek powers to grant baronetcies as to give degrees in medicine'.[92] As it was, too many bodies had powers to grant medical qualifications and the public was understandably wary of proliferation. There would be strong opposition from England, Scotland and Ireland which Parliament and Privy Council could not ignore. To teach anatomy and physiology at Cardiff from 1893 onwards was one thing; to establish a complete medical school quite another. The framers of the Victoria University had wanted the right to confer medical degrees – Victoria already had three fully equipped schools – but they had been required to state in their charter that they could not grant degrees in medicine and surgery until they had been given a supplementary charter, which, in fact, they received 'quietly',[93] thought Isambard, a few years later. The authorities were now fully alert and any attempt to secure such powers

would destroy all hope of receiving a charter for the University of
Wales. Common prudence held sway.

In October 1891 Cadwaladr Davies had told Tom Ellis that there was
no 'desperate hurry' to submit a draft charter to the Conservative
government: 'let us formulate some sort of scheme first, and when that
is ready, perhaps a Liberal Government will be in office.'[94] The return
of Gladstone to power in August 1892 had given promise of speedy
attention to the problems of Wales. The government majority was only
forty and Wales had returned thirty-one Liberal members and but three
Conservatives. For Gladstone's response to Welsh demands we are in
part reliant on the recollections of Stuart Rendel eighteen years later.
Rendel was still nursing bitter grievances, namely that Morley and
Harcourt had influenced Gladstone not to include him in his Cabinet
and that the authors of *The Welsh People* (1900) had treated him
shabbily by omitting references to his services to Welsh education, 'a
deliberate policy of suppression',[95] he told T. F. Roberts, to whom he
unburdened himself. The aged Gladstone, it appears, was staying
under Rendel's roof when he was forming the Cabinet from which he
was excluding his host. It was a piquant situation. Gladstone,
impressed with Rendel's unfailing loyalty, offered to settle with him at
once 'the Welsh policy of the Cabinet'.[96] However, matters were not
quite so simple; they seldom were with Gladstone. Of the three 'boons'
requested by Rendel, the Premier at first jibbed at the Suspensory Bill
(which Rendel regarded as an 'essential preliminary' to
disestablishment) and a Royal Commission on Land, but 'as to the
University I had no need to say a word beyond a request, at once
granted'. This pledge, Rendel believed, 'secured the whole policy'. He
added: '. . . had I wanted or accepted office for myself I should *not* have
got the first two for Wales.' To ensure that the promise was fulfilled
called for some persistence. When Gladstone opened the Cwm-y-llan
track up Snowdon in September 1892 he was greeted by a large
assembly. Amongst the loyal addresses he received was one from
Blaenau Ffestiniog Liberals who specifically asked for a University of
Wales. During a pause in his reply of thanks a quarryman in the
audience is said to have cried out: 'Tell us something of the University
of Wales.'[97] Gladstone does not seem to have obliged. By late October,
A. H. D. Acland, Vice-President of the Committee of the Council on
Education and a firm admirer of Welsh educational aspirations,
recommended that there should be an inquiry into the question of a

University before a decision was taken. Gladstone appears to have assumed that Acland was anticipating legislative action, but Acland replied that he was pressing the matter on educational grounds. Representative men of all kinds, he told Gladstone in November, were about to meet in Shrewsbury to consider steps to prepare a draft charter 'and we might as well anticipate the inevitable and just demand'.[98] Aware, no doubt that some favoured a royal commission and mindful also of the ensuing delay, perhaps lengthy, he asked to be allowed to name at a forthcoming meeting at Aberystwyth the commissioner he and Gladstone had agreed upon to conduct an inquiry. Gladstone evidently consented and spoke warmly of the 'excellently chosen person'.[99] He was Owen M. Edwards, whom Acland had earlier described as one who would discharge his task 'with great tact and judgement'; his appointment would 'give great pleasure to men of all parties in Wales, including... the Dean of St Asaph',[100] no small qualification in Gladstone's eyes.

Acland and Gladstone were right. Brought up in Llanuwchllyn, Merioneth, educated at Bala, and Aberystwyth in its early days,[101] at Glasgow and at Balliol College, Oxford, Edwards was now Fellow of Lincoln College, Oxford and was admirably equipped for the task. That he was a complicated man we cannot any longer doubt, but he had sovereign qualities which enabled him to serve his fellow-countrymen with a quiet passion. Two years earlier he had declined a chair at Sydney and a princely salary by the standards of the day; one of his reasons, he told a correspondent was because 'I could not leave Wales, its Manuscripts and its hopes.'[102] Edwards set about his duties with a will for he was expected to complete his work by January 1893. An air of mystery, however, surrounds his report. Tom Ellis thought that it was in government hands by March 1893 and his son T. I. Ellis (who evidently had his father's copy) remarked that everyone who had spoken of it did so 'in a very guarded way'.[103] Acland refused to place it on the table of the House of Commons, despite a protest by a Tory member that it should not remain in Acland's pocket.[104] For some arcane reason it was printed at the Foreign Office in June 1893; it was never published and it was headed 'Confidential'. It contains no spicy disclosures and, as might be expected, it was informative, orderly and constructive. At Aberystwyth, Acland told his audience that Edwards would be asked to compile 'such a Report as to the state of the facts and the state of the work already done in the Shrewsbury Conference which might in a reasonable space be useful reading and provide valuable information for members of the Cabinet'.[105] There may have been a further reason for secrecy. Acland had said that Edwards 'would not be asked to give an opinion'. Edwards, however, did give an opinion and we may reasonably surmise that the government did not care to make public Owen's financial recommendations which were far higher than the Treasury was ready to accept.[106]

Edwards began by demonstrating that objections to the formation of a university voiced at the Aberdare Committee had now been effectively dispelled. 'The prospects of the success of the University of Wales are very different from what they were in 1881.'[107] He then considered the proposals of R. D. Roberts, of the Principal of Carmarthen College and of the Shrewsbury Conference. Roberts's scheme had been rejected 'with almost perfect unanimity'[108] at Shrewsbury, mainly because it could not be successfully operated. Principal Evans's comparison between attached and private students in the proposed university, on the one hand, and collegiate and non-collegiate students at Oxford and Cambridge, on the other, was highly misleading; a federation of twenty colleges in Wales would differ wholly from the colleges at the older universities. Edwards then compared the draft charter as presented to the Shrewsbury Conference in January 1893 with the Victoria Charter, much studied by the framers of the Welsh Charter. He noted that the three constituent colleges of the Victoria University had not entered at the same time, that Manchester was its seat, whereas none of the Welsh Colleges, which were to unite simultaneously, was to be the seat of the University, that the Court and Guild of Graduates of the University of Wales were to meet at each college in succession, but that the Welsh Court was much larger and less academic, thus enabling it to keep in touch with the people of Wales and to exercise 'abundant power'[109] over the colleges. He was correct in saying that the executive committee of the Victoria University Court was defined by charter but incorrect in saying that the Court of the University of Wales was allowed to form its own executive 'council';[110] he should have said executive 'committee'. Wales did not have a council of any kind, whereas Victoria had both a court and a council.

In the third section of the report Edwards examined the institutions most likely to supply students to the new University. The three university colleges differed from all other colleges in Wales: they received a state grant, they were 'absolutely' undenominational, there were no religious tests and each was governed by a large court of governors reflecting the educational activities of Wales.[111] Where possible he praised the location of the colleges. Aberystwyth owed much to its 'salubrious situation', Bangor was 'in a beautiful spot by the Menai', and St David's (in a later section) 'in a pleasant valley'.[112] Brief surveys were given of the history and constitution of the colleges, of their standards of education and their annual resources, and an attempt was made (based on materials supplied by the colleges) to classify students according to their social origins. The only degree-awarding college in Wales was Lampeter 'essentially a Church of England College' and 'mainly a Theology College' where the teaching was 'of a University character and of a University standard'.[113] Of the other eight denominational colleges, seven were actively profiting from the creation of the three university colleges; the exception was the Presbyterian College at Carmarthen.[114] As to training colleges, Edwards was concerned that all prospective elementary and secondary teachers should in future avail themselves of university education. The private student was amply provided for by London University examinations.[115]

What were his conclusions? He evidently had no doubts as to the desirability of establishing a University of Wales. The objections advanced in 1881 could no longer be sustained. There were now sufficient students to give the new institution 'a solid status'.[116] The education was of university standard as tested by Oxford, Cambridge and London in 'at least' four colleges.[117] Three 'at least' of the colleges were giving 'very advanced education in the subjects of the older Universities, and in others for which Welshmen have a special aptitude',[118] a dark remark unillumined by further comment. The previous ten years had seen much progress which the new University would reflect.[119] He was in general agreement with the decisions of the University Conference of January 1893, but he made certain recommendations and observations. The new university should be a teaching, residential university and it 'should begin by being a federation of existing Colleges, on the model of the Victoria University'.[120] What force should be given to 'begin' in this context it is now impossible to say. Was he, in effect, anticipating independent development of the colleges? He believed that the University Court should be allowed, as in Victoria, the power of admitting other colleges in future and of excluding an inadequate college. He foresaw that the University Senate might become too large and cumbersome; membership should therefore be confined to college delegates. The University should have a fixed seat – here he is really thinking of a registry – to be selected by the Court. 'But it had better not be in any of the constituent College towns, and it would be preferable to have it in Wales.'[121] Concerning Lampeter, he was unequivocal. Its staff was very efficient, though inferior to those of the university colleges, and he evidently approved of a residential college modelled on Oxford and Cambridge colleges. Nevertheless, it was a denominational college without a representative governing body, its principal and tutors were subjected to religious tests and its constitution debarred it from becoming a constituent college. In short, 'the course fraught with fewest difficulties is to leave it as it is.'[122]

Adequate revenue was vital. 'A mere *honorarium*' would not do for external examiners and it would be wrong to 'neglect any important branch of study through poverty'.[123] Denuded of resources for these essential purposes, the new university would not stand upright in the eyes of the world or fulfil its purpose by properly organizing education in Wales. Therefore he recommended that the university should be given £10,000 per annum (quite apart from existing grants to the colleges), a sum arrived at by examining the financial systems of other universities in Britain. The higher branches of study should not be starved and the university should be empowered to organize extension lectures, to examine schools and to guide education in Wales. One curious feature deserves attention. He spoke in reassuring terms of the Victoria University; perhaps he was unduly influenced by the principals of Owens College and Leeds, who praised the federal system for having raised the standard of efficiency, for creating a strong corporate sense and for enhancing the reputation of each college in the eyes of the community. Edwards had visited both colleges, but not Liverpool, the other member of the federation, where there was a growing body of opinion which favoured separation. Had he done so, he might have hesitated before declaring that in the Victoria University 'there are no signs of disintegration';[124] within a few years it had dissolved into its component parts. It would be graceless, however, to end on a note of qualification. The report, lucid and workmanlike, undoubtedly influenced the government. Three years later Viriamu Jones was to write: 'The report was not published but I have heard, on the best authority, that we have every reason to be grateful to Mr O. M. Edwards for the service rendered by it to the cause we had in hand.'[125]

By the end of April 1893 the time was ripe for the University Conference to consider comments upon the revised charter. A marathon meeting at the Westminster Palace Hotel, London lasting eight consecutive hours need not detain us save perhaps to note that Viriamu Jones's insistence upon a right of appeal from Cardiff to the Privy Council was defeated by a large majority, influenced in no small measure by the arguments of his brother Brynmor.[126] In May the charter committee met members of both parties at the House of Commons, Bryn Roberts (Caernarfonshire, Eifion) and D. A. Thomas (Merthyr Tudful) being ominously absent. By early summer a number of petitions had arrived at the Privy Council Office which had them printed and also in parallel columns the replies of the solicitors acting on behalf of the drafters of the Charter, Faithful and Owen. In addition to those already noted there was a petition jointly signed by Bryn Roberts and D. A. Thomas who reflected the views of the Caernarfonshire and Glamorgan county councils. The two most important petitions were from R. D. Roberts and from Lampeter.[127] Roberts's arguments have already received sufficient attention and it is now opportune to consider Lampeter's standpoint in the light both of its petition and of the debate in August in Parliament, especially in the House of Lords.

Lampeter's case for inclusion was based on a variety of arguments.[128] No university could properly be regarded as the University of Wales if the oldest institution in Wales 'imparting education of a University character' were excluded. Standards were secured by the appointment by the vice-chancellors of Oxford and Cambridge of six of the seven external examiners for the degree of bachelor of arts; in no instance could the college appoint more than one examiner. Lampeter was affiliated to Oxford and Cambridge which recognized its method of education, of residence and of examining as equivalent in part to their own. The college took special pride in its tutorial system unequalled in any of the three university colleges. Much was made of the recommendation in the Aberdare Report that Lampeter and Aberystwyth, together with any college of advanced secular education yet to be established should form a 'syndicate' empowered to grant degrees in arts subjects. This proposal should 'hold the ground' until superseded by an inquiry as thorough as that of the Aberdare Committee. Between 1883 and 1892 more than a quarter of the college's graduates had taken non-theological courses, but in any case no Welsh college providing higher education should be disqualified from membership of the University of Wales solely because it was in origin a religious foundation. The real proof was the educational worth of the institution. Lampeter imposed no religious test upon its students, its scholarships were open to Nonconformists who were in no wise obliged to attend services in the college, and it had founded and supported an intermediate school in the district open to pupils of other religious persuasions.

These considerations merited serious attention, but the arguments against inclusion at length prevailed. The appeal to the Aberdare Report was not considered weighty. In 1881 Aberystwyth was in a parlous state, but it had since given evidence of recovery and of solid achievement, whilst Cardiff and Bangor were not even founded. In the House of Lords Aberdare himself said in August 1893 that he would not return to the solutions of 1881.[129] As to Lampeter, Nonconformists had been afraid of the *genius loci* and many argued that it was not a university college at all but a theological college. If it were allowed in, what of the eight theological colleges where arts courses were taught with varying degrees of efficiency? The danger, Aberdare continued, of admitting institutions maintaining different standards was to reduce all to the lowest common denominator. Indeed, doubts had been expressed as to whether all subjects at Lampeter were taught by suitably qualified specialists. Then again the government of the college told heavily against it: in effect the Senate of the college was its Council and the Court its Visitor, the Bishop of St David's, who exercised enormous power; popular representation was wholly absent, whereas the champions of the university charter held that the three university colleges were 'public property and controlled by Courts of Governors representing large public interests'.[130] Finally, there was severe criticism of Lampeter's apparent inability to state its position clearly until a very late stage in the proceedings. Aberdare insisted that during the crucial period from the first meeting of the University Conference in November 1891 until the Shrewsbury Conference of January 1893 he had been unable to determine what Lampeter desired; even in August 1893 he did not know whether the college was prepared to surrender its arts degree. During the course of the same debate the Bishop of St David's thought that his silence had been misconstrued;[131] he had had many debates with himself, but had at last come to the conclusion that the balance of advantage was on the side of inclusion. The trumpet had indeed given an uncertain sound.

Many Anglicans had resolutely supported the struggle for the Charter, Aberdare and Rendel, Reichel and G. T. Kenyon amongst them, but several clergy were unquestionably hostile. Hartwell Jones, who was to spend most of his life in a Surrey rectory, gives the distinct impression that Lampeter and Llandovery generated a heated atmosphere. As a member of the charter committee and later as crown representative on the University Court 'evidence accumulated before my eyes that certain of our influential ecclesiastics were violently prejudiced against our contemplated university'.[132] Even if he were not a strictly neutral observer of the clerical manouvering which disturbed his own career, it is difficult to set aside his testimony. On the other hand, it should not be forgotten that the clergy genuinely feared that the disestablishment of their Church was nigh. It is in this background that we must interpret the debates in Parliament on 29 August 1893. We have already noted that as far back as January there was concern that the second reading of the Irish Home Rule Bill might muddy the waters and that it was essential for the passage of the Charter to be as smooth and as tranquil as possible. It was also reported that had the government proceeded in the matter by bill Lord Salisbury, much opposed to the Charter, would have made 'wild work'[133] of it. Others thought that the news was too good to be true, for if Salisbury were to appear in opposition he would effectively ensure unity amongst some discordant elements. By late August, Aberdare commented upon the speed with which the Charter had arrived on the table of Parliament. Bishop Jayne of Chester (a former Principal of Lampeter) had offered certain dates for a debate in the Lords, amongst them 24 August, St Bartholomew's Day, which 'with grim pleasantry' he had suggested would be 'the most appropriate for the massacre of Lampeter'. Aberdare feared what might happen if the charter were debated in the presence of 'a mob of Peers'[134] summoned from distant shires to massacre the Irish Bill. A thin House was much safer. His wish was granted.

The tactics in the Lords of the 'casuistic bishops',[135] as Aberdare called them, were indeed less than saintly. Immediately before the Charter was considered they had seen fit to call attention to the unhappy dispute at Bangor concerning the Ladies' Hall, an affair which had struck the College with the fury of a water-spout and which had attracted a gross amount of public attention.[136] The Bishop of St Asaph (A. G. Edwards) asked for 'the indulgence usually accorded to one who addressed the House for the first time'[137] – he had been consecrated bishop four years earlier – and he thus chose to make his 'maiden' speech on the subject of the Ladies' Hall, a matter of acute embarrassment to the Bangor College. He rehearsed the circumstances leading to the resignation of six members of the College Council, including Lord Penrhyn, who had also put in an appearance in the House and who supported the Bishop's graceless curtain-raiser. When it came to the draft charter the first on the stage was the Bishop of Chester who moved that assent be withheld until such portions had been omitted which precluded the inclusion of Lampeter as a constituent college of the University; he was supported by the Bishops of London, Ely, Salisbury and St Davids. Episcopal innuendo persisted and the Bishop of St Asaph, in his second speech in the Lords, observed that had there been a Visitor at Bangor the difficulties relating to the Ladies' Hall would never have arisen. Aberdare found these antics tiresome.[138] The Liberal Lord Chancellor, Lord Herschell, was also impatient: should Wales be kept waiting for the proposed University 'until Lampeter shall make up its mind whether it wants to be admitted or not. According to those who have supported its interests today, it has scarcely made up its mind yet whether it will become a part of the University. Having been so dilatory, is it fair to ask that the establishment of the University so ardently desired by the Welsh people should be delayed until arrangements satisfactory to itself shall be made for the admission of Lampeter?.'[139] When the question was put, the Contents were forty-one the Not-Contents thirty-two.

Later that day, Bryn Roberts rose in the Commons to move that the Queen's assent to the Charter be withheld until amended to enable students 'connected with' the three colleges to present themselves for degrees. The arguments urged by him for non-attendance are too familiar to merit repetition. D. A. Thomas seconded the motion, but he did not speak. They were supported by Stanley Leighton (Oswestry) who declared that a large proportion of the students at Cardiff were English, that Bangor was under a cloud and that Aberystwyth was at a standstill. They might eventually do good work 'but at present they were simply sowing very wild oats'.[140] S. T. Evans (Mid Glamorgan), a former student at Aberystwyth, produced statistics relating to the social origins of students. Acland wound up for the government and Bryn Roberts's motion to withhold assent to the Charter was negatived without a division. It was decided by the government to ignore the vote in the Lords. A few days later the peers arrived in strength to demolish the Second Home Rule Bill. An exhausted Aberdare wrote to Isambard Owen to say that he would be assisting 'as a Mourner – and a Mute – at its obsequies'.[141] The Irish Bill was soundly defeated in the Lords, but Aberdare could rejoice that the struggle for the Charter had been won.

The Bishop of Chester had prophesied that the exclusion of Lampeter 'would leave a root of bitterness in Welsh life'.[142] The Principal of Lampeter, John Owen, was certainly cast down, for he had been a member of the University Conference and of the charter committee, both as Dean of St Asaph until 1892 and subsequently as Principal, and the prime mover of the petition to the Privy Council. Later, when he was Bishop of St David's, he won golden opinions and at the time of his death he was chairman of the influential departmental committee which published in 1927 the report on *Welsh in Education and Life.* Yet during the controversies which preceded the Charter his role was not entirely satisfactory, even to Churchmen, such as G. T. Kenyon. Owen, who had renounced Calvinistic Methodism, was sometimes tenacious and sometimes concessive. His instincts were to avoid religious and political disputation in matters concerning the welfare of Wales as a whole. In 1890 he told Tom Ellis that it was unnecessary to wait for the settlement of the disestablishment controversy before men of good will co-operated to establish a University. Yet by 1891 the Bangor Registrar was writing to Ellis to say that there were reactionary elements on the charter committee and that Owen was 'bamboozling the preachers'.[143] After the passage of the Charter through Parliament, Owen sought to justify his actions. It was well within the rights of the Lords, by the terms of the College Charter Act, 1871, to remove the University Charter from the table of the House of Lords at any time within the thirty days it was required to lie there by the Act.[144] Owen and his allies had no illusions as to the intentions of the government and they deliberately decided not to imperil the Charter by having it removed. Their purpose was to seek the moral support of Lampeter's friends in the Lords in favour of including the College within the University. It appears that when the Privy Council had rejected St David's petition to be admitted as a constituent college Owen had been instrumental in introducing an important clause in the draft charter. As Dean of St Asaph he had been on good terms with Gladstone and when Lampeter's petition to the Privy Council was rejected Owen consulted him. Gladstone had no wish to change government policy, but he was apparently responsible for inserting a clause in the Charter empowering the crown to add to the number of constituent colleges if it so desired. As the Earl of Cranbrook astutely observed in the Lords, the initiative in the Victoria University for subsequent inclusions lay with the University itself. Nearly thirty years afterwards, Owen, then Bishop of St David's, said that an opportunity was thus given to a Unionist government, should it so wish, to bring Lampeter within the University. He added that when Salisbury came to office in 1895 he, Owen, did not think it prudent at that time to take advantage of the clause inserted by Gladstone. The door was thus not firmly shut against Lampeter, but many years were to elapse before it was opened wide.[145]

The Charter of the University of Wales received the royal assent and was duly sealed on 30 November 1893. The real victory however, had been won four months earlier and Isambard Owen was to recall many years later the sultry midnight in August when, after a decisive debate in the Commons, 'we had the gratification of wiring Viriamu that the contest was over and that the end he had worked for so devotedly and so brilliantly was virtually achieved.'[146] Viriamu himself wrote: 'The University Charter is safe. So a new and great chapter begins in Welsh educational history.'[147]

1. The Castle Hotel, the first home of the University College of Wales. The squat structure to the left of the canopy is a portion of Castle House.

2. Sir Hugh Owen (1804–1881).

3. Thomas Charles Edwards (1837–1900), Aberystwyth's first Principal.

4. Lord Aberdare and family at Duffryn. The grandson to the left was killed in the early months of the Great War.

PRAYERS & THANKSGIVINGS,

To be used at discretion.

O GOD, the Creator and Preserver of all
mankind, we humbly beseech Thee
for all sorts and conditions of men ; that Thou
wouldest be pleased to make thy ways known
unto them, thy saving health unto all nations.
More especially, we pray for the good estate
of the Catholic Church : that it may be so
guided and governed by thy good Spirit
that all who profess and call themselves
Christiàns may be led into the way of truth,
and hold the faith in unity of spirit, in the
bond of peace, and in righteousness of life.
Finally, we commend to thy fatherly goodness
all those, who are any ways afflicted, or dis-
tressed, in mind, body, or estate ; that it may
please Thee to comfort and relieve them,
according to their several necessities, giving
them patience under their sufferings, and a
happy issue out of all their afflictions. And
this we beg for Jesus Christ his sake. Amen.

5.   The offending prayer, to be used at discretion, is from the University
College's *A Manual of Prayer and Praise,* 1873.

UNIVERSITY COLLEGE OF WALES.

7, QUEEN VICTORIA STREET,

LONDON, 25*th October*, 1875.

Rev. and Dear Sir,

Next Sunday, as you are aware, will be " Sul y Brifysgol," and I take the liberty, on behalf of the Council, of entreating that you will be so kind as to urge the claims of the College on your congregation. The complete success of this appeal to the people will not only help to place the Institution on a permanently secure basis, but will also supply evidence of its national character, and of the favour with which the people regard the placing of higher Education within the reach of the many. It may be added that the success of this appeal cannot fail also to reflect honour on our Country, and to exalt it in the estimation of the intelligence of the English nation.

I remain, my dear Sir,

Yours faithfully,

HUGH OWEN.

Please to observe the " Facts bearing on University Education" on the other page.

6. This leaflet was widely distributed in preparation for the 'University Sunday'.

FACTS BEARING ON UNIVERSITY EDUCATION.

"If knowledge is power, ignorance is weakness, and we are fallen upon times in which the ignorant and the weak go down before the force of organised knowledge more speedily and more surely than, perhaps, at any former period of the history of man."—Lyons, *Intellectual Resources of Ireland.*

"If there is one thing which my foreign experience has left me convinced of,—as convinced of as I am of our actual want of superior instruction,—it is this : that we must take this instruction to the students, and not hope to bring the students to the instruction."—Mr. Matthew Arnold, *Schools and Universities on the Continent.*

Scotland, with little more than twice the population of Wales, has for upwards of three hundred years been in possession of four great universities, where some 4,000 students are annually being trained.

To the early foundation of four universities in Scotland "is to be traced the commencement of that general intellectual culture, and that wide extension of education, which have enabled so many, even from the humblest ranks of her population, to climb to name, fame, and political influence in the mother country, in the empire at large, and in her possessions beyond the seas."—*Lyons.*

Ireland has three Queen's Colleges and two Universities. The Report for 1870 of the Galway Queen's College, one of the smallest colleges in Ireland, shows that since the opening of the College in 1850, 1126 students had entered for study in the faculties of Art, Medicine, and Law, and in the department of engineering. Of this number 95 had obtained Government appointments ; 3 had obtained studentships at the Inns of Court in Dublin and in London ; 356 had obtained degrees and diplomas in arts, medicine, law, and engineering ; and 147 were then on the books for the session.

Germany has about thirty universities, with an average number of students attending each of more than 900, giving a total of more than 27,000.

New Zealand even has one university ; Australia has two ; and Canada has several.

Wales, with a population of one million and a quarter, would now have more than twelve hundred students receiving university instruction if she occupied an educational position similar to that of Scotland.

7.   Hard facts to buttress the 'University Sunday' appeal.

8. Cardiff College's first home in the Old Infirmary, Newport Road.

9. Bangor College opened its doors in the Penrhyn Arms.

10. John Viriamu Jones (1856–1901), Cardiff's first Principal and the University's first Vice-Chancellor.

11. Sir Isambard Owen (1850–1927).

12. Sir Harry Reichel (1856–1931), Bangor's first Principal.

wasgaru syniadau cywir ynghylch addysg uwchraddol. 'Rwy'n gweled
yn glir na chaiff Cymru ei gwared o afael Llundain hyd nes y
cawn Brifysgol i Gymru. Yr wyf yn ddistaw gredu, pe bai y Colegau
ac addysgwyr Cymru yn gwneud egni, yn crynhoi eu nerth, ac yn
gwneud y trefniadau angenrheidiol, y gallem gael Prifysgol mewn
dwy neu dair blynedd. Gallai llawer Cymro fyned, fel mae'r Ysgolhaid
wedi myned er's llawer blwyddyn, i Rydychen gyda'u gradd eu
Prifysgol eu hunain ac yna mill rhai o wobrwyon goreu Rhydychen.

    One singularly contemptible argument is used by the advocates of
London. They say that Oxford undermines the nonconformity and
nationality of Welshmen. This is not only a false but a mean and
despicable plea. It assumes that Welsh nationality and Nonconformity
cannot stand a severe test. It further ignores the fact that it
is only by allowing young Welsh nonconformists to throw themselves
boldly into the life of Oxford that they will help to crush out the
mistaken and prejudiced notions entertained by Englishmen about the
people and language of Wales, to win the respect and even the affection
of great and influential Englishmen for Wales and its life, and thus
by reaction to increase the self-respect, the capacities and the
sturdiness of character of Welshmen themselves. I have always held
and still hold that when Wales is enabled to complete its own
national system of education, more Welshmen will be able and
anxious to distinguish themselves at Oxford & Cambridge — the chief
Educational heritages of the British races — than ever before, and
that they will succeed.

13.   Thomas Ellis to Owen M. Edwards, 12 February 1890. A university for
Wales was never far from Ellis's mind even when recovering from fever at Luxor.

14. The Earl of Rosebery, the Prime Minister, addresses the first meeting of the Court of the University, 6 April 1894, in the Privy Council Chamber, Whitehall.

15. Owen M. Edwards (1858–1920).

16. Thomas Francis Roberts (1860–1919), Aberystwyth's second Principal.

17. The first formal meeting of the University Senate, at Aberystwyth, 27–8 September 1894. In the centre is Viriamu Jones; to his right H. R. Reichel, to his left T. F. Roberts.

18. The Installation of the Prince of Wales as Chancellor, 26 June 1896. The carriages proceed through North Parade and Great Dark Street, Aberystwyth.

19. Isambard Owen presents an address to the Prince of Wales, now fully robed. To the left is the aged Gladstone; upstanding to the right, Ivor James, the University's first Registrar.

20. The Chancellor confers the degree of Music upon the Princess of Wales.

VII

The Royal Charter

The Charter at once declared that the name of the University founded 'in and for Wales and the County of Monmouth' was to be 'the University of Wales'.[1] Early speculation, which also hovered around the University of London, that it might be called the Albert University, as a counterpart, one imagines, to the Victoria University, happily evaporated in both cases.[2] The title 'Prifysgol Cymru' does not appear and is not, indeed, to be detected until the fifth supplemental Charter of 1967, at a time when the wind of change was blowing through countries large and small. It was then given precedence. The University motto 'Goreu Awen Gwirionedd' ('The Best Inspiration is Truth') is on the University Arms and Crest and upon the Common Seal designed by Sir Edward Burne-Jones;[3] but the Charter itself was innocent of Welsh words and of any reference to the Welsh language. Isambard Owen, at the end of his first draft of the charter, had been emboldened to specify the occasions when Welsh might be used, but this section disappeared with the 'Cabinets' and 'Chambers' he had designed for the Guild of Graduates.[4]

A Welsh version of 'universitas', it will be recalled, had appeared in a poem of the early fifteenth century.[5] Ellis Gruffydd, the Welsh soldier of Calais in Henry VIII's reign, had spoken of 'vnneuerseitti';[6] not dissimilar forms appear in the work of Rosier Smith in the next century and in the *Pantheologia* of Williams Pantycelyn in 1762. They gave way to 'prif yscol', used, it seems, for the first time in the early seventeenth century by Thomas Wiliems, the lexicographer. In 1715 James Owen was able to inform his Welsh readers of a young man who gave his soul to the devil in one of the 'prif ysgolion', or universities, of Pomerania.[7] By the early nineteenth century 'prifysgol' was well established and became the accepted Welsh form, in preference to 'prifathrofa' and to the deplorable 'cyfathrofa', which the genius of the language roundly rejected. In due course scholars noted that in Germany, as in Wales (though not in the Welsh language), there were two words for a university, 'Universität' and 'Hochschule'. In 1917

W. Rhys Roberts observed: '*Hochschule*, like *Prifysgol*, suggests a fine conception of a University, that of *high school, chief school, school of schools*. As *ysgol* does modern duty in Wales for the Latin *scala* as well as *schola*, *Prifysgol* might, I suppose, mean "ladder of ladders" as well as "school of schools".'[8] As to the term 'university' in the Charter, Isambard Owen said that it was originally intended to be an inclusive term embracing the 'entire apparatus of higher education in Wales',[9] that is, the three colleges, any bodies later to be affiliated or recognized, as well as those to be created by the Charter. Owing to certain unspecified objections, 'university' was restricted to the new corporation which was evidently to have the usual powers of a corporation as to property and in other matters necessary to discharge its functions.[10] It is a misfortune that Isambard, normally a model of clarity, did not develop this point. What he had in mind, doubtless, was that whereas the universities of Oxford and Cambridge existed before the colleges, and could in theory survive their extinction, the colleges in Wales had preceded the University; they had their own charters, their own property and endowments, and it was upon their joint petition that the Crown summoned the University into being. Isambard remarked that 'the extended use of the word is still common and often unavoidable'.[11] He was then writing in 1916.

Under the first clause of the Charter women were given complete equality with men for admittance to any degree. In the new universities this was common, though there were still some inequalities; the Victoria University, for instance, required women to wait several years before they were permitted to study medicine.[12] In the University of Wales there were no restrictions of any kind. Moreover every office in the University and membership of every authority was to be open to women equally with men. On this question, Isambard tells us, 'the promoters of the University felt no hesitation, and dreamed of no half-measures'.[13] From the first draft charter to the Charter itself this was the only clause that was never questioned or amended.

The authorities of the University were the Visitor, the Chancellor, the Court, the Vice-Chancellor, the University Senate and the Guild of Graduates. The Visitor was to be the monarch acting through the Lord President of the Council. The Chancellor, 'the Head and Chief Officer'[14] of the University, was to be appointed by the Court and was to preside over its meetings. In practice the Court by statute appointed deputies, a Senior Deputy-Chancellor and a Junior Deputy-

Chancellor. The Court was the supreme governing body and was to consist of 100 members, together with the Chancellor, six more than had originally been envisaged. Considered to be the most democratic body of its kind in the United Kingdom, its constitution reflected the popular origin of the University and also the need (though little was said of this at the time) to seek financial support from public authorities for several years to come. Apart from thirteen persons appointed by the Privy Council, thirty-six represented the courts, councils and senates of the three constituent colleges in equal proportion, thirteen the Guild of Graduates, twenty-six the county and borough councils of Wales, three the staff of intermediate schools and three the staff of primary schools, and, finally, six the so-called Central Board (as soon as it was formed) to control the intermediate schools.[15] The constitution of the University was thus drawn up on national rather than on strictly federal grounds. One of the two mandatory annual meetings of the Court was to be at a place chosen by the Court and was later known as the non-collegiate meeting; it was to be held alternately in north and south Wales.[16] The Vice-Chancellor was to be appointed from amongst the principals in rotation for a period of one year, subsequently extended to two years. He presided over the Senate, composed of heads of departments recognized by the University. The Guild of Graduates, comprising the graduates of the University and all the teaching staffs of the constituent colleges, was to meet at least once a year within five miles of one of the colleges in turn, a curious archaism.[17] It was allowed to make representations to the Court on any matter concerning the interests of the University. Isambard, who regarded the Guild as the 'third estate'[18] of the University was, however, dispirited when the Privy Council allowed but a '*frustum*'[19] (morsel) of the proposals in the draft charter to be included in the Charter itself, for he had wished the Guild to appoint trustees 'to hold property independently of the University Court'[20] to advance research in any branch of knowledge and to promote improvements 'in any of the practical Arts'.[21] The Privy Council evidently thought that such powers would later prove an impediment, and by Charter the Guild was allowed only 'to collect'[22] money to found scholarships and prizes, a power further diluted by the Charter of 1920 which permitted the Guild only 'to receive'[23] money for these and other educational purposes.

The balance of power within a federal university is not easily to be determined or maintained. It has been well said that federalism is a

specific which may be taken in varying doses.[24] As we have seen, the
Charter of 1893 provided one solution which at the time was believed
to command that general assent without which federal bodies are
doomed. The charter committee had not proceeded to create a
University of Wales in the fullest sense because the educational
apparatus was already established. A major purpose had been to
liberate the colleges from the burdensome restrictions of the University
of London by associating the colleges with a public body, namely the
Court, upon which they would be amply represented. It was clearly
intended that there should be an extensive measure of academic
freedom, *Lehrfreiheit*, liberty for the teacher, and *Lernfreiheit*, liberty
for the learner, qualities in the German system which Matthew Arnold
had long since extolled.[25] Curricula were not to be imposed from
above; the initiative for proposing courses lay with each college which
alone had the right to present students for examinations.[26] Nor was it
required that schemes of study should be the same for each college, a
freedom absurdly misinterpreted in the debates preceding the Charter
as tantamount to creating three universities. In permitting a measure of
liberty to colleges in academic matters the advocates of the Charter
hoped that they would avoid the uniformity imposed upon staff and
students at Victoria and also the burden of frequent travel, which, in
Wales would have been excessively punitive. On the other hand, as we
have also seen, the external examiner in Wales had a firmer control than
at Victoria and the Charter categorically stated that the University
would not receive a report upon examinations without the full
concurrence of the external examiner.[27] To return to curricula, even
though they had received the closest scrutiny of the Senate, the final
decision lay with the Court. It is true that the Charter stated plainly
that there should not be any changes in statutes relating to academic
matters unless the Senate had so recommended or until the Senate
'shall have had a reasonable opportunity of considering and reporting
thereupon'.[28] These words, however, could scarcely conceal the reality
that ultimate authority lay with the Court whose chief functions
concerned curricula and examinations. Why was it that a public body
was given absolute authority in academic affairs? The Court's
administrative duties were certainly scanty, for the colleges managed
their own business by and large. The real explanation lies in the fact
that one of the Court's duties was to ensure that there should be a
proper regard for 'the special mental characteristics'[29] of Welsh

students at a time when the majority of teachers of the University were unlikely to be Welsh by birth or training. The Court was thus expected to review the recommendations of the Senate from a national standpoint. Such a demanding responsibility was never fully appreciated and when the first generation of Court members disappeared this aspect of the Court's work so declined that the recommendations of the Senate, once challenged and referred back, were accepted without serious debate. The Senate virtually became a legislative body. Even at the outset, the Court had not matched Tom Ellis's exacting standard that it should be composed of the hundred best men in Wales; with the passing years the quality of members diminished. A contributory factor was the establishment of the Central Welsh Board in 1896.

It will be recalled that Viriamu Jones had in his inaugural address at Cardiff in 1883 stressed the unity of Welsh education. One of the fundamental principles laid down at the Shrewsbury Conference of November 1891 was that the University should have power to inspect and examine intermediate schools and other educational institutions, and to grant certificates of proficiency. In the Charter this principle appears in an emasculated form:

> The Court may undertake at the request of any person or persons having authority to make such a request the inspection and examination of any school or schools in Wales and may make report thereon to such person or persons.[30]

The Intermediate Education Bill had included a provision to create a Board of Education for Wales, but it was dropped from the Act itself, with unhappy consequences for the administration of education in Wales.[31] The sequel was that in September 1890 the first General Conference of the Joint Education Committees of Wales and Monmouth, under its newly-elected chairman A. H. D. Acland, passed a resolution in favour of a central education body, in essence the germ of the Central Welsh Board. A year later the University Conference passed the resolution to which reference has just been made. It appeared that Viriamu's aspiration in 1883 might possibly succeed and Isambard's view in 1916 was that the intention of the University Conference of 1891 was to secure 'the educational unity of Wales'.[32] The strange feature is that two representative bodies, comprising many of the same persons, were proceeding in different directions. The explanation appears to be that the Treasury, which provided a grant, obliged Wales to choose between a separate board and direct inspection from Whitehall and that under these circumstances it was natural to opt for independence.[33] This is why the clause in the Charter relating to inspection is a much attenuated version of the principle proclaimed in 1891. Shortly after the creation of the Central Welsh Board in 1896 the Joint Education Committees resolved that before the Central Welsh Board was seven years old 'a conference should be arranged between the Central Board and the University Court to consider whether or not it is advisable that the functions of the Central Board should be transferred to the University Court'.[34] But no such conference was held and the Central Welsh Board, whose formation had been much opposed by Viriamu Jones and John Rhys, continued upon its independent course so that there were two 'educational parliaments' in Wales, both conducting their own matriculation examinations. The champions of the Board in turn had good arguments on their side. The University Court was a novel, inexperienced body which needed to discover its true role in relation to the constituent colleges which had from their inception looked after their own affairs (apart, of course, from the large exception of the London examination). The intermediate schools had distinctive needs and problems and in many ways made a wider appeal to the general public. Independent development had two consequences. Able men who began to be impatient with routine business of the University Court (much of it academic in the proper sense) and who found no place on the Court's executive committee, discovered a more rewarding focus of attention as members of the Central Welsh Board whose deliberations intimately affected their own localities. The Court, therefore, tended to be less effectively manned. The second consequence, in the words of the Haldane Report, was 'the separation of the University Court from an important current of popular interest'.[35] The clause in the Charter, which has been quoted above, is, therefore, a memorial to Viriamu's vanished dream.

If the University was not required to inspect schools, the Charter did confer upon it inquisitorial powers to 'appoint any two or more of its Members to be Visitors of any Constituent College' to inspect and report upon its 'laboratories, class rooms, museums and other teaching material'.[36] We cannot doubt that attempts to execute these powers would have been firmly resisted. In many ways it is strange that the clause was ever included in the Charter. The draft charter committee had wisely rejected a proposal to remove from the colleges the responsibility for the control and appointment of staff and to place it in the hands of the University. At this stage – indeed at any stage – the colleges would have resented such interference, and it was not until the post-Haldane period that the University was represented on committees to appoint principals and professors.

The dispute which had been firmly settled in favour of a teaching university had left a lively, residuary concern for those unable to study at one of the colleges. In May 1891 Ellis Edwards had written to Viriamu Jones to say that the University should consider it 'an essential part of its work to spread the benefits of University education by some such means as those employed in the University Extension movement'.[37] This, he believed, would meet 'the difficulty which divided us when our undertaking failed' (in 1888). By Charter the Court, in consultation with the Senate, might institute and maintain extra-collegiate courses of instruction accompanied by examinations and might also exempt a student pursuing such courses from attendance for part of the term of study necessary for graduation, a period later specified by statute as no more than one year.[38] There was a similar concession at Cambridge, for instance, but there is no sign that the University of Wales ever provided courses of this kind. The empowering clause disappeared after the Haldane Report and the revised Charter of 1920 does not mention examinations in relation to extra-mural courses, henceforth to be promoted by the University.[39] The shades of R. D. Roberts were not even partially appeased for several decades.

The problem of theology had long seemed intractable, but the drafters of the Charter, quite without instruction from the University Conference, had been able, as we have seen, to make recommendations verging on the audacious which are enshrined in the Charter. Despite the fact that theology was not a subject taught in a constituent college the Court could admit to a degree in the Faculty of Theology now established any graduate of any university in the United Kingdom after study in a theological college *in Wales*.[40] The italicized words had caused disquiet in various conferences, particularly those of the Welsh Wesleyan Methodists who did not have a college in Wales but who received a hearing justly accorded to minorities.[41] It was at length decided, probably wisely, that it was imperative not to weaken the position of existing theological colleges in Wales by casting the net beyond the borders of Wales itself. By requiring a degree in theology to be preceded by an initial degree academic standards were preserved and the principle of attendance safeguarded. There was also provision in the Charter, to which scant reference appears elsewhere, that theology could be recognized as a subject for an initial degree in the Faculty of Arts, provided the necessary period in a theological college did not exceed one year.[42] The term 'associated' theological college, which later became familiar, is not once mentioned in the Charter, and the first statutes of the University speak only of 'approved' theological colleges.[43] Nine colleges, including Lampeter which did not much appreciate such an ecumenical gesture, could be 'accepted' as 'approved' colleges provided they gave instruction in all the subjects required for the theological degree. The Faculty of Theology was to be managed by a Theological Board to advise the Court on matters theological; it was to consist of members of the 'approved' colleges, of the University Court and Senate and of the Guild of Graduates.[44] Thus was devised a system which would have surprised members of the University Conference which had met but twenty months earlier.

The architects of the Charter punctiliously avoided giving even a semblance of precedence to any one of the colleges now entering the new organization 'on absolutely equal terms',[45] in Isambard Owen's words. One of the Court's two normal annual meetings, called the Annual Collegiate Meeting, was to be held at each college in rotation. The seat of the chief executive, the Vice-Chancellor, passed from college to college in turn. These 'ambulatory regulations',[46] as Isambard called them, unconsciously followed a precedent set by the University of New Zealand fifteen years earlier. A century later antipodean parallels were urged in relation to the nomenclature of constituent colleges wishing to be called universities within the University of Wales. The colleges are not once named in any of the clauses of the Charter and it was not deemed wise to seek even an alphabetical neutrality. In the historical preamble it was difficult to avoid such delicacy. Cardiff is described as the University College of South Wales and Monmouthshire, and Bangor as the University College of North Wales, but care had to be taken in the case of Aberystwyth, established in 1872, so the preamble runs, '*under the name* of the University College of Wales' (my italic). The battle of the sites had been followed by a lively skirmish over nomenclature and it is not surprising that the wise men of 1893 proceeded with grave circumspection.

It would be idle to pretend that the Charter received universal approbation. The gaitered clergy were for the most part hostile and not above a sneer or two; it was noted with some displeasure that the Privy Council had been unable to recommend a single bishop to the University Court.[47] Amongst Nonconformist bodies *Y Tyst*, the powerful organ of the Welsh Independents, had early questioned the immediate need to establish a university; there were other more clamant claims upon the attention of the nation, disestablishment and home rule amongst them.[48] Nevertheless there was general satisfaction. *The Times* had vastly changed its tone in the course of the decades, proclaiming that 'without distinction of creed and politics, all people will join in wishing success to the new Welsh University'; Lord Aberdare had good reason to be proud of his 'indefatigable exertions'.[49] The most public acclaim came in September 1893 from Chicago where five thousand Welshmen attending an International Eisteddfod at the World Fair enthusiastically resolved after the chairing ceremony and fortified by trumpets to express their gratitude to Gladstone and his government 'for acceding to the demand of the Welsh people for a National University'.[50] Some months later the resolution was presented to Gladstone at the House of Commons.

The University Conference was not immediately dissolved for it still had important functions to perform, chief of which was to present a petition to the Chancellor of the Exchequer. Before doing so, a deputation waited upon the Lord President of the Council, the Earl of Kimberley, in order to thank him personally for his support during the debate in the Lords. In his absence owing to ill-health the opportunity was taken to address A. H. D. Acland whose alert awareness of Welsh educational needs had sustained the supporters of the Charter through many vicissitudes.[51] Two days later a powerful deputation on behalf of the University was received by the Chancellor of the Exchequer. The largest room in the Treasury could not comfortably contain them all, one principal having to make do with a coal scuttle. Some recalled the small group which had met forty years earlier and which had moulded the key which now, it was hoped, would unlock the coffers of the Treasury. The Chancellor, Sir William Harcourt, had put on 'his most courtly air'[52] as he listened to Aberdare's presentation of the petition's twenty-eight clauses, several of them concerning the recent development of Welsh education. The essence of the matter, however, was to seek an immediate grant of £3,000 per annum, rising to £8,000 when the University was in full working order, an unduly modest sum, it might be thought, for it did not take account of moneys deemed necessary for advanced study, including the provision of fellowships. Harcourt in reply seems to have 'played the heavy father' for he began lugubriously by remarking that it was 'difficult for an empty sack to stand upright'.[53] Individual Welsh colleges were already receiving more from the state than English colleges and he took issue with the petitioners for seeking in due course a substantially greater sum to pay external examiners than was set aside for the purpose by the Victoria University, thus failing to recognize the imperative necessity for the new university to secure the best scholars as external examiners in order to achieve the highest academic standards at the outset. Nor did he refer to the large state grants to the Scottish and Irish universities. The outcome was that the University of Wales received the £3,000 requested for immediate needs, the Chancellor adding pensively that it was one of the few things he had been able to grant that year. A few years later it was raised to £4,000 but there was no further increase until 1909. The plea for an 'assured income' of £8,000 when the University was in full operation was ignored by subsequent administrations. It was by no means made financially secure.

The first official meeting under the Charter was that of the Guild of Graduates at Shrewsbury on 17 March 1894. The names of 300 graduates were read out and O. M. Edwards wondered how long the list might have been had Glyn Dŵr's two universities been founded. Thirteen members were elected to the Court representing the Guild as a body and not individual colleges, thereby establishing an important principle. Edwards, who became the first Warden, observed that 'there is no knowing what good the Guild of Graduates may do'.[54] We are indebted to him for an account of the first meeting of the Court on 6 April 1894 in the Privy Council Chamber at Whitehall.[55] In that 'dingy' room he found it difficult to realize that 'the hopes of so many years were being amply fulfilled'; yet, if Scotland, Sweden, Switzerland and Holland, all small countries, could point to decisive victories by land and sea, this day in the history of Wales could be 'placed side by side with their most glorious'. Such solemn musings were interrupted by the arrival of a *Black and White* photographer who captured in that dim light some semblance of the scene. Gladstone's successor as Prime Minister, Lord Rosebery, spoke warmly of the Welsh achievement. There were two features which particularly appealed to him. It would be a place in the main for poor students, the sons of a peasant, a farmer or a mechanic 'to grasp with a hard or even a horny hand the weapons with which he meant to carve out his career'. Secondly, in words which may not have altogether pleased ardent members of the Cymru Fydd movement: 'there is one form of nationality which appeals to all. I mean that form which insists, not in putting forward political schemes, but in endeavouring to preserve ancient traditions, ancient literature, ancient language, and to press forward in the race with other nations so as to make the nationality to which one belongs equal to any. As a sign of that high and just principle of nationality, I welcome the Welsh University. . .' The Court then settled down to the humdrum but necessary business of appointing committees to draft statutes, which had to be done within twelve months of the Court's first meeting, to recognize departments of study and to deal with the conferring of degrees in theology.

The first informal meeting of the Senate was held at Jesus College, Oxford in early July. No meetings lingered more vividly in the mind of C. H. Herford, Aberystwyth's distinguished professor of English, who left us this account:

> Around the long oak table of the College Hall, Cardiff and Bangor and Aberystwyth met to shape the inchoate body of the new University organism; and the stress of debate insensibly thrust local jealousies into the background; the conflict of argument, of subject with subject, of man with man, banished or obscured the rivalry of College with College. It was here that my friendship began with my late revered friend, C. E. Vaughan, the editor of Rousseau, then Professor of English at Cardiff. Some brilliant speeches of those days still live in my memory; one, in particular, in which Professor Sorley of Cambridge, then Professor of Philosophy at Cardiff, completely transfigured for most of his audience the abstract study of Logic by restating its scope and purpose in the terms of an idealist philosophy. Then, after the hours of strenuous and on the whole fruitful debate, came dinner in the College Hall when angles were rounded and attachments formed with or without the Celtic metheglyn, symbolically dispensed by the genius of the place; finally, for not a few, the genial hospitality dispensed by the President and his romantically named daughters in the College Lodge.[56]

As to the choice of officers, there had been no problem whatsoever in electing Viriamu Jones, the senior principal, to be Vice-Chancellor. The office of Senior Deputy-Chancellor was at first offered to William Rathbone who had been a tower of strength to Bangor from its inception and to the emerging University. Advancing years prohibited acceptance and a younger man, Isambard Owen, filled the office with distinction until 1910. The selection of Chancellor is usually a delicate matter. It seems that an informal approach was made to William Rathbone, who at once ruled out the possibility: 'You want a very distinguished "symbol and figurehead" to put the University of Wales on the same footing as other great Universities. It should not be an unlearned English commoner, but one of the great noblemen connected with Wales, and if possible, a learned man.'[57] In April 1887 Viriamu Jones had spoken with somewhat bated breath of the need to include the Queen or the Prince of Wales in the constitution of the University.[58] By Charter the monarch was Visitor and one imagines that Viriamu had the Chancellorship in mind. At all events, the first step was taken by the Marquess of Bute in the spring of 1894 when he wrote to Viriamu to suggest that Gladstone would be 'a very proper person'[59] to receive the honour. Bute, a Tory, had magnanimously cast aside all political considerations in the interests of one who was eminently learned and who had been Prime Minister when the Charter was granted. Aberdare may well have felt embarrassed in not having anticipated Bute, especially when he himself was invited to fill the office upon Gladstone's wish to be excused on grounds of failing health. In early 1895 Aberdare was deservedly elected the University's first Chancellor. The Welsh people, he told Isambard, could not have conferred upon him a greater honour 'unless, indeed, under the new regime of the disestablished church an archbishopric... should be created or unless, under the fervour of the national spirit, a successor to the unfortunate Prince Llewelyn should be insisted upon.'[60] Within a month he was dead. At length the 'peasants' University'[61] turned to the Prince of Wales (later Edward VII), the first of an unbroken line of royal Chancellors. For many the University would not be a formal reality or the colleges drawn together in a bond of unity until the Chancellor had been installed. Only then would the grand national enterprise be accomplished. To that day of public thanksgiving in June 1896 we must now turn.

It seems that the Prince of Wales accepted the invitation to become

Chancellor readily enough; according to his secretary, Francis Knollys, he had 'observed with much satisfaction the love of learning displayed by the Welsh people, especially as evinced by the creation of this University'.[62] However, before arrangements had been completed there was much uneasy fluttering. Where was this most august assembly to be held? The choice in practice lay between Cardiff and Aberystwyth.[63] The former had certain advantages listed with some gusto by Viriamu Jones's brother, Brynmor: for this special reunion the wealthy men of Cardiff were prepared to defray much of the costs, and Lord Tredegar had a substantial house to place at the disposal of the Prince and his entourage. The country houses within reasonable distance of Aberystwyth, on the other hand, Gogerddan, Nanteos, Crosswood and Plas Machynlleth, were minor seats hardly appropriate for an auspicious occasion. Cardiff, however, did not present its case with tact: Brynmor Jones is said to have acted snobbishly for he did not wish to be twitted by the smart set in London concerning the rustic poverty of the University, whilst the Cardiff spokesman at the Court meeting where the subject was fully ventilated did not help matters by suggesting that the Prince might open an exhibition in the town, thus appearing to relegate the University to second place. By the narrowest of margins, Aberystwyth was chosen.[64] The college undoubtedly had superior buildings, but the claim that they were well suited for the ceremony lost something of its force when the installation finally took place in a marquee outside the Town Hall and the large lunch in the pier pavilion. The true case rested on Aberystwyth's seniority and because it was 'the birthplace of the whole movement'.[65] It was a correct decision.

The problem of accommodating the Prince's party was resolved in favour of Plas Machynlleth, mainly because the owner's wife, Lady Londonderry, had links with the royal family. The townspeople of Aberystwyth responded with dextrous alacrity to the prospect of a large influx of visitors; good men were taken aback at the soaring prices for the hire of houses, so much so that Humphreys-Owen thought it cheaper for him and his friends to engage a special train from Montgomeryshire rather than stay overnight.[66] Beneath the surface contention simmered. Francis Knollys was disturbed that honorary degrees were to be conferred on three Liberals but not on a single Conservative. His suggestion that Joseph Chamberlain be included was firmly rejected and a further hint that Lord Londonderry be considered was privately declared to be 'still worse'.[67] Neither had done anything for Welsh education and Humphreys-Owen was certain that the Tories were coming to Aberystwyth to honour the Prince, not the University. Of the three Liberals no one could conceivably question Gladstone's high deserts, nor indeed those of Earl Spencer, Chancellor of the Victoria University, and Lord Herschell, Chancellor of the University of London. Gladstone hesitated before accepting the honour. The 'Ancient of Days' – he was in his eighty-seventh year – gnarled, though not withered, now found the large assemblies he had so long dominated and inspired both wearisome to the body and vexatious to the spirit. At length he succumbed to the persistent pleading of Rendel who was later to say that he had wrestled to bring Gladstone to Aberystwyth 'to save *Welsh* Wales from the humiliation of taking a wretchedly subaltern place on that occasion'.[68] In fact, according to one spectator, it was the aristocracy and Church dignitaries who looked 'abject'.[69] Of the four to be honoured, due precedence was given to the Princess of Wales soon to be raised by the land of song to the dignity of doctor of music. Not a single Welshman was included, a needless act of self-denial not frequently followed thereafter. Some thought, with good cause, that Aberystwyth's valiant first Principal should have been honoured, especially since theology was no longer held at arm's length.

The long-awaited day, 26 June 1896, was set apart throughout the Principality for public thanksgiving and joy.[70] It began at Aberystwyth when the royal train, described as 'a palace on wheels',[71] arrived promptly at noon. The Prince and Princess of Wales proceeded, to tumultuous applause, through streets decorated with coloured bunting and Venetian masks to a grand marquee incorporating on its western side four trees growing in the square outside. Over 2,000 guests, including representatives of various aspects of Welsh life, heard Isambard Owen and others address the new Chancellor, now robed in black satin damask, embroidered with gold and displaying in five places the dragons of Wales. After the conferment of degrees there was luncheon for 500 guests in the pier pavilion. In the afternoon Princess Alexandra opened the women's hall which bears her name. The royal party departed somewhat later than arranged and in the evening there was a splendid fireworks display. The *Western Mail* pronounced it the 'most brilliant pageant witnessed in Wales in modern times'.[72] Sharp observers commented upon matters large and small. It had been 'royal weather', the sea was an almost Mediterranean blue and the sun beat down fiercely. There were trappings of imperial power: detachments of yeomanry, guards of honour and the cruisers *Hermione* and *Bellona* which fired twenty-one gun salutes in Cardigan Bay. No expense had been spared. The Principal's room on the ground floor, reserved for the Princess, was furnished in Louis XV style, the suite having been specially manufactured in Paris. Since there was only one pickpocket, little injury was done to Wales's reputation as the 'Land of the White Gloves' (Gwlad y Menyg Gwynion). In the marquee the Prince held Gladstone's hand for a full minute before conferring a degree upon him. The new Chancellor was not always audible, being hampered by 'a troublesome little cough', and he was no doubt relieved when, according to practice, the Grand Master of the Freemasons of the Western Division of South Wales presented an address, but did not read it; the Chancellor in turn handed back a written reply, a silent signal of secret solidarity.

The speeches of the day were well received. Isambard Owen in his address affirmed that the Chancellor had 'graciously accorded the final element of completeness to a national institution; and [that] the University begins its career with the happy augury that the Prince and the people of Wales are united in its work'.[73] The Chancellor in response was 'persuaded that our University will not be national in name only',[74] adding that 'the future credit and welfare of Wales are in an exceptional degree bound up in the conduct of its educational institutions, and a great responsibility rests on the University by which the efficiency of similar establishments will in some measure be influenced.' Viriamu Jones, the Vice-Chancellor, sought hard to associate the Prince with the triumphs of university education. Had not his ancestor, George II, founded the University of Göttingen, renowned for its contribution to university life in Germany and to the advancement of learning?[75] Gladstone was rapturously welcomed and in a short speech the People's William greeted the People's University. There had been a great increase in wealth and he saw the danger of its unchecked dominance: 'This university represents the antagonism which is offered to it by mental cultivation.'[76] Owen M. Edwards, in Welsh on behalf of the Guild of Graduates, declared that the day had crowned many a noble effort. 'It is a day that begins a new period in the development of Wales, a period of greater service to the Empire and to mankind.'[77] The Prince, he later said, had performed a high service to the new University, causing

it to be respected in quarters where it had been misunderstood. The
University through its Chancellor had united Wales within itself. All
ranks of society from noblemen to collier now 'bent the knee to this new
power of the future'. Few were untouched by euphoria. Sir Lewis
Morris rejoiced in a celebratory ode which, apart from its fulsome
notes, may have permanently disqualified him from the Laureateship
he so ardently coveted:

> The long, long night of ignorance is done
> Triumphant o'er our land the Orient Sun
> Shines with renascent power
> Our little Wales that lay asleep
> In secular slumbers deep
> Awaken for whatsoe'er of nobler fate
> . . .
> Our lost Llywelyn seems again to come
> For love of learning to his ancient home.[78]

The installation of the Prince, said the *Western Mail*, marked 'a
starting-point in our national history' and 'means quite a fortune to the
Welsh University'.[79] However democratic the age might have become,
'a Royal Prince is a Royal Prince, and even the stoutest of Radicals, as
well as the silliest of Socialists, is prone to acknowledge that there is still
a divinity which hedges round a King'. The Prince had given the
University 'a fifty years' start'. Brynmor Jones thought that to have the
Prince as Chancellor was a 'great good fortune'. In his view 'it at once
raised the status of the university and made it impossible for any
reasonable person to assert that it was an institution of a party or
sectarian kind, or deny its national character'.[80] Looking back upon
the events of the day in *Cymru Fydd*, O. M. Edwards wrote: 'If I had
to decide which our national day of rejoicing is, I would decide on the
twenty-sixth of June.'[81] We should not question his sincerity. The
fortunes of the University meant much to him to the end of his life.
When an honorary degree of the University was to be conferred upon
him in 1917, the date of the Congregation conflicted with a meeting of
the Haldane Commission, then inquiring into the state of the
University. He decided that the interests of the University were best
served by attending the Commission meeting.[82] Nevertheless, he was
not uncritical of the University and he never spoke of it again with such
exuberance as on that bright day in June 1896.

VIII

The Achievement

The creation of a federal rather than a unitary University of Wales has been deplored by some men of judgement. In 1945 W. J. Gruffydd declared that it was a disastrous error to have raised four similar colleges in different parts of Wales.[1] In 1950 David Williams concluded that 'much university work is thus quadrupled in Wales, and the system has proved wasteful and inefficient. Had the departmental committee of 1880 decided upon one college for Wales numerous problems of administration and finance would not have arisen.'[2] Since both writers had extensive knowledge of the University their views command attention. Joseph Chamberlain, who insisted upon founding a unitary university at Birmingham in 1900, would have agreed with them, particularly upon the need to concentrate scarce resources to promote research.[3] In Wales, however, circumstances decreed otherwise. It is an inescapable conclusion.

Hugh Owen regretted that he had not for many years seen B. T. Williams's pamphlet of 1853 advocating a unitary university in Wales. Owen himself in the following year favoured 'one or more Queen's Colleges', after the Irish pattern, 'in some central part'.[4] This is somewhat ambiguous because the Queen's Colleges were in different places. In his outline constitution of 1854 Owen did not speak directly of a university, but it is a reasonable inference that he had in mind for Wales an institution comparable to the Queen's University to bind together the Welsh equivalent of the Irish Queen's Colleges. The plans which were fathered by Thomas Nicholas in the early 1860s and which won broad approval, envisaged one college for the whole of Wales 'in a central spot' or two colleges, one in north and one in south Wales brought together into an 'educational confederacy', of which the University, combining features of London University and the Queen's University, would be the 'crown and finish'.[5] In subsequent conversations with Lampeter it was agreed that a new unsectarian college together with St David's College, retaining its distinctive Anglican character, should form one university; other colleges would be affiliated if deemed prudent. It is clear, therefore, that by the mid-1860s the idea had won general acceptance that there should be at least two colleges in Wales and that they should be federated in a national university. Negotiations with Lampeter failed and when the opportunity came to purchase the Castle Hotel at Aberystwyth it was plain that the institution to be housed there was to be a university college. Since appeals to the public had been made on the understanding that there were to be two colleges, some feared that contributors would be resentful.[6] In the event such anxieties subsided, but not the aspiration to establish a university.

In 1892 Thomas Charles Edwards recalled that 'the original idea was that there was to be a university' and that 'the Welsh people . . . wanted a university and not merely a college'.[7] Hugh Owen never lost sight of the long-term goal. In March 1871 the London Committee considered whether an application for a government grant 'should be for a College with University privileges or for a College without such privileges'. The Committee concluded that it would seek the assistance of the state 'to establish a College which shall be of the status of the Queen's Colleges in Ireland, or the University and King's Colleges in London, and which eventually may assume a *University* character, being empowered by charter to grant Academic Degrees'.[8] This declaration of aims must be taken in conjunction with Hugh Owen's statement to the Committee that 'the proposed intention of the Promoters of this Undertaking from the outset was to obtain a University and one or more Colleges; and the Committee had never departed from that original intention so far as the question of a University is concerned . . .' It is evident that the intention to found two colleges had been allowed to lapse, but not the intention to create a university. Although the references to the Queen's Colleges and to the London Colleges rather darken counsel at this stage, we must conclude that the Committee was nourishing hopes that Aberystwyth might develop into a degree-awarding institution, in other words into a unitary university. When the Departmental Committee issued its report in 1881 it could well be argued that it had given insufficient recognition to the College's indomitable determination to survive, to the services of its Principal and staff and to the ailing fortunes of other young colleges in the United Kingdom. If it did not administer a *coup de grâce*, it had delivered a very palpable blow.[9] On the other hand, the Committee could not set aside the testimony presented to it, namely that the College had only fifty-seven students at the time of the inquiry, that one third of students from its inception had come from Cardiganshire, that the College's achievements (albeit in unfavourable circumstances) had been modest, that many deplored the creation of the College and that the urgent needs of the heavily populated areas of South Wales, especially, could not be ignored. The recommendation concerning a north Wales college was understandably interpreted as freedom to found a college there, and difficult though it was to speak positively at this stage concerning a future university in Wales, the Committee's tepid compromise involving a 'syndicate' puzzled many and pleased few.[10] This much, however, was certain: the last chance to establish a unitary University of Wales had evaporated. Twelve years after the Aberdare Report, Thomas Ellis reviewed the position. The opening of the college at Aberystwyth had been 'the first real step' towards creating a university. He believed that most Welshmen had at first firmly hoped that Aberystwyth would become 'the one centre of higher education, and ultimately become the University'. He added that 'the prospect of its becoming the University largely explains the marvellous and touching devotion and sacrifice of the people on its behalf.'[11] Ellis is evidently speaking of the dozen or so years following the purchase of the Castle Hotel. In 1887 Ellis told the students at Aberystwyth that since the 'vast commercial and industrial interest of Wales was in the extreme South and the extreme North' the Departmental Committee had been bound to recognize the inevitability of placing a centre of higher education in both north and south Wales. A single university centre in Wales was now out of the question: 'the facts and circumstances of the situation have made that impossible'.[12] It was idle to spend time on vain regrets. During his appearance before the Departmental Committee, Thomas Charles Edwards agreed that additional university colleges would be needed in Wales in due course, but he wished Aberystwyth to retain a certain primacy. A university should have a 'local habitation'[13] in his view and the arrangements at Manchester attracted him. In 1880 the Victoria University had received its charter, and Owens College became its first, and for a period, its only constituent college (until joined by Liverpool in 1884 and Leeds in 1887). Although other colleges within the University of Wales would be on terms of equality with Aberystwyth, nevertheless Aberystwyth would be the headquarters of the University as Owens was of the Victoria University. Twelve years later he still espoused this notion[14] which found a partial reflection in the justifiable retention of the title University College of Wales. It was also an ingredient in Aberystwyth's later objection to the placing of the University Registry at Cardiff. That, however, is another story.

Above and beyond all other considerations proximity to the seat of learning was the prime determinant in establishing a federal university in Wales. In the north of England during the seventeenth century, as we have seen, distance and expense prevented 'many choice wits'[15] from proceeding to Oxford and Cambridge; instead they went to the Scottish universities. At Oxford itself there was a particularly strong regional bias in the late seventeenth century when only twelve per cent of students came from the area north and east of the Thames Valley.[16] Despite improved travelling facilities to Dublin by 1892, half the students at Trinity College born in Britain came from Wales or the western counties of England.[17] In 1850, according to Rowland Williams, Vice-Principal of St David's College, Welsh youth could not afford to go to a university: 'It is idle to recommend an University Education to men whose whole families, if they were sold into slavery, would scarcely enable an Oxford undergraduate to pay his tailor and his wine merchant.'[18] He added that 'circumstances, stronger than opinions, have demonstrated to theoretical opponents that a large proportion of the Welsh clergy will henceforth be educated either at Lampeter, or nowhere.' Even so there were problems within Wales itself, underlined nearly two decades later by Basil Jones (a future Lampeter Visitor) writing from Bishopsthorpe Vicarage, his Yorkshire fastness. A glance at Bradshaw, he assured Joshua Hughes, showed that large parts of Wales were for practical purposes nearer to Oxford and London than they were to Lampeter and Aberystwyth. The geography of Wales was 'adverse to Welsh centralization and to Welsh unity. Most parts of the Principality have far more communication with the nearest English counties than they have with other Welsh districts... Most Welshmen who have ever been from home know more of Liverpool or Bristol than of the capital of the next county.' Basil Jones was, of course, exaggerating and it was a malicious overstatement to say that 'North Wales contemns South Wales, and [that] South Wales knows nothing of North Wales.'[19] Yet it had to be conceded that the fastest trains in Wales travelled to and from Euston and Paddington. Within Wales there were several leisurely lines and some who journeyed on the Cambrian railway became convinced that eternity was a reality. When

Lloyd George spoke at Aberystwyth's fiftieth anniversary he referred to
his early desire to enter the College (which he could see from Cricieth)
and of his inability to 'travel'[20] there (whether daily or not he did not
say). For many years after 1893, university meetings at Shrewsbury and
London were far more convenient for the majority than those held at
any single college. Both before and after the Aberdare Report,
Aberystwyth placed in a prominent position in its College Calendar the
telling words of Matthew Arnold: 'If there is one thing which my long
experience has left me convinced of, – as convinced of as I am of our
actual want of superior instruction, – it is this: that we must take this
instruction to the students, and not hope to bring the students to the
instruction.' Although not so intended by the college authorities, it was
the best advertisement imaginable for establishing colleges at Cardiff
and Bangor. Local colleges generated local loyalty and attracted local
contributions when they attended to local needs. But they were also,
assuredly, national colleges. In 1893 Thomas Ellis detected 'evidences
of the peoples' instinct as to the thoroughly national character and
purpose of these colleges',[21] soon to be bound together in a federal
university.

There was also the spirit of the age. The federal principle was much
favoured during the second half of the nineteenth century. In political
terms a federation may be regarded as a compromise between a national
government, in which there is direct representation by popular
suffrage, and a confederation, representing separate governments. In a
federation people and governments are represented, and Sheldon
Rothblatt, in an illuminating study, following E. A. Freeman in
applying the American model, stated the matter thus: 'in a perfect
federation, each member of the Union was independent in matters
which concerned it alone, but all members were subject to a common
power in matters that concerned the whole body collectively.'[22] In
university terms federalism reached its most extreme form in the
London University after 1858 when its examinations became open to
all candidates wherever they might be and whether they had studied in
an institution or privately. The power at the centre was clearly very
great for it determined curricula and examinations. This system was
exported to Toronto (1853), Madras, Calcutta and Bombay (1857) and
New Zealand (1874). In Ireland, in the north of England and in Wales
federalism was adapted in a modified form, for regular attendance was
required at specified courses in a recognized institution. Federations

were exceedingly popular in the 1880s at the time when the Welsh colleges were planning to organize themselves into a federal university. The Victoria University was spoken of with enthusiasm as the federation of the North and there was talk of a University of the East Midlands and of a University of the West Midlands. The modified federal system offered protection to young institutions and allowed them a minimum of freedom in devising courses not possible under the restrictive regime imposed by London examinations. There was another consideration which weighed with the government. Federations controlled tendencies to found 'Lilliputian universities',[23] as Bryce called them, and the consequent dangers to academic standards. New degree-awarding institutions were firmly discouraged. In fact, in mainland Britain only four universities were created throughout the whole of the nineteenth century, namely, Durham, London, Victoria and Wales. The dramatic change came in 1900 when Joseph Chamberlain succeeded in making Birmingham a unitary university.[24] There were speedy repercussions, many being affected (or afflicted, some thought) by 'the Brummagem spirit'; and it is highly significant that during the first decade of the twentieth century more degree-awarding institutions (all of them unitary) were founded in England than throughout the nineteenth century. Earlier the atmosphere had been very different. At the end of the debate on Hussey Vivian's motion in 1879, the Chancellor of the Exchequer had questioned Vivian's claim that a Welshman should be able to obtain a degree in his own country: '. . . it was very undesirable unnecessarily to multiply Universities. . . [and] there ought to be a case very clearly made out to justify the establishment of a fresh University.'[25] This was the challenge which faced the Welsh colleges. As Isambard Owen remarked laconically in 1916, 'the grant of a new University Charter . . . was a less easy matter to compass in 1893 than now.'[26]

The federal university was also to be a teaching university, but a protracted dispute as to its exact nature arrested progress. We have already considered in some detail the views of R. D. Roberts. They did not prevail because his plans omitted a fundamental requirement, namely, that schemes of study should be pursued *in* a constituent college. By January 1893 the overwhelming majority of those who assembled at Shrewsbury were convinced that the university must insist upon regular attendance at a course of instruction in one of the university colleges, in accord with the conclusions independently reached later by O. M. Edwards.[27] There was also unease amongst some leaders, such as H. R. Reichel, as to whether the public at large fully appreciated the nature of higher education.[28] In Aberystwyth's early days students had frequently drifted in and out of courses in the belief that a little of a good thing was better than none. Poverty, of course, was the prime cause, for in many cases it was a substantial sacrifice to remain even for one or two terms. Yet the misgiving remained. In 1876 it was evident that the College's most staunch supporter had little concept of the true purpose of the University College of Wales. In a letter to the Principal, David Davies said that 'my object in assisting this College was to give the Welsh poor or lower middle class a higher standard of education than they could get elsewhere on account of its cheapness to fit the young men of Wales for better situations in the mercantile world to compete with the English and Scotch. I understood it to be pure and simple a mercantile College or school purely Elementary.'[29] The redeeming feature of his letter was that he had at least spoken of the poor and of the lower middle class. For many years, from William Williams and William Davies, Ffrwd-y-fâl to Hugh Owen and Thomas Nicholas, appeals had persistently been made on behalf of the educational needs of the middle class, however defined, and not on behalf of the lower members of society who therefore did not feel committed to a movement from which they were apparently excluded. Nor was it easy to reach the conscience of the rich. In north Wales the Penrhyn family had derived untold wealth from the toil of quarrymen and tenants, but it was not a debt they were inclined to repay by promoting the cause of higher education. When due allowance is made for economic contraction and the fluctuating fortunes of the market, enlightened self-interest pointed to the endowing of a school of quarrying, of which the study of geology would be an essential part, in a college rooted, in Evelyn Waugh's words, in 'a highly geological country'.[30] It would be wrong to say that the Penrhyns gave nothing to the college and that the rent charged for the college's first home was exorbitant, but neither the first nor the second baron contributed a tithe part of what might have been expected. Their authority over a wide area was very great and in 1870 the quarrymen of Bethesda were reluctant to support Aberystwyth until they had received the approval of the first baron. When Hugh Owen called upon him in January 1873 he found him 'brim-full of prejudice'.[31] Industrial strife and the growing attachment of quarrymen to both Aberystwyth and Bangor exacerbated relations. The second Lord Penrhyn refused to contribute to a memorial fund to the College's first President, the Earl of Powis – a better Tory one could not find – because members of the College staff had accompanied Lloyd George in a carriage during his victorious progress through Bangor following the election of 1892. In the following year he told Lord Kenyon that he would be very sorry if Kenyon accepted the Privy Council's invitation to become a member of the College Council. With one brief interlude, the College has drawn all its presidents from north-east Wales.[32]

In the densely populated areas of south-east Wales industrialists were reaping a rich harvest. It was not unreasonable to hope that the captains of trade and commerce would respond to such challenges by handsomely financing a thriving school of mines at Cardiff in place of the frail department which limped hesitantly from 1891 onwards. A few years later at Birmingham Joseph Chamberlain could confidently appeal to local loyalty to raise £250,000 to endow a fund to maintain several professorships.[33] Despite Viriamu Jones's charm and eloquence the industrialists of south Wales were slow to show their hand. There were one or two exceptions, but by and large the tale is one of sorry disengagement. Perhaps it was not all loss. The college may have been spared unwelcome interference in their affairs. Rich alumni sometimes tyrannized American colleges and post-war Aberystwyth did not always find it easy to deal with a bountiful President.[34] It is often the case that benefactions are best received from Jordan's further shore.

Grievous religious divisions hindered progress. The evidence of several clergy to the departmental committee in 1880 revealed hostility to the university movement, and Aberdare once spoke of the danger that the Anglican Church might appear to detach itself from Welsh aspirations. Even an undoubted patriot like John Owen, Bishop of St David's, gave an impression of being equivocal on the subject and Aberdare became impatient with him at the Shrewsbury Conference. A. G. Edwards, Bishop of St Asaph, sneered at 'your precious University' and Hartwell Jones remembered a layman quoting to him at the Conference the famous saying of Gambetta: 'Le clericalisme, voilà l'ennemi.'[35] Nonconformists on the other hand, did not always appreciate that Lampeter meant a great deal to Anglicans. Attitudes such as those represented by David Davies were naturally resented. In

1876 he told Aberystwyth's Principal that 'the persons educated at Lampeter and Ystradmeuric [*sic*] have surfeited the people of Wales and that they are hated by the majority of people in fact by nearly all nonconformists'.[36] With so much brimstone in the air it was not easy to march together like Christian soldiers. Anglicans were not the only ones to conclude that Aberystwyth College was a Calvinistic Methodist preserve. It was not a reasonable charge. T. C. Edwards was far from being a narrow sectarian and was often misunderstood because he held broad ecumenical views. Nevertheless, an ordained Calvinistic Methodist minister, the son of Lewis Edwards, and the great-grandson of Thomas Charles, the founder of the Sunday School Movement, was seen as a powerful representative of a Calvinistic Methodist dynasty. Even in the late 1880s, Congregationalists were loath to contribute to the reparation of Aberystwyth College, in part because the principal collector was a Calvinistic Methodist.[37]

The raising of funds presented immeasurable difficulties. Direct appeals to rich individuals were straightforward enough, but public meetings, often sparsely attended, were not an efficient method. Administrative costs were disproportionally high; enthusiasm ebbed and flowed; those who made easy promises found it easier still to defer payment, and there were hard times. Devout Nonconformists had not spared themselves or their families to maintain a full-time ministry, to build and extend chapels, increasingly a familiar part of the Welsh landscape, and to establish theological colleges. Understandably enough, undenominational appeals – and they could not be otherwise – on behalf of university colleges did not arouse the same immediate sense of duty or of allegiance, especially if it were hoped that a theological college might itself develop into a degree-awarding body. Again, after 1889 the resources of local government were being concentrated upon the new intermediate schools, several of them in the course of time in the same county. Donations from beyond the seas were generally disappointing. Americans gave £1,050 to equip the new library at Aberystwyth and an Australian paid for the ornamental ceiling which created the indoor Quad.[38] It is not easy to discover further gifts from the United States to any of the colleges. We should not be surprised. Those who left industrial and rural Wales in the late nineteenth century faced a tough, uncertain future demanding self-reliance and resilience of a high order. They nourished expectations, largely fulfilled, that their children's children would melt naturally and comfortably into prosperous, white America. Nonconformist chapels and the Welsh language survived with remarkable tenacity for several decades until they were inevitably subsumed by the mellifluous sentimentality of the *cymanfa ganu*, the eisteddfod and the St David's Day dinner. The news that a university was to be founded in Wales was certainly received to the sound of trumpets at the Chicago Eisteddfod in September 1893; otherwise it was a case of *vox praeterea nihil*. At the same time it is fair to remember that Welshmen played no small part in the development of education in the United States.[39]

It had long been apparent that no university college in Wales could survive without state aid. It had been a perpetual grievance that Scotland and Ireland had long enjoyed substantial subvention from the government. During the debate in 1879 on Hussey Vivian's motion it was remarked upon that 'Scotland was clever enough to secure the maintenance of her Universities at the time of the Union'.[40] Indeed the Act of 1707 specifically stated that the universities should be preserved and it is at once evident that the legislation merging two sovereign states differed vastly from the Acts of Union of 1536—43 by which Wales was 'incorporated, united and annexed'[41] to the realm of England. There was resentment that a pacific nation such as Wales received none of the benefits conferred upon troublesome Ireland. An Independent minister residing at Cardiff felt moved to tell the Aberdare Committee that 'loyal and peaceable Wales should be on equality at least with Ireland'.[42] After all, the Welsh farmers 'pay their rent in silver and gold, and not in powder and shot'. Many years earlier, R. W. Lingen, one of the Blue Book commissioners, as will be recalled, had told Hugh Owen plainly: 'you Welsh deserve all the kicks that you get, because you do not assert your rights.'[43] Wales had, however, long turned her back on the direct action of Rebecca and of the Chartists. The voice of sweet reasonableness, on the other hand, carried little weight. Memorials to successive governments proved disappointing. Not much could be expected from Disraeli, whilst Gladstone's convoluted replies, though not devoid of sympathy, led nowhere. In fairness to government it must be allowed that once Welsh colleges received grants there would be similar demands from England. This is precisely what did happen. In January 1883 Lewis Fry, the member for Bristol, spoke in combative terms reminiscent of the early Friends. The university college at Bristol, he said, had close business links with south Wales, 'an important part of the field we were established to occupy'.

It had not then been easy to collect funds for the Bristol college 'and as we have not the good fortune to talk any barbarous language of our own, we don't look for Government help like our neighbours. All we ask is that you will be so good as to take our existence into account'.[44] The existence of Bristol and of other English colleges was taken into account in 1889, only a few years after grants were made to the Welsh colleges, but they did not receive as much. The Chancellor of the Exchequer, Sir William Harcourt, reminded a Welsh deputation in 1894 that whereas each of the Welsh colleges was given £4,000, only one of the English colleges received more than £1,800 and most of them only £1,200.[45] In this sense Wales could not complain. The real comparison, however, was always with Scotland and Ireland.

How are we to account for the success of the university movement? The prime motive force was undoubtedly Liberal middle-class Nonconformity. The advance of democracy enabled its voice to be heard not only from the pulpit, on the platform and in the press but on the floor of the Commons. The election of 1868 may not entitle us to speak of an *annus mirabilis*, yet there were mounting expectations, and although the Reform Act of 1884, followed in 1885 by the redistribution of constituencies, did not create a perfect democracy, yet it may justifiably be claimed that Wales was 'something resembling a political democracy for the first time'.[46] The petitioning of Parliament had earlier in the century been a useful safety-valve, giving a sense, often illusory, of participating actively in political affairs. The Liberation Society, in turn, had exerted a powerful influence. Yet it was in Parliament that the great decisions were to be taken, and from 1868 may be traced the growth of a buoyant, zestful radicalism. To be in a minority often strengthens individual qualities of independence and resolve, but membership of a majority generates confidence and enthusiasm. After the 1851 Census Nonconformists were demonstrably in the majority within Wales. In the elections of 1880 and of 1885 the Conservatives retained only four seats in Wales. In 1880 every candidate had pledged himself to remedy defects in the Welsh educational system; 1885, in one sense, may be regarded as having a greater significance than 1868, for Welsh members in their own persons reflected more clearly than before the nature of Welsh society.[47] All was not plain sailing. There was delay in introducing legislation for intermediate education in Wales, fundamental to the future of the colleges and of the university. There was impatience, too, with the reluctance of Welsh members to exert pressure on a premier consumed by Irish affairs. One college registrar wrote of 'this superstitious Gladstone-worship'[48] paralyzing the action of Welsh representatives. A year later he doubted whether progress was possible unless Welsh members sank their differences and created a 'Welsh question' much as there was an 'Irish question'.[49] Gladstone's vacillations often dismayed his followers, but to speak of 'Gladstone-worship' was not far from the truth for he was widely venerated in Wales. When he returned to power in 1892, with a thin majority, much was expected of him since he was heavily dependent upon the support of Welsh members. Moreover, there had been a remarkable degree of agreement between the two parties in 1889 in the debates on the Welsh Intermediate Act, passed under a Tory administration, which had 'revealed an unprecedented sympathy towards Welsh aspirations'.[50] There was a mood of euphoria and W. Cadwaladr Davies thought there should be an intermediate school in each town within reach of the children of the artisan and of the tradesman. 'There is no reason why the children of *Sir Fôn* should put up with three intermediate schools ... for the whole county, any more than the adults of Anglesey should be contented with three places of worship.'[51] At the University Conference at Shrewsbury in 1891 Aberdare expressed himself delighted with the readiness of members of the joint education committees to work together to establish schools, for they had hitherto been fierce opponents.[52] The Cymru Fydd movement founded in 1886 expressed the cultural, and for a time, the political aspirations of the new Wales. In the Welsh parliamentary party, reinforced at home by the Liberal county councils, there was a surge of optimism. In 1892, the year of the Liberal victory, John Morris-Jones wrote his *awdl* 'Cymru Fu, Cymru Fydd' to the resurgent Wales whose hour was at hand. A few months later Owen M. Edwards, in his report to the government, affirmed that 'the progress made in education in Wales within the last ten years is extraordinary. It is a period of awakening. Broadening and inspiring influences are at work. The tone of Welsh literature is improving every year − every month, it may almost be said, the University would reflect this progress, while helping and guiding it.'[53]

Inevitably there was an appeal to the English sense of justice. Wales was being taxed to support Scottish and Irish universities and was manifestly not receiving her due. She had, moreover, contributed substantially to maintain the English educational system. According to Tom Ellis in 1889 the tithes of Montgomeryshire alone had since the Reformation provided £800,000 to educate the English aristocracy at Christ Church, Oxford.[54] The sense of oppression was expressed in extravagant form by Henri Gaidoz in the *Revue Celtique*. Whilst welcoming the establishment of a 'university' at Cardiff in 1883, he believed that Wales had fared no better than Christians in European Turkey, for although the English had not been guilty of torture and of creating a body of janissaries they had for centuries taken over and assimilated the most promising youth of Wales.[55] More temperate champions insisted that Welshmen were a peaceable people, as we already have had occasion to notice. During the course of discussion in 1869 concerning a future university it was said that Wales cost less to keep in good order than any part of the kingdom. According to Watkin Williams, member for Denbigh District, 'Wales was most loyal and quiet; it needed not to be garrisoned; let them go beyond Chester, beyond the English border, and not a soldier would be found. But what had this quietness, loyalty and orderliness gained for Wales? Absolutely nothing from government.'[56] Naturally, on such occasions there was silence concerning crimes of drunkenness (higher than in England) and of the apparent failure of the strict Methodist ethic to restrain nocturnal gambollings in the stablelofts of Anglesey. D. Lleufer Thomas was later to produce reassuring statistics to show that there were fewer crimes in Wales than in England,[57] thus providing some basis for the much-vaunted claim that Wales was the 'Land of the White Gloves'. It has recently been shown in a penetrating study that Henry Richard and others who extolled 'innocent Wales' in the 1860s were writing at 'a convenient moment in history'[58] when indictable crimes were declining after a rapid rise during the first half of the century. What could not be seriously doubted was that Nonconformity had in general raised the standard of public and of private morality.

In an age when supposed racial characteristics held sway, Welshmen considered they had something of value to contribute to the composite British character. They knew that this sword was double-edged and the appeal was made only to the more flattering of Giraldus Cambrensis's assessments. Tom Ellis quoted Matthew Arnold's estimate of the Germanic, Celtic and Norman races. The defect of the Celtic genius lay in 'ineffectualness and self-will', a view more than echoed by O. M.

Edwards in 1892 when he spoke of the 'wild genius' and 'unstable character of the Welshman'.[59] But there were great qualities, and it was these which were usually canvassed. The Celtic genius, according to Arnold, had 'sentiment for its main basis, with love of beauty, charm and spirituality for its excellences',[60] admirable correctives to 'the commonness' and 'the humdrum' in the Germanic nature and to the 'hardness and insolence' of the Norman. The Earl of Powis told the Aberdare Committee that 'the peculiarity of the Scotch desire for education depends very much upon race';[61] in the Ulster Plantation the Irish Presbyterian had retained all his racial characteristics, 'his phrases, dialects and so on', as if he had not crossed the seas from the mainland in the reign of James I. The true Irish, however, presented a problem, understood better than most by the Bangor Principal. All the Celts had an intuitive imagination, but the Welshman, said Reichel, had 'caution and sanity which nature or history had denied to his brilliant but wayward and irresponsible Irish kinsman'.[62] He warmed to the judgement of Ernest Renan (of Breton parentage) who regarded the Welshman as 'the Teuton of the Celts'; he was 'likely, therefore, to play a more beneficent part in History than his Celtic confrères'. He would do well under palm and pine in the larger Britain overseas; he supplied an 'indispensable ingredient to the full prescription for Imperial well-being'.[63] This, too, was Rendel's view. There could be no better investment in the empire than by employing 'the great natural resources of Welsh genius lying dormant in the Welsh hills'.[64] Both Reichel and Rendel were prone to exalt rural virtues and appeared to appreciate neither the creative vigour of Welsh communities in industrial south Wales nor the social and cultural consequences of the vast internal migration since 1841.[65] During the decade 1881–91, within Wales itself, 87,200 had moved into Glamorgan and Monmouthshire and the rural depopulation of north and west Wales had strengthened Nonconformist values in south-east Wales, where two-thirds of the population now lived. Far older than Nonconformity was the martial tradition, a further gift in store. Though normally presented as pacific, the Welshman was a doughty fighter. His heroism at Rorke's Drift and Isandhlwana was fresh in the mind when Hussey Vivian's motion was debated in July 1879, for although the Zulu Wars were not generally popular in Wales, Vivian could not forbear to claim that there had not been a 'more gallant deed of arms'[66] since Thermopylae than that performed by the 24th Welsh.

It had long been apparent, and not only to their compatriots, that many Welshmen of lowly origin had a deep concern for education. In 1895 Viriamu Jones said that one outcome of the religious revival of the eighteenth century had been an awareness of spiritual values which had led to 'a real reverence for knowledge, a reverence that penetrated to the humblest homes'.[67] Associated with it was the democratic ideal of a state in which all should be cultivated citizens; from these twin impulses had sprung 'an intense longing for intellectual opportunity, for the means of acquiring knowledge, for a complete educational system'. In the Sunday School religion and education were intertwined: the 'opening' of the Scriptures, close examination and abstract discussion led to a pamphlet, a commentary and, at length, to a stiff volume of exegesis and to a blossoming book trade in which the Scots found it profitable to participate. Within such 'home-grown religious institutions'[68] – as Ieuan Gwynedd Jones has called them – there developed an élite leadership based not upon wealth but upon the gifts of nature. The educated, religious man was highly esteemed by his fellows. If he were outstanding he would be a national figure, such as the great Calvinistic Methodist minister Henry Rees (1798–1869) who had attended the meeting in 1854 and who was described by H. T. Edwards to Gladstone as one who 'wore no mitre and enjoyed no revenue, but [who] was, for all that, in his day the successor of St David in his authority over the religious mind of his country'.[69] The blend of scholarship and of preaching had a profound effect on Thomas Jones ('T. J.'). On the occasion of Aberystwyth's jubilee celebrations in 1922 he recalled that he decided to study at Aberystwyth rather than at Cardiff (a good deal nearer his Rhymney home), partly because there was a slight taint of infidelity about Cardiff, but mainly because the Aberystwyth Principal was one of the foremost preachers in the land. Although he did not include the following passage from the *Western Mail* when the article was reprinted, it is worth reproducing here: 'I am not ashamed to confess that in my teens I had gone to a meeting of the Calvinistic Methodist General Assembly at Merthyr to hear him, and at the end of the service I had pressed through the throng and touched him as he passed out of the chapel – such was my admiration for him before becoming one of his students. And I am sure I was typical!'[70] It is a simple tale, but eloquent in its simplicity. Thomas Jones's teacher at Glasgow, Henry Jones, remembered at his Llangernyw home 'when I was a big boy, waiting for hours for a BA to pass along the road, and failing, from very reverence, to speak to him'.[71] He added, significantly: 'The respect for learning was due to my father', the village shoe-maker. Earlier still, Lewis Edwards wrote to his future · wife in 1836 to say that she could not imagine the sensation created in south Wales when he graduated that year at Edinburgh (in three years instead of the usual four). The news had spread like wild-fire and 'I find it difficult to convince some of them that I am not the most learned man in the world.'[72]

Anecdotes of this kind may have had a marginal effect upon legislators. In the main, however, they sought compelling evidence. Lewis Morris, in 1888, after the unsuccessful attempt to secure a university for Wales, reflected on the conditions considered necessary by a government of whatever complexion before granting a charter.[73] It was, he thought, absurd to establish three colleges without completing the edifice, and whilst the authorities might under-standably dislike multiplying degree-awarding bodies, the matter could not be in serious doubt provided satisfaction were given on four matters. First, it had to be shown that there was an adequate supply of students. This would not be difficult. Four years later O. M. Edwards reported that there were 477 students in all at the three colleges, appreciably more than at Owens College when it became the first and only constituent college of the Victoria University. There were also the students of the theological colleges which had gravitated to the vicinity of the university colleges. At Edinburgh it appears that in 1888 there were ninety Welsh students and thirty-six at Glasgow. The second matter concerned adequate attainment. Here Edwards was able to give reasonable satisfaction. Of those who had proceeded from Cardiff to English universities a large proportion had taken first or second classes in honours. Over the years 'there is hardly a subject in the London University examinations in which an Aberystwyth student has not been placed in first class Honours'.[74] The third condition concerned real cases of hardship and the fourth the strength of the desire of the people to receive higher education. In both cases there was abundant testimony, to which we must now turn.

Osborne Morgan observed in 1892 that the government would never have given grants to the three colleges unless the people of Wales had successfully demonstrated that they were in earnest.[75] One of the most valuable and influential aspects of the Aberdare Report was the evidence concerning the endeavours of ordinary people. At Merthyr

Tudful miners and colliers were attending classes after work underground and were regularly sitting examinations and receiving certificates and prizes.[76] At Aberdare it was reported by a collier (examined in Welsh) that many of his colleagues kept their children at school as long as possible, some until they were twenty: 'Nothing would induce them to take their children away from school except want of food'.[77] A shearer at the Landore tinplate works spoke of a boy who had left school at nine to become a mason; at seventeen, having lived economically, he managed to enter Brecon Congregational College where he was maintained for four years; in order to prepare himself as a medical missionary he studied at Edinburgh for a further four years, but having qualified as a doctor he was obliged to relinquish his ambition because he had incurred heavy debts; in due course, he became a doctor in England, where he now had a flourishing practice.[78] Aberdare himself was fond of relating the fortunes of two brothers who were colliers. One succeeded in entering the Cardiff College before the other, but returned to the pit in vacations so that his brother could study until at length he too became a student at Cardiff.[79] A Caernarfonshire schoolmaster spoke of 120 scholars who attended his night school at Carneddi, Bethesda during the winter months; they came after the day's work and almost all were quarrymen aged between fourteen and twenty-one; some travelled long distances, a number throughout the year, arriving at five in the morning to receive tuition before work began at seven (and ended at half-past five); 'indefatigable labour and self-denial'[80] had enabled the brightest to become quarry managers, professional men, teachers and ministers of the gospel. 'The Bethesda booksellers', he said, 'could also tell a tale that would surprise our English friends', adding that it was not uncommon sight to see young quarrymen reading Mill and Macaulay during the dinner hour. The unsparing discipline which Henry Jones imposed upon himself during his early years was in part revealed in the Aberdare Report, where he is referred to as 'young Crispin', for he was following his father's craft. It became a familiar tale, but less familiar was his admission that had he failed he would have faced bankruptcy. 'The failure would have been ruinous. . . I thank God for the struggle, but would not like to see a dog try it again. There are scores of lads in Wales that would creep up, but they cannot. Poverty has too heavy a hand for them.'[81] Doubtless Samuel Smiles was an inspiration to many; indeed, he included Welsh examples in his *Men of Invention and*

Industry (1892) and sent a heartening message to the Bangor College upon its natal day.[82] This much, however, we may say with certainty: there were limits to the doctrine of self-help.

Many observers were impressed not only by the exertions of the young but by the sacrifice of members of an earlier generation who could never themselves directly profit. They contributed not merely to the founding of colleges, but to the maintenance of students for lengthy periods and to the erection of new buildings at Cardiff and Bangor. The oft-reiterated claim that colleges were established by the poor has more than once been repudiated. It is likely, too, that such phrases as 'the pennies of the poor', 'the rock from which we are hewn' and 'the romance of Welsh education' have by dint of constant repetition clouded true understanding. The contributions of collier and quarrymen were principally and naturally intended to establish a few scholarships, not to maintain a trinity of colleges, dependent in larger measure (except for Aberystwyth at first) upon the state and upon the gifts of prosperous members of the middle class. However, we are not here concerned with the arithmetic of the counting house. The sums contributed by the poor were small, but, as Viriamu Jones said on one occasion, these 'sums [were] not small to them'.[83] They gladly gave a great deal more than might reasonably have been expected of them, industrialists and landowners a great deal less in proportion to their resources. No one knew more of the circumstances of the founding of Liverpool University College than William Rathbone who never tired of singing the praises of impoverished Welshmen. In 1889 he told the Commons that 'the poor Welsh farmers and the quarrymen were, in proportion to their means, the most liberal supporters of the North Wales College, putting those of us who belong to the wealthier classes to shame by the largeness of their contribution.'[84] Ten years earlier Osborne Morgan informed the Commons that it might be very well to draw attention to what had been done in Lancashire for Owens College 'but what comparison was there between the Lancashire cotton lords and the poor colliers and quarrymen of Wales? When the Wigan colliers were found clubbing together their weekly wages to found an exhibition for Owens College, then, and not until then, would he admit that there was an analogy between the two cases.'[85]

Welshmen were naturally proud of the achievement. Percy Watkins, almost half a century later, believed that the years between the Aberdare Report and the formation of the Central Welsh Board in 1896 'represent the finest flowering period of statesmanship and effective performance in the whole history of Welsh Education'.[86] Wise planning and the acts of persuasion had elicited support bridging political and other divisions. The interests of the nation and of small localities had been served by 'constructive action'. At times there was a tendency to exaggerate. Thus, Viriamu Jones, in 1895, declared that 'the history of Wales during the last thirty years has been little else than the history of its educational progress.'[87] More revealing for our purpose are the verdicts of Englishmen speaking on English, rather than on Welsh platforms. Much was made of a rousing speech by Gladstone at Nottingham in 1877:

> I speak of the country of Wales, in which I have the happiness to spend a large portion of my time; and there is no part of the population of the country – and I say it freely and boldly in your hearing – there are few parts which can compete with Wales, and there is no part which can exceed it, from one end of the island to the other, in the earnest, ardent... passionate love of instruction. They are a religious people... enamoured of knowledge, and what they have done has been done with very little assistance, with no assistance at all from any public fund of any kind, they have, within the last five or six years, founded a large and important College at Aberystwyth. Is it possible for you to have a stronger proof that the existence of a love for primary education does lead on, and must lead on, to every great effort for the establishment of higher education.[88]

A. H. D. Acland in 1894, looking back upon his experience as chairman of the Welsh Joint Education Committees, said that the lessons he had learnt in Wales were of the greatest value to him as 'Minister of Education'. The concern for the Welsh nation and for the common good by men of all parties and creeds had taught him 'what enthusiasm people could have for education; he could only wish that England was less backward in these matters.'[89] D. R. Fearon, secretary of the Charity Commissioners, told his audience at Keighley in 1898 that no more remarkable reform than had been achieved in Wales during the previous fifteen years 'has ever been accomplished in any European country'.[90] It is true that he was speaking primarily of intermediate and technical education, but we may fittingly remind ourselves that advance in higher education was part of a larger movement which left its impress upon the whole system. Again, the Scottish example had always inspired Welshmen. Writing from the ruins of St Andrews Cathedral to Thomas Ellis in 1897, John Rhys said that 'I could not express a larger wish as to Welsh education than that it may do for Wales in the future as much as it has done for Scotland.'[91] Near the outer wall of the ruins may be seen memorials to the distinguished Playfair family. A member of that family, Lyon Playfair, later first Baron Playfair, was the last to speak in the debate on Hussey Vivian's motion in the Commons in 1879. He was then the member for Edinburgh and St Andrews universities, and it was appropriate that he should speak. He 'knew of no instance where such poor people as those of Wales . . . quarrymen and colliers, had subscribed for scholarships to send their sons to the Universities. Certainly, they had no instance of that kind in Scotland.'[92]

The final arbiters, however, were the Welsh people themselves. They had cause to be grateful to their leaders. Many had worked without stint, but four men gave exceptional service. Hugh Owen died twelve years before the University received its Charter (and only a few months after he was knighted), yet he must be accorded the premier place. That he was intensely disliked by some cannot be doubted; only an irredeemably sentimental Victorian could say with Lewis Morris, upon his death, that he had 'joined the ever-lengthening procession of the saints'.[93] There are no signs that he was deliberately unfair or unpleasant, but there was an element of ruthlessness in his dealings with lesser mortals, the inevitable ruthlessness, perhaps, of one who sees to the root of the matter and who is not to be deflected. His administrative skills had long been apparent. In planning the Reform Bill of 1867 Disraeli relied upon two men at Gwydyr House, one a Catholic, the secretary of the Statistical Society, and Hugh Owen the Nonconformist; Mrs Disraeli called them her husband's 'guardian angels'.[94] Owen, with some justice, has been called a philistine at heart, for to him 'the Welsh language represented a problem to be solved rather than a redoubt to be defended'.[95] Yet, when needful reservations have been made, it is difficult to think of any of his fellow-countrymen who could have performed such herculean tasks. His energy, a wonder to those who had themselves spurned delights and lived laborious days, was not squandered on rhetoric and vain conceits. He served the causes upon which he had set his heart with relentless self-discipline; in the face of defeat he was steadfast and like the first of the royal Tudors, what he minded he compassed.

Contemporaries spoke with admiration of Lord Aberdare. Viriamu Jones called him 'the commander-in-chief of the Welsh educational army';[96] that he should be the University's first Chancellor was entirely appropriate. He was a wise chairman and his social standing also helped to make him an effective leader of endless deputations to government concerning Welsh educational matters. He was not hidebound for he allowed his views to develop and mature. In 1875 he told the Lord President of the Council that he had not at first favoured the establishing of colleges in Wales but that he had become convinced of their need. In 1888 he said with some enthusiasm that changes during the previous eight years enabled him to speak 'very much more clearly and strongly'[97] upon the necessity for a University of Wales than he and his brother members of the Departmental Committee had ventured to do in 1881. In 1884 he wrote to Henry Richard: 'why can't we live 100 years − or rather, return here 100 years later − and see the results of that work for which we and our friends have laboured?'[98] His statute in Alexandra Gardens, Cardiff faces the University College; behind him lies the University Registry.

Isambard Owen's most notable contribution was to prepare the first draft of the University Charter which he fashioned clause by clause at his Mayfair home during the early hours of the morning after a day in the hospital or consulting room. Aberdare considered that no one else was 'so specially equipped'[99] for this arduous task. Viriamu Jones thought that 'were he not a physician [he] might have been a great lawyer, so nice is his appreciation of a difference and so perfect his gift of expression.'[100] This gift was much in evidence during his exposition of the draft charter to public bodies in Wales, especially college courts, and in his firm, lucid replies to querulous correspondents in newspapers and journals when the draft charter was exposed to intense, widespread scrutiny. To Reichel he was 'an academical statesman of the first rank' and 'in some respects the greatest member... of that remarkable little group of Welsh educationalists to whose labours the University of Wales owes its establishment'.[101]

It was a high tribute by a close, discerning observer. However, Reichel would have agreed that Viriamu Jones had the more original mind and that his influence was at its greatest during the period when the nature and purpose of the proposed university were receiving animated attention. By common consent Viriamu was the chief fount of inspiration. From the day of his arrival in Wales he made it clear that he had not returned to Wales simply to be Principal of Cardiff, important though this was in his eyes. He sought by eloquent reasoning and charm to convince his countrymen that the University must embrace the whole nation. In his view, too, it should lead the whole educational movement, though here he was to face disappointment.[102] In seeking support for the Charter in south-east Wales, Viriamu had perhaps the hardest task of all. There were, of course, several champions of the university in the two most heavily populated counties of Wales. Isambard Owen, however, well knew the nature of the challenge and we cannot do better than to quote the words he wrote many years later:

> To commend the scheme to the authorities of populous, industrial Glamorgan and Monmouthshire and their rising municipalities, to counter the many springs of disintegration these rapidly developing communities contained, to convince them of the advantages to be gained by educational union with rural Wales, of the danger of standing aloof, was Viriamu's work, and his almost alone. It was work which few men could have done, that none could have done so well. There was more concerned in the task than the question of a University scheme. The unity of Wales was really at stake; and Viriamu's statesmanship had other than merely academic issues.[103]

The tensions between industrial and rural Wales were ever-present and led to the collapse of the political aspirations of the Cymru Fydd movement in the mid 1890s. The University of Wales, however, the expression of cultural national consciousness, though exposed to crosswinds, endured.

The leaders of the university movement were not only inspired by high principles, they were also eminently practical men. Since the differences concerning the nature of the university had imperilled united action in 1888 it was thought best to defer serious consideration until November 1891. That it took eighteen months or so thereafter to prepare the draft charter and to consult extensively does not justify a charge of procrastination. C. H. Herford of Aberystwyth, no mean judge of men or of events, commented favourably upon the 'remarkable rapidity'[104] of the proceedings. Aberdare put the matter well when the draft charter was presented to the Shrewsbury Conference in January 1893 by quoting Dryden:

'Tis not the hasty product of a day
But the well-ripened fruit of wise delay.[105]

Proposals to request a royal commission had been sensibly dismissed in case of lengthy postponements and a change of government. Needless confrontation was avoided. The constitution of the university, for instance, was clearly designed to strike an acceptable balance between the independence of colleges already in being and an effective central control. No attempt was made to invade the rights of colleges to appoint their own staff and the potentially inflammable question of the University Registry was deferred until the dust had settled.[106] Time would tell whether it was wise to invest the representative Court with both executive and legislative powers. The decisions to include theology and to exclude medicine were undoubtedly wise. The charter committee, as we have seen, exceeded its authority in providing for the study of theology, initially at postgraduate level; a few experienced men shook their heads, but it was generally accepted that the din and clangour of sectarianism had perceptibly diminished and that an honoured place could now be safely given to the 'queen of the sciences'.[107] The unwillingness to admit any candidate to a degree in medicine or surgery at this stage caused understandable disappointment, but to have pursued the matter contrary to the wishes of government and of responsible medical opinion, as Isambard Owen fully recognized, would have led to the certain rejection of the Charter. A decisive majority favoured a teaching university, but it was reasonable to recognize that extra-collegiate courses followed by examination could count as part of the period of full-time attendance. A large portion of the grant to the university itself was to be used to secure the services of the best external examiners in order to establish and to maintain the reputation of the new university in the sure knowledge that 'debasement of the academic currency is a moral injury to the whole community'.[108]

The Charter which eventually won approval was practically identical with the draft charter. By contrast, elephantine labours to create a teaching University of London had proved futile, despite two royal commissions. These labours may be followed in part in Sir William Allchin's *Account of the Reconstruction of the University of London*.[109] His third volume dealt with the years 1891 and 1892 only; not for nothing was he an authority on indigestion. The promoters of the

University of Wales, on the other hand, had been clear-headed and tenacious, prudent and victorious. The *Educational Times* in March 1893 thought that when another opportunity came to attempt to establish a teaching university for London 'we shall find many a valuable hint in the charter which is being drafted for the proposed University of Wales'.[110] The dreamy, meandering Celt had indeed excelled himself. Yet the outcome had not been certain. In 1916 Isambard Owen speculated as to the probable alternative had the Conference of 1893 foundered. In 1880 affiliation with the Victoria University seemed to some the only realistic course.[111] In fact the attractions of Victoria were so great that a responsible reformer such as Sir George Young recommended that University College, London, should become one of its constituent colleges in order to escape the toils of the London examining system.[112] In Wales, failure to receive a charter and the clamant desire for academic freedom would have intensified the demand to affiliate with an English university or college. Isambard was firmly of this view. Many influential persons connected with the Welsh colleges, he tells us, believed that the colleges 'should individually seek federation for University purposes with such English Colleges as were nearest to their respective seats'. The consequences would of course have been dire and he stated categorically in 1916 that from the national standpoint 'the passing into law of the University Charter was probably a crucial event in the history of Wales'.[113]

The power of creating a degree-awarding body, initially by a papal or imperial bull, had in early modern times been transferred to sovereign states. In Britain a new university was established by royal charter granted by the sovereign in council upon the advice of the government. In order to persuade government to confer a charter the university movement in Wales was expected to demonstrate broad support. Divisions remained; as late as 1881 religious jealousy was described as a 'growing evil'.[114] Yet it was clear that the success of the movement depended upon the readiness of men of diverse opinions to unite in a common enterprise. Anglicans who contributed in the early days to Aberystwyth were doubtless in general wealthier than Nonconformists. Nevertheless, it is proper to remember that they contributed more than any other religious body.[115] Welsh clergy in Yorkshire were early advocates of a university, and Anglicans in the forefront of the movement included Osborne Morgan and Aberdare. Dean Vaughan gave excellent service to Cardiff, Archdeacon Griffiths of Neath and

McKenny Hughes, son of a bishop of St Asaph, to Aberystwyth. The Bangor Principal was a devout Anglican; the Vicar of Llandyrnog was one of two secretaries organizing the campaign to establish a college in north Wales, the other being Henry Jones, a Calvinistic Methodist. In short, there were many individual Anglicans who deserve the highest praise. Nor should we forget the Roman Catholic Marquess of Bute. Firm Tories such as Robert Jones, Rotherhithe, G. T. Kenyon and the Earl of Powis identified themselves with the cause of higher education in Wales, as did English Liberals representing Welsh constituencies, William Rathbone, the Unitarian, and Stuart Rendel, the Anglican.

During a time of intense denominational loyalty it had not been easy to arouse the enthusiasm of the *gwerin* of Wales, sometimes idealized, it is true, but who, nevertheless, were uncommon common people.[116] Persistent appeals to pursue the claims of the middle class were unlikely to elicit widespread support, but a vital stage in reaching the hearts and minds of the *gwerin* was the organization of collections upon a chapel basis. 'Sul y Brifysgol', the University Sunday, brought religion and higher education together. It was a powerful combination, as W. J. Gruffydd recognized in his poem to an old man of Tyn y Mynydd:

> Hard-earned mite gave he to found the College,
> Heavy heart to him who bore the Cross.[117]
>
> (Rhoes ei geiniog brin at godi'r Coleg
> Rhoes ei galon drwm i Wr y Groes.)

Such persons would be moved by Aberystwyth's struggle to survive, to fight injustice after the Aberdare Report and to face the consequences of a calamitous fire. Upon the basis of statistics, culled in part from O. M. Edwards's report, S. T. Evans (member for Mid Glamorgan) claimed that more than two-thirds of those who had attended the Welsh colleges since their inception came from 'the lowest walks of life'.[118] It is evident that he was here including small shopkeepers, tradesmen and farmers as well as labourers, and his claim was thus questioned by a writer in the *Western Mail*.[119] O. M. Edwards felt justified in describing the new university as 'Prifysgol y Werin', 'the Peasants' University'.[120] The founders of the university were convinced that the injustices of the past were being removed and that society would no longer be impoverished by the neglect of undiscovered talent. Many 'now holding the plough. . . might have been made more fit to steer the state'[121] said a writer in 1648, a view echoed by one of the university's benefactors, a Chester chemist who wrote in his will that 'I believe there is a large body of ability in the Welsh race which lies hidden under the surface and waiting for an opportunity to show itself.'[122] The plight of the poor student had long been recognized in England, from Chaucer onwards; three acts of Parliament in Henry VII's reign allowed him to beg, and the mendicant scholar was familiar in the seventeenth century. Fees in the colleges of the University of Wales were reduced to an absolute minimum and there was much heart-searching when increases became inevitable. According to David Williams, 'it was, without question, providential for T. F. Roberts and his contemporaries that the College was opened when it was, almost, so to speak, on their doorstep. It gave them an opportunity which would not otherwise have come to them.'[123] We cannot, of course, be certain that such an able man as T. F. Roberts would never have reached Oxford, but without the long preparatory period at Aberystwyth the policeman's son would have faced an intimidating challenge. There were others who wondered whether the presence of a university in Wales from medieval times onwards might have encouraged men of high ability to 'return home to the centres of life in Wales, which would have been the case had there been a university'.[124] Such was Aberdare's view, but it was fanciful to suggest that Archbishop John Williams, apart from the exigencies of civil war, might have come back to his native land rather than remain in his vast northern diocese. There was general agreement, however, that 'considerable men' through the ages had remained in undeserved, if not wholly barren, obscurity and that henceforth dormant gifts would be awakened in the lower ranks of society to the great enrichment of the whole nation.

Further satisfaction was derived from the complete equality given to women in the Charter. The issue had never been in doubt. Although the 'treason' of the Blue Books had long been placed in tolerable perspective, this enunciation of principle was the best riposte to those who had grossly traduced Welsh women in 1847. A woman's name was the first in the College Register at Bangor; the first graduate of the University was a woman student at Cardiff. Viriamu Jones, a fervent advocate of women's rights, despaired when he heard Bryce say of women's suffrage that 'this is an experiment so large and bold that it ought to be tried by some other country first.'[125] Viriamu insisted that women should not be made equal 'by degrees' alone; they should hold office or be members of any university authority equally with men. This provision in the Charter caught the attention of *The Times* which commented that 'in this important respect the new University is in advance of every British University', adding, rather waggishly 'that it may be that a woman may some day hold the office of Chancellor, and [that] the example of Italian universities, where in times past women have held professorships at the nomination of Popes, may be followed in our own days by Nonconformist Wales'.[126] Nevertheless, as W. Gareth Evans perceptively noted, a *de jure* right is not a *de facto* right.[127] Society's hoops and barriers caused endless difficulties so that in practice there were few women on university and college bodies. Yet the unequivocal assertion of equality and an apparent readiness to act accordingly placed the University upon more secure, just foundations.

It is evident, too, that widespread, thorough consultation during the process of shaping the Charter had given general satisfaction. Everyone, it appeared, responsible and irresponsible, had had his say. The principle of representation had been amply recognized in the composition of the University Court, a fitting reflection of the popular movement. The great weight of opinion had favoured a teaching, not an examining, university, and college staff rejoiced at the prospect of casting off the shackles of a system increasingly seen as tyrannical and stultifying. Freedom from external authority, however, was not to encourage narrow, introspective habits of mind. The University was janus-faced. It was, naturally, to attend to the needs of Wales, but it was also to be outward-looking, standing confidently, in the course of time, amongst the universities of other nations. It was in this spirit that Henry Griffiths had advocated a 'National University'[128] in 1849. Those prominent in founding the university had for the most part received their higher education outside Wales and were men of broad vision. T. F. Roberts said in 1894 that 'it is our first duty to lay down the methods and apparatus which will place our country, as regards the externals of higher study on a level with other countries.'[129] He did not minimize the challenge: 'It is the seed time of a distant harvest.' The establishing of a university in Wales heralded a new era, but universities were 'exacting in their requirements; to create living centres of learning even with every appliance in the most perfect form is a task of sufficient difficulty; to create them, and at the same time to struggle with incomplete buildings or an inadequate equipment is well-nigh hopeless.' Such reflections were a timely antidote to easy, comfortable words. One could not speak lightly of higher studies. 'It will be long before our country can make her presence felt in this difficult altitude. She must pass through a prolonged period of silent self-discipline carried on under principles derived from international experience.' He added that Wales must welcome the best teachers from whatever country they might come. In the same spirit students from England were gladly enrolled. According to Edward Anwyl (strangely reluctant at first to break away from London) Welshmen were bound to look beyond their own borders. There were few families who did not have relations in England and overseas. A maritime tradition had helped to create the 'vision of a greater Wales'. The new University must be 'an international institution'.[130] Viriamu Jones from the first believed in 'the national genius of the Welsh people, and in their capacity to make their University respected among the universities of the world'.[131]

Links with Oxford and Cambridge were to be strengthened, not weakened. The University of Wales would facilitate the entry of the ablest Welsh students into the older universities to a far greater extent than was possible under the London system whose requirements were a distinct hindrance. Thomas Ellis, recuperating in Egypt in 1890 and writing in both Welsh and English to O. M. Edwards, felt that a potent argument for a university in Wales was that Welshmen should follow the example of the Scots who for generations had gone to Oxford fortified with their own degrees and who had won the highest honours. The defenders of the London system had used 'singularly contemptible arguments'.[132] Oxford, they said, undermined the Welshmen's Nonconformity and nationality, which, Ellis insisted, could well stand 'a severe test'. Welshmen who threw themselves into Oxford life would not only extinguish the 'prejudiced notions' concerning the people, language and religion of Wales, they would win the respect and affection of Englishmen and strengthen their own self-respect. Upon the completion of its educational system 'more Welshmen will be able and anxious to distinguish themselves at Oxford and Cambridge – the chief educational heritage of the British races – than ever before, and ... they will succeed'. The question of self-assurance had been raised before. In May 1863 a writer in the *Baner* argued that Welshmen would not be imbued with sufficient ambition to rise in the world unless educated within Wales.[133] Some observers remarked that outside Wales they were disinclined to mingle with others. Alfred W. Hughes, lecturer in anatomy at Edinburgh and later professor of anatomy at Cardiff, said that 'my experience of Welsh students out of Wales is that with a few exceptions their chief associates are Welsh'.[134] In 1886 H. R. Reichel, basing his remarks on his Oxford days, found that Welsh students kept to themselves and were considered 'a peculiar people', rather like the early Methodists, we must suppose. Jones of Jesus was a puzzle, 'as is attested by many quaint and some uncomplimentary *bon mots*'.[135] According to one testimony, the situation was even worse: Cowbridge men clung together, as did Rhuthun men and Llandovery men.[136] Reichel, we may be sure, was not being skittish. He reported upon the situation as he saw it. The Scot had self-confidence in abundance, mainly because the standard of education in Scotland was higher than in England; imperfect acquaintance with the English language meant that Wales could not influence England as Scotland had done, or even 'backward Ireland'. Reichel's expectation was that Wales's 'choicer spirits', having taken their degrees in Wales, would proceed to Oxford and Cambridge, and 'no longer keeping timidly aloof in conscious inferiority, would throw themselves with confidence into the most intellectual society of the place'. Scholarships, and especially fellowships, would fall into their lap. Wales would enjoy a new intellectual life if her sons were to 'plunge fearlessly into the general life of Great Britain'.[137] Indeed, in a *cywydd* in 1887 it was said that the Cardiff College was a fine place to enable a Welshman to come to the fore in competition with an Englishman.[138]

Reichel took practical steps to initiate rural swains into the arcana of polite society. His formidable breakfasts, following the example of Jowett, encouraged punctuality, table manners and the art of conversation. Competitive games such as rowing and cricket were favoured, and especially tennis which permitted both sexes to participate in decorous proximity. It should not escape notice, however, that during the year in which Reichel reflected sombrely upon Welshmen at Oxford, a society, Cymdeithas Dafydd ap Gwilym, was founded, composed of Welshmen from various colleges. Henceforth Jones of Jesus would be less isolated. The early members were remarkable men, Owen M. Edwards, for example, John Morris-Jones and Edward Anwyl, who met under the presidency of John Rhys, first Professor of Celtic at Oxford (1877). Thomas Parry called them 'giants'.[139] In no sense insulated from the mainstream of Oxford life, they thought creatively of the new Wales to which they were profoundly committed.

It was, of course, not realistic to believe with Dyfnaint in 1830 that the new university would teach 'all the sciences known to man' or with Joseph Chamberlain in 1898 that at Birmingham there should be established 'a great school of universal instruction, not confined to any particular branch of knowledge, but taking all knowledge as its province'.[140] 'Universities' did not mean 'universal knowledge', a concept based on an error in Johnson's dictionary which had so disturbed Cardinal Newman that he would confer upon theology a central, unifying role.[141] 'Universitas' was originally a guild, deriving its name from the words of its charter, 'universitas vestra' ('all of you'). The origin of the modern university was the *studia generale* – in his Pennal Letter Glyn Dŵr speaks of *studia generalia*[142] – which sprang out of the efforts to educate priests and monks beyond the level of monastic schools. The main difference between the latter and *studia generale* ('schools of general resort') was the presence of scholars from foreign countries who banded themselves together as guilds or universities in the vicinity of *studia*, which were 'a centre of studies *for all fit persons* and *not* of *all things fit for study.*'[143] It follows that whereas an exceedingly strong case could be made for powers to grant degrees in medicine, surgery and obstetrics in the University of Wales, Viriamu Jones was not strictly correct when he said in 1886 that unless a medical school were founded at Cardiff the 'University element' would be 'sadly incomplete'.[144]

The essence of the new university, said W. Rhys Roberts in 1892, was that it should be the centre and the home of learning in Wales. This fundamental duty, he insisted, was to be borne in mind at the very outset during financial negotiations with the government. He was especially mindful of Lewis Edwards's plea that there should be a number of fellowships for the best students upon graduation. Without fellowships, Edwards had said, it was folly to contemplate a university in Wales. O. M. Edwards in his report had also pointed to the danger of 'starving the higher branches of study'; if these were neglected it would not be possible to acquire status 'in the eyes of the academical world'.[145] Partly with such considerations in mind he had recommended that the University should have an annual revenue of £10,000. Alas, exceedingly few fellowships were to be distributed for many decades, either by the University in its corporate capacity, or by individual colleges. The advancement of learning, nevertheless, remained an imperative. Rhys Roberts noted that the best American universities — John Hopkins was a case in point — had learnt these lessons from Germany. Roberts was inclined to be a purist. Learning in a university was to be sought for its own sake. Even the Germans, he said, had warned their students against *Brodstudien*, bread (and butter) studies.[146] However, within three years Hastings Rashdall, in his magisterial *The Universities of Europe in the Middle Ages*, would be recalling that vocational, non-liberal studies were in the high tradition of Western universities. The Scots had long been told by Knox that 'it is not to be supposed that all men will dedicate themselves and their children, that they look for no worldlie commoditie. But this cankered nature quhilk we bear is provokit to follow vertue, when it seeth honour and profeit annexed to the same.'[147] In 1962 Robbins, in his famous report, quoted an apparently authentic analect of Confucius which said that it was not easy to find a man studying for three years without aiming for pay.[148] In Wales, William Davies, Ffrwd-y-fâl, informed his countrymen in verse (of a kind) in 1849 that a university would make Wales 'a commercial nation'.[149] Before long Thomas Nicholas was urging them to awaken to the challenge, and to grasp the benefits, of the industrial revolution. The theme was endlessly repeated: there was no reason why Welshmen should not learn English, embrace the gospel of chemistry, get on in the world and eat white bread. The spectre of German competition became more menacing with each passing year. Behind the Prussian soldier was the Prussian schoolmaster. Mundella told a Welsh audience of a professor in a technical college in France who kept a German helmet at hand to remind sluggish students that 'the man who wore this helmet conquered France... Beware, that unless you apply yourself diligently to your studies they will conquer your industries, as they have conquered your provinces.'[150] The new English university colleges were responding with a will to the mounting needs of industry; in time, they became known as 'community service stations'.[151] However, ncither government nor industry in Britain invested as much in higher education as its rivals. Could Wales emulate the example of the smaller nations, Switzerland or Denmark? There were notable disappointments. Bangor had been unable to develop the study of geology, without which a school of Quarrying could not be contemplated. At Cardiff the Department of Mining had faltered and Engineering had not advanced as might have been expected. Nevertheless, the Technical School at the Collage had a staff of twenty-five teachers when O. M. Edwards surveyed the scene and he noted that the College's Higher Technical Department was maintained by the counties of Glamorgan and Monmouth, and by Cardiff, which together contributed £2,200 per annum. Agriculture, Wales's principal industry, felt the brunt of continental and American imports, and the colleges at Aberystwyth and Bangor helped the Welsh farmer, initially mistrustful of academic advice, to apply the lessons of science to open 'Nature's pantry'. Kiel butter, which had weaned the discriminating from the traditional salty home product, began to feel the force of competition.[152] The grant of a Charter in 1893 was welcomed the more readily because of the increasing awareness that the colleges, now to be federated, were addressing problems of immediate concern to the economy of Wales.

Several other aspects of Welsh life had received attention, such as her fisheries, and flora and fauna. The study of music, for which Welshmen were believed to have a natural aptitude, had made an early beginning at Aberystwyth and Cardiff. However, many were convinced that a university in Wales would be mortally wounded at birth if an honoured place were not at once accorded in all the colleges to the language, literature and history of Wales. Hitherto circumstances had not been propitious. The pressure to master English had quickened, especially after the Blue Books of 1847. Two years later, E. R. G. Salisbury, a firm advocate of Welsh colleges and the committed collector of Welsh books which later found their way to Cardiff, as we have seen, told the Marquis of Lansdowne that 'I am pretty well convinced that the extermination of the Welsh language (as a *living* one) would be the greatest possible blessing to Wales.'[153] The statement is all the more extraordinary since it was made by one who claimed descent from William Salesbury, the great Renaissance scholar who had translated part of the New Testament into Welsh (1567), and whose wife traced her ancestry to William Morgan, the translator of the Bible into Welsh (1588). Osborne Morgan in 1871 did not hesitate to tell the editor of *The Times* that the college at Aberystwyth was not 'designed to perpetuate, even encourage, the Welsh language, but solely to afford to the Welsh youth. . . the educational advantages now enjoyed by most Englishmen of the same age'.[154] Soon after the opening of the College the order of service prepared by the Principal gave no opportunity for students to sing praises in Welsh; even the two hymns by William Williams, Pantycelyn are in English.[155] Many years later the ailing compiler whispered from his bath-chair to the young R. T. Jenkins, about to enrol at Aberystwyth, that he should attend the English, not the Welsh, chapel, advice, it may be added, which withered on the vine.[156] A brief glance at the official Calendar of the colleges gives a distinct impression that both Aberystwyth and Cardiff were more Welsh in tone than Bangor.[157] At Aberystwyth Edward Anwyl had in 1892 succeeded J. E. Lloyd as professor of Welsh; at Cardiff Thomas Powell had been professor of Welsh since 1884. The main problem was that the three colleges were manacled to the degree requirements of London University which did not recognize Celtic as an examinable subject. In 1888 the Bangor Senate asked the University of London to encourage the study of the Celtic languages, largely then the preserve of foreign scholars, 'although it is chiefly within Great Britain and Ireland that living Celtic languages flourish'.[158] Celtic studies had 'a very important bearing not only upon investigations into the general structure and history of the Indo-European languages, but in particular upon the history of the literature of Western Europe in medieval and modern times'. London relented to the extent of allowing the Celtic languages to be added to the list of languages for the MA examinations. In practice the concession did not amount to much. Many years later John Morris-Jones, appointed to a lectureship at Bangor in early 1889, wrote: 'I prepared one or two students for the MA degree, but my ordinary lectures were attended only by a handful of impracticable people who, like myself, studied the subject because of the fascination it had for them'.[159] His salary was no more, it was said, than several members of the Bangor Council paid their coachman. In 1892 he was sufficiently downcast to apply for an inspectorship of schools. From this *pis aller* he was rescued by the University of Wales which at once included Welsh among subjects to be examined for its degrees. The number of students of Welsh increased dramatically in the three colleges and Welsh studies prospered to the great gain of the nation.

The University was seen by many as an educational Parliament for Wales. Although that ambitious dream was not wholly fulfilled, much else was expected. William Abraham, at the opening of the Cardiff College, announced, in a characteristic utterance, that whilst free libraries and mechanics institutes enlightened the people, refined their tastes and encouraged them to desert public houses, they could not instruct the children of the working class in the principles of political economy which, when taught by the best masters, 'would so influence their minds as to act as an antidote to useless strikes, disastrous lock-outs, and the inevitable results of overproduction'.[160] There was general support for Newman's view that a university 'aims at raising the intellectual tone of society, at cultivating the public mind, at purifying the national taste'.[161] Lewis Edwards had spoken of raising the standard of learning before the people; O. M. Edwards's reiterated hope was to set the old country on its feet again.[162] In the process it might sometimes be necessary to enlighten their countrymen as to the true purpose of a university. Popular institutions were not to be exempt from criticism. The duty of a university, said T. F. Roberts, was to establish 'standards of taste and judgement in matters of literature and art';[163] it was anticipated, therefore, that it would 'correct certain uncritical tendencies which are encouraged by the competitive methods of the Eisteddfod'. Pernickety spelling, curious grammar, inflated style derived from the pulpit and romantic, baseless notions of the past were early victims of an astringent scholarship which did not always promote harmony at the Eisteddfod or elsewhere. Extension lectures, not hitherto fully developed, and indeed in temporary decline, would bring the University within reach of a discerning public. Closer association with the theological colleges should act as a balm of Gilead to heal ancient abrasions. Teachers of primary and intermediate schools would be a permanent bridge between university colleges and schools in towns and villages. Rendel later detected a social solidarity at the three stages of education, primary, intermediate and university. 'There is no *social* break', he declared, 'in the whole educational ladder and system of Wales.'[164] Osborne Morgan, in an astronomical variant of Viriamu Jones's metaphor of the University as a magnet to iron filings, saw the colleges as planets revolving around the sun. E. P. Hughes argued that no force other than education was strong enough to keep Welsh nationality alive.[165] T. F. Roberts reminded a Cymmrodorion audience that in medieval times students at Paris and Oxford had been divided into 'nations'. In Wales there would be 'one university co-extensive with the whole national area'. The three colleges, in close touch with their immediate constituencies, would in time contribute more to the effectiveness and unity of the University than if it consisted of one central college. 'In a country much divided by political and religious differences it will be a symbol of that deeper national unity of thought and aspirations which lie below the surface.'[166] The University's first Vice-Chancellor in a letter to O. M. Edwards said that the University was 'the first of our national institutions'; he was anxious that it should unite, not divide, otherwise 'we lose perhaps the best of the good gifts it has to give'. It was not simply a matter of reconciling north and south Wales. True union, he told the Bangor governors, liberated an 'enormous additional force'.[167] Some years ago the present Vice-Chancellor of the University wrote that '"the People's University", *Prifysgol y Werin*, is a product of nineteenth-century democracy. It forms perhaps the most glorious monument to the national revival which revitalized Wales in the late Victorian era.'[168]

The University of Wales received its Charter after many struggles, some of them bitter, and after battles in both Houses of Parliament. The true victory, however, was won within Wales itself, over geography and particularism, over religious and political divisions, and, not least, over poverty. A determined, united people in an emerging democracy were not to be oppressed or defeated, and the University of Wales became for them the symbol of national unity. It is a heroic tale which deserves to be freshly remembered in each succeeding generation.

Appendix 1

The University Seal

The Seal of the Univeristy was designed by Sir Edward Burne-Jones. On the obverse of the Seal the field is occupied by a seated figure under an arcade holding an open book, and representing the teaching side of the University – that is to say, Wisdom or Knowledge as the instructor. On the right and left are two standing figures also holding books, representing the students or graduates of the University, together with three shields of the three constituent colleges, with their devices of the Rose, the Castle, and the Mace. The legend is from the Vulgate Latin version of Isa. lviii. 10 and 12, of which the following is the English authorized version: 'Then shall thy light rise in obscurity, and they that shall be of thee shall build the old waste places'; the allusion being to the creation of the University. The Welsh motto, 'Goreu Awen Gwirionedd', is the motto of the University, and may be translated, 'The best inspiration is Truth'.

On the reverse side is a building symbolizing the University, with cloisters below and classrooms above, and placed between the mountains and the sea. The legend here is a verse from 'Lucretius' Book II, line 8: 'Edita doctrina sapientum templa serena'. It may be translated thus: 'The serene regions (or mansions) of the wise raised high by learning.'

Appendix 2

The Social Origins of Students

Evidence relating to the social origins of students before 1893 is largely dependent upon two sources. The first appeared in O. M. Edwards's Report; the second was produced in the debate on the University Charter in the Commons on 29 August 1893 by S. T. Evans, member for Mid Glamorgan.[1] Both men were former students at Aberystwyth. Edwards received his information directly from the colleges, but in the case of Aberystwyth he provided statistics for 1892 alone. It is possible that S. T. Evans obtained his statistics from Edwards himself, but with one exception, for he was able to include information concerning Aberystwyth from 1872 to 1892. In the Commons, however, he dealt only with three groups, tradesmen, farmers and labourers, though he also included the total number of students from all classes. The two sets of figures are set down side by side:

Table A

O. M. EDWARDS		S. T. EVANS	
Aberystwyth 1892 only		*Aberystwyth* 1872–1892	
Gentlemen	12		
Clergy and Ministers	45		
Professional classes	67		
Farmers	25	Farmers	188
Tradesmen	70	Commercial class	413
Labouring class	12	Labouring class	184
		Total	785
Total	231	Total number of students of all classes	1214

Cardiff 1883–1892		Cardiff 1883–1892	
Noblemen	3		
Gentlemen	57		
Clergymen	86		
Professions	106		
Commercial	299	Tradesmen	299
Farmers	84	Farmers	84
Labouring class	285	Labouring class	285
		Total	668
		Total number of students of all	
Total	920	classes	940

Bangor 1884–1892		Bangor 1884–1892	
Higher classes	16		
Professional	144		
Mercantile	184	Tradesmen	183
Agricultural	78	Farmers	78
Labouring	142	Labouring class	143
		Total	404
		Total number of students of all	
Total	564	classes	564

There are one or two discrepancies. The totals for Cardiff differ, but the numbers given for the classes reported by both are identical. As for Bangor, Edwards has one more than Evans under mercantile/commercial and one less under labouring classes. We may reasonably assume that Bangor included clergymen and ministers under the professions, in contrast to Aberystwyth and Cardiff which listed them separately. Evans was not concerned with the professions for his immediate purpose and the percentages for the professions and the upper class in Table B are derived wholly from Edwards's Report.

Table B

	Aberystwyth		Cardiff	Bangor
Upper class	5.2	(1892)	6.5	2.8
Professional (including clergy and ministers)	48.5	(1892)	20.9	25.5
Commercial	30.3 34	(1892) (1872−92)	31.8	32.5
Farming	10.8 15.8	(1892) (1872−92)	8.9	13.8
Labouring class	5.2 15.2	(1892) (1872−92)	30.3	25.4

As might be anticipated, the proportion of the sons and daughters of farmers was higher at Aberystwyth and Bangor than at Cardiff. The labouring classes are more heavily represented at Cardiff and Bangor than Aberystwyth because of the proximity of the mining and quarrying industries and because of the facilities for daily travel which substantially reduced the cost of maintenance. It is likely that craftsmen, 'secure in their trades and beholden to none,'[2] in the words of Ieuan Gwynedd Jones, were included under the labouring class. In one of the more sophisticated returns to the Raleigh Committee in 1906−7 artisans and mechanics were entered separately from labourers but under the broad umbrella of 'Working Men'.[3] Again the designation 'farmer', for instance, does not enable us to distinguish between large, comfortable farmers owning their own land and the small tenant farmer extracting a bare living from the soil. In the Commons S. T. Evans declared that when he spoke of the 'commercial class' he had in mind 'the sons . . . not of the wealthy middle class, but of the class of shopkeepers and small tradesmen'. Further, by 'lumping' the three colleges together he concluded that the offspring of tradesmen, farmers and labourers numbered 1,857 out of the 2,718 students at the three colleges since their foundation and that, therefore, 'more than two-thirds of the whole' (in fact, 68.3 per cent) had come from 'the lowest walks of life'.[4] The interpretation was not at all liked by D. Rhys Jones in the *Western Mail* who believed that it was 'entirely misleading'[5] to group these classes together; only one in five students in the colleges were of working-class origin. He was near the mark, the actual figure being 22.5 per cent.

It is clear that by 1893 we have travelled some distance from Thomas Nicholas and Hugh Owen who intended the proposed university to be a middle-class institution, providing Wales with 'a professional and specialised middle class, a type of positivist Nonconformist *clerisy*'.[6] Social divisions are, of course, notoriously difficult to define with precision. A. G. Edwards, the future archbishop, was ready to tell the Aberdare committee that there were no middle classes in Wales: 'I mean what is commonly called the middle classes in England; that is to say, the wealthier tradesmen.'[7] Doubtless he was reflecting upon such families as the Rathbones and the Cottons of Liverpool or the Chamberlains of Birmingham, but we may be certain that the Davieses of Treborth and of Bodlondeb, near Bangor, and the Davieses of Llandinam would have been disconcerted at their exclusion. The proprietor of 'the Middle Class School' at Brecon cast his net far wider. The parents of the boys under his care were 'professional men, farmers, tradesmen and the better class of mechanics'.[8] The Aberdare Report itself, as we have seen, recognized that the middle and lower classes in Wales, tradesmen and farmers, were usually poorer than their counterparts in England.[9] We have also seen that Hugh Owen considered that students at Aberystwyth were mostly drawn from the middle class;[10] in speaking thus he had in mind many members of the commercial and farming classes whom S. T. Evans now consigned to 'the lowest walks of life'. Evans's purpose was to convince the Commons that the university shortly to be established was broadly based. We are witnessing a process which led O. M. Edwards some years later to speak of the 'peasants' University'.[11]

Abbreviations

Aber.   E. L. Ellis, *The University College of Wales, Aberystwyth,*
                 1872–1972 (Cardiff, University of Wales Press, 1972).

Aberd., *Rept.* *Report of the Committee appointed to inquire into the condition*
                 of Intermediate and Higher Education in Wales and
                 Monmouthshire, Vol I.

Aberd., *Evid.* Vol. II, *Minutes of Evidence and Appendices* (C.3047),
                 Parliamentary Papers, vol. XXXIII (London, HMSO, 1881).

Baner   *Baner ac Amserau Cymru.*

Bangor   J. Gwynn Williams, *The University College of North Wales:*
                 Foundations, 1884–1927 (Cardiff, University of Wales Press,
                 1985).

Cardiff   University College, Cardiff: A Centenary History,
                 1883–1983, edited by S. B. Chrimes (unpublished).

DWB   *Dictionary of Welsh Biography down to 1940*, edited by John
                 Edward Lloyd and R. T. Jenkins (London, 1959).

Haldane, *Rept.* *Report and Minutes of Evidence of the Royal Commission on*
                 the University of Wales. Appendix to First Report, Minutes of
                 Evidence, Parliamentary Papers, 1917, Vol. XII, Cd 8507
                 (London, HMSO, 1917). *Appendix to Second Report, Minutes*
                 of Evidence, Parliamentary Papers, 1917, Vol. XII, Cd 8699,
                 (London, HMSO, 1917), *Final Report, Parliamentary*
                 Papers, 1918, Vol. XIV, Cd 8991 (London, HMSO, 1918),
                 Appendix to Final Report, Parliamentary Papers, 1918, Vol.
                 XIV, Cd 8993 (London, HMSO, 1918).

Lamp.   D. T. W. Price, *A History of Saint David's, University*
                 College of Lampeter, Volume One: to 1899 (Cardiff,
                 University of Wales Press, 1977).

Man. Guard.   *Manchester Guardian.*

NLW   National Library of Wales.

NW Chron.   *North Wales Chronicle.*

NW Obs.   *North Wales Observer.*

Mins. and
Mem.   'The University for Wales Minutes and Memoranda', the formal record in manuscript of the proceedings of the Committee of the University of Wales, in the college archives of the University College of Wales, Aberystwyth.

PRO   Public Record Office.

SWDN   *South Wales Daily News.*

Trans. Cymm.   *Transactions of the Honourable Society of Cymmrodorion.*

W. Mail   *Western Mail.*

Notes

I Aspirations

1. E. V. Arnold, 'A University for Wales', *Cymru Fydd*, 1, rhif 11 (1888), 334.
2. Ibid, 335. It was said, however, of William Jones that he 'knew every language except his own'. *DWB*, 523.
3. R. R. Davies, *Conquest, Coexistence and Change, Wales 1063–1415* (Clarendon Press, Oxford; University of Wales Press, 1987), 450.
4. *Welsh Records in Paris*, edited by T. Matthews (Carmarthen, 1910), 54, 98.
5. *DWB*, 785.
6. John Hackett, *Scrinia Reserata. A Memorial offered to ... John Williams, D.D.* (London, 1693) I, 7.
7. *DWB*, 355; *Bangor*, I, n. 2; *Calendar of State Papers, Ireland, 1586–98* (London, 1877) 473–4.
8. *The Fairfax Correspondence*, edited by G. W. Johnson, ii (London, 1848), 272.
9. Ibid., 274–6.
10. Charles Webster, *The Great Instauration* (London, 1975), 239, 241.
11. 'The Correspondence of John Lewis, Glasgrug, with Richard Baxter and with Dr John Ellis, Dolgelley', edited by G. F. Nuttall, in *The Journal of the Merionethshire Historical and Record Society* ii, ii (1954). 120–34.
12. Ibid., 132, and n.1. See also John Lewis, *The Parliament Explained to Wales 1646* (reprinted by Cymdeithas Llên Cymru, Cardiff. 1907), 35, where Lewis refers to distance and expense.
13. Ibid., 131.
14. Ibid., 132.
15. Below, 70.
16. H.P. Roberts, 'Nonconformist Academies in Wales, 1662–1682', in *Trans. Cymm.*, 1928–9, 1–98.
17. *Y Ffydd Ddi-ffuant*, edited by G. J. Williams (Caerdydd, 1936), 212.
18. Theophilus Evans, *Drych y Prif Oesoedd*, edited by S. J. Evans (London, 1902), 236, 257.
19. E. Gibbon, *The Decline and Fall of the Roman Empire*, edited by J. B. Bury, iv (London, 1944), 62.
20. W. Cadwaladr Davies and W. Lewis Jones, *The University of Wales and its Constituent Colleges* (London, 1905), 29–30.
21. Glanmor Williams, *The Welsh Church from Conquest to Reformation* (Cardiff, University of Wales Press, 1962), 393.
22. Davies and Jones, op. cit., 31.
23. G. Williams, op. cit., 393.
24. Aberdare, *Evid.*, Q. 19,041.
25. *Bangor*, 36.

26. See, for example, *College by the Sea*, edited by Iwan Morgan (Aberystwyth, 1928), 4.
27. *Lamp.*, 1.
28. Ibid., 3.
29. Ibid., 5.
30. Ibid., 12–14, 21, 25.
31. Rowland Williams's letter in *The Times*, reproduced in the *Welshman*, 3 Jan. 1851. £20,000 is the sum usually given, but the total cost, including the house for the Vice-Principal, appears to have been £22,500. *Lamp.*, 33, 80–81.
32. *Lamp.*, 45.
33. *Wales: The Language, Social Conditions, Moral Character, and Religious Opinions of the People* ... (London, 1849), 315–29.
34. Ibid., 326–7.
35. Ibid., 328.
36. Idem.
37. I. Morgan, 'A Preliminary Investigation into the Origins and Development of the University Movement in Wales... in the period 1804–89' (Univ. of Wales MA thesis 1929).
38. *Lamp.*, 91.
39. Their *Reports* from 1852 to 1856, published at Caernarfon, have been bound in one volume at the National Library of Wales. They are now a rarity.
40. *Report*, 1 March 1856, 42.
41. Ibid., 18.
42. Ibid., 1 March 1856, 62; see also 1 March 1852, 27.
43. Ibid., 1 March 1853, 36.
44. H. P. Roberts, *Trans. Cymm.*, 1928–9, 1–98. See also an important article by R. Tudur Jones, 'Diwylliant Colegau Ymneilltuol y Bedwaredd Ganrif ar Bymtheg', in *Ysgrifau Beirniadol*, V (Dinbych, 1970), 112–49.
45. F. J. C. Hearnshaw, *Centenary of King's College, London 1828–1928*, (London, 1929), 41.
46. Ibid., 132.
47. The authority on Hugh Owen is B. L. Davies. See below, 236, 239.
48. For his career, see Daniel Evans, *The Life and Work of William Williams* ... (Llandysul, 1940?), a portmanteau of varied information.
49. Ibid., 309.
50. *Aber.*, 15.
51. Ieuan Gwynedd Jones, *Mid-Victorian Wales* (Cardiff, University of Wales Press, 1992), 109.
52. Darlith Flynyddol y BBC yng Nghymru, 11–12.
53. I. G. Jones, op. cit., 163.
54. Quoted by W. Gareth Evans, *Education and Female Emancipation: The Welsh Experience* (Cardiff, University of Wales Press, 1990), 50.
55. The *Welshman*, 6 Nov. 1863.
56. *A Second Letter on the present Defective State of Education in Wales* (London, 1858). Pamphlet.
57. *Education for the Welsh* (Whitefriars, 1849). Pamphlet.
58. *Y Traethodydd*, 1885, 6.
59. *Brud a Sylwydd*, Rhif 1 (1828), 15–17.
60. *Seren Gomer*, (1830), 298. He includes here a note in English.
61. Ibid., 364–5.

62. Ibid., (1831), 12–14.
63. *The Character of the Welsh as a Nation.* (London, 1841), 6.
64. *DWB*, 525.
65. Op. cit., 8.
66. *Y Drysorfa Gynnulleidfaol*, VII (1849), 61-2.
67. *Y Traethodydd* (1849), 434.
68. *Yr Haul* (1849), 127-9.
69. *Ysgolion a Cholegau yr Annibynwyr* (Llandysul, 1939), 83.
70. Above, especially 8, 14–17.
71. Printed at Carmarthen.
72. Aberdare, *Evid.*, Q. 307. The other references in this paragraph are to be found in B. T. Williams, op. cit., 19, 22, 23.
73. Above, 9.
74. R. J. Derfel, *Traethodau ac Areithiau* (Bangor, 1864), 134.
75. Above, I.

II Seed-Time

1. Aberdare, *Evid.*, Q. 307; Appendix, 865–6.
2. T. W. Moody and J. C. Beckett, *Queen's University, Belfast, 1845–1949; the History of a University*, (The Queen's University of Belfast, 1959), I, 1–137.
3. Negley Harte, *The University of London, 1836–1986* (the Athlone Press, University of London, 1986), 96, 98.
4. Aberdare, *Evid.*, 865.
5. Ibid.
6. Ibid.
7. E. Fiddes, *Chapters in the History of Owens College and of Manchester University 1851–1914* (Manchester University Press, 1937), 190.
8. Aberdare, *Evid.*, 865.
9. The *Welshman*, 18 Oct. 1972. The account was also separately printed as a pamphlet.
10. Harte, op. cit., 105.
11. Hywel Teifi Edwards, *Gŵyl Gwalia: Yr Eisteddfod Genedlaethol yn Oes Aur Victoria, 1858–1868* (Llandysul, 1980), 64.
12. David Thomas, *The University College of Aberystwyth* (London, 1863), 4.
13. *Middle and High Schools and a University for Wales* (London, 1963), 13.
14. Ibid.
15. Ibid., 14.
16. Ibid., 15.
17. Ibid., 14, 26.
18. Ibid., 25.
19. Ibid., 22.
20. Ibid., 23–4.
21. Ibid., 27.
22. Ibid.
23. Ibid., 30.
24. Ibid., 31.
25. Aberdare, *Evid.*, Q. 307.
26. Mins. and Mem., 4.

27. R. T. Jenkins and Helen Ramage, *A History of the Honourable Society of Cymmrodorion* (London, 1951), 3.
28. *Aberystwyth Observer*, 1 March 1885.
29. Jenkins and Ramage, op. cit., 174–5.
30. *DWB*, 586.
31. *DWB*, 644.
32. Jenkins and Ramage, op. cit., 180.
33. *Thomas Charles Edwards Letters*, transcribed and edited by T. I. Ellis (Aberystwyth, National Library of Wales, 1952–3), 68.
34. Above, 24. *DWB*, 942.
35. D. Thomas, *The Univ. Coll. of Aberystwith*, 2.
36. *DWB*, 251.
37. Quoted by Jenkins and Ramage, op. cit., 181.
38. *DWB*, 294–5; Jenkins and Ramage, op. cit., 179–80.
39. *A University for Wales* (London, 1864). The original address and the fuller version are to be found in Mins. and Mem., 2–3, 6–8. Both were printed together under the above title in August 1864. Substantial portions of the latter are included in W. C. Davies and W. L. Jones, *Univ. of Wales*, 79–84. My references are to the printed publication of August 1864, a copy of which is in the University College of Wales archives.
40. *A Univ. for Wales*, 5.
41. Ibid.
42. Ibid.
43. Ibid., 6.
44. Ibid., 7.
45. Ibid.
46. Ibid.
47. Ieuan Gwynedd Jones, *Explorations and Explanations* (Gwasg Gomer, 1981), 293–4. The author admirably demonstrates that politicians and reformers deliberately set out to create a middle class in Wales in order to break the social distance between the high and the low. Ibid., 292. See appendix 2.
48. Hywel Teifi Edwards, *Gŵyl Gwalia*, 77.
49. Nicholas, *Univ. of Wales*, 3–4.
50. Ibid., 4.
51. Ibid., 3, 4.
52. *A University of Wales* (Dowlais and London, 1863), 14.
53. *Lamp.*, 93–4.
54. Ibid., 93.
55. Mins. and Mem., 9.
56. Ibid., 18.
57. The *Welshman*, 28 Feb. 1868, quoted in *Lamp.*, 114, n.14.
58. *Lamp.*, 115, n. 19.
59. Ibid., 120.
60. G. Hartwell Jones, *A Celt Looks at the World* (Cardiff, 1946), 51; K. O. Morgan, *Wales in British Politics*, 33.
61. Mins. and Mem., 194.
62 Ibid., 195.
63. Lamp., 116; D. Emrys Evans, *The University of Wales* (Cardiff, University of Wales Press, 1953), 107.
64. St David's Univ. Coll. Archives, Basil Jones to Joshua Hughes, 14 Oct. 1869,

f.5. The Revd D. T. W. Price very kindly sent me a xerox copy of this lengthy letter.

65. Ibid.
66. The *Welshman*, 18 Oct., 1872.
· 67. Above, 22
68. Both articles are included in *Traethodau Llenyddol* (Wrexham, no date), from which I quote.
69. Ibid., 187.
70. Ibid.
71. Ibid., 188.
72. Ibid.
73. Ibid., 189 '. . . y pethau hyny sydd o'r golwg wrth wraidd pob celfyddyd.'
74. *Univ. of Wales*, 13.
75. Quoted by Alun Llywelyn-Williams, 'Lewis Edwards ac Urddas Cenedl', *Ysgrifau Beirniadol*, II (Dinbych, 1966), 118.
76. T. C. Edwards, *Bywyd a Llythyrau . . . Lewis Edwards* (Liverpool, 1901), 446.
77. Trebor Lloyd Evans, *Lewis Edwards, ei fywyd a'i waith* (Abertawe, 1967), 116.
78. Edwards, op. cit., 368.
79. Ibid.
80. Ibid., 549–50.
81. *Baner*, 18 March 1863.
82. Ibid., 3 June 1868.
83. B. L. Davies, 'The Aspirations and Innovations of a Dissenting Radical; Henry Richard and Education in Wales' (Univ. of Wales M. Phil. thesis 1990), 129.
84. *Y Cronicl*, xxxvii, 349–51. 'Nid teg trethi y tlodion/I brentisio boneddigion/ Dylent dalu am ddysgeidiaeth/Fel rhai ereill am brentisiaeth.' I am indebted to Dr B. L. Davies for this reference.
85. *Aber*, 26 and note 46. See also Bangor (Yale) MS, no 42, 29 March 1871. Hanmer did somewhat relent thereafter, Hanmer to Roger Edwards, 3 April 1871. Ibid.
86. Richard Griffith, *Y Gohebydd, Cofiant* (Dinbych, 1906), 121.
87. The *Welshman*, 18 Oct. 1872.
88. Griffith, op. cit., 120.
89. Below, 51.
90. Y Cymmrodor III (1880), 133.
91. Ibid., *Y Beirniad* (1865), 175.
92. H. P. Roberts, 'Nonconformist Academies. . .', in *Trans. Cymm.* (1928–9), 73; G. D. Owen, *Ysgolion a Colegau yr Annibynwyr*, 127.
93. Mins. and Mem., 116; *Baner*, 20 Ion. 1969.
94. John Davies, 'Early Recollections', in *The Welsh Gazette*, 22 June 1899.
95. *Baner*, 20 Ion. 1869.
96. Mins. and Mem., 22.
97. Ibid.
98. Ibid., 43.
99. Ibid.
100. *Seren Cymru*, 22 Hydref 1869, 4.
101. Mins. and Mem., 44.
102. Nicholas to Henry Richard, NLW MSS. 5505C, f. 29, 21 Oct. 1972. He added on 24 Oct. that 'I have not met such depth of scheming and duplicity in my short course of life as I have seen in the noble H.O.'. Ibid. 30a.
103. *T. C. Edwards Letters*, 9.

104. D. Thomas, *The Univ. Coll. of Aberystwith*, 2.
105. Jan. to March, *Baner* 1869.
106. David Thomas, op. cit., 5. He added: 'Until the University College of Aberystwith raises a monument in grateful memory of his services, its honourableness will not be stainless.'
107. There is a good account by Iolo W. Williams, 'Coleg y Gnoll', *Y Gwyddonydd*, IV (1966), 152–7.
108. *Aber.*, 20.
109. Mins. and Mem., 52.
110. Ibid.
111. Ibid., 49.
112. *Bangor*, 19–20.
113. Mins. and Mem., 39.
114. Ibid., 40.
115. Ivor Thomas, *Top Sawyer: A Biography of David Davies of Llandinam* (London, 1938), 40–1, and passim.
116. Henry-Russell Hitchcock, *Architecture: Nineteenth and Twentieth Centuries.* Pelican History of Art (London, 1958), 187. An authoritative survey of the architecture of the College is being prepared by Emeritus Professor R. J. Webster.
117. Ibid.
118. *Baner*, 3 Chwefror 1969.
119. *Report, Royal Commission in University Education in Wales*, Cd 8991, (HMSO London, 1918), 4. It goes on to speak of 'the calculated audacity' of the founders. Ibid.
120. Mins. and Mem., 53.
121. Below, 166
122. K. O. Morgan, *Wales in British Politics*, 36.
123. Baner, 31 Rhagfyr, 1868. There is a copy of the meeting on 25 February in the University College of Wales archives under 1869.
124. Mins. and Mem., 93.
125. Fiddes, *Owens College ...*, 190–1; Mins and Mem., 101.
126. Mins. and Mem., 125–6.
127. Ibid., 131.
128. Fiddes, op. cit., 191.
129. Mins. and Mem., 154–6; Brit. Library, Gladstone Papers, Additional MSS 44616, f. 82.
130. Mins. and Mem., 158–9.
131. Ibid., 159.
132. Ibid., 125.
133. Ibid., 170.
134. *Baner*, Ion.–Mawrth, 1969.
135. Ibid., 24 Chwef. 1969.
136. Mins. and Mem., 114.
137. Ibid., 178–9.
138. Lewis to William, 5 Oct. 1857, *The Letters of Lewis, Richard, William and John Morris*, edited by J. H. Davies, II (Aberystwyth, 1909), 27.
139. Mins. and Mem., 180.
140. Ibid., 186.
141. Ibid.

III   The First College

1. The *Welshman*, 18 Oct. 1872.
2. Ibid.
3. The *Cambrian News*, 13 Oct. 1876. Quoted in *Aber*, 54.
4. *Aber.*, 43–4.
5. *The Letters of the Rt. Hon. Lord Aberdare*, edited anon (Oxford, 1902), ɪ, 13.
6. Ibid., ɪɪ, 303; Aberdare to A. J. Mundella, 21 April 1884, A. J. Mundella Papers,
    University of Sheffield Library, 6P/17/14/1; 'The Bard and the Cuckoo', Wales
    ɪ, No.1 (1894), 22; *Cymru Fu II*, No.1 (1894), 115. 'Lord Aberdare, of course,
    we regard as a Welshman', said O. M. Edwards in *Wales*, ɪ (1894), 40.
7. *Letters of . . . Aberdare*, ɪɪ, 31–2.
8. Ibid. I, 203–4.
9. *DWB*, 197–8.
10. *T. C. Edwards Letters*, 16.
11. Ibid.
12. Ibid.
13. Ibid., 22.
14. *Coll. by the Sea*, 68.
15. Ibid.
16. There is a copy in the College Library, Bangor.
17. *T. C. Edwards Letters*, 36.
18. Thomas Gwynn Jones, *Cofiant Thomas Gee* (Dinbych, 1913), 381–391.
19. *T.C. Edwards Letters*, 55.
20. Ibid., 93.
21. Ibid., 72–3.
22. *Coll. by the Sea*, 72. Cardiff wisely appointed him Head of the Music
    Department. He was there from 1882–1903.
23. Ibid., W. R. Evans in *Coll. by the Sea*, 55. He was grandfather to Bangor's third
    Principal.
24. T. T. Lucius Morgan, *Rupert of Glamorgan* (Dolgellau, no date), 62; *Aber.*, 48.
25. *Coll. by the Sea*, 71.
26. W. J. Gruffydd, *Owen Morgan Edwards, Cofiant* ɪ (Aberystwyth, 1937), 182.
27. *T. C. Edwards Letters*, 40.
28. *Coll. by the Sea*, 71.
29. Gruffydd, op.cit., 178.
30. T. T. Lucius Morgan, *The Rev. J. Gwynoro Davies*, Barmouth (Llandysul, 1941),
    10.
31. T. F. Roberts in *Y Traethodydd* (1899), 273.
32. Thomas Jones, *A Theme with Variations* (Gregynog Press, 1933), 129.
33. *T. C. Edwards Letters*, 154.
34. Ibid., 158.
35. Ibid., 163.
36. *Aber.*, 60.
37. *T. C. Edwards Letters*, 162.
38. *Aber.*, 34–5.
39. The *Welshman*, 18 Oct. 1872.
40. B. L. Davies, 'Hugh Owen . . .', 435, 446–8, and passim, chapter 7.
41. Aberd. *Evid.*, Q 307.
42. *T. C. Edwards Letters*, 95.

43. Ibid., 77.
44. See, for example, the College Calendars for 1878–79 and 1879–80.
45. Below, 183
46. 'Report of a Deputation', 27 July 1875, Minutes of the Court of Governors, 35–8.
47. Ibid.
48. *Aber.*, 52.
49. 'Report of a Deputation'.
50. Ibid.
51. *Coll. by the Sea*, 347.
52. *T. C. Edwards Letters*, 144, 146.
53. Hugh Owen to Henry Richard, 19 Nov. 1878, NLW, Richard MSS, 5505B; also *Coll. by the Sea.*, 347.
54. Ibid.,
55. Quoted by B. L. Davies, 'Hugh Owen . . .', 558, who gives a good account of the Association, 556–64.
56. Ibid., 564; *Bangor*, 208–9.
57. H. T. Edwards to Henry Richard, 6 March 1879, NLW, Richard MSS, 5503B.
58. *Hansard's Parliamentary Debates*, 3rd Series, ccxlvii, 1142–1183. There is a fuller account, separately published, under the title *Higher Education in Wales* (London, 1879), from which the following passages are taken.
59. Ibid., 4–5.
60. Ibid., 7.
61. Ibid., 57.
62. Ibid., 24.
63. Ibid., 46.
64. K. O. Morgan, *Wales in Brit. Politics*, 48.
65. *Higher Education in Wales*, 39.
66. Ibid., 39, 41.
67. Ibid., 42.
68. Ibid.
69. Ibid., 53.
70. Ibid., 52.
71. Ibid., 60.
72. Ibid., 60–1.
73. K. O. Morgan, op. cit., 48.
74. *Higher Educ.*, 37.

IV The Aberdare Report

1. Aberd., *Evid.*, Q. 3677.
2. Ben Bowen Thomas, 'The Establishment of the "Aberdare" Departmental Committee, 1880: some Letters and Notes', *Bulletin of the Board of Celtic Studies*, part IV (May 1962), 319.
3. B. L. Davies, 'Hugh Owen . . .', 480; *W. Mail*, 15 March 1882. Special Reprint.
4. B. B. Thomas, op. cit., 322.
5. Ibid., 324.
6. Ibid.
7. Ibid., 327; *Aber*, 69.

8. B. B. Thomas, op. cit., 329, 331.
9. B. L. Davies, op. cit., 490; *Baner*, 25 Awst 1880.
10. Thomas, op. cit., 334.
11. Aberd., *Rept.*, xvii.
12. Aberd., *Evid.*, Q 307.
13. Ibid.
14. Ibid., Q. 320.
15. Ibid., Q. 9562. Four at London, if the first M.B. is included.
16. Aberd., *Rept.*, xviii.
17. Aberd., *Evid.*, Q. 333.
18. Ibid.
19. Ibid., Q. 2366.
20. Ibid., Q. 2737.
21. Ibid., Q. 13713.
22. Ibid., Q. 18160.
23. Ibid., Q. 3761.
24. Aberdare to Gladstone, 18 Dec. 1882, Brit. Library, Gladstone Papers, Additional MSS, 44,087, f. 136.
25. Aberd., *Evid.*, Q. 15,544.
26. Ibid., 9801.
27. Ibid., Q. 334.
28. Aberd., *Rept.*, xvii.
29. Aberd., *Evid.*, Q. 9914.
30. Ibid., Q. 7727.
31. Ibid., QQ. 7683, 17,538.
32. Ibid., QQ. 19,544, 19,556.
33. Ibid., Q. 9973.
34. Ibid. Q. 336. The remarks concerning love of education and an inadequate appreciation of higher education were made by W. J. Craig, QQ. 7698, 7731. The statistics concerning attendance are in Appdx. 19 to Aberd., *Evid.*
35. Ibid., Q. 3293.
36. QQ. 11,184, 11,191, 11,306.
37. Q. 923.
38. QQ. 18,204, 18,163, 18,204, 18,363.
39. Aberd., *Rept.*, xxxi.
40. Aberd., *Evid.*, Q. 10,524.
41. Ibid., 15,004.
42. Ibid., Q. 17,928.
43. Ibid., Q. 3737.
44. Ibid., Q. 12,667.
45. Ibid., Q. 279.
46. Ibid., QQ. 4087–8.
47. Ibid., Q. 7118.
48. Ibid., Q. 17,873.
49. Ibid., Q. 325.
50. Aberd., *Rept.*, xxxii.
51. Aberd., *Evid.*, 19044.
52. Aberd., *Rept.*, xxxiii.
53. Aberd., *Evid.*, Q. 8586.
54. Ibid., Q. 2989.

55. Ibid., Q. 2351.
56. Ibid., Q. 18,311.
57. Ibid., Q. 13,961.
58. Ibid., 18,229.
59. Quoted by Don Carleton, *A University for Bristol* (University of Bristol Press, 1986), 14.
60. Aberd., *Evid.*, Q. 7182.
61. Ibid., Q. 1380.
62. Ibid., Q. 11,700.
63. Quoted by J. Simmons, *New University* (Leicester University Press, 1958), 28.
64. Aberd., *Evid.*, Q. 9617.
65. Ibid., QQ. 3758, 3761−5.
66. Ibid., Q. 14,716.
67. T. W. Moody and J. C. Beckett, *Queen's, Belfast, 1845−1949: The History of a University*, I, 286−7; T. W. Moody, 'The Irish University Question of the Nineteenth Century', *History*, XLIII, No. 147 (1958), 102.
68. Aberd., *Evid.*, QQ. 344, 360.
69. Ibid., Q. 13,961; above, 72.
70. Ibid.
71. Aberdare to Gladstone, 18 Dec. 1882, Brit. Lib., Gladstone Papers, Additional MSS 44087, ff. 131−2; Aberdare to Mundella, 21 April 1884, Sheffield University Library, Mundella Papers, 6P/17/14/1.
72. *Lamp.*, 144.
73. H. D. Harper, Principal, Jesus College, Oxford and T. McKenny Hughes, Aberd., *Evid.*, QQ. 958, 1334.
74. Aberd., *Evid.*, QQ. 17425, 3778.
75. Ibid., Q. 8453.
76. Ibid., Q. 10,588.
77. Ibid., QQ. 10,387, 15,986, 3760. Below, 167
78. Ibid., 11,391−3.
79. Ibid., Q. 2349.
80. Ibid., Q. 13,961.
81. Ibid., QQ. 6491, 6421.
82. Aberd., *Rept.*, xx.
83. Ibid., xxi.
84. Ibid.
85. Ibid., xxiii.
86. Ibid., lxv.
87. Ibid.
88. Ibid., lxvi.
89. Ibid.
90. Ibid., lxvi−lxvii, for the above quotations.
91. Ibid., lxvii−lxviii.
92. Ibid., lvxii.
93. Aberd., *Evid.*, QQ. 19,038−9; 17,572.
94. Ibid., Q. 424.
95. Aberd., *Rept.*, xlviii.
96. Ibid., xlix.
97. *Aber.*, 66.
98. Above, 63.

99. *Aber.*, 69, note 11.

100. Aberd., *Evid.*, Q. 10,669.

101. Above, 64.

102. Below, 104.

103. J. R. Webster, 'The Place of Welsh Secondary Education in Welsh Society, 1800–1918' (University of Wales Ph.D. thesis, 1959), 330. This study remains indispensable.

104. H. H. Bellot, *University College, London, 1826–1926* (London, 1929), 252.

105. F. J. C. Hearnshaw, *Centenary History of King's College, London* (London, 1929), 206.

106. M. J. Tuke, *History of Bedford College for Women* (London, 1939), 95, 100.

107. H. B. Charlton, *Portrait of a University, 1851–1951* (Manchester University Press, 1951), 57.

108. Ibid., 57.

109. Aberd., *Evid.*, Q. 18,203, despite a net income from the John Owens legacy of £96,654.

110. D. Carleton, *A University for Bristol*, 7. Simmons, *New University*, 39.

111. Aberd., *Evid.*, Q. 9608. The charters of 1852 and 1865 were, of course, in addition to the original Charter of 1828.

112. *University of Wales*, 31.

113. Aberd., *Rept.*, lxviii.

114. Ibid.; above, 78–80

115. *Aber.*, 108. The view of J. R. Webster deserves close attention. The Report, he says, 'has all the marks of having been hurriedly put together. Indeed, occasionally it is difficult to determine exactly what the committee is recommending'. 'The Welsh Intermediate Act of 1889', *The Welsh History Review*, 4, No. 3 (1969), 274.

116. *Lamp.*, 143.

117. T. C. Edwards to Ellis Edwards, 11 June 1884, NLW Yale, Llanbedrog MSS, 83.

118. Aberd., *Evid.*, 19645.

119. Ibid., Q. 7538. Morris, in fact, made many contributions to Welsh historical studies, not least as editor of *Archaeologia Cambrensis*, 1907 to 1918 *DWB*, 666.

120. Ibid., 7910 (Wrongly numbered as 9710).

121. Ibid., QQ. 8152, 8154.

122. Ibid., Q. 2604.

123. 'Adroddiad Pwyllgor y Llywodraeth ar Addysg yng Nghymru', 473–496.

124. Aberd., *Evid.*, QQ. 15,025, 15,035–8.

125. *Bangor*, 61, 63.

126. Aberd., *Evid.*, Q. 17,474.

127. Below, 180–82

128. Aberd., *Rept.*, xlvi. For the remainder of the paragraph, see xlvi–1.

129. Ibid., xlvii.

130. J. R. Webster, op. cit., 274.

131. Aberd., *Evid.*, appendix 2,867.

132. Below, 85.

133. B. L. Davies, 'Hugh Owen . . .', 524, where he speaks of the *Western Mail's* 'general vendetta against Aberystwyth'.

134. Above, 85.

135. *Y Traethodydd* (1881), 491 ('yn felltith ac yn rheg'); see also, 474.

136. T. I. Ellis, *The Development of Higher Education in Wales* (Wrexham, 1935), 54. For further tributes, see W. Gareth Evans, 'The Aberdare Report and Education in Wales, 1881', *Welsh History Review*, 11, No 2 (1982), 150. This article presents a balanced survey of all aspects of the Report, whereas in this chapter attention has necessarily concentrated upon higher education.

V The Three Colleges

1. *Cardiff*, 17. For the purpose of this volume, two essays in *Fountains of Praise* are full of insights. See below, 235–6. For an important analysis, see Neil Evans, 'The Welsh Victorian City: the Middle Class and Civic and National Consciousness in Cardiff, 1850–1914', *Welsh History Review*, 12, No. 3 (1985), 350–87.
2. Lewis Fry to Lord President of Council, 21 Jan. 1883, PRO, ED 119/74.
3. See especially, Gwynedd O. Pierce, *Fountains of Praise*, 25–40.
4. Undated memorandum, PRO, ED 119/74.
5. Ibid., also undated.
6. Ibid., Award of Arbitrators, 14 March 1883.
7. *Cardiff*, 21.
8. Above, 78.
9. *Exchequer Proceedings concerning Wales in tempore James I*, compiled by T.I. Jeffreys Jones (Cardiff University Press, 1955), 91.
10. Above, 67.
11. A. J. Mundella to W. E. Gladstone, 31 May 1882, Brit. Lib., Gladstone Papers, Additional MSS 44258, ff. 186–7.
12. *Hansard's Parliamentary Debates, 3rd Ser.,* 272, 1541–2.
13. *NW Chron.*, 25 Oct. 1884.
14. Ibid.
15. *Bangor*, 26–31.
16. Draft Copy, 9 Dec. 1882, PRO, ED 119/71.
17. *Bangor*, 35.
18. Ibid., 41. For the battle of the sites, see ibid., 35–45.
19. 'Minutes of the Arbitrators', f.11, PRO, ED 119/70.
20. *NW Chron.*, 5 May 1883, 25 Oct. 1884; *Bangor*, 48.
21. Aberdare to Mundella, 27 August 1883, University of Sheffield Library, Mundella Papers, 6P/16/33.
22. Gladstone to Mundella, 27 April 1880, Brit. Library, Gladstone Papers, Additional MSS 44258, ff. 163, 165–6.
23. *Hansard's Parliamentary Debates, 3rd ser.,* 285, 1612.
24. *T. C. Edwards Letters*, 183.
25. *Aber.*, 76 n. 42.
26. *NW Chron.*, 27 Jan. 1883.
27. *Coll. by the Sea*, 24.
28. *Bangor*, 32. Lewis Morris had been in the van of a scheme to convert the college into a high school or college for girls. It is fully dealt with by W. Gareth Evans. *Education and Female Emancipation*, (University of Wales Press, Cardiff 1990), 212–16.
29. Ibid., 50.
30. Ibid.
31. Ibid., 51.

32. Ibid., 50.
33. K. V. Jones, *Life of John Viriamu Jones*, 133.
34. Aberdare to Richard, 19 Aug. 1883, NLW, Richard MSS 5505C.
35. T. H. Waterhouse to Lord Pres. of Council, 8 Nov. 1883, PRO, ED 119/68.
36. *Bangor*, 32. 1 Jan. 1884, PRO, ED 119/68.
37. Burgesses of Swansea to Gladstone, 15 Feb. 1884, PRO, ED 199/68.
38. David Williams, Llandyrnog, extract from *The Aberystwyth Observer and
     Merioneth News*, 3 Feb. 1883, PRO, ED 119/68.
39. *NW Chron.*, 25 Oct. 1884.
40. Ibid.
41. *Aber.*, 82.
42. *NW Chron.*, 25 Oct., 1884.
43. 11 July 1994, NLW, J. H. Davies (Univ. Coll. of Wales) MSS, quoted in *Aber.*,
     83, n. 67.
44. *SWDN*, 17 March, extract in PRO, ED 119/68.
45. *Aber.*, 81.
46. There is an excellent assessment by K.O. Morgan, ' "The member for Wales":
     Stuart Rendel (1834–1913)' in *Trans. Cymm.* (1884), 149–71.
47. K. V. Jones, *Viriamu Jones*, 132.
48. *Aber.*, 81.
49. 'Memorial of the University College of Wales . . .' to Gladstone, 14 March
     1884, *Univ. Coll. of Wales Reports* (1863–91); B. L. Davies, 'Henry Richard',
     172.
50. *Hansard's Parliamentary Debates, 3rd. ser.*, 285, 1606.
51. Mundella to Richard, 17 March 1884, NLW., Richard MSS 5505C; *Aber.*,
     81–2.
52. Richard to Rendel, 16 July 1885, NLW, Rendel MSS 19454D.
53. *Coll. by the Sea*, 352; *Aber.*, 87.
54. T. I. Ellis, *Higher Education in Wales*, 64.
55. *W. Mail*, 10 July 1885, quoted in *Aber.*, 87.
56. *Aber.*, 87.
57. *Coll. by the Sea*, 40.
58. *W. Mail*, 10 July 20 July 1922. Lloyd George was speaking at the Jubilee
     celebrations at Aberystwyth, where he received the freedom of the town.
59. *Aber.*, 88.
60. Bangor MSS 5540, f. 213.
61. Ibid., ff. 218–19.
62. Ibid., f. 250.
63. Ibid., ff.261, 276.
64. Thomas Jones, *A Theme with Variations*, 121.
65. Ibid.
66. *Coll. by the Sea*, 90.
67. *Bangor*, 237.
68. *Aber.*, 106.
69. *Coll. by the Sea*, 124–5; *Aber.*, 103.
70. *Aber.*, 104–5.
71. Ibid., 105–6; *Bangor*, 86, 167, 181.
72. Above, 98
73. K. O. Morgan, *Trans. Cymm.*, (1984), 170.
74. *T. C. Edwards Letters*, 247.

75. Bangor Council Minutes, 130, 134; *Bangor*, 112, n. 146.
76. T. C. Edwards to T. Gee, 8 March 1889, NLW., Gee MSS, 8305D.
77. Ibid.
78. *Bangor*, 112.
79. David Williams, *Thomas Francis Roberts* (University of Wales Press, 1961), 29.
80. Lewis Morris to Education Office, Whitehall, 2 Oct. 1884, ED 199/68.
81. W. J. Gruffydd, *Owen Morgan Edwards, Cofiant, Cyfrol 1*, 1858–1883, 177.
82. Ibid. It was in fact an undenominational college where the teaching of theology was forbidden.
83. *W. Mail*, 20 July 1922.
84. *A Theme with Variations*, 126.
85. David Williams, op. cit., passim.
86. Thomas Jones, *Leeks and Daffodils* (Newtown, 1942), 50.
87. D. Williams, op. cit., 46.
88. K. V. Jones, *Viriamu Jones*, 12.
89. Ibid., 111.
90. *A History of Modern Wales* (London, 1950), 277.
91. E. B. Poulton, *John Viriamu Jones and other Oxford Memories* (London, 1911), 37.
92. Undated petition of April 1886 to the Lord Pres. of the Council, PRO, ED 119/74; also a letter from Viriamu Jones, undated, May 1886 to Earl Spencer.
93. J. B. Thomas, 'The Origins of Teacher Training at University College, Cardiff', *Journal of Educational Administration and History*, xvi No. 1 (1984), 11.
94. Ibid., 12.
95. K. V. Jones, *Viriamu Jones*, 124.
96. A. H. Trow and D. J. A. Brown, *A Short History of the University College of South Wales and Monmouthshire* (Cardiff, 1933), 79.
97. *DWB*, 423.
98. *W. Mail*, 25 Oct. 1883.
99. *Cardiff*, 25.
100. Ibid., 43.
101. Ibid., 44. These are the words of Lewis Williams.
102. Above, 14. There is a very good brief account by B. James in *Cardiff*, 413. See also *DWB*, 899.
103. *Bangor*, 102.
104. *Sir Harry Reichel, 1856–1931* (University of Wales Press, 1934), edited by J. E. Lloyd; *Bangor*, 63–72.
105. *Bangor*, 71.
106. Ibid.
107. *Univ. of Wales*, 53.
108. *Bangor*, 61.
109. Ibid., 299.
110. Ibid., 87.
111. *NW Chron.*, 25 Oct. 1884.
112. Bangor, 104–11.
113. Ibid., 97–8.
114. N. Harte, *Univ. of London*, 130.
115. O. M. Edwards, Report, 22–37. Below, 138–43
116. Memorial by Cardiff's Council elect to Lord Carlingford, 4 July 1883, PRO, ED 119/74. Carlingford saw the force of Cardiff's argument. By charter, however,

there were to be nominees of five universities, in the first instance, on the Cardiff Court.

117. *Cardiff*, 63, n. 8; The Rector of Llanbedr to Powis, 14 Oct 1883, Bangor, Univ. Coll. Library, Powis MSS, 4428; *Bangor*, 54.
118. Edwards, Report, 23.
119. Ibid.

VI The Struggle for the Charter

1.   K. V. Jones, *Viriamu Jones*, 112–13.
2.   Poulton, *John Viriamu Jones . . .*, 305. The principals and senates of the three colleges had met at Shrewsbury in 1886, the first of a series of conferences, to plan the campaign. K. V. Jones, op. cit., 223.
3.   Poulton, op. cit., 305–6.
4.   *The Future Development of the Welsh Educational System*, being the proceedings of the Cymmrodorion Section of the National Eisteddfod of 1887, was reprinted from the *Schoolmaster* (London, 1887). There is a copy at the National Library of Wales.
5.   Ibid., 4.
6.   K. V. Jones, op. cit., 376.
7.   Ibid., 375.
8.   Ibid.
9.   *The Future Development of the Welsh Educational System*, 5.
10. K. V. Jones, op. cit., 379. *The Proceedings of the Welsh Educational Conference* at Shrewsbury on 5 and 6 Jan. 1888 was reprinted, with additions, from the *Oswestry Advertizer and Border Counties Herald* of 11 Jan. 1888. There is a copy at the National Library.
11. G. A. Jones, 'Isambard Owen'. See below, 236, 239; Harry R. Reichel, *Henry Isambard Owen*, reprinted from the *Welsh Outlook*, March, 1927.
12. *University of Wales Court Minutes*, May, 1909, appdx 11, 3.
13. Quoted by G. A. Jones, op. cit., 141.
14. K. V. Jones, *Viriamu Jones*, 228.
15. *Oswestry Advertizer*, 21 March 1888.
16. *Transactions of the Liverpool Welsh National Society* (1886–87), 17.
17. *Oswestry Advertizer*, 21 March 1888.
18. K. V. Jones, *Viriamu Jones*, 228.
19. Ibid., 229, 380; *Bangor*, 113.
20. *SWDN*, 18 July 1888, for an account of the meeting; *Aber.*, 109.
21. Poulton, *Viriamu Jones*, 306.
22. 'The Proposed University for Wales' in *Y Cymmrodor*, XI (1892), 225.
23. *Trans. of the Liverpool Welsh Nat. Soc.* (1886–7), 16.
24. *W. Mail*, 16 March 1888. Above, 118
25. *Oswestry Advertizer*, 18 Nov. 1891.
26. *Bangor*, 113; Univ. Coll. of N. Wales *Court Minutes*, 41; Davies and Jones, *Univ. of Wales*, 183.
27. *A University for Wales*, report of the conference at Shrewsbury, 11 Nov. 1891 (Caernarfon, 1891).
28. Ibid., 9.
29. Above, 70
30. *A Univ. for Wales*, op. cit. (1891), 10.
31. Ibid., 5. In Davies and Jones, *Univ. of Wales*, 184–5 these appear as seven

resolutions, whereas the first resolution of the conference incorporated a rider which should not be listed as a separate resolution.

32. *A Univ. for Wales* (1891), 8.
33. Ibid., 10.
34. Ibid., 11. A rider was added to ensure that there should be four representatives elected by each of the constituent bodies. The Conference itself was to consist of fourteen members from each of the Colleges and twenty-two from the Intermediate Education Committee.
35. I. Owen, *The University of Wales and its Educational Theory* (London, 1898), 1; *W. Mail*, 7 Jan. 1893.
36. Reichel, *Univ. of Wales Court Mins.*, May, 1909, Appendix 11, 2.
37. *Liverpool Mercury*, 7 April 1892.
38. W. A. Darbishire.
39. R. W. Phillips.
40. Ibid.
41. See, for example, *The Development of Theological Education in the University of Wales* (Bangor, 1917), 5.
42. *Mins., Univ. Court*, May 1909, appdx. 2, 2.
43. Humphreys Owen to his wife, 5 July 1888. NLW, Glansevern MSS, not numbered. Above, 119.
44. *Trans. Liverpool Welsh Nat. Soc.*, (1886–7), 14, 16.
45. Negley Harte, *The University of London, 1836–1896*, 93.
46. W. J. Gruffydd, *Owen Morgan Edwards*, 181.
47. T. Hudson Williams, *The Magazine of the University College of North Wales*, Dec. 1927, 7.
48. *Trans. Liverpool Welsh Nat. Soc.* (1886–7), 16.
49. K. V. Jones, *Viriamu Jones*, 18.
50. *Royal Commission on University Education in London, First Report* Cd. 6717 (London, HMSO, 1913), 36.
51. Ben Bowen Thomas, 'R. D. Roberts and Adult Education' in B. B. Thomas (ed.), *Harlech Studies* (Cardiff, University of Wales Press), 1–35. *DWB*, 878.
52. Memorandum, 3. There is a copy in the Library of the Univ. Coll. of N. Wales; the file is entitled 'Proposed University for Wales, 1891–5'.
53. Ibid.
54. *Suggested Outline of a Charter to constitute the University of Wales* (London, 1892). A Copy was in due course sent to the Privy Council, PRO, PC1/2922, no. 4.
55. In the section dealing with clause 2.
56. These are conveniently summarized by O. M. Edwards in his report, 9–10. For the Report, see below, 138–43.
57. *W. Mail*, 6 Dec. 1892.
58. *Man. Guard.*, 24 April 1893.
59. *Royal Commission in University Education in Wales, Appendix to First Report*, Cd 8507 (London, HMSO, 1917), 252.
60. D. D. Williams, *Thomas Charles Edwards* (Liverpool, 1921), 38.
61. Above, n. 54.
62. *Caernarvon and Denbigh Herald*, 20 Jan. 1893; *SWDN*, 6 April 1893.
63. B. B. McDowell and D. A. Webb, *Trinity College Dublin, 1592–1952* (London, 1982), 115–16. Determining considerations were the comparatively tender age of the undergraduates, fear for their safety in a large city and college expenses.
64. *SWDN*, 6 April 1893.

65. Ibid.
66. *Eighth Annual Report of the National Eisteddfod Association* . . . 1888 (1889), 53.
67. *Cambrian News*, 13 Jan. 1893; see also the *Carnarvon and Denbigh Herald*, 13 Jan. 1893 for an attack on the 'three-legged University'.
68. *W. Mail*, 6 Dec. 1892.
69. *SWDN*, 11 March 1893.
70. *The Oswestry and Border Counties Advertizer*, 28 Dec. 1992.
71. *W. Mail*, 25 Nov. 1892; *Cambrian News*, 31 March 1893, for report of a meeting of Aberystwyth's Court of Governors at Haverfordwest, where Professor Genese stated that the Aberystwyth Senate was 'strongly of the opinion that it was desirable in case of disagreement that responsibility for the issue should rest with external examiners'. The colleges would then be above suspicion.
72. The *Report of proceedings of the General Conference*, which included representatives of the Joint Education Committees and which met on 6 Jan. 1893, were printed at Cardiff. I have used the copy in Univ. of Wales Registry, H1130, 203. See below, 237–8. Cadwaladr Davies's remarks and those of Aberdare are on page 29 of the printed version of the proceedings.
73. *Report of Proceedings of the General Conference*, 30.
74. *Prif Benau Gweithred neu Freinlen* (Dinbych, no date).
75. This volume was printed at Manchester in 1892. The quotation is on page 19.
76. *W. Mail*, 1 May 1893.
77. Quoted in *W. Mail*, 4 Sept. 1893.
78. The petitions of Caernarfon County Council, the inhabitants of Aberystwyth and Glamorgan County Council are at the PRO, PC1/2922, nos. 3, 6 and 7 respectively.
79. 3 March 1893.
80. *W. Mail*, 2 Dec.
81. *SWDN*, 11 March 1893.
82. Ibid.
83. K. V. Jones, *Viriamu Jones*, 226.
84. There is a copy marked 'Private and Confidential' in the College Library at Bangor in the File entitled 'Proposed University for Wales, 1891–5'.
85. Ibid.
86. *The Univ. of Wales*, 45.
87. Below, 151. Isambard held the office of Senior Deacon as a freemason in the Province of Bristol, Bangor MSS, 6358.
88. The petition of Lewis Morris, PRO, PC 1/2922, no. 9.
89. Ibid.
90. The matter was admirably presented by A.W. Hughes, then lecturer on anatomy at Edinburgh (later as professor, at Cardiff) in the *12th Annual Report of the National Eisteddfod Association, together with the Transactions of the Cymmrodorion Section of the Rhyl National Eisteddfod, 1892*, (1893), 49–54.
91. Above, 17.
92. *SWDN*, 9 March 1893.
93. Isambard Owen to Ivor James, 13 Dec. 1892, Univ. of Wales Registry, H1130, 117. Isambard said that 'many people were unpleasantly surprised at the celerity with which the Victoria supplemental Charter was slipped through'. It is important to note that when the Victoria University was established there were 'three full medical schools under its wing'. He added that 'it is *certain* that graduating powers in Medicine cannot be got till there is a well established School of Medicine in Wales'.

94. W. Cadwaladr Davies to T. Ellis, 24 Oct. 1891, NLW, Ellis MSS 3345.
95. The authors were John Rhys and Brynmor Jones. Rendel to T. F. Roberts, 18, 27, 25 Oct. 1906, NLW MSS, 19442E, ff. 140–1. On this issue, see also, Rendel to T. F. Roberts, 3 Sept. 1903, NLW MSS 19441E, f. 68.
96. NLW MSS 19442E, f. 142.
97. K. V. Jones, *Viriamu Jones*, 235 note; Alun Llywelyn-Williams, *Crwydro Arfon* (Llandybïe, 1959), 123–4; *Baner*, 14, 21 Medi 1892.
98. A. H. D. Acland to W. E. Gladstone, 6 Nov. 1892, Brit. Library, Additional MSS 44516, f. 250.
99. Gladstone to Acland, 7 Nov. 1892, ibid., 44549, f. 36b.
100. Acland to Gladstone, 20 Oct. 1892, ibid., 44516, ff. 192–5.
101. Above, 55.
102. O. M. Edwards to Ellis Edwards, 18 Feb. 1889, NLW MSS, N. Lewis, Bournemouth.
103. T. I. Ellis, *The Development of Higher Education in Wales*, 97. Subsequent writers have been dependent on the author's references on page 96–102. He did not indicate the provenance of the report, but it has now come to light and is to be published by the National Library of Wales, to whom it was recently presented by Mrs Mari Ellis. Tom Ellis later indicated that Edward's report was not in government hands in April when he wrote to Edwards, NLW, O.M. Edwards MSS. 18 April 1993.
104. *Hansard's Parliamentary Debates, 4th ser.,* xvi, 1448.
105. *Cambrian News,* 18 Nov. 1892.
106. Below, 194–5.
107. Edwards, Report, 3.
108. Ibid., 9.
109. Ibid., 21.
110. Ibid., 20. Reichel and several others would have preferred to have had a small council, in addition to the court, but on this issue Tom Ellis and Isambard won the day. H. R. Reichel, *Isambard Owen,* reprinted from the *Welsh Outlook,* March 1927, 8.
111. Ibid., 22–3.
112. Ibid., 24, 33, 39.
113. Ibid., 40.
114. Ibid., 44.
115. Ibid., 46.
116. Ibid., 46.
117. Ibid., 46. Edwards added that 'the feeling in favour of a University is exceedingly strong among all classes, and there is practical unanimity as to the form it should take.'
118. Ibid.
119. Ibid.
120. Ibid.
121. Ibid.
122. Ibid., 48.
123. Ibid., 49.
124. Ibid., 18; Armytage, *Civic Universities,* 245.
125. K. V. Jones, *Viriamu Jones,* 233, note 1.
126. *W. Mail.,* 1 May 1893.
127. PRO, PC 1/2922, nos. 4 and 5.

128. Ibid., no. 5.
129. *Hansard's Parliamentary Debates, 4th ser.*, XVI, 1323.
130. PRO, PC 1/2922, no. 5, for the reply of the University soliciors to the Lampeter petition.
131. *Parliamentary Debates, 4th ser.*, XVI, 1320–1.
132. G. Hartwell Jones, *A Celt Looks at the World*, ed. by Wyn Griffith (Cardiff, 1946), 58.
133. Aberdare to Ivor James, 28 Dec., 1892, Univ. of Wales Registry, H1130, 163.
134. Aberdare to Isambard Owen, 20 Aug. 1893, Bangor MSS 6239.
135. Same to same, 27 Aug. 1893.
136. Above, 111. Edwards's view was that 'this small matter' had received far too much attention. Within a short time it would be totally forgotten. *Cymru*, V (1893), 243.
137. *Parliamentary Debates, 4th ser.*, XVI, 1310.
138. Ibid., 1310–38.
139. Ibid., 1334–5.
140. Ibid., 1442–56, especially 1442–7, 1451–3. For Evans's statistics see appendix 2, above, 202–5.
141. 3 Sept. 1893. Bangor MSS 6239.
142. *Parliamentary Debates, 4th ser.*, XVI 1317.
143. W. Cadwaladr Davies to Tom Ellis. 24 Oct. 1891, NLW, Ellis MS 3345; John Owen to Ellis, 4 June 1890, Ibid., 1595. It is evident that the Tory Anglican, G. T. Kenyon, was perturbed that Owen appeared to be severing himself from 'the National Aspirations', adding that 'I have always regarded you as holding these same views as myself. Will you think me unkind or inquisitorial if I ask you if a change has come over the spirit of your dream?' Eluned E. Owen, *The Early Life of Bishop Owen* (Llandysul, 1958), 165.
144. For a somewhat waspish dispute on the subject between Owen and Osborne Morgan, see Bangor MSS 6236. It is evident that Owen's interpretation of the College Charter Act, 1871, 34 and 35 Victoria c.63 sec. 2 was correct. I am indebted to Lord Cledwyn and to Mr D. L. Jones, the Librarian of the House of Lords, for elucidating the procedure of the time. Mr Jones also kindly sent me a copy of the relevant section of Erskine May, *A Treatise on the Law, Privileges, Proceedings and Usage of Parliament*, 10th edition (London, 1893), 514.
145. *Parliamentary Debates, 4th ser.*, XVI, 1334, for Cranbrook's remarks. John Owen's recollections of these events are to be found in *Y Llan and Church News*, 8 Medi 1922, 'Atgofion gan Esgob Tyddewi'. See also, Eluned Owen, op. cit., chapter XIV.
146. Poulton, *Viriamu Jones*, 309.
147. K. V. Jones, *Viriamu Jones*, 233.

VII   The Royal Charter

1. Clause I.
2. Harte, *The Univ. of London*, 143, 150, 154: *Aber*, 110.
3. See appendix I, 201.
4. Above, 135–7. It is worth noting his initial recommendation, under the heading 'Language':

It will be provided –

That all public notices or published acts, ceremonial or otherwise, of the University Chamber, shall be delivered in Welsh and English both, and in Welsh first.

That in all such publications the title of the Chamber or of the University, if set forth, shall be set forth in Welsh and English both, the Welsh being placed first.

That the same shall apply to similar publications by any Cabinet or Delegacy of the Chamber.

That the proceedings of the University Chamber shall for the present be conducted, and its records kept, in English.

That any Cabinet, Delegacy, or Committee appointed by the University Chamber may, by consent of all the members of such Cabinet, Delegacy, or Committee, conduct the whole or any part of its deliberations in Welsh; but that its records shall for the present be kept, and its communications to the Chamber made, in English.

That the above regulations shall apply equally to the Guild of Graduates.

5. Above, 5
6. NLW, Mostyn MSS 158, f. 491 a.
7. I owe the above references to Mr Gareth Bowen, editor of *Geiriadur Prifysgol Cymru*, who allowed me to see the relevant slips: Rosier Smith, *Theatr du Mond* (London, 1615), 116; William Williams, Pantycelyn, *Pantheologia* (Caerfyrddin, 1762), 525; Thomas Wiliems, Dictionary, NLW, Peniarth MS 228, I, 1604–7(7); James Owen, *Trugaredd a Barn* (Llundain, 1715), 95.
8. 'University Education in Wales' , *Trans. Cymm.*, 1917–1918 (1919), 145–6.
9. Haldane, *Rept., Appdx to 1st Rept.*, 259.
10. Ibid. 219, for the evidence of Brynmor Jones.
11. Ibid, 259.
12. Fiddes, *Owens College*, 121.
13. Isambard Owen, *The University of Wales and its Educational Theory*, 24.
14. Cl. v.
15. Cl. vi.
16. Cl. xi (8); Statute xiv.
17. Cl. ix.
18. I. Owen, op. cit., 23.
19. Ibid.
20. Cl. 84 of the Charter as adopted by the Shrewsbury Conference in Jan. 1893.
21. Ibid., Cl. 90.
22. Cl. xiii (3).
23. Cl. xvi (3) of the Supplemental Charter of 1920.
24. D. Emrys Evans, *Univ. of Wales*, 42.
25. Quoted by Rhys Roberts, *British Universities*, 26.
26. Owen, *Univ. of Wales and its Educational Theory*, 13.
27. Above, 172–3. See also the Memorandum prepared by Isambard Owen to guide the Conference of Jan. 1893, page 2. There is a copy in Univ Reg. MSS, H1130, 170–73. It is dated 28 Dec. 1892.Cl. xv (2) deals with the authority of external examiners.
28. Cl. xviii (l).
29. Haldane, *Rept., Appdx to Ist Rept.*, 259.
30. Cl. xvii (2).

31. J. R. Webster, 'The Welsh Intermediate Act of 1889', *Welsh History Review*, 4, No. 3, 284, 290, 291.
32. Haldane, *Rept., Appdx to Ist Rept*, 258.
33. Isambard Owen firmly attributed the blame for limiting the powers of the University Court to the Treasury. Ibid., Q. 4734. There is an important retrospective section on this subject in Haldane, *Final Rept.*, 15. D. Emrys Evans, 'The Welsh Intermediate Education Act, 1889', *Trans Cymm.* 1939 (1940), especially 102–8.
34. Strictly speaking, the Shrewsbury Conference consisted of the Joint Education Committee of Glamorgan and the county governing bodies. T. I. Ellis, *Higher Education*, 107.
35. Haldane, *Rept.*, 15.
36. Cl. xvii (4).
37. K. V. Jones, *Viriamu Jones*, 231.
38. Cl. xiv (3); Statute xxiii (9).
39. Cl. xxiv, 1920 Supplemental Charter.
40. My italics; Cl. xiv 7 (b).
41. See, for example, the concern expressed by the Revd Thomas Hughes on 4 Jan. 1893 to the promoters of the Charter, Univ. Reg. MSS H 1130. Later, the North Wales Wesleyan Education Committee met at the Brunswick Schoolroom, Rhyl, to protest. *NW Obs.*, 17 Feb. 1893.
42. Cl. xiv (6); Stat., xxiii (9).
43. Stat. xx, and note.
44. Stat. xxi (2).
45. Owen's Memorandum, Dec. 1893, 3. See note 27 above.
46. Ibid., 4.
47. See successive Calendars of the University, where members are listed.
48. There is an extract in Univ. Reg. MSS H 1130, f. 147.
49. Quoted in *SWDN*, 9 April 1894.
50. *NW Obs.*, 20 Oct. 1893. For the meeting with Gladstone, SWDN, 17 Feb. 1894.
51. *SWDN*, 17 Feb. 1894.
52. *W. Mail*, 13 Jan. 1894.
53. Ibid.
54. *Wales*, I (1894), 27.
55. Ibid., 39–40; Rosebery's remarks are in *Man. Guard.*, 7 April 1894.
56. *College by the Sea*, 99.
57. William Rathbone to Ellis Edwards, 27 March 1895, NLW, Calvinistic Methodist Archives, MSS 15900.
58. K. V. Jones, *Viriamu Jones*, 226.
59. Ibid., 244.
60. Aberdare to Isambard Owen, 1 Feb. 1895, Bangor MSS 6239. He expressed similar sentiments to his daughter, 11 Feb. 1895, *Letters*, 11, 337.
61. These are the words of O. M. Edwards, *Wales* I, (1894), 39.
62. *Univ. Court Mins.*, July 1895, 4.
63. *Aber.*, 118–19.
64. *Univ. Court Mins.*, Feb. 1896, 7–8. Aberystwyth said that it was the only collegiate centre which possessed 'magnificent buildings'. Ibid.
65. Humphreys Owen, quoted in *Aber.*, 119.
66. Humphreys Owen to his wife, 8 June 1896. NLW, Glansevern MSS, not numbered.

67. *Aber.*, 119.
68. Rendel to T.F. Roberts, 25 Oct. 1906, NLW MSS 19442E, f.142.
69. Llywelyn Williams in *Young Wales*, II (1896), 172.
70. There is a lengthy account in *SWDN*, 27 June 1896, from which I have freely drawn.
71. Geraint H. Jenkins, *The University of Wales: an Illustrated History* (Cardiff, University of Wales Press, 1993), 11.
72. Quoted in *Aber.*, 120.
73. Davies and Jones, *Univ. of Wales*, 197.
74. Ibid., 198.
75. *SWDN*, 27 June 1896.
76. *Daily Chronicle*, 27 June 1896.
77. Ibid.; *Wales*, III (1896), 339.
78. *Young Wales*, II (1896), Welsh University Celebration Number, 121.
79. *W. Mail*, 24 June 1896.
80. Brynmor Jones's views were given many years later in Hald., *Rept.*, *Appdx to lst Rept.*, 220.
81. *Wales*, III (1896), 338.
82. *Univ. Court Mins.*, July 1917, 148.

VIII   The Achievement

1. W. J. Gruffydd, *Prifysgol Newydd i Gymru* (Caerdydd?, 1945), 3.
2. David Williams, *Modern Wales*, 277.
3. E. J. Somerset, *The Birth of a University: a Passage in the Life of C. A. Sonnenschein* (Oxford, 1934), 8, 15–16.
4. Aberd., *Evid.*, 865.
5. Above, 28: *Address*, Aug. 1864, 5.
6. Thomas Nicholas in *Baner*, 7 Mawrth 1867.
7. *Cambrian News*, 18 Nov. 1892.
8. Mins. and Mem., 152, 155.
9. Above, 78.
10. Above, 83–4.
11. *SWDN.*, 11 March 1893.
12. Ibid. Ellis is referring here to his address to Aberystwyth students in 1897.
13. Aberd., *Evid.*, Q. 9614.
14. *SWDN*, 11 March 1893.
15. *Bangor*, I; above, 3.
16. Lawrence Stone, *The University in Society*, 1 (Princeton University Press: London, Oxford University Press, 1975), 35–7.
17. R. B. McDowell and D. A. Webb, *Trinity College, Dublin. 1592–1952*, 324.
18. The *Welshman*, 3 Jan. 1851, reprint of an article in *The Times*; Iwan Morgan 'A Priminary Investigation into the Origins and Development of the University Movement in Wales . . .' (MA, University of Wales, 1929), 29.
19. Basil Jones to Joshua Hughes, 14 Oct. 1869, St David's Univ. Coll. Archives, f. 5.
20. *W. Mail*, 20 July 1922.
21. *SWDN*, 11 March 1893.
22. 'Historical and comparative remarks of the federal principle in higher education', *History of Education*, 16, No. 3 (1987) 151–2.

23. Quoted by Sheldon Rothblatt, ibid., 162.
24. Id.
25. *Hansard's Parliamentary Debates*, 3rd ser., 247, 1181.
26. Haldane, *Rept., Appdx to First Rept.*, 258.
27. Edwards, Report, 47.
28. *W. Mail*, 22 Sept. 1891. Reichel thought that 'a ludicrously exaggerated value' was attached to a pass degree throughout the Principality. Ibid.
29. *T. C. Edwards Letters*, 97.
30. *Diaries*, edited by Michael Davie (Penguin Books, 1979) 201.
31. *T. C. Edwards Letters*, 37.
32. *Bangor*, 187.
33. Somerset, *The Birth of a University*, 15–16.
34. *Aber.*, 258–9.
35. Hartwell Jones, *A Celt Looks at the World*, 44.
36. *T. C. Edwards Letters*, 97.
37. Above, 100.
38. Univ. of Wales Reg. Archives, H 1130; *Aber.*, 103.
39. I am grateful to Dr Eirug Davies, Cambridge, Massachusetts for sending me a copy of *Cyfaill yr Aelwyd*, XII, Rhif 3 (1891), where T. L. James, Postmaster General to President Garfield, spoke of the free atmosphere and of the educational opportunities to Welshmen in America. See particularly the articles by Bob Owen on 'Cymru ac Addysg America' in *Lleufer*, 13 (1957) and 14 (1958).
40. *Higher Education in Wales*, 1 July 1879, 12. Special report, see above, 215, note 55.
41. 'Anne c.11, 1706, art. xxv, secn. 2, 'for the greater security' of the Protestant religion. Glanmor Williams, *Recovery, Reorientation, and Reformation, c.1415–1642* (Clarendon Press, Oxford, University of Wales Press, Cardiff, 1987), 268. He adds that constitutionally this was not an innovation.
42. Aberd., *Evid.*, Q. 17,911.
43. Lingen to Hugh Owen, 19 Nov. 1878, *Coll. by the Sea*, 347. Above, 59.
44. Lewis Fry to Mundella, 21 Jan. 1883, PRO, ED 119/74.
45. *W. Mail*, 13 Jan. 1894.
46. K. O. Morgan, *Rebirth of a Nation, Wales, 1880–1980* (Clarendon Press: University of Wales Press, 1981), 27.
47. Morgan, *Wales in British Politics*, 65–6.
48. W. Cadwaladr Davies to Dilys Davies, 20 April 1886. Bangor Archives, Dilys Glynne Jones Papers.
49. *Carnarvon and Denbigh Herald*, 15 April 1887.
50. Morgan, *Wales in British Politics*, 101.
51. *Carnarvon and Denbigh Herald*, 18 April 1890.
52. *Oswestry Advertizer*, 18 Nov. 1891.
53. Edwards, Report, 46–7; John Morris Jones, *Caniadau* (Rhydychen, 1907), 70.
54. *Hansard's Parliamentary Debates*, 3rd ser., 336, 154.
55. 'Une Université en Galles', *Revue Critique*, 11 Juin, 1883, 476.
56. Univ. Coll., Aberystwyth, Archives, for report of meeting at the Westminster Palace Hotel, London, 25 Feb. 1869.
57. Morgan, *Wales in British Politics*, 42, n.5.
58. David D.V. Jones, *Crime in Nineteenth-century Wales* (Cardiff, University of Wales Press, 1992), 241.
59. 'The influence of the Celt in the Making of Britain', *Speeches and Addresses* (Wrexham, 1912), 90.

60. *Welsh Pictures, drawn with Pen and Pencil*, edited Richard Lovett (London, 1892), 135. I am indebted to Mr Donald Moore for this reference.
61. Ellis, op. cit., 90; Aberd., *Evid.*, Q. 8555.
62. *Patriotism, Local and Imperial* (Bangor, 1921), 10.
63. Id.
64. *Man. Guard.*, 31 Oct. 1896.
65. Gwyn A. Williams, *Fountains of Praise*, 5–6; *Bangor*, 226.
66. *Higher Education*, 1879 debate, special report, 23.
67. K. V. Jones, *Viriamu Jones*, 374.
68. I. G. Jones, *Explorations and Explanations* (Llandysul, 1981), 293.
69. H. T. Edwards, *Wales and the Welsh Church* (London, 1889), 160.
70. *W. Mail*, 19 July 1922; Thomas Jones, *A Theme with Variations*, 114–36.
71. Henry Jones, *Old Memories* (London, 1922), 29–30.
72. Thomas Charles Edwards, *Bywyd a Llythyrau ... Lewis Edwards*, 157.
73. *Eighth Annual Report of the National Eisteddfod Association ... 1888* (1889), 53.
74. Edwards, Report, 27. The numbers at Glasgow and Edinburgh are taken from Lewis Morris, op. cit., 57. See note 73 above.
75. 'Prifysgol i Gymru', *Y Geninen*, x, Rhif 1 (1892), 1.
76. Aberd., *Evid.*, Q. 15,180.
77. Ibid., Q. 15,011.
78. Ibid., Q. 14,494–7.
79. K. V. Jones, *Viriamu Jones*, 162.
80. Aber., *Evid.*, Q. 2730.
81. Ibid., Q. 2731. The full version of the letter dated 23 Oct. 1880 and quoted by W.C. Davies to the Aberdare Committee is at NLW, Thomas Jones MSS, U, vol. 2.
82. *Bangor*, 14.
83. K.V. Jones, *Viriamu Jones*, 374.
84. *Hansard's Parliamentary Debates*, 3rd ser., 336 (1889), 140.
85. Ibid., 3rd ser., 247, 1173.
86. Percy Watkins, *A Welshman Remembers*, (Cardiff, 1944), 58.
87. 'Wales as a University', *Young Wales*, iii (1896), Welsh University Celebration Number, 130.
88. This extract was quoted in a prominent position for many years in Aberystwyth College Calendars.
89. *SWDN.*, 17 Feb. 1894. This is Acland's description of his office. He was in fact a Vice-President of the Committee of Council on Education and thus a forerunner of Presidents, Ministers and Secretaries of State.
90. Quoted by Watkins, op. cit., 58.
91. John Rhys to Ellis, 21 July 1897, NLW, Ellis MSS 1754.
92. *Hansard's Parliamentary Debates*, 3rd ser., 247, 1183.
93. Report of speech by Morris in the *Liverpool Daily Post*, 30 Nov., 1881 in PRO, ED 119/71.
94. B.L. Davies, 'Hugh Owen ...', 630.
95. Gwyn A. Williams, 'Hugh Owen', *Pioneers of Welsh Education* (Swansea, 1962), 69, 77. This is a most stimulating article.
96. K. V. Jones, *Viriamu Jones*, 382.
97. Report of a Deputation, 27 July, 1875, Mins. of the Court of Governors, 35–8; *Oswestry Advertizer*, 21 March 1888.
98. Aberdare to Richard, 11 Feb. 1884, Glamorgan Record Office, D/D Br 162/11.

99. Aberdare to Isambard Owen, 29 March 1893, Bangor MSS 6239.
100. K. V. Jones, *Viriamu Jones*, 382–3.
101. Univ. of Wales Court Mins., 1908, appdx. 11, 1; *Isambard Owen* (1927), 1.
102. Above, 153–5.
103. Poulton, *Viriamu Jones*, 309.
104. *Coll. by the Sea*, 98.
105. Univ. Registry Archives, H 1130, Report of Proceedings of the Second University Conference, 6 Jan. 1893, at Shrewsbury, 3.
106. No attempt was made to implement Clause xvii (4), which gave the Court powers of inspection of teaching facilities at the colleges. Above, 142, 154–5, 156.
107. H. Reichel, *The Development of Theological Education in the University of Wales* (Bangor, 1917), 4–5.
108. C. Grant Robertson, *The British Universities*, 12.
109. Harte, *The University of London ...*, 148.
110. 1 March 1893.
111. Aberd., *Evid.*, QQ. 2604, 15,380.
112. Armytage, *Civic Universities*, 225.
113. Haldane, *Rept., Appdx to 1st Report*, 259.
114. Aberd., *Evid.*, Q. 16,666–7.
115. Above, 66.
116. Glanmor Williams, 'Wales – the Cultural Bases of Nineteenth and Twentieth century Nationalism' in *The Roots of Nationalism: Studies in Northern Europe*, edited by Rosalind Mitchison (Edinburgh, 1980) 122–3.
117. *Caneuon a Cherddi* (Bangor, 1906), 51. The translation is by Caradog Prichard.
118. See appendix 2.
119. Ibid.
120. *Wales*, 1 (1894), 39. 'The People's University would have been a better rendering "Prifysgol y Werin."' Below 199.
121. W. A. L. Vincent, *The State and School Education 1640–1660 in England and Wales* (London, 1950), 33–4.
122. John Eyton Williams, *Man. Guard.*, 1 Nov. 1907.
123. David Williams, *T. F. Roberts*, 18.
124. *W. Mail*, 13 Jan. 1894.
125. K. V. Jones, *Viriamu Jones*, 151.
126. *The Times*, 7 April 1894.
127. *Education and Female Emancipation: The Welsh Experience*, 211.
128. Above, 16.
129. *The University of Wales in its Relation to the National Life* (Liverpool, 1894), 4–5.
130. *Wales* iv (1898), 275. For some time after the proposal to found a university in Wales was bruited he was not enthusiastic. 'I felt there was no great need for one.' Univ. Coll. of Wales *Magazine*, xv No. 1 (1892), 1.
131. K. V. Jones, *Viriamu Jones*, 385.
132. Ellis to O. M. Edwards, 12 Feb. 1890.
133. *Baner*, 20 Mai 1863: 'nid oes gymmaint o ysbryd codi yn uchel yn y Cymry mewn colegau tramor a phe baent yn eu coleg eu hunain'.
134. *12th Annual Report of the National Eisteddfod Association* 1893, 52.
135. *Trans. of the Liverpool Welsh National Society* (1886–7), 5–6.
136. Aberd., *Evid.*, Q. 7548.
137. Trans., *Liverpool Welsh Nat. Soc.* (1886–7), 21–2.
138. 'Prifysgol Deheudir Cymru a Mynwy' in *Y Gweithiwr Cymreig*, 16 Mawrth

1887. I owe this reference to Professor Hywel Teifi Edwards. Note the loose use, common enough, of 'Prifysgol' to describe a college.

139. *The Oxford Companion to the Literature of Wales*, compiled and edited by Meic Stephens (Oxford University Press, 1986), 109.
140. Above, 14; Somerset, *The Birth of a University*, 14.
141. Armytage, *Civic Universities*, 215–16.
142. Above, 2.
143. Grant Robertson, *The British Universities*, 2.
144. Viriamu Jones to Earl Spencer, no date May 1886, PRO, ED 119/74.
145. Above, 142, 158.; Edwards, Report, 49.
146. *British Universities*, 30.
147. Quoted by Grant Robertson, *The British Universities*, 41.
148. *Higher Education, Report* (1963), Cmnd. 5154, 6.
149. 'Os rhydd y Llywodraeth ddysgeidiaeth i'r Cymry,/Hwy ddeuant yn ganadl [sic] fasnachol cyn hir'. *Yr Haul* (1849), 128.
150. *NW Chron.*, 25 Oct. 1884.
151. Armytage, *Civic Universities*, Chapter 11.
152. Edwards, Report, 29; *Cardiff*, 46–7. For Agriculture, see *Bangor*, 82–8, 167–73.
153. *Education for the Welsh* (Whitefriars, 1849), 8.
154. 14 Nov. 1971.
155. Above, 52.
156. R. T. Jenkins, *Edrych yn Ôl* (Llundain, 1968), 131.
157. *Bangor*, 216–17.
158. Ibid.; *NW Obs.*, 28 Dec. 1888.
159. Ibid.; Univ. Court Mins., July 1926, 149–50.
160. *W. Mail*, 25 Oct. 1983.
161. Newman, *Prose and Poetry*, edited G. Tillotson (London, 1957), 521–2.
162. See, for example, Lewis Edwards, *Traethodau Llenyddol*, 31. O. M. Edward's *Cymru* had on its title page the words 'I Godi'r Hen Wlad yn ei Hol'.
163. 'The Proposed University for Wales', *Y Cymmrodor*, XI (1892), 245.
164. Rendel to T. F. Roberts, 18 Oct. 1906. NLW MSS 9442E, ff. 140–1.
165. *Y Geninen*, x, Rhif 1 (1892), 1; *Young Wales*, 11 (1896), Celebration number, 148–50.
166. *Y Cymmrodor*, XI (1892), 245.
167. *Man. Guard.*, 31 Oct. 1895.
168. 'The People's University in Retrospect' in *The University of Wales Review* (The Welsh Anvil), Summer 1964, 7.

Appendix 1

1. This authoritative description is taken, with one brief addition, from W. C. Davies and W. L. Jones, *The University of Wales*, 213.

Appendix 2

1. For the Report, see above, and for his statistics, 25, 32, 35. For S. T. Evans, see above 55; *Hansard's Parliamentary Debates*, 4th series, XVI, 1893, 1452.

2. *Explorations and Explanations,* 293.
3. *Bangor,* 289.
4. *Hansard,* id., 1452.
5. 1 Sept. 1893.
6. Gwyn A. Williams, *Pioneers of Welsh Education,* 70. Above, 211, note 47.
7. Aberd., *Evid.,* Q. 11319.
8. Ibid., Q. 16491.
9. Above, 81; Aberd., *Rept.,* xlviii.
10. Above, 68.
11. Above, 160.

A Note on Sources

This note is selective, not exhaustive. Its purpose is to indicate the nature of the sources examined. For example, it does not include references to government publications which are separately noted in the table of abbreviations or in footnotes.

University and College Histories

It is not proposed here to list the histories of British universities which have been consulted, but it is necessary to refer the reader to an admirable survey, entitled *Work in Progress and Publications* edited by John M. Fletcher, begun in 1978 and published for the International Commission for the History of Universities. A most useful source for the Welsh movement is part three of Iwan Morgan's thesis (see below) where he included 567 works, not all of which are significant but a few of which would almost certainly have eluded me. Of journals, *the History of Education*, the *Welsh History Review*, *Transactions of the Honourable Society of Cymmrodorion* and *Cof Cenedl* have important articles.

W. Cadwaladr Davies and W. Lewis Jones wrote from first-hand knowledge *The University of Wales and its Colleges* (London, 1905), which should not be neglected. D. Emrys Evans, *The University of Wales* (Cardiff, University of Wales Press, 1953) is a crisp, judicious survey of the first sixty years which repays careful reading. The first in Wales to examine sources relating to his College at the Public Record Office and at the National Library was E. L. Ellis, *The University College of Wales, Aberystwyth, 1872–1972* (Cardiff, University of Wales Press, 1972). He skilfully placed its history, at times turbulent, within a broad perspective. I am deeply indebted to this admirable work. The unpublished 'University College, Cardiff: A Centenary History, 1883–1983', edited by S. B. Chrimes has many merits, not least of which is the substantial section devoted to departmental histories. No Welsh college has a comparable survey. The editor's treatment of sources at Cardiff is clear and authoritative. The need to place the college in its social setting was much in the mind of Gwyn Jones and Michael Quinn, editors of *Fountains of Praise, University College Cardiff 1883–1983* (The University College Cardiff Press, 1983): amongst those who wrote notable essays were Gwyn A. Williams ('Odd

Man Out') and Gwynedd O. Pierce ('The Welsh Connection'). Both volumes are valuable in different ways. The first may be likened to a cask of wholesome home-brewed ale; the second to a draught of champagne. Lampeter is fortunate in its historian, D. W. T. Price; I have frequently consulted his illuminating first volume, *A History of Saint David's University College Lampeter, Volume One: to 1898* (Cardiff, University of Wales Press, 1977). The early history of Bangor was written by J. Gwynn Williams, *The University College of North Wales: Foundations 1884–1927* (Cardiff, University of Wales Press, 1985). Most germane to the history of the colleges is the rewarding study by W. Gareth Evans, *Education and Female Emancipation: the Welsh Experience, 1847–1914* (Cardiff, University of Wales Press, 1990), who has a thoughtful chapter on women in the university colleges during this period.

Of those prominent in the university movement pride of place must be given to *Hugh Owen*. It is greatly to be hoped that B. L. Davies's slim volume *Hugh Owen* (Cardiff, University of Wales Press, 1977) is but the forerunner to a substantial biography based upon his scholarly thesis, noted below. Daniel Evans, *The Life and Work of William Williams M. P.* (Llandyssul, ?1940) is scarcely a systematic biography but the author assembled much miscellaneous information. There are two biographies of David Davies, Llandinam: Ivor Thomas *Tom Sawyer* (London, 1938) and Herbert Williams, *Davies the Ocean: Railway King and Coal Tycoon* (Cardiff, University of Wales Press, 1991) which incorporates new material. *The Letters of the Rt. Hon. Lord Aberdare*, edited anonymously (Oxford, 1902), in two volumes, cast light on Aberdare's approach to people and his reaction to events. There are good portraits of Isambard Owen by Gwilym A. Jones and of Henry Richard by B. L. Davies in their theses. Though frequently regarded as a gadfly in the years preceding the Charter, R. D. Roberts receives sympathetic, balanced treatment in 'R. D. Roberts and Adult Education' by Ben Bowen Thomas in *Harlech Studies: Essays presented to Dr. Thomas Jones, C. H.* (Cardiff, University of Wales Press, 1938). Eleanor Rathbone's study of *William Rathbone* (London, 1905) deals with her father's long service to higher education in Wales as well as in Liverpool. John Griffith's career was recalled by his brother Richard Griffith in *Y Gohebydd, Cofiant . . .* (Dinbych, 1905); pages 118–39 are directly relevant to the early struggles, as also are several passages in Thomas Gwynn Jones, *Cofiant Thomas Gee* (Dinbych, 1913). T. I. Ellis wrote two volumes on his father; *Thomas Edward Ellis, Cofiant I* (Liverpool, 1944) deals fully with his student days at Aberystwyth. W. J. Gruffydd's *Owen Morgan Edwards, Cofiant, I, 1858–1883* (Aberystwyth, 1937) was at once regarded as a classic upon publication; it includes a penetrating chapter on Edwards at Aberystwyth. The continuing challenge to write the sequel is formidable. In the meantime there is an outstanding interpretation by Hazel Davies,

O. M. Edwards in the Writers of Wales series (Cardiff, University of Wales Press, 1988).

Of the four principals (to 1893), Viriamu Jones has been best served. Several years after his death his wife, Katharine Viriamu Jones wrote the felicitous and wide-ranging, *Life of John Viriamu Jones* (London, 1915). Neville Masterman reassessed his career in *J. Viriamu Jones, 1856–1901, pioneer of the modern university: an appreciation* (Llandybïe, 1957). E. B. Poulton, *John Viriamu Jones and other Oxford Memories* (London, 1911) is a collection of essays; those by Isambard Owen and H. R. Reichel are especially rewarding. D. D. Williams's *Thomas Charles Edwards* (Liverpool, 1921) is still useful, if a little dated. David Williams's lecture on *Thomas Francis Roberts* (Cardiff, University of Wales Press, 1961) is a shrewd, just estimate, spiced with touches of irony. It is a serious deprivation that H. R. Reichel was unable to fulfil his apparent intention to write the memoirs of which we have but a foretaste in *Sir Harry Reichel 1856–1931*, edited by J. E. Lloyd (Cardiff, University of Wales Press, 1934), a volume consisting largely of tributes, amply deserved, by those who knew him well.

There is a very good study of the young John Morris-Jones by J. E. Caerwyn Williams, 'Syr John Morris-Jones; y Cefndir a'r Cyfnod Cynnar', Rhan 1 a 2, in *Trans. Cymm.* 1965 and 1966. Henry Jones's time at Aberystwyth and Bangor are sketched by H.J.W. Hetherington, *The Life and Letters of Sir Henry Jones* (London, 1924). Jones himself recalled his early years in *Old Memories* (London, 1922). Others who wrote lively accounts in their declining days were G. Hartwell Jones, *A Celt Looks at the World* (Cardiff, 1946), R. T. Jenkins, *Edrych yn Ôl* (Llundain, 1968) and Thomas Richards, *Atgofion Cardi* (Aberystwyth, 1960) particularly section two. Thomas Jones ('T. J.') included several memorable pieces on Aberystwyth in such volumes as *Leeks and Daffodils* (Newtown, 1942) and *A Theme with Variations* (Gregynog Press, 1933); his whole career is treated in masterly fashion by E. L. Ellis, *T. J.: A Life of Dr Thomas Jones C. H.* (Cardiff, University of Wales Press, 1992). There are, of course, many recollections in college magazines and in various other publications. By far the best compendium produced by any of the colleges is *University College of Wales Aberystwyth: The College by the Sea*, edited by Iwan Morgan (Aberystwyth, 1928). It is full of fascinating sidelights which might otherwise have vanished into oblivion.

Manuscript Sources

In general the University Registry is not as rich a repository as might have been expected. Owing to the services of Huw Flynn Hughes as archivist it was possible to reach this conclusion without undue delay. There is, however, one volume of first importance for the present purpose consisting of many original letters, newspaper cuttings, the proceedings of the University Conference and much else deemed significant by Ivor James, a joint secretary of the Conference and Cardiff's registrar; it is referred to as Vol II, University of Wales, H 1130.

Aberystwyth has an impressive collection of college archives, most of them in Yr Hen Goleg and some in the Sir Hugh Owen Library. Those in Yr Hen Goleg include the 'Minutes and Memoranda' of the first University Committee, a wholly indispensable mine of information. One or two items available in 1970 cannot now be retrieved despite the best efforts of the staff; they must therefore be regarded as 'lost'. The printed University College of Wales Reports (1863–91) is a case in point. Fortunately, wherever necessary, I have been able to rely on Dr Ellis's thorough investigations. It is also curious that whereas Bangor and Cardiff have an unbroken set of volumes of newspaper cuttings extending, respectively, to the 1920s and 1930s, such volumes are but thinly represented at Aberystwyth. The oldest college has, however, conspicuous advantages, for its first two principals carefully preserved their correspondence. T. I. Ellis deserves lasting gratitude for transcribing and editing the Thomas Charles Edwards Letters (Aberystwyth, the National Library of Wales, 1952–3). The letters of Thomas Francis Roberts are at Yr Hen Goleg and have been put in some semblance of order. At Bangor it is evident that H. R. Reichel did not take steps to ensure the survival of communications sent to him ex officio; ironically, letters written by him have been preserved by several of his correspondents. Of the three colleges Bangor has undoubtedly the greatest number of individual deposits relating to the early years, the Powis Papers being especially fruitful. The College, too, was exceedingly fortunate in receiving the papers of Isambard Owen, invaluable to an understanding of the struggle for the Charter. Cardiff's records were put in excellent order by Susan Bellamy, who derived much encouragement from the late S. B. Chrimes. Recent developments, however, have not facilitated enquiries. It seems that Viriamu Jones's papers, which formed the basis of his wife's biography, were not placed in the care of the College. Only at Bangor is there a full-time professional archivist in charge of college collections.

At the National Library there are rich deposits essential to an understanding of the development of higher education in Wales. The papers of J. H. Davies, O. M. Edwards, T. E. Ellis, Thomas Gee, Humphreys-Owen and Stuart Rendel are but examples of sources which illumine significant matters which might otherwise have remained in undisturbed obscurity. At the Public Record Office the files of the Department of Education and Science deal with the Colleges and the University during a formative period (ED/119). The following papers have also been consulted; those of Gladstone at the British

Library, of A. J. Mundella at Sheffield University Library and of William Rathbone at the Liverpool University Library.

Theses

Bryn L. Davies, 'An Assessment of the Contribution of Sir Hugh Owen to Education in Wales' (Univ. of Wales Ph.D. thesis 1971).

Bryn L. Davies, 'The Aspirations and Innovations of a Dissenting Radical: Henry Richard and Education in Wales' (Univ. of Wales M. Phil thesis 1990).

Gwilym Arthur Jones, 'The Life and Work of Sir Isambard Owen (1850–1927)' (Univ. of Wales MA thesis 1983).

Iwan J. Morgan, 'A Preliminary Investigation into the Origins and Development of the University Movement in Wales ... in the period 1804–90' (Univ. of Wales MA thesis 1929).

Robert Owen Roberts, 'The Life and work of Dean Henry Thomas Edwards (1837–1884)' (Univ. of Wales thesis 1977).

Roger J. Webster, 'The place of Secondary Education in Welsh Society, 1800–1918' (Univ. of Wales Ph.D. thesis 1959).

Index

William Hazledine
Pioneering Ironmaster

William Hazledine
Pioneering Ironmaster

Andrew Pattison

BREWIN BOOKS

BREWIN BOOKS
56 Alcester Road,
Studley,
Warwickshire,
B80 7LG
www.brewinbooks.com

Published by Brewin Books, 2017

A CIP catalogue record for this book is available
from the British Library

ISBN: 978-1-85858-562-8

Printed in Great Britain by
Hobbs The Printers Ltd.

Contents

Acknowledgements

It is impossible to list all the people who have freely given their time and trouble to assist me in the research that led to this book. I would, however, particularly like to thank Tim Booth for invaluable help with the section on mills and millwrighting, and Peter Brown for the chapters on canals.

Archivists of the various Archives I have consulted have been invariably helpful, but I would particularly pay tribute to the staff of Shropshire Archives – your patience and professionalism are greatly appreciated.

The basis of this book was an MPhil at Birmingham University; for that I am grateful for the help of Roger White my supervisor and financial support by the trustees of the Pagett Bursary.

None of this would have been possible without Lois, who has patiently read and re-read every word (and many more), as well as being a brilliant support and encouragement – thankyou!

Chapter 1

Early Life

WILLIAM HAZLEDINE (Figure 1) was born on Wednesday April 6th 1763, the second son of William and Mary (nee Morgan) in Shawbury, a small village about five miles northeast of Shrewsbury, Shropshire (Figure 2). William senior was a millwright, as were his older brother John and father, also called William (Figure 3). Millwrights have been called 'the aristocracy of the working class', since they had to be familiar with the building and maintenance of the engines of the day – watermills and windmills. The best millwrights had a good knowledge of mathematics and technical drawing, the ability to design and build structures of stone, brick and wood, and an understanding of how to harness and control wind and water power. The Hazledines were good at their job, judging by the fact that they worked on mills as far away as South Wales and Cheshire, as well as all over Shropshire.

In addition to being a millwright, William senior was also a money lender. He usually lent small amounts of a pound or two, though occasionally it could be up to £40 at 5% interest, for as long as the client was willing to pay.[1] In later years the family also ran a shop, presumably some sort of general store, in the village. William senior kept meticulous records, which show that in 1777, the first year recorded, his income was £254, which would equate to perhaps £30,000 today, and by the time of his death in 1818 he earned £1000 for the year, which equates to about £65,000.[2] The family were thus by any standard comfortably off.

When William junior was aged three his grandfather John died, so William's family took over the lease of his grandfather's house (rent 6d a year) which was at nearby Moreton Forge. The forge was situated on the River Roden, and had been set up by the Corbets, the landowners, in the early 1600s, and was one of a number of similar forges along the River Tern and its tributaries (Figure 2). Their purpose was the conversion of 'pig' or cast iron to 'bar' or wrought iron. Traditionally pig iron was produced in furnaces from iron ore, heated with charcoal (later coke) and limestone to remove impurities. These furnaces tended to be situated near the iron ore supplies (in Shropshire's case around the area that is now Telford). The next stage of converting pig iron to bar iron needed a plentiful supply of water power so it was economic to transport it to forges such as Moreton. These forges were situated where a main road passed near the river; in this case it was the confluence of roads from East Shropshire via Roden and the main Shrewsbury to Market Drayton road.

For many years Moreton Forge had been run by members of the Russell family, whose ancestors had first brought modern ironworking techniques to England from the northeast of France over 200 years before (Figure 3).[3] William Hazledine's grandfather had married into the Russell family, which is presumably why they lived near the Forge. John Hazledine also acted as 'forge carpenter', which meant that he not only made and repaired the forge machinery, but also supplied patterns on which the workers hammered the iron into the required shape. The forge must therefore have provided a constant backdrop to their lives. Not least, it was extremely noisy, which is why forges tended to be built in isolated areas. The Hills of Tern Hall, later Attingham Park, found this out to their cost. In the early years of the eighteenth century they tried to make money by allowing the conversion of an old corn mill on the River Tern below their house into a forge. They soon regretted giving the owners a 50 year lease when they realised the noise that often went on day and night for 6 days a week. (Upton Forge, on the other side of the Attingham Estate, could be clearly heard in Atcham, at least two miles away.)

We know little of William Hazledine's very early life, but we do know that there was a school run by the Corbets at Moreton Corbet, so it is highly likely that William went there.[4] During this time he became proficient in the 'three Rs' and also developed an interest in science and poetry. On May 11th 1778 at the rather late age of 15 he began his apprenticeship to his uncle John, a skilled craftsman and kindly man. As Uncle John only had daughters it appears that he treated William as a son. The young man quickly became highly proficient at his trade, at the age of 16 or 17 earning praise for excellent work at Upton Forge.[5] By the age of 22 he had finished his apprenticeship and was ready to make his way in the world. As well as having technical ability, his appearance and personality were also impressive (Figure 4).[6] Tall and broad-shouldered, he was immensely strong. His facial features were heavy and rather forbidding, but he had a ready smile when pleased or amused. He was a man of few words, with a bluff manner and unpolished Shropshire accent, but he had a ready wit and was convivial in company. He had considerable ambition, but this was always tempered with caution in business affairs. This enabled him to build up a successful business while many other people went to the wall in the turbulent political and economic circumstances of the day. He could be ruthless in business, like his father, but he was sympathetic to the needs of his workers, unlike many of the employers of the day. Above all, he was a man of immense energy, throwing himself into a bewildering array of different branches of work. But this was balanced by attention to detail, which enabled him to generally maintain a reputation for accuracy and prompt-itude in his business dealings.

The world of the mid-1780s was experiencing rapid change. Internationally, the Treaty of Paris, signed in 1763, the year William was born, confirmed the status of Great Britain as a world power, and set the stage for rapid economic growth and prosperity. James Cook discovered Australia in 1770, and during that decade the American war of independence was fought, culminating in the Treaty of Versailles in 1783. The first bill to promote parliamentary reform was rejected in 1785, and the cataclysm of the French Revolution followed in 1789. On the industrial and scientific front, during the first 20 years of Hazledine's life James Watt patented his steam engine, Richard Arkwright revolutionised the cotton industry, Joseph Priestley discovered oxygen, and Henry Cort took out his first patent for producing wrought iron by 'puddling'.

Transport was also beginning to change; the first modern canal (the Bridgwater) was opened in 1761, and ever more ambitious ones followed soon after. While he was doing his apprenticeship, no doubt William took the newly-turnpiked road from Attingham to Leighton for the benefit of sightseers to watch the erection of the new Iron Bridge at Coalbrookdale.[7] The roads were still very slow, however; the New Fly left the Raven Inn in Shrewsbury at 5am on Monday, Wednesday and Friday, and got to London the next day 'for dinner' – nearly two days of extremely uncomfortable travel.[8] By the end of Hazledine's life, however, this coach journey had been reduced to just one long day, a change in which Hazledine was to play a small part. Agriculture, too, had been undergoing develop-ment. William Hazledine's involvement in that is the subject of the next chapter.

Endnotes

1 Information from William Hazledine senior's notebooks, kindly loaned to the author.

2 www.measuringworth.com, accessed July 2016.

3 Chris Evans, 'A skilled workforce during the transition to industrial society: forgemen in the British Iron Trade, 1500–1850', *Labour History Review*, Vol. 63, no 2, Summer 1998, pp.143–159.

4 Evelyn Lea, *Shawbury, the village and its people*, 2005, p.33.

5 Obituary of William Hazledine, Shrewsbury Chronicle (SC), 30.10.1840.

6 This description is compiled from the tribute in SC *Notes and Queries*, Nov 8th, 15th, 22nd and 29th, Dec 6th 1901. There is a copy in Phillips, W, *Shropshire Men*, Vol. 5, pp.268, Shropshire Archives (SA) Microfilm 167.

7 Anthony Blackwall, *Historic Bridges of Shropshire*, Shropshire Libraries, p.18.

8 SC 9.5.1778.

Chapter 2

The Young Millwright

ASSUMING that he completed his full seven-year appren-ticeship, William Hazledine was free to set up on his own in May 1785, when he was 22. To further his ambition in both the iron and millwrighting trades he decided to move to the county town of Shrewsbury. His progress in the iron trade will be considered in the next chapter. To establish a millwrighting business must have been a challenge, since many other experienced men, such as his father and uncle, were already well known. However, agriculture was developing rapidly, stimulated by the 'improve-ments' of large landowners and the progress of enclosures. The increase in cereal production and improvements in transport enabled landowners to concentrate their milling activities in fewer, but larger, mills. As a result, many mills were enlarged or improved, and a number of new ones were built in the late eighteenth and early nineteenth centuries.

Evidence for this is provided by the following advertisement for the mill at Shinewood (SJ 615027), 'lately [1806] erected...under the directions of Mr Hazledine.'[1] The mills comprised both a longstanding watermill, which William senior had worked on 30-odd years before, and which his son presumably modernised, and a windmill, which appears to have been designed and built by Hazledine junior. The advert further explained,

> The above mills, which drive six pairs of stones, have been lately erected, upon the most approved principles, under the directions of Mr Hazledine, and no expense spared to make them as convenient as possible.
>
> The situation for the purchase of corn, as well as the sale and delivery of flour, is very eligible, not being more than one mile distant from the River Severn, ten from Shrewsbury, seven from Wellington, and the iron and coal works in that neighbourhood, and two from Wenlock, all capital wheat markets, and to which places there are good turnpike roads from the mill...

In summary, the landowner who redeveloped the mill expected the new tenant to buy wheat and other cereals in significant quantities from the markets in the surrounding towns. From this he would produce flour which he would sell on to bakers in the nearby populous industrial area of East Shropshire. Things had moved a long way from mills being used almost entirely by local subsistence farmers simply for their own personal needs.

In 1785 the young William Hazledine needed to establish his reputation in order to share in these developments. Being of an entrepreneurial nature he realised that one thing that Shrewsbury lacked was a maker and supplier of millstones, especially the French burrs that produced the finest white flour then becoming popular. The young William had heard that a cargo of French burrs had recently arrived in Bristol, and were up for auction. But he certainly couldn't afford the £80 or so that would be needed to buy them, so he asked his mentor Uncle John for the loan of the money. John, generous as always, agreed. What he said next made a deep impression on the young man.

"Have you any security," asked his uncle, "that you will repay me the money?"

"None," said William, "except my own conduct."

"That's enough lad," said the generous donor, "but one guarantee I shall require, which is this – name your day for repayment, but let it be distant or near as best suits you; for if you wish to please me, or succeed in the world, attend punctually to your promise, and you will never lose a friend and very seldom require one."

The borrowed money was punctually returned on the promised day, and the advice of his uncle was the rule of his conduct through life.[2]

Having bought his stones and transported them to Shrewsbury, he had to make them into the finished article. French burrs had been known to produce the finest millstones for centuries, but it was only in the previous hundred years that they had been imported into Britain in significant quantities. The stone is an unusual form of chert (a quartz-like rock) that occurs most commonly in the Paris basin, especially around La Ferté-sous-Jouarre.[3]

The stone mostly occurs in quite small pieces buried in clay, which means that the standard millstone of between 4 foot and 4 foot 6 inches diameter has to be made up of smaller pieces. The reason this stone is so good is that it is 'porous' (having small holes), which means that, even untreated, the surface will grind satisfactorily. The stone is also so hard that the amount of surface stone ground off with the flour is negligible. If the surface of the stones is worked on, the furrows so produced will last without further attention for weeks.

The consequences of these qualities were that the best millstones, well maintained, could operate quite subtly on the grain so that the bran would be sliced and travel separately through the stones instead of being churned up with the white flour, and thus it could subsequently be sifted out.[4]

Hazledine's French millstone making workshop was near the English Bridge in Shrewsbury. His trade advertisement shows how they were manufactured (Figure 5).

The millstone was made in an upright position, perhaps leaning against a wall. The pieces were fitted together like a jigsaw, in two concentric circles, starting at the centre or eye of the stone. The stone illustrated has about 19 pieces, quite a usual number. The pieces were joined with plaster, and the whole was tightly bound around the outside with two iron hoops, applied hot, like a blacksmith making a wagon wheel. The lower (or bed) stone had its underside set in a layer of plaster, flattened to fit on the floor of the mill. The upper stone (or runner) had its upper surface finished with a convex layer of plaster, which made it run better, since there is more weight in the middle. The runner also had pieces of stone set into it to achieve balance. Both stones were pierced centrally for the spindle on which the runner turns. The runner also had fixing holes for the rynd, the iron pieces that fix it to the spindle. Making French millstones was slow and laborious, and it is estimated that one man would probably have made only 8–12 of these in a year.[5] Once the stones had been made, their grinding surfaces were prepared. Hazledine's trade advertisement also shows this being done (Figure 6). This involved incising the surface with sharp pick-like instruments called 'bills'. This made a pattern that had been found from long experience to work best for both grinding the corn and separating it from the bran.

The cost of burrs at the time depended on quality, but was probably around £15-20 a hundred.[6] Hazledine paid £80 for his initial consignment; if they cost £15 per hundred, it follows that he obtained around 600 stones. If he used 20 pieces per stone, this produces 30 complete millstones, or 15 pairs. In 1785 the cost of these stones was around £25 a pair, so he would have sold his original millstones for about £375. Taking into account transport, labour (men earned around £15 a year) and wastage, he must still have made a handsome profit on his initial outlay of £80 (his father made around £50 profit a year from his millwrighting work). No wonder he could afford to pay his uncle back promptly.[7] He certainly prospered, for in November 1789 he was able to take over the shop and workshop of a whitesmith in Wyle Cop.[8] He presumably transferred his millwrighting and millstone making business there, as well as maintaining the whitesmith's shop. The property comprised a good sized house (in which he probably lived), another smaller house, a brewhouse, workshops and other outbuildings. The whole site was on the north side of Wyle Cop at the western end of the English Bridge, adjoining the river Severn (SJ 495124). In 1805 he purchased the freehold of the two houses and the rest of the site for £200.[9] In the autumn of 1804 he was also able to purchase Jones' Mansion next door for about £5,575, with a mortgage of at least £4000. This medieval property was quite run down, especially since the level of Wyle Cop had been raised after the building of the English Bridge in 1769. After May 1805, Hazledine made both Jones' Mansion and his original property one site. He and his partner, the builder John Simpson, demolished Jones' Mansion and in its place built several houses, workshops, a laundry, stables, and warehouses, and this became the hub of his growing business.[10]

However William Hazledine would not become significantly wealthy just by making millstones and repairing and renovating mills like his father and uncle. He needed connections with large landowners to have any success in obtaining the contracts to build the new mills that would bring in big money and make his reputation. Progress in this direction arrived from an unexpected source, Thomas Telford. Telford was appointed by Sir William Pulteney, reputedly the richest commoner in England, to rebuild

Shrewsbury Castle as a family home. Telford probably arrived in Shrewsbury in late 1786.[11] Not long after this he was appointed County Surveyor for Shropshire through the influence of William Pulteney, and he quickly began to mix with large landowners through his surveying and architectural work. When Telford met Hazledine we do not know. One writer, having described Telford's arrival in Shrewsbury, wrote,

> Telford and Hazledine soon made each other's acquaintance, much to their mutual advantage. They were both thoroughly practical men who had risen from the ranks by the force of character and mental endowments.[12]

In time this acquaintance became a lifelong friendship, and William Hazledine probably obtained the contacts he needed from Telford's access to Sir William Pulteney and other landowners. Hazledine himself also worked directly for Pulteney, who numbered among his estates the Manor of Deytheur in Montgomeryshire. In 1788 Pulteney obtained a parliamentary act to enclose 2600 acres on this and neighbouring estates.[13] Much of the area required drainage, which was done by damming or rerouting existing watercourses and digging new 'trunks'. For this the commissioners who oversaw the act appointed Hazledine as the surveyor, which meant he was responsible for doing both the original drainage work and also maintaining it for five years.[14] How much he was paid we do not know, but his contract stipulated a bond of £700, so considerable sums of money were involved.

At the same time as he was doing this work, Hazledine was beginning to obtain contracts to build new mills. This is documented in a treatise that Telford wrote for the Board of Agriculture in 1798, entitled *On Mills*, which appears never to have been published.[15] Presumably Telford got the writing commission via Pulteney, but quite why he was considered expert enough to advise landowners and others on the current best practice in relation to mills is obscure. At that time Telford was as much an architect as an engineer, and there is no evidence that he was ever involved in agriculture, far less mills. So he must have been heavily reliant for his information on his friend Hazledine, a fact that he freely recognised, calling him *a very ingenious practical millwright*, in whose designs the reader could have confidence, since his *mills were sanctioned by experience.*[16] Telford and Hazledine must have had many conversations on the subject, and so the treatise gives a good insight into Hazledine's knowledge. The subjects Telford covered included a detailed history of mills of all types, and the theory and practice of millstones. He also discussed waterwheels, including John Smeaton's experimental work, tables of size, velocity etc, and the latest thinking of William Strutt. The latter half of the treatise covers windmills, and includes further reports of Smeaton's experiments, and finally there is a description of Andrew Meikle's thrashing machines. He also gave detailed information, with drawings and measurements, on both watermills and windmills designed and built by Hazledine. Assuming that Hazledine had a significant input into the treatise, this supports the view that he was not just a practical millwright, but was thoroughly versed in the history and theory of the subject as it was then understood. Telford described three sample watermills and four windmills that Hazledine had built by 1798, and stated that this was not an exhaustive list (Figure 7).

None of the mills he built survives in working order, and any parts that do remain may also have had replacements or additions over the years. The most complete watermill survival is Broadstone, built in 1794. This is now a private residence, but the surviving machinery has been preserved, and the mill was well documented just prior to conversion.[17] All the gearing is of wood, mostly oak, but the stone nuts are of elm, bound by iron hoops, and the wallower is wholly of iron. The pitch (the distance between the centres of the cogs) is too fine for this to be original. The waterwheel has been missing for many years; it is possible that it was made of iron, since Telford refers to the 'practice now begun of making water wheels of iron'.[18]

During Hazledine's lifetime more and more components were made of iron. This development can be seen in the estimate for the rebuilding of Long (Longdon-on-Tern) Mill in 1816.[19] This was a double mill, with two wheels working four pairs of millstones. Most of the two waterwheels (except the arms) were of cast iron, as were the pit wheels, wallowers, great spur wheels, and the spurs for sack tackle and dressing mills. The cogs of the great spur wheels, crown wheels and spurs for driving the sack tackles and dressing mills were, however, made of wood.[20] The reason for this is that, being slightly less hard than iron, wood tended to run more smoothly at high speed, and individual wooden cogs could be replaced if they got broken or worn.

These mills were well constructed and built to last. Their design incorporated the latest thinking, but on the other hand they used tried and tested technology, which would enable them to be maintained by any competent tradesman. The design was adaptable, for example everything could be duplicated by the addition of another waterwheel on the other side of the building, a common practice at the time. Their cost was also reasonable – if erected in Shropshire or Cheshire, Hazledine charged £350 for a mill like the one Telford illustrated in his treatise, or £650 for a double one. This included all the building work, also done by Hazledine's firm to a high standard. In 1816, despite the inflation that had occurred during the French wars, Hazledine's estimate for the building of Long Mill was just £594 13s 9d – less than he charged 20 years before. Perhaps that reflected the amount of iron work he then used, which was much less labour-intensive than making everything of wood, and the iron work for different mills could be reproduced from existing patterns. Being such a large firm he was able to undercut the opposition. For example the other quote that Lord Gower obtained for Long Mill came in at £677.[21]

The only windmill that is proven to have been built by Hazledine and is still standing is Hawkstone. This was built for Sir Richard Hill as part of the 'Follies' in Hawkstone Park. Its Dutch style made it a picturesque addition to the view beside the newly formed Hawk Lake, but the mill also served a practical purpose. Originally it was used to grind flax for linseed oil for cattle food and for pumping water from a nearby spring to Hawk Lake; later it became a bone mill for grinding animal bone for fertiliser.[22]

Once Hazledine was well-established he would have had little time to do the practical work himself. One of his skills, however, was building a team. Having done the initial survey, he passed on the detail of writing the contract to his clerk. This is shown in the estimate for the Toft Windmill at Trentham, where Hazledine just wrote the covering letter and added a detail that the clerk had missed.[23] He also employed a number of other millwrights on a permanent basis. Three such were Robert Lambert, William Townrow and Thomas Jones, who all lived in Coleham, Shrewsbury, and whose children were baptised in St Julian's Church in the period 1805 to 1812.[24]

When it came to the building work, Hazledine's style was not just to let the millwrights and other workers get on with it; he actively managed the work by ensuring that they had the materials they needed, and also gave them detailed practical advice as to how the job should be done. This he did both by frequent letters and also by visiting them on site. Hazledine's attention to detail is shown in a series of letters to Thomas Thomas, who supervised the building of the wharf at Market Drayton in the period 1834–37.[25] 'The mahogany hand rail must be cleaned off **and not** [his emphasis] varnished until you have cleaned the house down and done painting it,' Hazledine wrote on April 11th 1837, as if Thomas was an apprentice. Perhaps Hazledine was getting pedantic in his old age (he was 74 at the time), and Thomas probably just smiled to himself, knowing the genuine concern his employer had shown for him and his family over the years. For example, when Thomas Thomas senior had been in Bath helping to build the Cleveland Bridge, Hazledine had written a postscript to a letter on practical matters, 'I called on Mrs Thomas on Monday. She is well.'[26] Clearly Hazledine knew what it was like to spend long periods working away and did his best to support his workers and their families. This genuine rapport with his workforce was noted by his contemporaries.

Endnotes

1 Salopian Journal (SJ), 12.2.1806.
2 SC 8.11.1901.
3 Martin Watts, *Corn Milling*, Shire 2008, p.31; O Ward 'Millstones from La Ferte-sous-Jouarre, France, Industrial Archaeology Review **VI(3)**', 1982.
4 Ward, p.205.
5 G Tucker, 'Millstone making in England', *Industrial Archaeology Review*, **IX**, 1987, pp.167-188.
6 H Aplin, *Norfolk Corn and other Industrial Windmills*, Norfolk Windmills Trust, 1984, p.15.
7 Figures from William Hazledine senior's notebooks and Tim Booth.
8 SC 27.11.1789.
9 SA 311/39, 40, 41.
10 SA 311/10, 11, 12, 13, 14.
11 T Rolt, *Thomas Telford*, Pelican edition 1979, p.32ff; A Burton, *Thomas Telford*, Aurum, 1998, p.19 – I have used these sources for general information on Telford.
12 SC 8.11.190.
13 SA D3651/B/9/5/8/16; approximate grid reference is SJ 260180.
14 SA D3651/D/14/120.
15 T Telford, *On Mills – report for the Board of Agriculture*, 1798, Institution of Civil Engineers; T Telford and E Burne, On Mills, *Trans Newcomen Soc* 1936, **17**:205-214.
16 Telford 1798, pp.38ff and 120ff.
17 C Boucher, Broadstone Mill, Corvedale. *Trans Newcomen Soc* 1963, **36**:159-164.
18 Telford 1798, p.60ff.
19 Staffs RO D593/L/4/7.
20 I have used the more modern terms for the various wheels to avoid confusion.
21 Staffs RO D593/L/4/7.
22 RK Morriss, *Hawkstone Park Windmill, an Archaeological Analysis and Survey*, Mercian Heritage Series 1997.
23 Staffs RO D593/L/1/19/3.
24 SA, St Julian's fiche 256/A/1.
25 SA 901/1.
26 Letter to Thomas Thomas senior, August 9th 1826, SA 901/1.

Chapter 3

Man of Iron

AT THE same time as William Hazledine was making his mark in the millwrighting world, he was also taking his first steps as an ironmaster. Soon after he moved to Shrewsbury he entered into partnership with Robert Webster (1755–1832), and together they set up a small foundry for the production of cast iron near Mardol, Shrewsbury.[1] Quite how the two men came to be in partnership is not clear, since Robert Webster was a well-known local clockmaker.[2] Possibly Webster was looking for a partner to help him develop and manufacture a washing machine that he patented in 1792.[3] Sadly, this machine never caught on, and the only known example perished in a fire. As well as his washing machine, Webster also made spinning wheels of a new design, three of which were presented to Queen Caroline.[4]

Items Hazledine made for the new St Chad's Church, the first of which was delivered in the late summer of 1792, can be dated to this period. Hazledine was paid £35 12s 4d for iron rails for the gallery and the tower and various lead castings for the roof.[5] But the main payment of £180 was for the railings around the churchyard and the banisters for the back stairs.[6] In 1793 he supplied railings round the vestries, and a final set of railings was made round the portico in 1807. Most of these railings have now been removed or replaced, but there are probably some surviving ones still attached to the church.

Perhaps the main significance for William Hazledine of the rebuilding of St Chad's church was that through this he first met John Simpson (1755–1815), a Scot, who arrived to supervise the building of the church in May 1790.[7] (Figure 8) William Hazledine and Thomas Telford presumably met Simpson soon after he arrived, and the three became close friends and business partners in many enterprises.[8] Fittingly, Hazledine and Simpson are commemorated together in St Chad's church.

At the same time that Hazledine was working in partnership with Robert Webster producing cast iron in Shrewsbury, he also took his first steps into the production of bar (now known as wrought) iron. This was at Pitchford Forge (grid reference SJ 533056), which is situated about 10 km to the south east of Shrewsbury near the hamlet of Eaton Mascott, on the edge of the Pitchford Hall Estate. The forge was on the Cound Brook about 5km from its junction with the River Severn, and in close proximity to the route that passes from Shrewsbury to Acton Burnell, and thence to South Shropshire. Hazledine took over the forge in May 1789, before signing a formal lease for 42 years at £40 a year in June 1790.[9]

Always the realist, Hazledine included in the lease a clause allowing him to remove the machinery in the event of the enterprise not being a success, and the forge being converted to a different use. Evidently Hazledine did make a success of the forge, which continued in operation till at least 1811.[10] Pitchford Forge was the smallest of Hazledine's enterprises, and it seems slightly surprising that he should have been interested in leasing it. Perhaps the answer may lie in the fact that in November 1784 it was one of the earliest places where Henry Cort demonstrated his new 'puddling and rolling' method of making bar iron using coke in a reverberatory furnace.[11]

Just after he entered into the lease for Pitchford Forge, Hazledine entered into an altogether more important contract – that of marriage. On 14th January 1790 he married Eleanor Brayne (or Brain) at St Mary's Church, Market Drayton.[12] Eleanor's mother was also called Eleanor. She had married Samuel Brain, a farmer from the parish of Hodnet, on July 1st 1761, and her maiden name was Hazledine, so it is probable that William and Eleanor were distantly related.[13] Eleanor was baptised at St Mary's, Market Drayton on June 1st 1762, so was about 10 months older than William.[14] They had probably known each other since childhood, but William waited till he felt he was well enough established in business to tie the knot. It is likely that they made their home in the house attached to his millwrighting business in Wyle Cop, which is in the parish of St Julian.

The only description we have of Eleanor is that she was described as 'an uncommonly strong minded woman', when she organised the rescue of books, papers and other valuable items when her husband's foundry caught fire in 1804. This was after she had been awoken from sleep, while her husband was away.[15] She appears to have been an ideal helpmeet for her husband – strong and capable in her own right, and able to take responsibility for bringing up their family during his frequent absences. She was soon busy with domestic duties, since their first daughter, Mary, was baptised at St Julian's on 29th December 1790. Mary was followed by John (baptised 25.9.1793), Elizabeth (2.10.1794), Ann (17.4.1797), Eleanor (19.5.1799) and Fanny (20.5.1801). Eleanor died when she was about a year old, but the others all survived into adult life, though Fanny was only 20 when she died.[16] Family life seems to have been very happy, since,

> His strong affections for the members of his family rendered his fireside one of the most happy round which an English family ever gathered. He was ever devising some simple means

of increasing their enjoyments; and he attended personally to everything in which their comforts were involved.[17]

But all this was in the future – in 1790 he had barely begun in the iron trade. By this time Hazledine's partnership with Robert Webster was becoming strained. Hazledine was keen to expand the business, but Webster was not. So the partnership broke up, and Hazledine looked for a new site for his foundry. He found this in the Shrewsbury suburb of Coleham, beside the River Severn (SJ 495121). He appears to have bought the land in four parts over a three year period from 1790–93.[18] The total cost of the four pieces of land was £1805, most of which was covered by a mortgage. The land already contained a number of houses and other buildings, most of which he appears to have retained, but some were demolished to make way for the foundry. This he built up gradually as business grew, until it had a frontage onto Coleham of 305 feet (92.96 metres), and spread over an area of 5204 sq yards (approx 4350 square metres).[19] In addition to the foundry itself, there was a large timber yard, saw mill, storage areas for ironwork, a smith's shop, a landing stage from the river, offices and other associated buildings.

The foundry was used for the production of cast iron, which is essentially the same as the pig iron produced from iron ore in a furnace. Pig iron, however, tended to contain impurities, and pouring it directly from the furnace made it difficult to cast. Despite these drawbacks, the latter years of the eighteenth century saw a steady increase in the production of cast-iron items, particularly armaments, but also such large items as cranks and pistons for steam engines, tram wheels, and rollers, as well as smaller domestic items such as pots and pans and fire grates. The production of cast iron was greatly boosted, however, by the invention of the cupola furnace, patented by John Wilkinson in 1794. A cupola is a brick-lined furnace charged from the top with pig (or scrap) iron, coke (or charcoal) and limestone. The coke or charcoal is lit and the temperature is raised by means of an air blast introduced through tuyeres. The molten metal is then run off into moulds, either directly or via ladles (Figure 9). Coleham foundry had a number of cupola furnaces. In 1821 a visitor noted that two cupolas were employed doing just one order for the Dublin docks, the assumption being that there were others doing other work.[20] The air blast was produced using a Boulton and Watt steam engine, which were just becoming powerful enough for this purpose, indicating that Hazledine was abreast of the times.

So what was made at the Coleham foundry? The answer is almost anything that could be made of cast iron! Many years after Hazledine's death, when the foundry was taken over by Arthur Lowcock, the new owners advertised that they still had the patterns used by the foundry in Hazledine's time. Among the items they advertised were the following – gearing, bevel and spur wheels and pinions, pulleys, brackets, flywheels, pedestals, columns, caps and brasses, roof castings, builders' girders, complete sets and sizes of outlet pipes, drain pipes, well covers, tidal valves, sluice valves, trolley, tram and barrow wheels, sash weights, range castings, street curbings, fire irons, firebars, and gratings. Hazledine drain pipes (thought to be some of the earliest recorded cast-iron rainwater pipes in the world) are still in use at the Old Market Hall in the Square, Shrewsbury (Figure 10).[21]

As well as these 'off the shelf' items, the foundry provided all the cast-iron and brass items for Hazledine's millwrighting business, and made many things to order. Some of these are unfamiliar to us, such as a clay mill, fitted up and provided with all its parts, which the Earl of Powys ordered in 1826.[22] (Clay mills were horse powered, and were used for mixing and tempering clay prior to making bricks.) Coleham Foundry employed 300–400 people at its height. Nothing of it now remains, except some buildings at the front which were probably offices, and are now incorporated into shops, and there is evidence of a landing stage from the river at the rear.

Endnotes

1   SC 30.10.1840.
2   DJ Elliott, *Shropshire Clock and Watchmakers*, Phillimore 1979, pp.129-130.
3   Elliott, 1979, p.6.
4   Ibid.
5   SA 1048/63, 67.
6   SA 1048/68.
7   SA 1084/67.
8   A Pattison, Thomas Telford's Shrewsbury Team: Thomas Telford, William Hazledine and John Simpson, *Journal of the Railway and Canal Historical Society*, 2007 199, 664.
9   National Library of Wales (NLW), Pitchford Hall collection 2103–4.
10 NLW Pitchford Hall, Vol. 1 139/6/13 – a survey of the Estate in 1807 details Hazledine as the lessee. The forge, buildings, houses, gardens, etc occupied 1 acre and 1 rood. The last entry relating to the Forge in the Parish Register is of Charles Morgan aged 5 from the Forge, who accidentally drowned in 1811.
11 Staffs RO D695/1/12/36.
12 SA Drayton-in-Hales Parish Records, fiche no P97/142.
13 SA Drayton-in-Hales Parish Records, fiche no P97/125.
14 SA Drayton-in-Hales Parish Records, fiche no P97/82.
15 SC 30.10.1840.
16 SA St Julian's Shrewsbury, fiche P256/A/49 for births; burial of Eleanor, SA St Chad's Shrewsbury (transcript) S9/230H, p.1625; burial of Fanny, SA St Chad's fiche P253/A/31.
17 SC 30.10.1840.
18 SA D3651/D/5/214, D3651/D/14/113, D3651/D/5/228 & 246; these documents are all draft deeds, which show a number of alterations. The first is dated 29.7.1790, in which Hazledine's name has been crossed out, but he has also signed it, so it may or may not be that this transaction happened at that time.
19 Sale notice in SJ 20.10.1841.
20 Institution of Civil Engineers (ICE), Thomas Telford correspondence, T/EG 96, 21.12.1821.
21 http://www.oldmarkethall.co.uk/Accessible/AboutOMH/repairs.htm (accessed 2012).
22 SA 552/12/386.

Chapter 4

Innovative Structures

CAST IRON is a rather unfamiliar material to us, and it is especially difficult therefore to understand the way that ironmasters like Hazledine worked with it. Did he rely on experience, intuition, and even trial and error, or did he try to apply the latest thinking of the then infant discipline of metallurgy to his work? The metallurgical differences between the forms of iron were just beginning to be understood when Hazledine was starting his career. In 1786 a number of continental chemists realised that the basic difference in the types of iron was due to the amount of carbon they contained. During Hazledine's lifetime, further strides were made in understanding iron, and what evidence we have suggests that he was abreast of the latest thinking. Hazledine's contemporaries remarked that, despite his lack of formal education, he was extremely well read, enjoying such authors as Isaac Newton.[1] This joining of intellectual curiosity, technical knowledge and practical experience enabled him to excel at iron making and push the boundaries of cast iron production forward. A contemporary wrote that 'the strength [of cast iron] depends on the skill and experience of the founder',[2] and history was to prove Hazledine one of the best.

Because he left no records of his procedures, we can only pick up some hints as to how he did this. The first thing he did was to be very careful in the source of his materials. The quality of pig iron could vary considerably, depending on the source of the iron ore, the fuel used in smelting, and the expertise of those who produced it. For much of his career he did not make his own pig iron, but bought it from others, such as the Botfields at Old Park in Dawley and the Lilleshall Company, and it was then transported via the Shrewsbury Canal.[3] However, during the period when he leased the Calcutt works near Ironbridge (c1817–31), he did produce his own pig iron.

In 1818 James Thomson, a visitor on behalf of Thomas Telford, wrote that,

> At Calcutt, the materials from which the iron is made are those called the best all over that quarter. And from examinations I made the iron is certainly the strongest I have met with.[4]

Thomson then went on to Upton Forge, where, he wrote,

> From the trials I made on several bars of different sizes, I have no hesitation in saying I would prefer this iron for the fitting up on such work [as Telford proposed] to Swedish iron.[5]

Finally Thomson moved on to Shrewsbury, where he reported that

> The foundry at Shrewsbury is extensive, and the castings are principally made from Calcutt iron, using the weakest for small and general castings.[6]

It is clear from this last remark that Hazledine's iron founders were well aware of the different qualities of the iron they were using, and used it appropriately.

Hazledine purchased coal for ironmaking from the East Shropshire Coalfield, which he brought to Coleham via the Shrewsbury Canal. In 1813 he formalised an agreement with the Lilleshall Company for the provision of 20,000 tons of coal yearly 'free of slack'.[7] Hazledine also leased 100 tub boats from the Lilleshall Company, which were based at Donnington Wood.[8] Such large quantities of coal suggest that these arrangements had been going on for some time prior to 1813. The agreement also specifies the types of coal to be supplied – Hazledine was well aware of coal and its varying qualities. He set up in business as a coal merchant, presumably using the best coal for his own use and then selling on the remainder for the domestic market.

Wood was also a significant raw material for the ironmaster, being a source of both timber for pattern making, and charcoal for iron production. Much of this charcoal came from the Wenlock Edge area and it is likely that Hazledine employed it regularly. It is often thought that when coke technology really took off, and especially with the introduction of Henry Cort's puddling and rolling technique around the turn of the nineteenth century, charcoal rapidly became obsolete as a fuel. It has, however, been demonstrated that this was not entirely the case in Shropshire. Wrought iron made with charcoal was used to produce wire (and products made of wire), tinplate, gun barrels, scythes and other articles of the best quality.[9] David Mushet confirmed this when he wrote that,

> There is still no question of the superior effects of charcoal in the iron trade, in producing through the whole process a more perfect metallic result.[10]

This was presumably also the case with cast iron, since the purer the form of carbon (charcoal is virtually pure carbon) used for re-melting pig iron, the less the impurities that will be introduced.

Hazledine was also able to benefit from considerable improvements in casting techniques. The cupola furnace meant that much more liquid iron of purer quality for casting was available at one time, and hence much larger structures could be produced. Traditionally, liquid iron had been cast into the required shape using a wooden pattern smeared with 'loam', a mixture of sand, clay, straw and horse manure, which then had to be thoroughly dried to avoid the production of steam when in contact with the hot metal. Later dry sand was used, and later still 'green' sand, which is sand with a small proportion of clay and 'sludge'. Using this type of sand enabled much larger structures to be cast on the foundry floor, rather than just using a wooden box to enclose the casting material.

Iron casting is a highly skilled occupation, with pattern makers forming the required wooden pattern just a little larger than the final article, and moulders or founders actually doing the casting. Evidence for the existence of these trades in Hazledine's foundry is provided in the St Julian's Parish registers, which records the occupations of those recorded in the register.[11] Occupations detailed include 'iron founder', 'brass founder' (Hazledine also produced brass goods), 'cast iron moulder', 'model maker', 'pattern maker' and 'moulder'. One man who fathered three children was called 'iron founder' in 1822, 'moulder' in 1826, and 'brass founder' in 1829, so evidently the terms could be interchangeable. The most intriguing one is a lady, Mary Hill, who died in 1805, and is termed an 'iron founder', so the work was not limited to men.

Many things could go wrong with the casting process, such as the following[12]

- Blow holes due to poor venting of the moulds
- Residual stresses caused by differential cooling rates
- Contamination by sand becoming detached from the mould
- Weaker and coarser material at the centre of the casting
- Cold joints due to interruption of the casting

Fig 1: William Hazledine as Mayor 1836 (Shropshire Archives).

Fig 2: Sites associated with the early life of William Hazledine (author's collection).

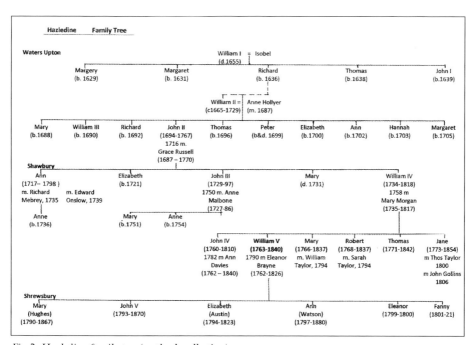

Fig 3: Hazledine family tree (author's collection).

i

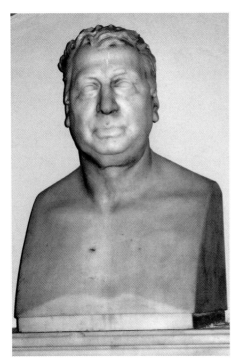

Fig 4: Bust of William Hazledine (author's collection).

Fig 5: French millstone making (Shropshire Archives).

Fig 6: Preparing the milling surface (Shropshire Archives).

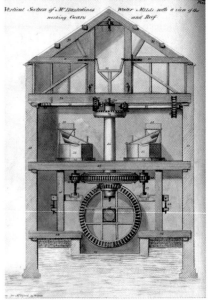

Fig 7: A Hazledine water corn mill (author's collection).

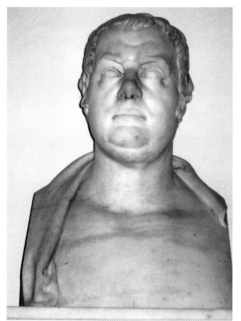

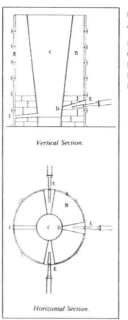

Early cupola
A – Cast-iron plates forming outside of furnace
B – Fire brick
C – Cavity for fuel and iron
D – Tuyere hole for air blast
E – Blowing pipe for air blast
F – Taphole for liquid metal

Vertical Section.

Horizontal Section.

Fig 8: John Simpson (author's collection).   *Fig 9: Cupola furnace (author's collection).*

Fig 10: Downpipe at the Old Market Hall, Shrewsbury (author's collection).

Fig 11: Ditherington Flax Mill (author's collection).

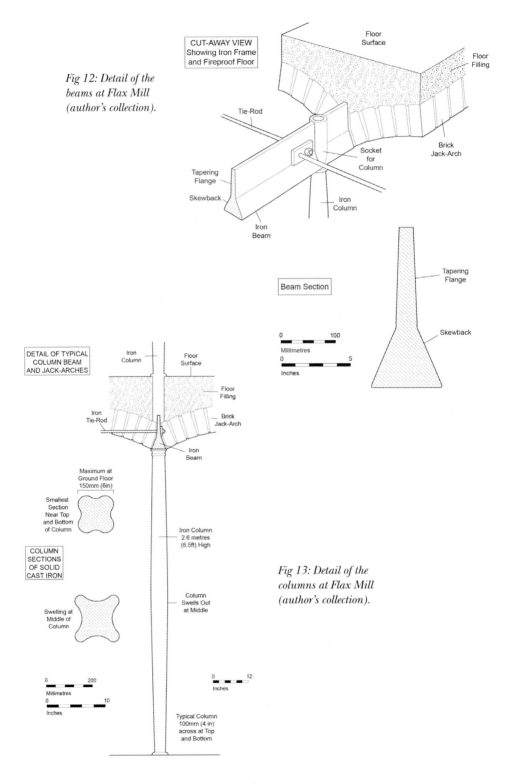

CUT-AWAY VIEW
Showing Iron Frame
and Fireproof Floor

Floor
Surface

Floor
Filling

Tie-Rod

Socket
for
Column

Brick
Jack-Arch

Tapering
Flange

Skewback

Iron
Column

Iron
Beam

Fig 12: Detail of the beams at Flax Mill (author's collection).

Beam Section

0   100
Millimetres
0   5
Inches

Tapering
Flange

Skewback

DETAIL OF TYPICAL
COLUMN BEAM
AND JACK-ARCHES

Iron
Column

Floor
Surface

Floor
Filling

Iron
Tie-Rod

Brick
Jack-Arch

Iron
Beam

Maximum at
Ground Floor
150mm (6in)

Smallest
Section
Near Top
and Bottom
of Column

Iron Column
2.6 metres
(8.5ft) High

COLUMN
SECTIONS
OF SOLID
CAST IRON

Fig 13: Detail of the columns at Flax Mill (author's collection).

Swelling at
Middle of
Column

Column
Swells Out
at Middle

0   200
Millimetres
0   10
Inches

0   12
Inches

Typical Column
100mm (4 in)
across at Top
and Bottom

iv

Fig 14: Attingham Hall - cast-iron ribs with 1974 glazed cover (Sarah Kay).

Fig 15: Thomas Telford, with Pontcysyllte Aqueduct (ICE).

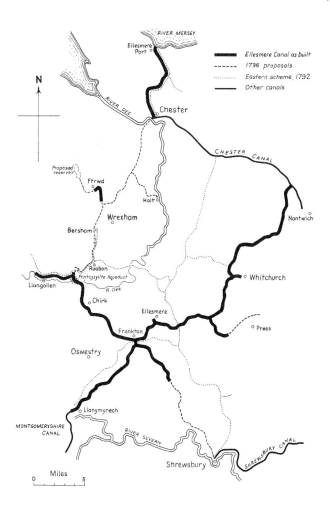

Fig 16: The line of the Ellesmere Canal (Charles Hadfield).

Fig 17: Construction of Pontcysyllte Aqueduct (public domain).

Fig 18: Ironwork at Pontcysyllte (author's collection).

Fig 19: Map of Plas Kynaston ironworks (Charles Hadfield).

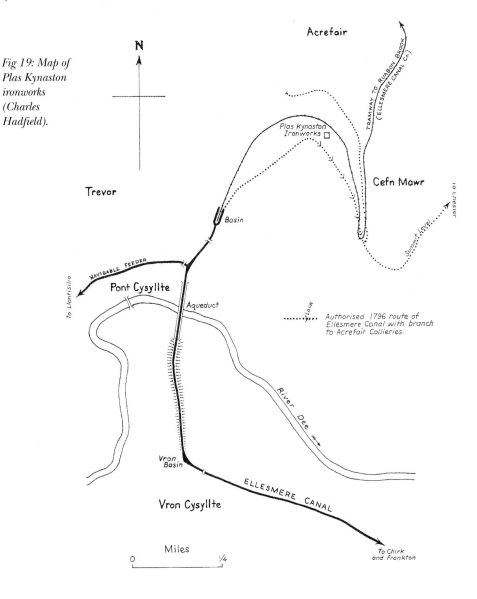

Fig 20: Pontcysyllte (Shropshire Archives).

Fig 21: Vyrnwy Aqueduct (author's collection).

Fig 22. Market Drayton Wharf (author's collection).

Fig 23: Berwick Wharf (author's collection).

Fig 24: Welshpool Town Hall (Welshpool Museum).

Fig 25: St John's Market Hall, Liverpool (public domain).

Fig 26: Cantlop Bridge (author's collection).

Fig 27: Cound Bridge re-erected in Telford Town Centre (author's collection).

- Variations in section thickness
- Surface defects caused by damaged moulds
- Cold-spots where earlier splashes of molten iron have cooled and solidified without subsequent absorption
- Impurities trapped in the body of the metal can act as stress raisers
- Incorrectly repaired castings

Hazledine certainly needed all his skill for the firm's biggest challenge, producing the castings for a new Flax Mill at Ditherington, just north of Shrewsbury (SJ 499139). This was the first totally iron framed building in the world (and hence the forerunner of all skyscrapers). Since its acquisition by English Heritage in 2005 its story has become well known, so it will only be outlined here.[13] John Marshall (1765–1845) was a flax mill owner from Leeds, and in order to increase his capital in 1794 he introduced the brothers Thomas (1762–1833) and Benjamin (1763–1834) Benyon into the partnership. The brothers came from Shrewsbury, and were keen to set up a flax mill in their home town. So in 1796 the partnership purchased land in Ditherington, close to the site of the proposed Shrewsbury Canal (opened in early March 1797).[14] In 1796 a mill owned by Marshall and the Benyon brothers in Leeds caught fire, resulting in a loss of around £5,000. Fires in mills were common at that time due to the inflammable nature of the materials used in spinning and weaving, and especially since the introduction of steam engines to power machinery. The partnership therefore decided to make the new Shrewsbury mill as fireproof as possible by constructing it of iron and brick, not wood. To oversee this new type of construction they turned to a Shrewsbury man, Charles Bage (1751–1822), the new mill being finished by late summer 1797.[15] At first sight Bage seems a most unlikely choice. He was probably born in Derby and moved as a child to Elford near Tamworth, where his father Robert (1728–1801) set up a successful business as a paper and cardboard manufacturer.[16] Charles Bage moved to Shrewsbury sometime in the early 1770s, where he made his living by a curious combination of being a wine merchant and a surveyor. Quite how he became interested in iron as a structural material is a mystery. One clue is that, as well as being in the paper trade, his father was also a partner in a business making high quality ironwork at Wychnor, Staffordshire, which opened in 1764.[17] One of the other partners was Erasmus Darwin, a leading light in the Lunar Society, whose members included Matthew Boulton and James Watt. After Erasmus Darwin moved from Lichfield to Derby he set up the Derby Philosophical Society in 1784, whose members included Robert Bage, who joined in 1788.[18] Darwin's deputy in the Philosophical Society was William Strutt (1756–1830), a mill owner from Belper, Derbyshire, who was 'the first to utilise iron components as a means of making textile mills fire-resistant.'[19] Charles Bage and Strutt became friends after Bage had initiated a correspondence in 1796 asking for advice about the construction of the Ditherington mill.[20] From the content of these letters it is clear that Bage was already conversant with the most up-to-date thinking on using iron as a structural material in textile mills.

The evolution in the use of structural cast iron in mills has been well documented.[21] Bage's part in this is that, in addition to the cast-iron columns and brick arched floors that Strutt had pioneered in Derby, he was the first to also use cast-iron beams. His other major contribution was the development of theories and mathematical formulae to test the strength of cast-iron columns, which turned out to be remarkably accurate.[22] He developed these theories partly by experiments. Some of his later experiments were carried out at William Hazledine's works, but it is not known whether he performed any experiments before the building of the Ditherington Flax Mill. He may just have relied on Strutt's experience, the experiments at Coalbrookdale, and his own mathematical work. If the appointment of Bage as architect and engineer appears a gamble to us, commissioning William Hazledine to do the ironwork would also seem to have been rather risky. The foundry at Coleham had only been in operation for 3–4 years, and there is no evidence that he had attempted anything on this scale before.

The original Ditherington Mill has five storeys, and measures about 54 x 12 metres (177x39ft)[23] (Figure 11). The external brick walls are load-bearing, and the internal structure is supported by a grid of columns, spaced at equal intervals, with 17 rows of three columns along the length of the building. Thus each floor has 51 columns, making a total of 204 columns in the first four storeys. For the attic storey, just the central columns from the fourth floor (not the side ones) extend up to roof level, which gives the roof its distinctive 'saw-tooth' appearance. The columns at each level support brick jack-arches (which in turn support the floors), and cast-iron beams. The jack-arches are strengthened by the insertion of wrought-iron tie rods (Figures 12 and 13). The columns are of cruciform cross section and are wider in the middle than at the top and bottom for maximum strength (Figure 13). The columns at ground level are wider (127mm/5in at mid-height) than those at the upper floor levels (114mm/4½in), and the capitals of the central columns at the ground and fourth floor levels are cast in the shape of a rectangle to accommodate drive shafts for machinery that ran the length of the building.

Each floor has 17 lines of beams, each cast in two lengths bolted together in the middle. There are thus 34 separate beams on each floor, a total of 136 in the whole building. The beams run over the side columns, to which they are connected via cylindrical sockets in the beams and spigots in the tops of the columns (Figure 12). The beams are of an inverted T cross section with a skewback, and have a slight hogback, varying in depth from 175mm (7in) at the external walls to 250mm (10in) over the side columns and 275mm (11in) where they join at the middle columns. The beams are also perforated at different points to allow drive shafts to run between the different floors. At the wall end, the beam is shaped into a plate which sits between two timber pieces, the whole being bolted together with wrought-iron rods. These timber pieces, though covered with other materials, were a potential fire risk, as was the roof, which is really a series of pitched roofs based on cast-iron beams that slope up from the valley of each section to the points of the columns that reach from the centre of the floor below. The ceilings are brick jack-arches like the floors, and these are covered with timber rafters and battens to which the slates are attached. In addition, all the windows and doors were made of iron, though none of the originals now remain.

This description of the ironwork is brief, but it does give us an indication of the scale and complexity of the castings needed, which were all done at Coleham. In summary, there were 204 columns of a number of different patterns, and 136 beams. The beams in particular required precise and complex casting, especially where they fitted with the columns, the walls and the machinery. The pairs of beams also required bolts to join them together. Assuming there was originally a window at either end of each bay, there would have been 136 windows in the whole building, each of which required casting, as did an unknown number of doors.[24] There were 19 separate roof sections (one for each bay, and one for one end); each of these was supported by cast-iron trusses. The wrought-iron tie rods supporting the jack-arches and wall plates were presumably done at Pitchford, and also required careful forming. There must also have been many smaller wrought-iron pieces – door furniture, banisters, and the like. The whole complex structure needed to fit together like a giant Meccano set, and also to fit precisely with the brickwork. We do not know who the brickwork contractor was, but in all probability it was Hazledine's partner John Simpson, since he is credited with later work on the site, such as the Apprentice House and Clerk's House, both built before 1800.[25] One can imagine the two friends spending many hours planning and puzzling how they could bring Charles Bage's scheme to reality!

So how has history judged the ironwork? The first observation is that the building, after over 200 years of use (and sometimes misuse), is still standing. This is definitely an achievement for a structure that was in some ways a prototype. As for the ironwork, recent surveys have provided an opportunity to examine both its composition and how it has stood the test of time. Samples from various parts of the mill have been tested (Table 1). The carbon equivalent value is based on the amount of carbon, silicon and phosphorus present in the sample; higher values suggest less tensile capacity.

> As much historic cast iron used in structures has been found to have a carbon equivalent value above 4.3%, many of the results show the tensile strength of the iron tested is higher than is typically found.[26]

Alternatively, one can try to directly measure the tensile strength of the material; in the samples tested this varied between 200 and 230 N/mm^2 (Newtons/square millimetre).

> The current recommendation for assessing historic cast-iron structures is to adopt a tensile strength of $123N/mm^2$ when no other data is available. This shows that the iron is of above average quality.[27]

In summary, the weaknesses of the building in its present condition are due primarily to the slender design of the iron frame and the decay of the structural timber, not the original ironwork, which is of exceptional quality.

Table 1 – Metallurgical tests on iron from Ditherington Flax Mill[28]

Sample origin	Carbon equivalent value %	Tensile strength N/mm²	Carbon %	Sulphur %	Silicon %	Manganese %	Phosphorus %
Column	3.8	230	2.88	0.063	2.04	0.63	0.73
Beam	4.1	200	3.18	0.057	0.98	0.68	1.77
Beam	4.02	215	3.48	0.039	0.95	0.69	0.67
Beam	3.86	230	3.29	0.064	0.87	0.73	0.84
Beam	4.01	215	3.43	0.041	0.82	0.76	0.82

Another innovative structure that Hazledine was involved with at this period was the Attingham Hall picture gallery roof. Attingham Hall, near Shrewsbury, is now a National Trust property, but was then the seat of the Berwicks. Between 1805 and 1807 the 2nd Lord Berwick (1770–1832) made alterations to the heart of Attingham Hall in order to house his Grand Tour collections.[29] To do this he employed the eminent Regency architect John Nash (1752–1835), later of Brighton Pavilion and Regent's Street fame. Nash swept away George Steuart's original entrance hall and grand staircase and built in its place Attingham's Picture Gallery with its innovative use of cast iron, and the theatrical drum staircase. The Picture Gallery is an iconic, ground-breaking piece of architectural design. Nash's clever solution provided top-lighting in an entirely internal space at the heart of the mansion. Supported on his structure of metal and glass, the central bed of the ceiling appears to float above the space. All the internal, high-level decorative elements were gilded so that the overall effect would have shimmered spectacularly.

Nash's solution for the Gallery's lighting was unique in terms of technique and materials: the roof structure was a very early example of the use of cast iron, in the form of curved 'ribs' supporting continuous glazing (Figure 14). The curvature ensured that the light fell over a wide area, so that the lower pictures were better lit than by the more customary lantern-style top-lighting. It was also innovative because Nash was using iron in a domestic interior, rather than an engineering or industrial context. However, it was risky – early structural uses of iron were very much experimental, with many failures as well as successes.

The ironwork was supplied by William Hazledine – the cast iron coming from his Coleham foundry, and the wrought iron from Upton Forge, just up the River Tern from Attingham. In the second week of March 1806, the first 55 cast-iron 'bars' (sections) for the roof were delivered to the site.[30] Two of Hazledine's men (Richard Parkes and James Nugent) started work fabricating the roof on Monday 10th March. Some of their equipment, such as bolts and cramps, was supplied to them by the on-site blacksmith Mr Farnall. They appear to have run into problems with the fabrication, as there is a note dated March 29th for a payment to alter the patterns. A further 26 cast-iron bars (presumably to the new pattern) were delivered on March 28th. A further 2 bars followed on April 8th and the final 52 on April 25th. There were also a number of deliveries of wrought iron bars. In the last week of April, Francis Plowden and John Humphreys joined the other two workers, and the four of them were employed until July 2nd. This means that over a 16½ week period about 320 man-days of work were needed for the construction of the roof.

On June 11th they took delivery of a 'round cast skylight frame', presumably the skylight for the top of the stairs. During the week ending Saturday June 21st, the four men were joined by Benjamin Cox and Richard Griffiths when they worked together to put up this skylight, which took just 1¼ days. Quite how the fabrication was done without modern lifting gear and in the confined, double-height space is impossible now to say, but probably some of the men on Hazledine's team had fabricated Ditherington Flax Mill so had considerable experience in this type of work. Hazledine's total bill was £345 15s 6d, though a later document that summarised how much all the tradesmen were paid for the Picture Gallery, indicated that he was finally paid £479 5s 6d.[31]

The small panes of glass turned out to be a fundamental design flaw, and so the roof leaked almost from the outset. For this reason, there has been a major renovation recently, with a new cover over the entire roof. As part of the project, sections of Nash's roof were opened up in order to check the condition and also better understand its construction. It was discovered that the central roof is supported on a curved cast iron structure that is a continuation of the curved cast iron 'ribs' above the skylight. Despite appearances to the contrary, the roof of the Gallery is effectively an 'arched' structure, not a flat 'beam' structure as an earlier report had suggested. The curved cast iron 'arches' taper to a remarkably slender profile at the centre of the roof, compared to the deeper section that is visible above the skylight. Computer modelling by a structural engineer found this to be a very efficient and elegant design, which enables the structure to be concealed within a relatively thin overall roof thickness. Whether this part of the design was Nash's own or whether he had advice from Hazledine is not known. Either way, even though elements of Nash's innovative design were arguably flawed, Hazledine's ironwork was still serviceable after 200 years.

Endnotes

1 C Hulbert, *Manual of Shropshire Biography, 1839,* appendix.

2 T Tredgold, *A Practical Essay on the Strength of Cast Iron and other materials,* 1824, p.10.

3 SC 28.6.1839, records the theft of Lilleshall pigs bound for Hazledine's Coleham Foundry.

4 ICE, letter from James Thomson to Thomas Telford, 8.5.1818, T/EG 306.

5 Ibid.

6 Ibid.

7 Ironbridge Gorge Museum Trust (IGMT) Lilleshall Company Collection 1998.320 (DLIL/3/236).

8 IGMT, DLIL/3/247.

9 R Hayman, Charcoal ironmaking in nineteenth-century Shropshire. *Economic History Review* 2008 **61(1)** pp.80-98.

10 D Mushet, *Papers on Iron and Steel,* 1840, p.65.

11 SA St Julian's fiche 256/A/1 and transcripts St Julian's 5b.

12 Alan Baxter and Associates, *Ditherington Flax Mill, Shrewsbury, Structural Engineering Appraisal,* 2006, main report, section 3.

13 See, for example Malcolm Dick, http://www.revolutionaryplayers.org.uk/ditherington-flax-mill/ (accessed 2016).

14 SJ 1.3.1797.

15 SC 1.9.1797.

16 Dictionary of National Biography (DNB) articles on Charles and Robert Bage, Oxford, 2004.

17 D King-Hele, *Erasmus Darwin,* DLM Press, 1999, pp.52-3.

18 King-Hele 1999, p.198.

19 B Tinder, Ditherington Flax Mill, Shrewsbury, a re-evaluation, *Textile History* 1992 **23(2)** p.193.

20 SA 6001/2657/2; the letter, though undated, was almost certainly written in the Summer of 1796.

21 For example, Trinder 1992.

22 Baxter 2006, Appendix F, has a useful explanation of Bage's work.

23 All descriptions from Baxter 2006, main report, p.5 ff.

24 RR Angerstein, *Illustrated Travel Diary 1753–55,* Science Museum 2001, noted 40 years earlier that 'the people [of Shrewsbury] use window-frames of iron. These are welded at the corners and then riveted together with a thin piece of sheet-iron, to make them safer for the window-glass panes. For high windows, espagnolettes [hooked bolt-rods that engage in slots at the top and bottom of the main frame, so locking and tightening the opening light] are also used in order to make it possible to close them tightly and uniformly both at the top and the bottom. On the outside there is a spring that supports the weight of the window when it is opened, and which is also provided with a catch to hold the window in position' (p.329). Presumably the large factory windows of the Flax Mill, which were needed to let in as much light as possible, were of the latter type.

25 Trinder 1992.
26 Baxter 2006 section 5, p.12.
27 Baxter 2006 section 5, p.12.
28 Baxter 2006, Appendix H.
29 Sarah Kay, Emma Nock and Andrew Pattison, 2016 in press.
30 SA 112/6/256/290.
31 SA 112/6/256/291.

Chapter 5

'A Stream in the Sky'

S IR WALTER SCOTT described the Pontcysyllte Aqueduct as a 'stream in the sky', and 'the most impressive work of art I have ever seen'.[1] It is still the highest aqueduct in Britain, and a stupendous monument to those who created it, chief of whom was Thomas Telford. In recent years an attempt has been made to play down Telford's role in favour of the engineer in charge, William Jessop.[2] However, there seems little doubt that Telford should take the primary credit for the structure, which is celebrated in his formal portrait at the Institution of Civil Engineers (Figure 19).

Local landowner Rowland Hunt, who had been involved in the project since its inception, was chosen to give the oration at the opening of the Aqueduct. He said,

> We will mention, as concerned in the scientific and practical construction of the works, our General Agent [Resident Engineer] Mr Telford; who, with the advice and judgment of our eminent and much respected Engineer, Mr Jessop, invented, and with unabating [sic] diligence carried the whole into execution...In such a history will be found deservedly

mentioned, the names of Mr Hazledine, the spirited founder
of the Duct itself; of Mr Simpson, the accurate mason, who
erected the pillars; the well-computed labours of Mr Davies, who
constructed the mound and tunnels adjacent; and the careful
and enlightened inspection of Mr Davison [sic], who over-
looked the whole.[3]

This, then, was a collaborative enterprise, and this chapter seeks to
discover the contribution that William Hazledine made to the
project.

Among many canals being promoted in the early 1790s was one
that was projected to join the Rivers Severn, Dee and Mersey, and
which would also link the important towns of Shrewsbury and
Chester. After an initial survey, public meetings quickly galvanised
support for the idea, and an organising committee was set up, which
first met on June 28th 1791.[4] They formed the Ellesmere Canal
Company, and later that year William Jessop was appointed
consulting engineer and asked to draw up detailed plans for the
route.[5] After considerable discussion a route was agreed and the
relevant bill guided through Parliament by Jessop in 1793. Once
this was done Thomas Telford (Figure 15) was appointed resident
engineer in October 1793.

In February 1794 Telford secured the appointment of his old
friend Matthew Davidson as Superintendant of the Works.[6] Work
started immediately, originally on the northernmost section across
the Wirral, and also a branch linking the line of the proposed canal
to the limeworks at Llanymynech. Both these works were fully
opened in 1797 (Figure 16). At the same time as the Llanymynech
section was being built, another canal, the Montgomeryshire, which
was approved by Parliament in March 1794,[7] was being constructed
to link Llanymynech to Welshpool, and eventually, Newtown. The
main purpose of both canals was to transport heavy goods, such as
coal, iron ore, limestone and timber, from where they were mined

or produced to the centres of agriculture and population. Local landowners hoped to make a great deal of money from the Ellesmere Canal. For example, in September 1795 the Plas Kynaston estate, which is adjacent to the Pontcysyllte Aqueduct, and which contained coal, iron and clay deposits, was offered for sale. The advert stated,

> It is not to be calculated how great an extent the works are capable of being carried, or to what amount the demand may be increased, when the Ellesmere Canal, which will unite the Severn, the Dee and the Mersey, passes through it [the Estate], and opens a way to all the markets of the world. There is a vast rock of light-coloured free-stone [i.e. sandstone], through the centre of which the canal is intended to pass, and which thereby will become an object of very great consideration.[8]

Despite the enticements of the advert, it appears that there were no takers, since the estate was offered again the next year, this time to rent.[9] There were probably two reasons for the initial lack of interest in the estate. The first was the ongoing economic difficulties resulting from the war with France, and the second was that the building of this part of the canal was running into difficulties. William Hazledine, however, always alert for a money-making opportunity, took up the lease on a part of the Estate and the collieries sometime before 1799, probably in 1796.[10] His long term plan was to export the coal via the Ellesmere and Montgomeryshire Canals to the markets of Welshpool and Newtown and their surrounding areas, and also in the other directions to Shrewsbury, North Shropshire and Cheshire. But in the meantime, he had to be content to supply the local area until the canal building got going again.

That was going to take some time, as the engineering challenges of taking it over the Ceiriog and Dee Valleys were immense. The plan of the earliest surveyors was to take the canal up and down the valleys by means of locks, with low level aqueducts of the traditional type lined with puddled clay over the rivers. Jessop and Telford soon realised that this was impractical (not least because of water supply problems), and so looked for other solutions, particularly using an iron trough. Both Telford (at Longdon on the Shrewsbury Canal) and Jessop (on the Derby Canal) were getting acquainted with the idea of using iron in this way, and so, no doubt after much discussion, this is what Jessop recommended to the Canal Committee in July 1795.[11] The Committee wasted no time in approving the plan and the foundation stone of the Pontcysyllte Aqueduct was laid on 25th July 1795.

James Varley of Colne, Lancashire, was given the contract to build the piers in 1794, so he had already been at work cutting stone and preparing the site for some months when the foundation stone was laid.[12] But by the end of 1795 it became clear that Varley was not up to the job, so Telford arranged for his friend John Simpson to partner Varley.[13] The two worked together till 1797, when work stopped on the piers and Varley decided he had had enough, and left Simpson to it. Simpson was joined in this work by another exceptional mason, John Wilson of Dalston, Cumbria.[14] Simpson was also jointly responsible for the section of canal from Chirk Bank to Pontcysyllte. This included the digging of two tunnels (one a quarter of a mile long), and making stone bridges and culverts.[15] In December 1795 Simpson built a house for Matthew Davidson, just to the north of the Pontcysyllte Aqueduct, which is still there and is now known as the Thomas Telford Inn.[16]

The foundation stone for the Chirk Aqueduct was laid on 17th June 1796, and the contract for building the piers was also awarded to John Simpson, this time in partnership with William Hazledine. Hazledine's involvement initially had nothing to do with the ironwork, but was a recognition that, in addition to all his other accomplishments, Hazledine is described on legal documents as a 'master builder.'[17]

The team of Telford, Davidson, Simpson and Hazledine provided the essential core for a highly disciplined and creative workforce. The four men were close friends, whose mutual respect and trust would carry them through the many challenges ahead. Telford and Davidson had known each other since childhood. Telford persuaded Davidson to leave their native Eskdale and go first to Bath to benefit from the building boom there, and then join him in Shrewsbury to supervise the construction of Montford Bridge, Telford's first foray into bridge building, which was built between 1790 and 1792.[18] John Simpson arrived in Shrewsbury to build St Chad's Church at the same time, and Davidson and Simpson quickly became close. They were also united in tragedy, for Mary Simpson, who died on 26th October 1792 aged 1 year and 4 months, and Thomas Davidson, who died on 14th February 1793 aged two years, share the same burial plot at Swan Hill Congregational Chapel, Shrewsbury.[19] After his work on the Ellesmere Canal Davidson moved back to Scotland to superintend the building of the Caledonian Canal, and later his son Thomas returned to Shropshire to be apprenticed to an apothecary in Oswestry. During this time John Simpson kept a fatherly eye on the young man.[20] No wonder that when Simpson died unexpectedly and prematurely in 1815, Matthew Davidson wrote to Thomas that 'I mourn him [Simpson] deeply indeed.'[21] The friendship between Telford, Hazledine and Simpson has been described elsewhere,[22] and doubtless they and Matthew Davidson had many discussions about how the aqueduct could be constructed.

Telford's relationship with Hazledine is illustrated (and perhaps has been misunderstood) by an incident in early 1796. Telford was in London helping to get a new bill to amend the line of the canal through Parliament, and he wrote to Matthew Davidson,

'The moment I was conjuring about a spring for the coffee house door this morning, who should make his appearance but the Arch Conjuror himself Merlin Hazledine. This was one of the most singular instances I have met with. We have been considering about the arch over the roadway...'[23]

This is popularly taken to indicate that Telford had such a high regard for Hazledine's skill as a manipulator of iron that he regarded him as a magician like Merlin. In reality in early 1796 Hazledine had never made anything in iron for Telford. In the author's view all Telford is saying is that Hazledine's unexpected appearance was that, like Merlin the magician, he seemed to appear out of nowhere.

In the meantime work on the aqueducts stopped and started. In February 1797 the committee asked the two foremost Shropshire Ironmasters William Reynolds and John Wilkinson,

...what terms they will either jointly or individually agree to furnish the ironwork for Pontcysyllte and fix up and compleat [sic] the same.

There is no evidence that this was forthcoming, so in June it was agreed that newspaper advertisements should be placed for executing the ironwork.[24] But because of the escalating cost work was halted, and the committee dithered as it tried to decide what to do next. During this break Hazledine was able to concentrate on the Ditherington Flax Mill in 1797, and Telford and Simpson spent the whole of the 1798 construction season building a splendid new bridge at Bewdley. If Telford wasn't convinced already of Simpson's excellence, this project demonstrated to him that his friend was 'a treasure of talents and integrity.'[25]

The committee, if not the contractors, had cold feet about the whole iron aqueduct idea. As Hughes has written,

All the previous and relatively experimental iron aqueducts, such as Longdon (completed in 1796) and Outram's [William Jessop's business partner]...Holmes Aqueduct at Derby, were fairly small and the trough of the high and long upper aqueduct at Cyfarthfa [the first and then the longest iron aqueduct] was only 3ft 6in (1.07m) wide and 16in (0.41m) deep.[26]

When one considers that Pontcysyllte Aqueduct is 1007ft (306.9m) long, 11ft 10in (3.6m) wide, and 5ft 3in (1.52m) deep, one can understand their hesitation. In 1797 the committee looked at the possibility of substituting a railway for part of the canal, including using the piers designed for the aqueduct to take the railway over the river.[27] In the end the committee and the contractors decided on a compromise. Chirk Aqueduct would be built first and would have a base made of 1" (2.5cm) thick cast-iron plates bolted together transversely.[28] These plates would tie the side walls together, which were to be made of hard burnt bricks, sealed with waterproof Parkers Cement, and the outside faced with stone blocks. William Hazledine came in with the lowest tender for the ironwork, which was £10 10s a ton for cast-iron plates and 6d a pound for wrought-iron screws, exclusive of fixing. The tender was accepted in November 1799.[29] It has generally been assumed that Hazledine was able to tender more cheaply than the previous preferred bidders John Wilkinson and William Reynolds because he made the iron at his Plas Kynaston foundry (see page 52). In fact the foundry had not been built by then, but the Weston arm of the Ellesmere Canal was opened in 1797, so it was relatively straightforward to transport the iron the 8 miles (12.9km) from Shrewsbury to Weston Lullingfields and then via the canal to Chirk (Figure 16).

From then the work on Chirk Aqueduct proceeded rapidly, so that by May 1801 a visitor could write,

I found the canal much advanced and the fine aqueduct of ten arches, which traverse the vale beneath Chirk nearly finished...The other fine aqueduct over the Dee which will be a still grander object than the one before mentioned, has not advanced so much, but the canal is brought up to it, and the lime works above. There are 17 piers erected to bear the arches.[30]

The ironwork at Chirk was a success,[31] and so the contractors were emboldened to take the next obvious step and make the whole trough for Pontcysyllte of iron. Hazledine's tender for this was accepted in March 1802, according to the following minute,

Mr William Hazledine of Shrewsbury having proposed to execute the cast-iron work at Pontcysyllte Aqueduct on the following terms (viz.) the castings at £11 per tons, the wrought iron at 8d per pound [i.e. £74 13s 4d per ton], and being allowed £30 for cast-iron keys to connect the plates of the aqueduct over and above the price of £11 per ton upon the whole weight and to perform the work in every respect **according to the conditions and specifications now produced and signed by the said William Hazledine** [author's emphasis] ... this Committee accept of the proposal...[32]

The phrase emphasised in the minute can be read two ways. Either the conditions and specifications had been produced by the committee (presumably via Telford) and then signed by Hazledine, or, perhaps more likely, Hazledine himself had produced the conditions and specifications. Either way, Hazledine had a significant input into the detailed design of the ironwork.

Further light on the detailed construction of the aqueduct is shed in a report that James Thomson wrote for Thomas Telford in 1818 relating to work on the three proposed aqueducts for the

Edinburgh and Glasgow Union Canal. Telford sent Thomson to examine Hazledine's ironworks and also Pontcysyllte Aqueduct, presumably to help Thomson draw up detailed plans for the aqueducts on the Edinburgh and Glasgow Union Canal. Part of Thomson's report to Telford explained how the ironwork at Pontcysyllte was made watertight. He wrote,

> The jointing is done with very coarse flannel in the state it comes from the loom, cut into pieces to suit the flanges, and well covered with white lead of the normal consistency for jointing. And more or less of the pieces are needed in according [accordance] to the inequality of the joints which come together. The one also cut a little narrower than the flanges so as to leave a space on both sides to be caulked firmly up with good hemp rolled in tar, and hence well caulked and pitched over. I know of no simpler or cheaper method of jointing for cold water...I have never seen a piece of cast iron work more watertight than this aqueduct.[33]

Thomson also reported how the ironwork was installed. He wrote,

> The scaffolding and centering [sic] was done by leaving square holes in the piers two courses from the top, and running beams along from pier to pier in these holes, supporting each beam by diagonal braces under, and raising trestles over the beams.[34]

This has been confirmed by recent surveys, and is shown in animation in a video. (The animation does not show any centring to support the arches, so exactly what Thomson meant is not clear, as the ironwork would not need wooden centring in the way that a stone bridge does) (Figure 17).[35]

The ironwork comprises the following,

The trough is constructed in 18 sections, each 44ft in length, and is 7ft 6in high and 11ft 10in wide. It is made up of ¼in thick plates bolted together along the flanges... Each section of trough is designed to imitate a flat stone arch, the side plates shaped to imitate the voussoirs. Supporting each section are four ribs, cast in three sections and bolted together with connecting plates, the outermost ribs having infill plates which give the impression of a solid span. These ribs sit on cast-iron springing plates built into the stonework near the top of each pier. The trough is not directly attached to the ribs or the piers, but is instead prevented from moving laterally by a number of brackets and lugs cast onto the underside of trough base plates and which straddle the top edges of the ribs.[36]

Figure 18 shows the trough and guard rail (notice how the lateral trough supports are angled to continue the lines of the 'voussoirs' below).

The amount of iron that was needed was staggering. The 19 piers support 18 arches, each made up of four ribs cast in three sections. This is a total of 216 castings. Similar calculations give a total of 216 'voussoirs', 240 infill plates, and so on – literally thousands of major castings, before all the bolts, fixings, and so on are added. To do all this ironwork, Hazledine used his new works at Plas Kynaston. The Plas Kynaston foundry was built on the estate that he leased, and was about ⅓ mile (600m) from the Pontcysyllte canal basin. In 1803 it was proposed to build a 'railway' (tramroad) from the Pontcysyllte Basin to Ruabon Brook that passed near the foundry, but it took until November 1804 for the committee to organise Hazledine's contract for supplying the castings (at £11 a ton) for the double railway (tramroad), and also laying down the tracks.[37] (Figure 19) In the meantime all the ironwork from the new foundry would have to be taken to the aqueduct by horse and cart.

Hazledine himself oversaw the casting and erection of the ironwork, but to assist him he was fortunate to recruit William Stuttle. Stuttle came from the Black Country, and had been the Manager of the Wednesbury (Hallen's) Ironworks. Hazledine and Stuttle were soon hard at work, and Telford was able to report in 1804 that,

> The iron-work of the Trough-part of the Aqueduct of Pontcysyllte over nine arches is now put up, being nearly one half of the whole length. Many plates being now cast and brought to the bank at the north end of the Aqueduct – the workmen being familiar with the operations of putting the plates together and the operations at the foundry being in a very regular train, and well supplied with metal, there is reason to expect that the whole of the trough-part will be completed about Midsummer next.[38]

This work necessitated much time away from home for Hazledine, though he was presumably able to stay at Plas Kynaston House, since this was part of the estate he leased. But while he was away, on Friday November 16th 1804 he suffered a near disaster through fire at Coleham. The Shrewsbury Chronicle reported,

> Some timber kindling by the heat of the chimney of the fire [steam] engine is supposed to have been its origin, and communicated to the shop, where the models for casting were deposited. Happening in the dead of night, it was not perceived till it had raged some time, when the roof fell in, and presented a grand and dreadful spectacle, for the whole atmosphere was reddened with the blaze! The watchmen's rattles, ringing of bells, and beating of the drum soon alarmed the inhabitants and Volunteers; many of the latter appearing accoutred and in uniform, and their Colonel, Sir C Oakeley, who was present,

inspiring them with steadiness and promptitude, on occasions of this kind, as well as to the protection of the property that was removed. The night was fortunately calm; a quantity of salt added to the water in the engines was observed to have very great efficacy in extinguishing the fire. By the cheerful cooperation of all, it was prevented from spreading, and completely subdued by four o'clock. The damage is estimated at near £1500, about two-thirds of which are covered by insurance. Happily no lives were lost, nor any other kind of damage or injury sustained except the above. The proprietor is now rebuilding the premises with his usual resolution and dispatch.[39]

Hazledine was also greatly indebted to his wife Eleanor, who, when roused with the rest of the locality, 'immediately getting up gave directions for saving the books, papers, and other valuables, which caused their rescue from the flames.'[40] The mention of the 'Volunteers' is a reminder that in 1804 the country was at war with France. Hazledine was captain of a company of the Shropshire Militia, the commander of the whole corps being Colonel Sir Charles Oakeley, Bart. Hazledine's company was chiefly drawn from his own workmen, and were accordingly given the nickname of 'Vulcans', after the Roman god of fire and metal working. Hazledine's enthusiasm for the militia was such that during the construction work he organised his workers at Plas Kynaston into another company. As Rowland Hunt remarked at the official opening of the Aqueduct,

> Mr Hazledine, while engaged in an undertaking which would
> have absorbed the time, the attention and the capital of almost
> any other man – yet found resources, in an active and patriotic
> disposition, to lead and instruct the very artificers who craft the
> materials or erected this structure – in the practice of arms –

for the internal defence of that country, which he was enriching by the result of his and their labours.[41]

But military manoeuvres only took up a very small proportion of their time. Assembling the ironwork must have been both exhausting and frightening work for men unaccustomed to working at heights with no safety gear and up to 126ft (38m) above the stream below. Each arch rib section had to be lifted by means of pulleys attached to A-frames onto the trestles, manoeuvred into place, and then bolted first onto the piers, and then the middle section joined to the two ends, perhaps using wooden centring as a support. Once the ribs were in place it would have been easier to add the trough, but still an alarming experience when the weather was cold, wet or windy. The recent computer-aided simulation[42] is helpful in showing the sequence of construction, but the TV programme of the reconstruction of the erection of the Iron Bridge gives more of an idea of the effort involved.[43] The accuracy to which the piers were built is astonishing – there was almost no margin for error with fitting the precast ironwork sections.

As regards the finishing of Pontcysyllte Aqueduct, it appears that Hazledine and Simpson were mostly left to their own devices. Telford had moved his base from Shrewsbury to the Salopian Coffee House in London in 1800.[44] In 1803 he was appointed, jointly with Jessop, to design and build the Caledonian Canal, and much of the summer of 1803 he was engaged in the work of surveying for the canal in Scotland.[45] Telford managed to persuade Matthew Davidson to return to Scotland to supervise the building of the eastern end of the Canal, so once the work on the canal was due to start, in late summer 1804, Davidson left Pontcysyllte for good.[46]

While Hazledine was busy finishing Pontcysyllte, Simpson, in collaboration with John Fletcher (d.1820), the engineer for the Chester Canal, extended the Ellesmere Canal from Tilstock near Whitchurch to join the Chester Canal at Hurleston, near Nantwich, finally completing the canal, though not on the line originally intended (Figure 16). This section of the canal included several lift bridges, with castings provided by Hazledine.[47] Both the Aqueduct and the eastern extension of the canal were finished by the autumn of 1805, just in time for the whole country to be cheered by the news of Nelson's victory at Trafalgar on 21st October (Figure 20).

The official opening of the Aqueduct was on Tuesday November 26th 1805, a ceremony which was widely reported, both locally and nationally.[48] Early in the morning the Aqueduct was filled with water, and by midday the threatening clouds had given way to bright winter sunshine. Every road and path leading to the area was filled with onlookers, till the numbers swelled to an estimated 8000. Just before 2pm six barges assembled at the Vroncysyllte Basin at the southern end of the Aqueduct. In the first were the Lords and Ladies and other notables, and in the second were the members of the committee, among them Thomas Telford. The third barge contained the band of the Shropshire Volunteers playing patriotic music, while all the contractors, supervisors and their families crammed into the fourth. Among them was William Hazledine, who took the opportunity for a bit of free advertising, having had a flag made with the inscription, 'Success to the iron trade of Great Britain, of which Pontcysyllte Aqueduct is a specimen'. The fifth and sixth barges were filled with anybody else who could get aboard. When the first barge entered the Aqueduct the Artillery Volunteers let off the first of sixteen rounds from guns captured at the Battle of Seringapatam in 1799, and between the volleys the cheering of the workmen and onlookers echoed around the river valley. The dignitaries went off for their lunch and to hear the oration by Rowland Hunt, who had been chairman of the committee during most of its existence.[49] During lunch a train of five wagons, each loaded with two tons of coal, and the whole drawn by just one horse, trundled down the newly built railway from collieries on the Plas Kynaston Estate. Willing workers loaded this coal, together with more already waiting on the quay, into two empty barges which had followed the procession. These then tagged onto the barge procession as it returned to Vroncysyllte. The first of these coal barges had a banner which read, 'This is the first trading boat which passed the great Aqueduct of Pontcysyllte, loaded from Plas Kynaston Collieries of the 26th day of November 1805.' Hazledine certainly milked the advertising possibilities of the day! But he also ensured that the workers, not just the dignitaries, were looked after, for while all the festivities were going on two sheep were being roasted nearby. Once they were ready, all those who had actually built the aqueduct crowded into the Plas Kynaston foundry to enjoy the feast, washed down with copious quantities of beer and ale. Hazledine knew how to look after his workforce, and they, in turn, rewarded him with loyalty.

Hazledine could afford such celebrations. Table 2 details what he was paid for his work on the Ellesmere Canal. In addition to this, he and John Simpson, as joint contractors, were paid £19,055 0s 10d for the masonry work on Chirk Aqueduct. If Simpson and Hazledine were equal partners in this firm, Hazledine's total income would have been around £35,000 (around £1,200,000 at today's prices [50]). As none of Hazledine's records survive, we do not know what his expenses were, and the whole contract took ten years to complete, but there seems little doubt that he made a handsome profit.

Table 2 – Payments to William Hazledine for work on the Ellesmere Canal[51]

Work performed	Cost (£ s d)
Castings for swivel bridges etc	70 18 08
Ironwork for Chirk Aqueduct	1843 11 11
Rails, wagon wheels etc for building embankment	219 19 00
Ironwork for Pontcysyllte Aqueduct	17284 17 05
Iron rails, nails etc for railway	3643 10 02
Ironwork for 'water line' (canal to bring water supply from Bala Lake via Llangollen)	98 07 10
Lime kiln building	683 10 00
Boats, weights and repairs	637 04 09
Total	**24481 19 10**

He not only profited financially, but the building of the canal, and especially the Aqueduct, propelled him into the local, if not national consciousness, enabling him to gain other contracts. Also the canal enabled him to move his products – coal, limestone, building stone, slate, and possibly ironstone – from his mines and quarries, and ironwork from the Plas Kynaston foundry, to customers in Shropshire, Cheshire, mid-Wales and beyond.

Endnotes

1 I have not been able to find the original source for this quotation.
2 C Hadfield, *Thomas Telford's Temptation*, M+M Baldwin 1993.
3 Oration to mark the opening of Pontcysyllte Aqueduct 26.11.1805, published by J&W Eddowes, 1806, SA WD25.7.
4 Details of the progress of the project can be found in many sources, e.g. Rolt 1979; Hadfield 1993, p.20ff provides more details on certain items, but does not give a strict chronological sequence. The originals of the Ellesmere Canal Minute Books are in The National Archives (TNA) RAIL 827/1-7. Some of these are on microfilm in SA Mic. 94.
5 RAIL 827/1-4, 7.11.1791 & 9.1792.
6 Rolt 1979, p.58.
7 TNA, Montgomeryshire Canal Minute Books, RAIL 852/11.
8 SJ 16.9.1795.
9 SJ 14.9.1796.
10 Hazledine took out a formal lease in 1799, but this document states that the land is 'now or late in the occupation of William Hazledine' SA D3651/D/31/85.
11 Hadfield 1993, p.33.
12 Rolt 1979, p.62.
13 Ironbridge Gorge Museum Trust (IGMT) 1981.3587, letter from Telford to Davidson, 25.12.1795.
14 Rolt 1979, p.64-5.
15 RAIL 827/7 – final accounts.
16 Rolt 1979, p.64; Rail 827/7 – final accounts show that Simpson built all the houses along the canal.
17 SA D3651/D/5/228.
18 Rolt 1979, pp.40 & 47.
19 SA transcript of Swan Hill Independent Chapel records.
20 IGMT 1981.3588, letter from Matthew Davidson to Thomas Davidson, 29.4.1809.
21 Ibid, letter from Matthew Davidson to Thomas Davidson, 24.8.1815.
22 Pattison 2007.
23 IGMT 1981.3587, letter from Thomas Telford to Matthew Davidson, 19.2.1796.
24 RAIL 827/2, 10.2.1797 & 28.6.1797; the advertisements probably never happened, since a search of the relevant newspapers has failed to find them.
25 Rolt 1979, p.48.
26 S Hughes, *The Archaeology of the Montgomeryshire Canal*, RCAHMW 1988, p.21.
27 Rolt 1979, p.69.
28 http://www.engineering-timelines.com/scripts/engineering Item.asp?id=781, accessed 2016.
29 RAIL 827/2.
30 Tour Journal of Sir Richard Colt Hoare, Vol. 1, 1801, NLW, Cardiff Library Deeds, 3.127; the lime works were presumably kilns for burning lime to

make lime mortar. These were built by Hazledine (RAIL 827/7, final accounts).

31 In the longer term, Chirk Aqueduct tended to leak badly enough for the ironwork to be replaced by an iron trough in 1869 (R Quenby, *Thomas Telford's Aqueducts on the Shropshire Union Canal,* Swan Hill Press, 1992, p.108ff).

32 Rail 827/2.

33 Ibid, T/EG 306; James Thomson was evidently so impressed with Hazledine's work that he joined him at Calcutt's, making lock gates for the Gotha Canal, among other things – see Thomas Telford correspondence IGMT 1982.471.19; Burton 2007.

34 ICE, Thomas Telford correspondence, T/EG 306.

35 http://vimeo.com/2267361, accessed 2016.

36 www.rcahmw.gov.uk/HI/ENG/Heritage+of+Wales/World+Heritage+Wales/ Pontcysyllte+Aqueduct+%26+Canal – this website is not currently available (2016).

37 SA Bridgwater Papers 212/Box 366; Rail 827/2.

38 SA Bridgwater Papers 212/Box 366.

39 SC 23.11.1804.

40 SC 8.11.1901.

41 Oration to mark the opening of Pontcysyllte Aqueduct 26.11.1805, SA WD25.7.

42 http://vimeo.com/2267361.

43 BBC 'Timewatch' 2002 – it is even more astonishing when one considers that the reconstruction was done at ground level at half linear scale, and the weight was one-eighth scale.

44 http://www.engineering-timelines.com/who/Telford_T/ telfordThomas7.asp.

45 Burton 1998, p.77ff.

46 Davidson last appears in the attendance records for the Ellesmere Canal subscribers in June 1804.

47 Rail 827/5, the final report, probably incorrectly, referred to these as swivel bridges.

48 For example, SJ 4.12.1805; *Gentleman's Magazine,* Dec 1805, p.1228; the same report, and the oration by Rowland Hunt at the formal banquet for dignitaries, was later printed (SA WD257). This description including quotations, is taken from the *Salopian Journal.*

49 SA WD257.

50 https://www.measuringworth.com/ukcompare/ accessed 2016.

51 RAIL 827/5, final report; I have ignored halfpennies (but Hazledine didn't!).

Chapter 6

More about Canals

THE ELLESMERE Canal was not Hazledine's first involvement in canal building, nor would it be his last. At the same time as the Ellesmere Canal was being built, plans were advanced to build the Montgomeryshire Canal, which would start from the Ellesmere Canal at Frankton (between Oswestry and Ellesmere) and run through what was then Montgomeryshire, terminating at Newtown. The main purpose would be to supply lime for the rich agricultural countryside, and coal, stone, slates, and other large items for the developing towns and villages along the way.

The first structures to be built on the Montgomeryshire Canal were aqueducts over the Rivers Vyrnwy and Rhiw. The contract for building the Vyrnwy Aqueduct (SJ 254197) was given to William Hazledine and his partner John Simpson.[1] This five-arched aqueduct was built in the style of canal pioneer James Brindley, with massive masonry foundations supporting a canal bed of puddled clay. The foundations, however, were built on the soft gravels of the broad River Vyrnwy Valley, and the season was exceptionally wet, so part of the parapet and towpath walls gave way soon after it was built.[2] As a result the Canal committee called in William Jessop for advice.[3] He sympathised with the engineer John Dadford, having had similar problems himself on the Cromford Canal, and repairs made the aqueduct serviceable. But this was not the end of Hazledine's involvement with the structure. In 1823 further repairs were undertaken, during which the Aqueduct nearly collapsed completely, and it had to be strengthened with wrought-iron rods and tie bars supplied in an emergency by Hazledine's foundry (Figure 21).[4] There seems little doubt that the problems encountered at Vyrnwy encouraged Jessop and the rest of the team planning the aqueducts at Chirk and Pontcysyllte to opt for an iron trough.

Before the work on the Ellesmere Canal was even finished, Telford had been appointed as engineer for the proposed Caledonian Canal, where work was begun in 1805, and was not completed until 1822. The purpose of this was to link the west and east coasts of Scotland via the Great Glen, joining existing lochs and providing a seaway large enough for ocean-going ships. This was an extremely ambitious project, since no canal on this scale had been attempted in Britain before and the remoteness of the Highlands made working there especially challenging.

Until his death in 1815, John Simpson acted as one of the main contractors for the western half of the canal, for which Hazledine supplied the ironwork. This consisted of 14 pairs of cast-iron lock gates and an unknown number of turn-bridges. Telford was forced to use cast iron for the lock gates because of the shortage of oak. Their size was unprecedented – the locks were 40ft (12.2m) wide and 20ft (6.1m) deep. The castings were made at Plas Kynaston, and first taken along the Ellesmere Canal to Chester, from where they were taken by sea to the western end of the Caledonian Canal. Sadly none of the original lock gates and only one of the turn-bridges, the one at Moy, survive (NN161826).

The next canal with which Hazledine was associated, albeit in a small way, was the Gota Canal in Sweden, which is part of a link between the North Sea and the Baltic. Thomas Telford was the consulting engineer and it proved even more challenging than the Caledonian Canal.[5] Apart from the difficulty and remoteness of the terrain, one of the main challenges was the lack of expertise amongst both the engineers and the workers. To help overcome these obstacles, Telford sent examples of tools and other equipment for the Swedes to copy, and also sent experienced workmen to help with the project. One area of expertise that the Swedes lacked was in the production of cast iron, which is perhaps surprising considering that their foundries had long been famed for producing bar iron of the highest quality. So Telford sent his assistant James Thomson to set up a foundry near the canal. He then returned to Calcutt's and in 1819 supervised the casting of a pair of lock gates and all the materials and equipment he would need for the erection of the gates. The whole order was then sent down the River Severn and shipped to Sweden. Hazledine received £537 11s 2d for this, which seems a lot, but it included such items as 10,000 fire bricks, 120 reverberating bricks (made in a hot current of air), fire clay and so on.[6] The Swedes proved more than capable of copying the gates, and the foundry became the basis of an important industrial complex at Motala. Thomson, meanwhile, returned to Calcutt's, where he supervised the works for a while.

Hazledine was a frequent user of the Shrewsbury Canal (which linked the East Shropshire coalfield with the county town). He leased part of Berwick Wharf (Figure 23), near Attingham Park, where he had a warehouse and a crane.[7] But his main activity was at the Canal Basin in Shrewsbury, where he had a large warehouse and a coal wharf. He seems to have been frustrated at the slowness of the Canal Committee in coming to decisions, being reprimanded for building a swivel bridge and a new warehouse without permission.[8] He not only used the wharf, but acted as a contractor for making alterations and improvements. For example, in 1833 he made a new cut to enable long boats to turn and in 1835 he was employed to enlarge this basin. This involved building a new warehouse for £550, sheds for £380, opening a new waterway opposite the canal basin (£169) and a new boundary wall (£225).[9] He was also involved in extending the canal to the new Butter and Cheese Market just opening on Howard Street.

All this extra activity in the Shrewsbury Canal Basin was the result of the Shrewsbury Canal being linked to the national canal network for the first time. This was via the Birmingham and Liverpool Junction Canal, which was opened in 1835 and joined the Shrewsbury Canal at Wappenshall (north of modern Telford). During the construction of other canals, Hazledine had just been a contractor – this time he was part of the management team and a major shareholder. Thomas Telford was the consulting engineer, but he was too ill to actively oversee the work, so Hazledine seems to have been often used for technical advice. One project he reported on was a new wharf at Market Drayton, the contract for which he undertook in 1834.[10] This involved a large warehouse, and a number of associated cottages and other buildings (Figure 22). For these and other works he was eventually paid £1,316.

In addition, Hazledine was contracted to supply the ironwork for two of the major aqueducts on the Birmingham and Liverpool Junction Canal – at Nantwich and at Stretton (on the Staffordshire/Shropshire border). These were accomplished with commendable speed, but at Stretton, with some degree of controversy. The Stretton Aqueduct was completed in 1832. The central panel on both sides of the elegant structure bears the inscription, 'Thomas Telford, F.R.S.L. and E. Engineer', but on the Shropshire side can just be made out the words, 'William Hazledine, Contractor', which have been painted out. When and why this happened is unknown. Quenby[11] suggests John Wilson and his brother, who were responsible for the masonry work, might have done it. The reasoning is, "why should Hazledine get all the credit, when their work had been just as important?" Maybe – but I wonder if a more likely explanation is that Telford's supporters used it as a way of attempting to 'airbrush' Hazledine out of the story and increase Telford's prestige, which would enhance their reputation as well? By this time Telford was 75 and two years away from death. The changes could even have been made after his death, to avoid giving him offence. We shall never know!

During the Birmingham and Liverpool Junction Canal we see Hazledine working with the aristocracy (such as the Marquis of Stafford and Viscount Clive) in the planning and management of the project. It is a reminder of how far he had risen in life, and of the way that all classes of society were drawn by his straightforwardness, competence and approachability. The humane way he dealt with his workmen is illustrated by two amusing incidents.

The first concerns a workman who objected to being told what to do. "Who are you," he said, "what better are you than I am? I can remember the time when you carried your wallet [containing his lunch] on your back to work." "Why, Tom," replied Hazledine, "Can you remember no longer than that? I can remember when I had no wallet to carry!"[12]

The other incident is best described by his obituarist,

Mr Hazledine had less than most men of the rank to which he had elevated himself of that false pride which would lead him to pass by an old friend because he was poor. A laughable incident, characteristic of all his conduct in cases of this description, took place on one occasion in Chester. He had been constructing a bridge for the Marquis of Westminster [Eaton Hall Bridge] near that city, and being the race week he drove out to the course in his gig. The first man he met whom he recognised was a workman of his own, a soul endowed with an unquenchable thirst, who had gathered around him a crowd intently listening to the warbling of the mellifluous song of

"Giles Scroggin courted Molly Brown". Hazledine was wonder-struck at the spectacle of his own workman whom he had left comfortably at work in Shrewsbury thus engaged on the Chester Race Course, and stopping his gig till the song had ceased, he roared out with his stentorian voice, "Jack, lad, what bring'st thee so far from home? Dost na' thee want a jug of drunk to clear they pipes?" "Aye, bless thee, Master," was Jack's reply, "or I'le never see ou'd Coleham again. For the ruck o' these cheese-chawers here have only give me a half-penny in two hours' singing!" Hazledine desired him to step into his gig, and, taking him to the stand, crammed him full of what was there to be obtained, telling at the same time all his friends of the queer manner in which he had fallen in with his old fellow-workman. Next day he clothed him in a new suit and sent him off by the coach to Shrewsbury.[13]

Endnotes

 1 Hughes 1988, p.15ff, 152.
 2 RAIL 852/11.
 3 Hughes 1988, p.22.
 4 RAIL 852/5.
 5 Burton, 1999, p.199ff, especially p.130.
 6 ICE, T/GC.208.
 7 William Hazledine's will SA D55.5 v.f.
 8 TNA RAIL868/1, 12.10.1833.
 9 TNA RAIL868/1, 13+22.7.1835.
10 SA 901/1.
11 Quenby, 1992, p.83.
12 SA 901/1.
13 SC 29.11.1901.

Chapter 7

Challenges and Opportunities

RUNNING your own business at any time is a difficult occupation; it is hard for us now to imagine the immensity of the challenges Hazledine faced. For over 20 years (1792–1815) Britain was almost continually at war with France. While not on the scale of the World Wars of the twentieth century, this resulted in immense disruption, with gains as well as losses for businessmen such as Hazledine.

Because it was not possible generally to import food from the continent, prices of British produce, especially grain, were high. This produced a boom in agriculture, and hence the need for more and better mills, and consequently much work for millwrights, such as Hazledine. But after the end of the war agriculture became less profitable, resulting in few orders for new or improved mills. No doubt there was a continued need for repairs and renewals, but that side of the business presumably just 'ticked over'.

One new mill contract that he eventually got became a talking-point in the town. It concerned Cound Mill (SJ 556056), then owned by Shropshire MP and noted eccentric John Cresset Pelham

(1769–1838). The story behind this Hazledine later often recounted with much glee. Hazledine's obituary explains what happened,[1]

> These two originals met one day near the Post Office, and Mr Pelham told Hazledine that as he wished to remove Cound Mill nearer to the water which drove it, he would be glad if Hazledine would immediately set about the job. Hazledine, somewhat astonished, said, "Wouldn't it be better to bring the water nearer the mill, than to demolish the building to bring it nearer the water?" "I don't want your advice," says Mr Pelham, turning on his heel and walking off. "I don't want your job," replied Hazledine, driving his gig onwards to his residence. And the pair continued shouting, "I don't want your advice," and "I don't want your job," till they were out of each other's hearing.
>
> Eighteen months thereafter, not a word having passed them on the subject during all that time, Mr Pelham walked into Mr Hazledine's office, and briefly asked him to "do the job at Cound," which Hazledine answered with a nod. And the work, involving an expenditure of many hundred pounds, was completed without another word passing between them!

As a footnote to the story, for some reason Hazledine himself leased Cound Mill from about 1830. Quite why he did is not obvious, but presumably he saw it as a money-making opportunity.[2]

The wars with France were a mixed blessing for ironmasters. Those who supplied cannon and other ordnance to the military became very rich. One such was Alexander Brodie (1733–c1805), who purchased Calcutt's Ironworks, on the River Severn near Jackfield, in 1786 where they specialised in boring cannon.[3] This was so lucrative that when he died he was worth £100,000 (over £7m today). Calcutt's was taken over by his nephew, but declined rapidly, until the lease was taken over by Hazledine in about 1816. Such a transaction was typical of Hazledine – buying up or leasing properties that came up at a knockdown price, when he thought they had the potential to be a business proposition or at least increase in value.

Calcutt's, though, seemed to be a mixed blessing. It was a complete ironworks, producing pig iron from coke, ironstone and limestone, bar iron of high quality and also cast iron. Its position allowed him to tender competitively for contracts over a wider area. An example of this was a large cast-iron reservoir for Worcester Waterworks, which he tendered for in July 1817, stating that 'it will be cast at my works at Calcutt'.[4] In the event his wasn't the cheapest tender, but the competition was stiff, with no less than eight firms putting in a bid. Despite much hard work, it seems that Calcutt's never prospered, and Hazledine relinquished it around 1831. Charles Hulbert summed up Hazledine's involvement thus,

> Mr Hazledine occupied a foundry here for 14 years; but such was the unpropitiousness of the period, even his master talents could not ensure success. He consequently lost some thousands on the adventure.[5]

Hazledine grew his business gradually, a process which is exemplified by the development of his headquarters at the bottom of Wyle Cop, Shrewsbury. In late 1789 he leased the property previously occupied by a whitesmith.[6] This comprised a good sized house (or messuage), possibly another smaller house, a brewhouse, workshops and other outbuildings.[7] The whole site was on the north side of Wyle Cop at the western end of the English Bridge, and adjoined the River Severn (SJ 495124). It is probable that he himself lived in the 'messuage', since his children were baptised at St Julian's, in which parish the house was. His millwrighting business was run from there, as was the whitesmith's, which continued. By 1805 he had purchased the freehold of the two houses for £200.

In the autumn of 1804 he was also able to purchase Jones' Mansion next door for about £5,575, with a mortgage for at least

£4000. This medieval property had become quite run down, especially since the level of Wyle Cop had been raised after the building of the English Bridge in 1769, which resulted in part of the building being below street level, and hence prone to flooding. After May 1805, he combined Jones' Mansion with his original property to make one site. On this he and his partner, John Simpson, built several houses, workshops, a laundry, stables and warehouses, and this became the hub of his growing business. During this rebuilding they also demolished whatever was left of the old town wall that ran across the site.

Despite his business success he sometimes ran into financial difficulties, such as when he lost money on the contract for Bonar Bridge in 1812. On one such occasion in 1815 he had to use these premises as collateral to raise a further loan to tide him over. However, his business strength was such that he paid the loan off in four years.

Another way of growing his business was to use his enormous talents and energy to diversify into other fields. One such was the timber trade, which he was involved in from at least 1795.[8] His ironworks needed much timber, both for pattern-making and as charcoal for the production of the finest cast iron. Hazledine not only bought timber for his own use, but he, in partnership with others, bought and sold it. A typical arrangement concerned the sale of 292 fir trees on the estate of Robert More at Linley in 1815.[9] For this Hazledine and his partner paid £73 10s as a down payment and then £661 10s in two half-yearly instalments, a total of £1396 10s. The vendors had to fell and carry away the timber themselves, but had permission to sink sawpits and erect cabins for the workers to stay in. They could not, however, make fires for the production of charcoal. It is possible that each tree could fetch £50,[10] in which case the contract could make £14,600, so, even allowing for the labour-intensive work of chopping down the trees, and sawing up and transporting the wood, there was a considerable profit to be made.

Occasionally, rather than paying money for trees, Hazledine treated them as payment for work done. For example, when he did the work on the Attingham Picture Gallery roof (Figure 14), as well as his monetary payment Hazledine accepted timber (both standing and cordwood for charcoal), in part payment. This came from Sutton Wood, near Madeley, then owned by the Attingham Estate.[11] 'Bartering' in this way would have saved time and money for both parties.

While he was basically concerned to make a profit from these deals he also couldn't resist the odd quirky or speculative deal. His obituarist explains,

> Mr Hazledine was always open to an odd and speculative bargain... In 1808 he made purchase at Ruyton-XI-Towns of an oak tree growing a short distance from Ruyton Hall, over 60 feet high, and about 18 feet circumference a short distance above the ground. He gave 145 guineas for this tree, and out of it was made an altar table and altar rails for Ruyton Church, and a hall table for Ruyton Hall, leaving no doubt a satisfactory balance to the profit of the buyer.[12]

This is confirmed by a receipt in the Powis Castle archive, showing that in 1817 Hazledine was paid 5 guineas for a pillar stand table made from part of the Ruyton Oak.[13]

Another of the raw materials needed in the production of iron was limestone. This was added to the coke and ironstone in the furnace and many of the impurities in the ironstone became attached to the limestone, and the whole could be removed as slag. The same process happened with the production of cast iron, when further impurities in the bar iron were removed by the addition of limestone to the furnace. Hazledine thus needed good quality limestone, and as well as buying it for himself he also traded in the material. Lime was also much used for both building (as mortar) and in agriculture to improve acid soils. For the latter two uses the limestone had to be burned in kilns at a high temperature to produce quicklime.[14] Hazledine had interests in these activities from at least 1798.[15] Some of the limestone he obtained from his own Plas Kynaston Estate, while the rest he purchased from the quarries at Llanymynech or elsewhere. With a partner he owned limeworks near Llanymynech, Belan near Welshpool, Porth-y-waen near Llanyblodwel, and Garthmyl near Berriew. The reason for these locations was their proximity to the Montgomery Canal. The kilns were built into the banks of the canal to allow easy access for the limestone.[16] Carts would then carry it from the barges to the charging hole at the top of the kiln and then collect the quicklime from the kiln below. Quicklime, however, cannot be transported by water, as it has a violent reaction with water if any is spilled, so it had to be bought direct from the kiln and transported by the farmer to his land nearby. The process was coordinated from Welshpool or Newtown, where Hazledine had warehouses at the canal basins.[17]

The same route was used for coal and stone products from Plas Kynaston. These were loaded onto barges at the basin beside the Pontcysyllte Aqueduct and then transported to the communities along the Montgomery Canal. There are incidental records of slates, coping stones, 'crests' (ridge tiles) from big landowners such as Powis Castle and Glansevern Hall, but no doubt whole communities were supplied in this way. In addition, the warehouses at the basins at Welshpool and Newtown acted as distribution points for coal and stone products for the towns and surrounding area.

Another sideline for William Hazledine was speculation in mining. At that time there was a great deal of hope that significant amounts of lead, copper and barytes might be discovered under the Shropshire soil, and various consortia were set up to raise money for exploration. For example, in 1801 Charles Muckleston, Lord of the Manor of Brownlow and Meadowtown (in south west Shropshire), entered into an agreement with a consortium of nine men, headed by Hazledine, to exploit his land for lead, copper, tin, calamine [zinc], Black Jack [zinc blende] etc.[18] Nothing is known about the further history of this enterprise, so presumably it was a failure. Another lease Hazledine took out on his own account in 1803 related to the Manor of Roden (beyond Shawbury on the edge of the East Shropshire Coalfield) for the extraction of stone, coal, ironstone and limestone.[19] Since there is no evidence that such mines or quarries were actually dug, presumably nothing came of this venture either.

A more successful involvement in mines was an agreement Hazledine entered into in 1824 to lease mines in Wrockwardine.[20] This agreement did not appear to last long, as Hazledine seems to have found it easier to purchase from others. For example, in 1813 he entered into an agreement with the Lilleshall Company to buy 20,000 tons of coal yearly, the coal to be delivered to the Donnington Wood Canal.[21] Hazledine also purchased 90 tub boats from the Company, which he used to transport the coal on the Shrewsbury Canal to the county town. On the way, the canal passed beside Upton Forge, which was the destination for some of the best coal for iron production, and Berwick Wharf (just north of Attingham Park), where some was offloaded for local consumption. (Figure 23) At the Shrewsbury Canal Basin (now the British Rail car park), Hazledine had a large base with wharves and warehouses, from where the coal was delivered to the town and surrounding area.

Hazledine is styled 'a master builder' in one contemporary document,[22] and he used this aspect of his training to good effect. For much of this work he was in partnership with his friend John Simpson, an example being the rebuilding of the Welshpool Town Hall and Cloth Market, completed in 1804.[23] (Figure 24) There are probably a number of properties in Shrewsbury built by him, but the only one we have documentary evidence of is what is now known as Old Mount Pleasant. These are five large Georgian-style houses tucked in between what is now Mount Pleasant Road and Whitemere Road in the north of the town. They were built in the late 1830s to a high specification and originally had large gardens and stables to accommodate 30 horses.[24] Quite why Hazledine should have built these houses in what was then the outskirts of the town is hard to know, but presumably he bought the land cheaply and could see that the area was ripe for development.

Another property he was involved in, though did not build, was the Armoury, between Wenlock Road and London Road in Shrewsbury. This building had a chequered history, and was never fully utilised for its original purpose. In 1827 it was offered for sale, and Hazledine picked it up for £2,700.[25] Hazledine rented out the associated houses, but seems to have done nothing with the main Armoury, selling it in 1835 to the 3rd Lord Berwick (1773–1842) for £3292.[26] In addition to buying the property, Lord Berwick also paid Hazledine £317 12s 2d (the equivalent of £30,000 today) for grand cast-iron entrance gates.

But there were many challenges along the way. As has been noted with the Worcester Waterworks, Hazledine must have failed to obtain many contracts. Examples of this are Overton Bridge (1812) and the Grosvenor Bridge in Chester (1825). In both cases he provided estimates for iron bridges, but the proprietors preferred to go with traditional stone.

One contract that he did obtain that proved to be a great source of trouble to him was for the ironwork for the Custom House Docks in Dublin. While this was not Hazledine's finest hour, his work on Dublin docks illustrates the complexities of undertaking major contracts at that time. The project also demonstrated Hazledine's close friendship with, and indebtedness to, Telford who acted as a consultant for the dock work. Hazledine's contribution was to supply the roof, columns, beams and other ironwork for the west store. Contracts were signed in October 1820, with a completion date of December 1821.[27] By December 1821 it was clear that Hazledine was well behind schedule, and the resident engineer, John Aird, was despatched to Shrewsbury to investigate. Despite a favourable report, the Admiralty Board quickly began demanding compensation from Hazledine and applied to Telford for a report. Telford produced this in March 1822, stating that 'if consulted I should have advised the Board to allow another year [for the contract]'. Telford reduced the claim to £500, going on to state that 'I have from 20 years' experience found him [Hazledine] very industrious and capable of great exertion and performing his work well.' Telford also cited in mitigation 'the excess anxiety of transporting by sea as ... evidenced by a cargo containing all the ironwork having been shipped at Chester 6 weeks ago, and not yet arrived in Dublin ...' The roof was shipped in June 1822, but quite what happened to some of the other ironwork is not known, for Hazledine later wrote that he had had to have some components cast again in Dublin 'at great cost' and the items cast in Shrewsbury were not used.

The work was eventually completed in 1823, but the dispute over the size of the penalty rumbled on. In the end Hazledine travelled to London to be interviewed by the Lords of the Treasury. They were evidently sympathetic to his problems and reduced the penalty by £250. After this visit to London Hazledine wrote to Telford, 'I was in hopes of seeing you in person ... I am very sorry to have given my friends so much trouble in this business, but the balance will be of essential service to me.'

A contract with a happier outcome was St John's Market, Liverpool, opened in 1822. Here, Hazledine's Foundry supplied 116 cast-iron pillars each 25 feet high, which helped to produce a very light and airy ambience, much admired by artists and travellers (Figure 25). Sadly, the city council allowed the structure to deteriorate and it was demolished in 1964 as part of the redevelopment of the city centre.

Endnotes

1   SC Nov 6th 1840.
2   William Salt Library, Stafford 350/40/3.
3   John Randall, *Broseley and its surroundings*, 1879, Salopian and West Midland Journal, p.119.
4   Worcester Archives, Box 4965/9369/U9/95.
5   Hulbert, 1837, p.343.
6   A whitesmith was 'a worker in tinned or white iron; a tinsmith; a polisher or finisher of metals'.
7   SC 27.11.1789.
8   SC 19.4.1795.
9   SA D3651/D/5/624.
10 http://www.usbornefamilytree.com/timberimports.htm (accessed 2016).
11 SA 112/6/Box53/315.
12 SC 8.11.1901.
13 National Library of Wales, Powis Castle Deeds (5), 7174.
14 Richard Williams, *Limekilns and Limeburning*, Shire, 2004.
15 SJ 2.5.1798.
16 Hughes, 1983, p.55ff.
17 Pigot's North Wales Directory 1829.
18 SA D3651/D/31/183.
19 SA D3651/D/31/184.
20 SA D3651/D/20/698.
21 IGMT Lilleshall Company Collection 1998.320 (DLID/3)/236.
22 SA D3651/D/5/228.
23 Letter in *Archaeologia Cambrensis*, 13:51 (1882:July), p.235.
24 SA 901/1.
25 SC 5.12.1827; SA D3651/D/1/378; SA 112/5/19/48-9.
26 SA 112/5/19/50-1.
27 References for this section are from the Telford Correspondence at the Institution of Civil Engineers.

Chapter 8

Bridges

I T TOOK a long time for cast-iron arch bridges to become commonplace after the erection of the Iron Bridge at Coalbrookdale, which opened on January 1st 1781. The reasons for this included cost, the difficulty of transporting iron components manufactured at a distance, and the well-publicised failure of bridges at Staines, Middlesex, and Yarm, Yorkshire in 1803 and 1806 respectively. These failures were due to both design and construction faults. At this time there was a growing realisation that, as the strength of cast iron was established by tests such as those described in Chapter 4, bridges made of this material had to be well designed and the components made to the highest standards if they were not to fail. The combination of Thomas Telford as designer and William Hazledine as manufacturer fulfilled both these criteria. The success of the Pontcysyllte Aqueduct seems to have reassured the two men that cast-iron arch bridges were safe, but it was a further six years after Pontcysyllte was opened in 1805 before they built their first iron bridge together. This was quite a modest affair at Meole Brace on the southern outskirts of Shrewsbury (SJ 491107).

The original documents have been lost, but it appears that Telford did the preliminary sketch, while his assistant Thomas

Stanton did the detailed drawings. Hazledine's estimate for the ironwork was £360, and John Simpson was employed to build the stone abutments for £1,825.[1] The ironwork consisted of four ribs, each cast in two halves, which were mirror images of each other. The ribs sprang from sloping stone abutments, and consisted of a curved lower member and a straight upper member. Between the two was another member of a lesser curvature to the lower one, pierced by holes for cross members to join the arches together. The three horizontals were joined by uprights shaped to be reminiscent of the voussoirs of a stone bridge or the sections of the Pontcysyllte Aqueduct. The cast-iron roadway was bolted onto the upper members of the arches. This provided further stability for the bridge, which had a span of 55ft (16.8m). Opened in 1811, apart from routine maintenance, Meole Brace Bridge survived till 1933, when it was demolished to make way for a modern concrete bridge.

The next significant bridge built by the same team was at Cantlop (SJ 517063) (Figure 26), which spans the Cound Brook on the road south from Shrewsbury to Pitchford, and was built in 1813.[2] It was also built to Telford's design, and it is most likely that Hazledine and Simpson built it.[3] Like Meole, it has four arch ribs, but a shorter span of 31ft (9.5m), and is the only surviving bridge of this design still in its original location. As such it has its original railings, which are of a typical design that Hazledine used on many other bridges. Hairline cracks were noticed in Cantlop Bridge in 1974, so it is now bypassed.

The last of this group of Hazledine bridges was built on the main Shrewsbury to Bridgnorth road at Cound (SJ 558057) in 1818. William Hazledine was contracted to produce the ironwork for £494, the stonework being erected by local builder John Carline, since by this time John Simpson had died.[4] The four ribs of 55ft (16.8m) were exactly the same dimensions as Meole Brace. This bridge survived until 1967, when it was replaced by one designed to carry modern traffic. The ribs and railings, however, were preserved, and two ribs were incorporated into a pedestrian bridge over Hall Park Way in Telford Town Centre in 1988 (Figure 27).[5]

Hazledine's obituary stated that he had been responsible for 'several small iron bridges in this county, and many others all over the kingdom,'[6] which suggests that there may be other as yet unrecognised examples of his work. One such is the Dolforgan Estate Bridge in Kerry, Powys (SO 144901), restored in 2002/3. This bridge was erected by 1818, and incorporates the trademark Hazledine railings, though the four arch ribs (cast in two halves) incorporate different designs from those in Shropshire (perhaps a reflection on their small size and the lesser strength needed for an estate bridge) (Figures 28 and 29).

A 'one-off' Telford Bridge for which Hazledine supplied the ironwork is at Tenbury Wells on the Worcestershire/Shropshire border, which by 1812 urgently needed action to make it wider. Taking down and rebuilding the bridge with stone would have cost £7000–£8000[7], so in April 1812 Telford proposed an ingenious way of widening the bridge using 12 cast-iron arches set into each side of the stonework of each side of the 6 arches of the bridge to carry a new roadway and so allow a total increased width of 5ft 4in. Hazledine got the ironwork contract[8], and John Simpson did the building work. The design for the cast-iron arches and hand rails for Tenbury appears to have been on a smaller scale but very similar to that for the other small Shropshire bridges, though the iron arch for Tenbury is single. The work was completed in 1815, and lasted until 1871 when the bridge was widened again.

At the same period as these small cast-iron Shropshire bridges Telford was also designing much more ambitious structures in the same material, beginning in Scottish locations where the nature of the terrain made stone impractical. The first of these was at Bonar Ferry (NH 609917), and spanned the Kyle of Sutherland north of

Inverness.[9] This bridge has been described as 'epoch-making'[10], and the poet Robert Southey wrote that,

> I could see no bridge. At last I came in sight of something like a spider's web in the air. If this be it, thought I, it will never do! But, presently, I came upon it; and oh! it is the finest thing that ever was made by God or man!

What had struck Southey was the design of the spandrel bracings to form lozenges, which made the bridge look like a spider's web from a distance (Figure 30). But this was just part of Telford's revolutionary design to produce a strong, lightweight arch of 150ft (45.7m). For this to succeed he needed the best contractors, so he naturally turned to his friends John Simpson, for the approach roads and abutments, and William Hazledine, for the ironwork. The two men reluctantly agreed with Telford on a fixed price contract, of which Hazledine was to get £3,100 15s for the ironwork.[11] Telford wrote in July 1811 that Simpson and his partner John Cargill 'are miserable about undertaking Bonar Bridge at a closed sum, and to undertake to uphold [keep to] it.' Hazledine was likewise 'miserable' and would gladly have relinquished the project.[12] Their misgivings were understandable. In 1811 the country was exhausted after nearly 20 years of war with France, with many working men away fighting. In addition, the north of Scotland was extremely remote and inaccessible, and all the bridge castings, which were to be made at the Plas Kynaston foundry, had to be sent by canal to Chester and then undertake the long and dangerous sea voyage round the north of Scotland. Finally, such a bridge had never been made before – to expect Hazledine's men to erect the first in such a difficult location must have seemed a very risky undertaking. In the end the main problem with the bridge was that Telford hadn't surveyed the foundations adequately and had to hastily redesign it with two masonry arches in addition to the iron arch.[13] All this extra work meant that Telford had to give way on the financial details and Hazledine was eventually paid £3947.[14]

As planned, the ironwork was cast at Plas Kynaston, under the supervision of William Stuttle. In early June the bridge was erected in front of the foundry to ensure that it all fitted into place, and there it became 'a new object of attraction and wonder' according to the local paper, which went on to describe it as 'an admirable union of strength with neatness and elegance.'[15] At the end of the month it began its long journey north, followed soon after by Stuttle and two of his colleagues who were to erect the bridge. By mid-November they had finished the ironwork, in 'a masterly manner', according to Matthew Davidson.[16] Bonar Bridge survived until it was washed away in a flood in 1892. It became the template for others, a number of which are still standing.

The first of these was Craigellachie Bridge (NJ 285452), which spans the River Spey 19km above Fochabers.[17] The arch of 150ft (45.7m) is identical in size to Bonar and of the same construction, and like Bonar it was cast at Plas Kynaston, before making the even longer voyage round the north of Scotland to Speymouth, finishing its journey by horse and cart. Again William Stuttle and assistants did the erection, which took just two months, August and September 1814. But first they had to check and repair any damaged items in a smith's shop they built nearby. The bridge remained in full use until 1963, when it had to be dismantled above arch level due to some of the components working loose. As much of the ironwork as possible was retained, and the rest replaced with identical parts in steel.[18] This provided an opportunity to understand the bridge's construction, the complexity of just part of which is demonstrated in Figure 31.

A metallurgical analysis of the castings was done, the results of which are detailed in Table 3. The table also shows average metallurgical values of the ironwork at the Ditherington Flax Mill. Even making allowances for the small number of samples and possibility of changes in analytical methods, the results show an increase in purity, with less sulphur and phosphorus, and an increase in the beneficial manganese. In 1963 it was stated that the metal bore some of the characteristics of 'primitive steel', but it was cast iron of the highest quality.[19] In summary, Lowson, the engineer in charge of the reconstruction project, stated that,

> 'It did not seem possible that this [design] could have worked at all, but it did!'[20]

Table 3 – Comparison of the metallurgical analysis of beams at Ditherington Flax Mill (1797) and Craigellachie Bridge (1814)[21]

Element	Ditherington Flax Mill Beams (average) (%)	Craigellachie Bridge (%)
Total carbon	3.35	3.61
Silicon	0.91	0.98
Manganese	0.40	0.72
Sulphur	0.19	0.05
Phosphorus	1.02	0.62

The next bridge of this type designed by Telford and built by Hazledine is the 'Waterloo' Bridge at Bettws-y-Coed (SH799557), erected as part of the remodelling of the Holyhead Road. The bridge bears the date 1815, but was not erected until late 1816.[22] Like Bonar and Craigellachie, it was cast at Plas Kynaston; it then went by canal to Chester, by sea as far up the Conwy River as possible, and finally by horse and cart. With a span of 105ft (46m), the main feature of the bridge is the magnificent castings (doubling as spandrel bracers) of the emblems of the four countries of the Union – the leek, thistle, rose and shamrock, which surmount the words, 'this arch was constructed in the same year the battle of

Waterloo was fought'. On the opposite side of the bridge are two plaques, one to Telford, the other to Hazledine and Stuttle. Hazledine was paid £2,577 (around £108,000 in today's prices) for this contract.

The River Esk Bridge (locally known as the Metal Bridge) (NY 354649) is the least documented of this group. It was erected in 1820 as part of Telford's work on the Carlisle to Glasgow main road (now the M6/A74) just south of the Scottish border.[23] It had three cast-iron spans; the southernmost span measured 150ft (46m), like Bonar and Craigellachie, while the other two were 105ft (32m), like Waterloo. Evidently Telford used these dimensions as a way of saving money, knowing the patterns were already made. Once more the casting was done at Plas Kynaston. In 1911 the bridge was found to be severely corroded, and replaced with a modern ferro-concrete one. Considering that at this point the Esk is as broad as the Thames in London, and has a tidal range of over 16ft (5m), this bridge was a considerable engineering and constructional achievement.

The next bridge of this type that the Hazledine team erected was in 1824 and it spanned the River Dee on the Duke of Westminster's estate at Eaton Hall, near Chester (SJ 418601).[24] The bridge has an arch of 150ft (46m), which is the same as Bonar and Craigellachie, and also has four ribs cast in seven sections.[25] The ironfounders were able to indulge in fancy spandrel lattice decorations. Unlike the other bridges of this type, there is no evidence that Thomas Telford was involved in the design. Plaques on the side of the bridge mention William Crosley (surveyor), William Stuttle (resident engineer), William Stuttle Junior (founder) and William Hazledine (contractor). William Crosley was a well-respected engineer, whom Hazledine presumably used to do the survey, while he supplied the bridge 'off the shelf', as it were. It was also cast at Plas Kynaston, and then sent the short canal journey to Chester. Being an estate bridge meant that it has not had to deal with heavy traffic, and so it remains as originally built.

The last two bridges of this type for which Hazledine did the ironwork are both over the River Severn. They are Mythe, which now carries the A438 route out of Tewkesbury, Gloucestershire (SO 889337), and Holt Fleet, which carries the A4133 road near Ombersley, Worcs (SO 824634). The former was opened in 1826, the latter in 1828, and both are still in use, albeit after strengthening. It has been suggested that these bridges were cast at Coleham, but since we know that Laira Bridge (see below) was cast at Calcutt's, they may just as well have been cast there. Either way, transport was easy down the Severn. Holt Fleet is a standard Telford/Hazledine design and construction, with the usual 150ft (46m) arch with five ribs (Figure 32).

Telford reluctantly became involved at Mythe in 1824 after a disagreement between the previous architect and the Trustees.[26] Part of the 'deal' with him coming on board was that Hazledine should do the ironwork, as he wrote,

> As Mr Hazledine has at his works some of the apparatus used in the three [he seems to have meant 'four', as he had written four earlier in the report] similar bridges he has constructed for me, and his works being adapted and his workmen accustomed to the management of all the parts, he will execute the proposed plan of one arch of 170ft [51.8m] span for the same sum as his former proposal contained, that is to say £4,500.[27]

In addition to being 20ft longer than the others he had designed, this bridge was also seven feet wider to allow for toll-paying pedestrians. To accommodate this, there are six arch ribs, rather than five, and to further strengthen the structure the spandrel lozenges are vertically aligned.

The two major cast-iron arch bridges of a different pattern for which Hazledine provided the ironwork were both opened in 1827.

The first was the Laira (or Lary) Bridge (TA 044882), over the Estuary of the River Plym, near Plymouth. The original plan was for a suspension bridge, for which Hazledine had obtained the ironwork contract, but that was abandoned in favour of a cast-iron bridge with five arches, each having five ribs (Figure 33). The central arch had a span of 100ft (30.5m), while that of the adjoining arches was 95ft (30m) and that of the outer two 81ft (24.7m). The bridge was designed by up and coming architect James Rendel (1799–1856), a protégé of Telford, who travelled to Shrewsbury in August 1824 to clinch the ironwork contract for the newly-designed bridge.[28]

In March 1825 the patterns were ready and Hazledine made the long journey to Plymouth to make final arrangements before casting began at Calcutt's. The building work was subject to delay from many directions, such as antagonistic nearby landowners, a disgruntled contractor, and problems with foundations. All these delays were probably just as well, as Hazledine was struggling to provide the ironwork on time. His works were very busy, and over the summer of 1826 the water level in the River Severn was so low that it was impossible to ship anything. But in addition, Hazledine himself was involved in a serious accident early on Monday September 18th 1826 when a runaway cart collided with his gig on Wyle Cop, Shrewsbury.[29] Both he and his young granddaughter were thrown out of the gig. She was unharmed, but he had a compound fracture of his arm and a dislocated elbow. The dislocation had to be reduced and the arm manipulated without anaesthetic.[30] It is said that the shock of this accident precipitated the sudden death of his wife Eleanor just three weeks later, on 4th October.[31] Astonishingly, Hazledine had only about six weeks off work, and he was soon able to oversee the shipping of the ironwork down the Severn to Bristol, from whence it sailed round Land's End to Plymouth. Having more or less fulfilled the agreement that he would supply the ironwork by the end of 1826, Hazledine hoped that Lord Morley, who was financing the bridge, would allow his men to wait until the spring for the work of erection to start. Lord Morley, however, would have none of it, as he was in seriously straitened financial circumstances, so Hazledine had no option but to send William Stuttle to supervise such a foolhardy venture. Some days the wind was so strong that it was impossible for them to work, and at other times frost had the same effect. Perhaps inevitably, Stuttle, worn out by years of overwork and far from young, succumbed to pneumonia from which he didn't recover, dying on February 23rd 1827. Hazledine was devastated, but had no option but to substitute Stuttle's son, also William, for his father. Stuttle junior proved an able and energetic replacement, and the ironwork erection proceeded rapidly enough for the bridge to be officially opened on July 14th 1827. Perhaps Hazledine wondered if the £13,761 he received for the ironwork was worth it. This bridge lasted until 1962 before it was replaced – a testimony to excellent design and workmanship.

Hazledine's last major cast-iron arch bridge contract was that for the Cleveland Bridge, Bath (SO 753657), designed by architect Henry Goodridge. It is built in neo-classical style with four symmetrical 'tollhouses' (only one was actually used for the purpose). The span is 110ft (33.9m), with seven ribs, each made from five segments, cast at Coleham.[32] At 36ft (11.1m) this is the widest Hazledine bridge (Figure 34). A newspaper report recording the finding of Roman coins during the excavations for one of the abutments of the bridge states that the workmen were employed by Hazledine, and a plaque on the bridge records Hazledine as the contractor, not just as having supplied the ironwork.[33] The bridge was opened in October 1827,[34] and is still in daily use. Because it carries the heaviest of traffic, the bridge has had to be strengthened twice in the last 80 years. Hazledine's original ironwork has been tastefully retained, but now carries almost no weight.

Hazledine's foundries also cast a number of swing (more correctly 'turn') bridges. These were favoured for little-used routes over relatively narrow channels, and so allowed the free passage of boats. The only example still in use is Moy Swing Bridge on the Caledonian Canal (NN 162826), which was originally one of several on the canal, all of which were cast at Plas Kynaston.[35] Moy Bridge was erected in 1820, and has a span of 40ft (12.2m) and is 10ft (3.05m) wide. It has two counter-balanced arms turned by hand, which pivot on horizontal bearings. The arms meet at the middle, which means that the lock keeper has to row to the other side to close the bridge for road traffic. Hazledine also supplied swing bridges for Princes and Georges Docks in Liverpool in 1820, and the Shadwell entrance of the Eastern Dock in London in 1830–31. These bridges have been demolished. It is possible that a study of the records of other docks may reveal more such Hazledine bridges.

The final group of Hazledine bridges are small ones, either built of stone, or using simple iron girders. The best documented of these were for the Kington Tramroad.[36] This was part of a tramroad system that linked the border areas of Wales and Herefordshire to the Brecknock and Abergavenny Canal at Brecon. The contract for the 12-mile section from Burlingjobb to Kington was won by Hazledine in partnership with local surveyor Morris Sayce. Hazledine obviously provided the iron rails, and he also made some rather crude iron bridges, such as one over the River Arrow. There is no record of who designed the stone bridges – it may well have been Hazledine also.

Another project for which Hazledine was responsible was the construction of a towpath along the River Severn from Coalbrookdale to Shrewsbury. The scheme was agreed in February 1809, and the £5000 that Hazledine reckoned it would cost was raised by subscription, to which he contributed £500.[37] Hazledine was appointed surveyor, which involved designing and building gates, bridges, culverts and a house for the collector of tolls at Underdale.[38] Among the bridges were two over the Cound and

Leighton Brooks, both quite substantial rivers where they join the Severn. The towpath was opened by early December 1809,[39] a remarkable achievement considering that an Act of Parliament had to be obtained, as well as doing the construction. The path has long since fallen into disuse, but it is still clearly visible in places; the bridges no longer survive.

Endnotes

1 SA DP108.
2 SA DP33.
3 Blackwall, 1985, p.49; see also SJ 14.5.1812.
4 SA 227/5.
5 Dates from Blackwall 1985, p48 and plaque on footbridge. A bridge of exactly the same design was erected at Stokesay (SO 438818) in 1823, but this time the ironwork contract went to the Coalbrookdale Co (SA PH/S/30/8). When the bridge was dismantled in 1965 the intact ribs were given back to Coalbrookdale, one of which is on display at the Museum of Iron near the Darby furnace.
6 SC 30.10.1840.
7 SA DP180/1 – Q/E/7/1/180/1-2.
8 Worcester Archives Box 4965/9360/U9/95.
9 R Paxton and J Shipway, *Civil Engineering Heritage, Scottish Highlands and Islands*, Thomas Telford, 2007, pp.211-13.
10 Paxton and Shipway 2007, p.212.
11 SA D3651/D/5/562.
12 A Gibb, *The Story of Telford*, Alexander Maclehose 1935, p.156.
13 Gibb 1935, p.156.
14 Paxton and Shipway 2007, p.212.
15 SC 5.6.1812.
16 Matthew Davidson to Thomas Davidson 14.11.1812, IGMT 1981.3588.
17 Paxton and Shipway 2007, pp.130-132.
18 WW Lowson, 'The Reconstruction of the Craigellachie Bridge', *The Structural Engineer* 1967 **45**, pp.23-29 and pp.287-289.
19 Lowson 1967, p.289.
20 Lowson 1967, p.288.
21 Alan Baxter & Associates 2006, Appendix H; Lowson 1967a, p.26.
22 SJ 7.8.1816 records that the parts for the bridge were shipped the previous week.
23 http://www.engineering-timelines.com/scripts/engineeringItem.asp?id=883, accessed 2016.
24 Chester and Cheshire archives, Eaton Estate Account Book, EV387, 1824.
25 http://www.engineering-timelines.com/scripts/engineeringItem.asp?id=785, accessed 2016.
26 W Mackenzie, Account of the Bridge over the Severn..., *Transactions of the Institution of Civil Engineers* **2 1838**, pp.1-14.
27 Mackenzie 1838, p.5.
28 J Rendel, Particulars of the Construction of the Lary Bridge, *Transactions of the Institution of Civil Engineers* **1(1836)**, K Perkins, William Hazledine, Ironfounder of Shrewsbury, *Rendel's News,* Jan/Feb 1979, a copy of which is in SA C24.1 v.f.
29 SC 18.9.1826.

30 SC 30.10.1840; Probably the only man brave enough to perform this manoeuvre at that time was William James Clement (1804–70), pioneering surgeon, and a radical politician, like Hazledine.

31 SC 6.10.1826.

32 SC 5.10.1827.

33 SC 4.8.1826.

34 SC 5.10.1827.

35 Paxton and Shipway 2007, p.32.

36 G Rattenbury and R Cook, *The Hay and Kington Railways*, Railway and Canal Historical Society, 1996, pp.84-95.

37 SC 24.2.1809; SA 7112 (sundries) 17.2.1809.

38 SA 7112, 4.7.1809, 25.9.1809.

39 SC 15.12.1809.

Chapter 9

'The Magnificent Menai Bridge'[1]

T HE NIGHT of 30th January 1826 was pitch black and blowing a typical Welsh gale, but even so it was decided to open the new Menai Suspension Bridge. There was no official opening ceremony, just a decision that the Holyhead bound coach that night would cross the straits via the bridge rather than using the ferry. A contemporary described what happened.

[WA Provis] took charge of the mail [coach] across the bridge. It took up on its way to the bridge Mr Akers, the mail coach superintendant, Mr Hazledine, the contractor for the ironwork, Mr J Provis, the superintendant for proving and examining it, Mr Rhodes, who had the charge of erecting the iron and timber work, Messrs W & J Wilson, sons of the contractor for the masonry, Mr Esplen, an overseer, and as many more as could either be crammed in, or find a place to hang by. Thus loaded, amidst the blaze of lamps, the cheers of those assembled, and the roaring of a heavy gale of wind, the gates were thrown open, and the mail passed triumphantly across![2]

This was slightly anti-climactic conclusion to what would later be viewed as William Hazledine's greatest achievement – providing the ironwork for what was then by far the longest suspension bridge in the world, and which remains a magnificent memorial to the genius of Thomas Telford and his team.

Hardly surprisingly, Menai Bridge was a long time in the gestation. While everyone agreed on the need for a bridge to cross the treacherous Menai Strait, the contours would not allow an ordinary bridge to be built, and suspension bridge technology was still in its infancy. However, by about 1815 Captain Samuel Brown (1776–1852) had developed a system of 'chains', which were flat jointed pieces of wrought iron[3] linked together, which were strong enough for a large bridge. Thomas Telford adopted a similar system for the proposed bridges at Menai and a similar one nearby at the mouth of the Conwy River.[4]

Telford initially planned to use cables formed from ½ inch (1.25cm) square bars welded together in segments. But before the ironwork contract was awarded to William Hazledine in July 1821, the design was totally changed to an improved version of that of Brown, who used long eye-bar chains in single lines.[5] This design consisted of,

> Sixteen eye-bar chains, with each half of the deck being suspended at each side by two pairs of four vertically arranged chains. Each chain comprised five parallel flat-plate eye bars measuring 2.78 m [about 9 ft 1 in] between the centres of the eyes [the whole bar was about 2.9 m (9½ ft) in length], and having a cross section of 83 mm [3¼ in] by 25 mm [1 in]. These were joined to the next group of eye bars by six short connecting plates, to which the hangers were attached. Single 75 mm [3 in] diameter pins [which were 406 mm (16 in) long] passed through all eleven piles[6] at each connection.[7]

This arrangement is illustrated in Figure 35, while Figure 36 shows the whole bridge (Conwy has been pictured because it still has its original (refurbished) wrought ironwork, which was replaced with steel at Menai). Conwy has only one carriageway, whereas Menai has two, and Conwy's span is 100m (328ft), while that of Menai is 176m (579ft).

Since the whole ironwork specification was changed just before Hazledine was awarded the contract, it begs the question as to how much input he had into the final specification. Day has written that,

> Telford recognised the horrendous task of completing as many as 50,000 hammer welds in the wrought-iron bars [the original specification] to achieve continuity, and erecting such intractable cables over such a great span.[8]

In all probability his ironmaster friend would have left him in no doubt about the impracticality of the original design!

As it was, the revised specification presented Hazledine with probably his greatest challenge. For Menai alone the sixteen main chains (each 1710ft (521m) long) consisted of 14,960 eye-bars, around 16,000 connecting plates, and 6,000 screw-pins.[9] The chains needed a saddle at each end to allow them to pass over the masonry towers, and then had to be firmly anchored into rock. The saddles consisted of cast-iron rollers with brass bearings, designed to allow for expansion and contraction of the chains with changes in temperature. The chains were anchored by being attached to cast-iron plates, which were then screwed into the bedrock by means of wrought-iron bolts 9ft 6in (2.9m) long (Figure 37).

All the wrought iron for these bridges was formed at Upton Forge (SJ 559113), which is situated on the north bank of the River Tern about 2km from its confluence with the River Severn. This confluence lies just south of the Attingham Estate, whose northern edge is the south side of the River Tern, opposite the Forge. Upton

Forge is about 5km north east of the outskirts of Shrewsbury by road, and 1km south east of the ancient village of Upton Magna (SJ 555125) (Figure 38).

This had been an important site for iron manufacture since the 1660s, but the owners had gone bankrupt in 1794. This was partly due to the severe economic downturn occasioned by the war with France, and also that such remote rural forges were struggling with high transport costs and outdated methods. So Upton Forge was put up for sale, and the advert describes three fineries, two balling furnaces (chaferies) and two puddling furnaces[10] and 'every accommodation for carrying out an extensive trade, plentifully supplied with water, and capable of making about 30 tons of iron per week'. There was also a dwelling house for a 'genteel family' and 12 houses for workmen.[11]

There was no buyer for the forge, so the Commission against Bankruptcy decided that in order to preserve the business, and thereby possibly repay the creditors, they would assign the estate and effects of the previous proprietor Richard Watson to William Maybury, his clerk, described as 'ironmaster of Upton Forge'.[12] For the nominal sum of five shillings Maybury promised to keep the business going and then assist a new buyer appointed by the Commissioners. This situation appears to have continued for the next six years, until 1800. Then an advertisement appeared in the press which reads as follows,

> Whereas William Maybury, late of Shifnall [sic] in the County
> of Salop, ironmonger, hath by deed of assignment bearing the
> date the 28th of October last part, assigned over all of his effects
> to William Hazledine, of Shrewsbury, Ironmaster, for the benefit
> of such of his creditors who shall sign the said deed...[13]

The question is whether this William Maybury, 'ironmonger of Shifnal' was the same person as the one who took over Upton

Forge? On balance it seems most likely since the Maybury family and Hazledine were already well acquainted via Pitchford Forge, where some of Maybury's relatives worked. Maybury may have made this arrangement in order to secure the future of the forge, since in 1800 the Attingham Estate was expanding, and they were actively considering purchasing Upton Forge.[14] On May 14th Lord Berwick of Attingham received an urgent letter from his attorney Robert Pemberton that Pemberton's assistant John Dodson had made calculations on the cost of a lease or purchase of the forge. Pemberton wrote that,

> The reimbursement of the principal part of the money is to arise from the increase in value to the lands of different properties adjoining by the forge being taken down... If Dodson is correct as to the deficiency, it does not strike me as being a large sum for the price of such a nuisance.[15]

So the whole idea of the purchase was to demolish this noisy neighbour, which was a blot on their northern boundary, and so to increase the value of the adjoining properties.

But this proposed purchase fell through, and instead, John Dodson himself, in partnership with William Hazledine, took over the lease.[16] Dodson's capital enabled the two men to pay off the old creditors and develop the business that had been 'ticking over' for the past six years. John Dodson of Cound (1767–1831) is variously described as a 'builder' and a 'gentleman'.[17] He designed and built the first iron bridge at Cound in 1795.[18] He was also effectively the administrator of the Attingham Estate, being the assistant to local attorney (solicitor) Robert Pemberton, who was much too busy to be involved in day-to-day management.[19]

Hazledine was evidently well respected by Dodson, having been used as the final referee in a building dispute that Dodson and another arbiter could not settle.[20] The precise date of the takeover

Fig 28: Dolforgan Bridge,
Kerry (author's collection)

Fig 29: Dolforgan Bridge, Kerry (author's collection).

Fig 30: Bonar Bridge by William Daniell, 1769-1837, (Tate Gallery).

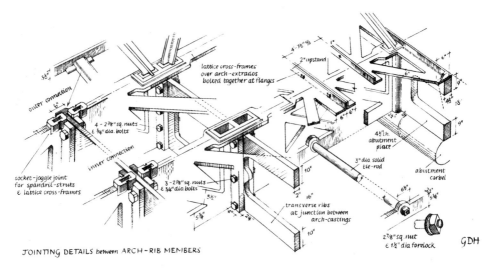

Fig 31: Craigellachie Bridge – joint detail (RCAHMS).

Fig 32: Holt Fleet Bridge (public domain).

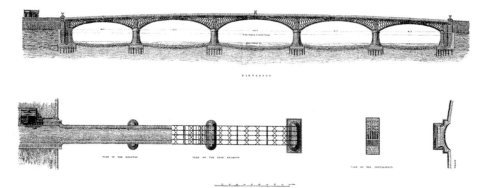

Fig 33: Laira Bridge (public domain).

Fig 34: Cleveland Bridge in 1841 (public domain).

Fig 35: Conwy Bridge design (author's collection).

Fig 36: Conwy Bridge (author's collection).

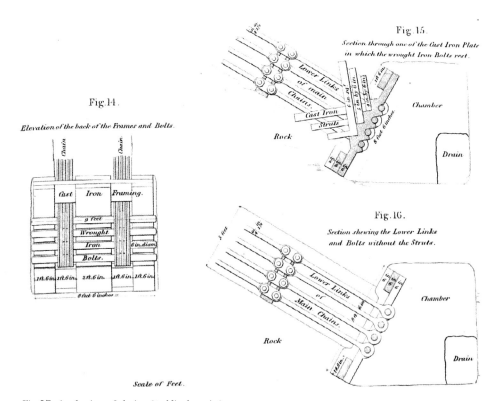

Fig 37: Anchoring of chains (public domain).

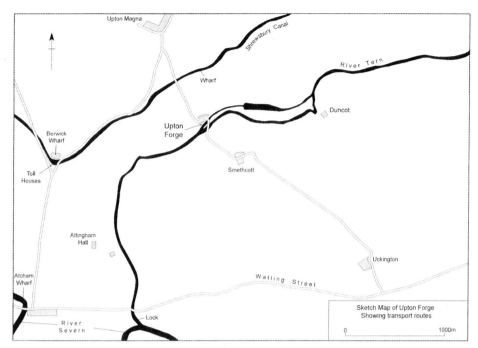

Fig 38: Upton Forge area (author's collection).

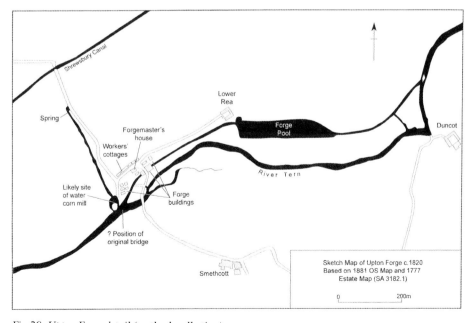

Fig 39: Upton Forge detail (author's collection).

Fig 40: Marlow Bridge (author's collection).

*Fig 41: William
Tierney Clark
(public domain).*

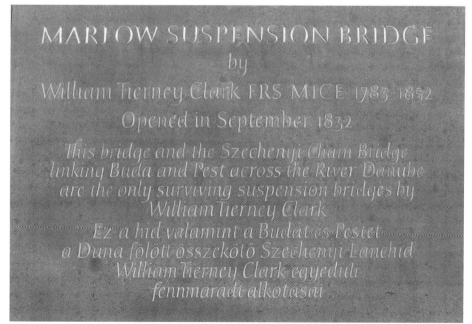

MARLOW SUSPENSION BRIDGE
by
William Tierney Clark FRS MICE 1783-1852
Opened in September 1832

*This bridge and the Szechenyi Chain Bridge
linking Buda and Pest across the River Danube
are the only surviving suspension bridges by
William Tierney Clark
Ez a hid valamint a Budat es Pestet
a Duna fölött összekötö Szechenyi Lanchid
William Tierney Clark egyeduli
fennmaradt alkotasai*

Fig 42: Marlow Bridge plaque (author's collection).

Fig 43: Pencil drawing of William Hazledine (National Portrait Gallery).

Fig 44: John Hazledine as Mayor (Shropshire Archives).

is not stated in the documents, but a minute of the General Committee of the Shrewsbury Canal dated 8.10.1800 states that 'the Upton Forge Co shall be at liberty to cut through the towing path of the canal at Upton Wharf...', which suggests renewed activity at the forge at this time.[21] The partnership between Dodson and Hazledine was eventually dissolved in 1819, leaving Hazledine as the sole partner.[22]

So why was Hazledine interested in Upton Forge? Probably it was Upton's much better communications that encouraged him to give up the lease on Pitchford and move his wrought iron operations to Upton. What made Upton attractive was the Shrewsbury Canal, which had been opened in 1797, and passed close by. He transported coal and pig iron from East Shropshire to Upton via the canal in a fleet of tub-boats that he had leased from the Lilleshall Company. What wasn't used at Upton carried on to Shrewsbury, either for the Coleham foundry or for his retail coal merchant's business. Finished products from Upton could then be sent on to Shrewsbury by the canal, or else they could be sent to their final destination by river or road. By this time, the iron industry was being concentrated near the centres of raw material production, such as East Shropshire and the Black Country. By ensuring his supply of raw materials and minimising transport costs Hazledine was able to compete, even though his facilities were more spread out.

The new centres of the iron industry also relied increasingly on steam power, which could be generated cheaply by the use of substandard slack coal which was mined nearby. On the other hand, Upton's power source, water, was free, and, because of extensive improvements to the water supply, (Figure 39) was reliable, except in times of flood. Being a millwright himself, presumably Hazledine was also more comfortable dealing with a power source that he understood well, rather than relying on the vagaries of early steam engines.

It appears that Hazledine continued to work Upton Forge as he found it, using the three fineries, two chaferies and two puddling furnaces, and employing a combination of coke and charcoal technology depending on the quality of iron required. He himself was a frequent visitor to the site, as a Mr Caswell recalled many years later.[23] Caswell grew up down the road at Atcham, and what most struck him about Hazledine was that, when the famous ironmaster's carriage passed by, the young boy noticed 'his invariable courtesy in returning my salute when I doffed my cap.'

The writer contrasted this with 'those who considered themselves entitled to a "bow" from their subordinates in rank or position [who] claimed it as a right, and the courtesy was seldom acknowledged.' The young Caswell's abiding memory of the forge was, he wrote, 'the thump, thump of the forge hammer [which] still reverberates to my memory.' If the hammer could be heard so clearly a mile or so away, what must it have been like to work at the forge day after day?

An example of the way Hazledine worked is recorded in two letters, handwritten by himself to Thomas Evans of Prescott, Baschurch, in May 1834.[24] Hazledine's assistants, Thomas Thomas and Nathaniel Evans, had evidently asked his advice about work they were doing to insert tie bars to strengthen the church tower. In his letters (one written on a Sunday) Hazledine advised inserting two extra bars. 'I shall go to the forge [Upton] early in the morning to have the iron drawn, and will endeavour to have the whole finished on Saturday,' he wrote. Even at this stage (he was 71 by then) he clearly remained 'hands on'.

Work began at Upton soon after the contract for Menai and Conwy Bridges was signed, but it quickly became clear that to make all the pieces to the required tolerances would require a completely novel approach. The first thing Telford did was to dispatch John Provis, the brother of resident engineer William, to Shrewsbury to supervise the testing of all the ironwork. To do this he (presumably

98

with Hazledine) designed and built a 'proving machine', which took from January to June 1822.[25] This was based at Hazledine's headquarters on Wyle Cop, to which all the ironwork was brought from Upton via the Shrewsbury Canal. Once the proving machine was working, the first consignment of bars for the main chains was delivered to Menai by October 1822.[26] After testing it was sent overland to Weston Wharf, then via the Ellesmere Canal to Chester, and finally by sea to Menai.[27] Not surprisingly, on arrival it was found that most of the anti-rust treatment (baked linseed oil), had been knocked off by this journey. Floods in the winters of 1822–23 and 1823–24 also delayed the work, but another challenge that had to be overcome was the forming of the eyes in the eye-bars. Doing this under the hammer could result in irregular eyes with weaknesses where the metal had been worked, so it was decided to drill the eyes once the metal was cold using another specially designed machine.

This work necessitated the installation of a new, more powerful steam engine, which, as well as punching the eyes of both main chain plates and links, was also able to turn the rollers for the saddles (they weighed 9 cwt (457 kg) each), and cut screw-pins. The introduction of these innovations took time, but the last links for the two bridges finally left the forge in March 1825.[28] John Provis kept a meticulous record of all the tests he performed (Table 4). This is probably the first project for which the materials had been so extensively tested, and considering that the iron was forged using 'old' technology, the production of over 35,000 items with a rejection rate of less than 7% speaks volumes for the skill of all those involved.

This contract also added considerably to Hazledine's fortune, since he was paid £53,050 for Menai and £9,345 for Conwy, a total of £62,395 (over £3m in today's prices).[29]

Table 4 – Results of tests on ironwork for Menai and Conwy Bridges[30]

	No. tested	Rejected – visual imperfections	Cracked under test	Broke in two under test	No. sent to site	% rejected
4in x 1in bars for chains in tunnels etc	5,032	60	0	0	4,972	1.2
Connectors for ditto	6,238	175	0	0	6,063	2.81
3¼in x 1in main chain bars	10,476	249	100	47	10,080	3.78
Connectors for ditto	13,903	1438	225	90	12,150	12.61
Total	35,649	1922	325	137	33,265	6.69

These bridges not only increased Hazledine's fortune, but his fame as well, reaching even the Royal Family. In 1832 the thirteen-year-old Princess Victoria, as the heir to the throne, was taken on a nationwide tour. This included Shrewsbury and was in the company of her mother, the Duchess of Kent. The host for their time in Shrewsbury was Lord Liverpool of Pitchford Hall. Lord Liverpool had leased Pitchford Forge to Hazledine and the two struck up an unlikely friendship. So Hazledine was summoned to Pitchford to meet the royals and tell them all about the building of the Menai Bridge.[31]

Hazledine was petrified lest his lack of breeding and eloquence be shown up. Lord Liverpool had instructed him to be sure to call them "Your Royal Highnesses", and Hazledine confessed afterwards that he had practised saying this to every gatepost between Shrewsbury and Pitchford! In the event all went well. Even the young princess was entranced, gazing up at him with her bright blue eyes as she stood under the big man's arm while he pointed out all the details of the bridge from a plan on the table. The Duchess gave him a present of a silver bridle, and when she later visited Menai she examined the bridge minutely, even going into the caves which surround the fixings of the chains to the bedrock.

Endnotes

1 Hulbert, 1837, p.308 footnote.
2 T Howell, *Shrewsbury to Holyhead,* T Howell 1826, p.27.
3 It had to be wrought iron, rather than cast iron, because the bridge components in a suspension bridge are in tension, rather than compression as in an arched bridge. Cast iron is not strong enough in tension to withstand the forces involved.
4 RA Paxton, *Menai Bridge, Evolution of Design,* in *Thomas Telford Engineer,* Ed A Penfold, Thomas Telford Ltd, 1980, pp.84-116.
5 Paxton 1980, pp. 94,102, illustrations pp.100-101.
6 'A set of wrought-iron bars placed together for welding' (Chambers Dictionary).
7 W Day, *Telford's Menai and Conwy Suspension Bridges, Wales,* Proceedings of the Institution of Civil Engineering, 2007, **160(5)**, p.28 – items in square brackets are author's additions.
8 Day 2007, p.28.
9 Paxton 1980.
10 This means that the forge used both old (charcoal-fired) and new (coke-fired) technology.
11 SC 18.4.1794.
12 Staffs RO D695/3/49.
13 SJ 28.10.1800.
14 SA 112/5/10/3-4, 7-8.
15 SA 112/14/70/75.
16 SA D3651/D/9/6/1-8.
17 SA 227/4; 112/5/43/7-8.
18 SA 227/4; Blackwall 1985, pp.48, 50.
19 SA – summary of Attingham administrative history.
20 SA D3651/D/13/17.
21 TNA RAIL 868/1. Dodson had been on the General Committee of the canal since 1798, so the nominal payment of one penny a year that the Upton Forge Company had to make for this canal access probably reflects his 'insider' status.
22 SA D3651/D/9/6/1-8.
23 SA 901/1.
24 SA P22/B/3/4,5.
25 W Provis, *An Historical and Descriptive Account of the Suspension Bridge Constructed over the Menai Straits in North Wales,* Alexander Maclehose, 1828, p.33ff.
26 Provis 1828.
27 Ibid, p.35.
28 ICE – Thomas Telford correspondence T/EG 125, 27.2.1825.
29 B Trinder, *The Holyhead Road – an Engineering Project in its Social Context,* Thomas Telford Ltd, 1980, Appendix 2, pp.148-9.
30 Provis 1828, Appendix 3, p.87.
31 SC, *Notes and Queries,* Nov 8th, 15th, 22nd, 29th and Dec 6th 1901.

Chapter 10

Engineers in Conflict

AFTER a working life of nearly forty years, by the 1820s William Hazledine was more than just a supplier of ironwork for others. Though not an engineer himself, his vast practical experience, allied with his no-nonsense personality, had the potential to bring him into conflict with members of the newly-emerging profession of civil engineering. The building of Marlow Bridge (SU 851860) is a good example of that.

In 1825 the old timber bridge that united Marlow in Buckinghamshire on the north bank of the River Thames with Berkshire on the south side, was close to collapse. In response to this, the magistrates of the two counties set up a joint committee to take responsibility for rebuilding the bridge. After much discussion, in 1828 the committee decided to opt for an iron bridge, rather than using the traditional materials of wood or stone.

The chosen designer and engineer of the bridge was John Millington (1779–1868). Millington, who owned a foundry in Hammersmith, was perhaps a surprising choice, since he had been dismissed as engineer for the West Middlesex Waterworks in 1810 for incompetence.[1] It appears that Millington produced designs for both a suspension bridge and an iron arch, though the original drawings have not survived. The suspension bridge design was like Telford's design at Menai and Conwy, with chains formed from links of wrought iron bolted together and slung over cast-iron towers erected on either shore of the river, with the ends of the chains fixed securely deep into the banks. Eventually in the spring of 1829 the committee decided to opt for the suspension bridge, though not before tenders had been invited for both the suspension and iron arch designs. Amongst the tenders received for the ironwork was one from William Hazledine, who for the suspension bridge offered to supply the cast iron at £11 a ton and the wrought iron for £21 a ton, with erection costing £450. Alternatively, he would supply a cast-iron arch of 200 foot span and 20 feet width for a total of £6,500.[2] After some negotiation, the committee agreed on 24th April 1829 that Hazledine would supply all the ironwork for the suspension bridge for £3650.

Contracts were signed, and after receiving the detailed plans, Hazledine's firm started work in September 1829. The wrought iron was produced at Upton Forge, and the cast iron was made at Coleham. Then in October Millington suddenly resigned to take up a post in Mexico, though whether he 'jumped' before he was 'pushed' is hard to gauge, since it appears that the committee were beginning to doubt his competence. William Tierney Clark (1783–1852) was appointed in his place, though the committee was unhappy that he would not be resident to supervise the work. Clark (Figure 41), though 20 years younger than Hazledine, had a similar background.[3] After training as a millwright in the Bristol area, he moved to Coalbrookdale, where he had a thorough grounding in the practicalities of the iron trade. No doubt he was aware of William Hazledine from his time there, though it is not known if they were personally acquainted. The great engineer John Rennie offered the young man a situation at his ironworks in London and during the next few years the two men became close. In 1811 Rennie recommended his protégé for the post of engineer at the

West Middlesex Waterworks, which he joined after the sacking of John Millington. Under his supervision the works were transformed into one of the most important in London, and such was the esteem in which he was held, that his employers allowed him to take on consulting work as well.

Clark's first excursion into suspension bridge design and execution was the bridge over the Thames at Hammersmith, which was built between 1824 and 1827. The ironwork for this bridge was supplied by the foundry of Captain Samuel Brown, and it was presumably as a result of the success of this venture that Clark was employed at Marlow. Immediately after he was appointed in November 1829 he made modifications to the design of the bridge, though as the original plans have not survived it is difficult to know how extensive these alterations were. One thing he certainly did was to replace the cast-iron towers with masonry ones. These alterations were agreed by the committee later in November, and the following month Hazledine travelled to Hammersmith to see Clark, and the two men agreed on the necessary alterations to the ironwork. The final design for the suspension system,

> ...comprised four wrought-iron eye-bar chains arranged in vertical pairs on either side of the carriageway, each chain consisting of four eye-bar links...arranged horizontally and joined by sets of five connector plates and wrought-iron pins. Wrought-iron suspender rods attached alternately to the upper and lower chains carried the deck bearers...[4]

The specification detailed 3526 separate pieces of wrought iron of 12 types, and 452 pieces of cast iron of seven types. Presumably boring machines designed for the Menai and Conwy Bridges could be reused to drill the holes for the connecting links.

Detailed drawings took a while to produce, but by March 1830 Clark was able to report to the committee that he expected to meet

Hazledine in Hammersmith that week for the ironfounder to look over the plans and inspect the proof patterns. No record of this meeting survives, but it appears that the two men disagreed strongly about the plans. As a result Hazledine refused to sign the amended agreement necessitated by the changes in the design, for Clark's next letter to the committee secretary on 8th April asked,

> Have you received Mr Hazledine's agreement, and is it signed?
> If not, it should be, for I think he would have no objection to give us some trouble.

So what was the problem? Hazledine's objection to the design was related to the links of the main chains. His problems were twofold. First the bars were supposed to be of circular cross section, a design which had already been rejected at Menai as almost impossible to forge. The second problem was that Hazledine felt that the eye bars would be too thin to support the structure. Hazledine's objections were well-founded, since a disaster that occurred to a new suspension bridge at Montrose in Scotland the previous year was fresh in the memory of bridge engineers and contractors. This bridge, engineered by Captain Samuel Brown, was of similar design to Marlow, with chains consisting of just four sets of iron bars (Menai Bridge had five bars in a set). Soon after Montrose Bridge was opened, a large crowd gathered upon it to watch a boat race. As the boats went under the bridge, the crowd surged to the other side to follow them, and the oscillations so produced caused one of the upper chains to break, whereupon the bridge partly collapsed and a number of spectators were killed.[5]

Clark, though, was unmoved by Hazledine's arguments – presumably he felt that his position as engineer and his experience at Hammersmith gave him the last word. Hazledine, though, was a stubborn man. He could point to his experience in producing the ironwork for the Conway and Menai suspension bridges. Above all, he was concerned for the safety of those who would use the bridge. So a stalemate ensued. Initially Hazledine played for time, asking for more detailed plans, which were duly delivered in July 1830. The following month the masons had finished work on the towers, and so the ironwork was urgently needed. By September Hazledine reported that all the ironwork was ready, but Clark was unwilling to accept it until Hazledine signed the contract. Hazledine wrote via his solicitors that,

> ...of course he was desirous of finishing the bridge, and that if Mr Clark will send a person to inspect [the ironwork that] is now here... [he would] agree upon the contract.

In other words, Hazledine was saying to Clark, "if this bridge fails, the fault is yours, not mine." Clark was incensed, writing to the committee that,

> ...you will not sanction any further alteration in the agreement with Hazledine... He has treated us very unhandsome in every stage of this business as such to deserve the least favour whatsoever...

At the same time Clark was making tentative enquiries about an alternative supplier for the ironwork.

Hazledine could see that his only chance of getting his way was to discuss the matter directly with the committee, so he and his solicitor travelled to Buckinghamshire on October 6th 1830 for a face to face meeting. Clark had hoped to be there, but was delayed at one of his other projects, but it appears that the meeting between the committee and the Shrewsbury men went well. No doubt Hazledine used his considerable experience and persuasive powers to bring the magistrates round to his view. Though unwilling to go against Clark's wishes and change the contract, the committee persuaded Clark to send his assistant Thomas Young to test the ironwork in Shrewsbury. Young began his work in late November. Initially his reports were encouraging, but early in the New Year he was unhappy with progress and asked Clark to come to Shrewsbury to check things for himself. Clark was so busy with other things that it took him till late March to make the trip, and receive Young's report. The gist of the matter was that, whereas virtually all the cast-iron parts were ready, Hazledine had obviously instructed his workmen not to produce any links or connecting pins for the main chains of the size that Clark wanted. Not surprisingly, Clark's report to the committee was very negative, and it wasn't long before Hazledine received a letter threatening legal action.

Hazledine's reply contradicted Clark's report in many respects. Clark said he spent three days in Shrewsbury, Hazledine replied that Clark was in the town for just an afternoon. Clark said that a bar he tested failed, whereas Hazledine replied that it more than passed the test. Hazledine maintained that the ironwork was much further on than Clark's report suggested. Hazledine also accused Clark of making 'ridiculous demands', of delay in sending Young, and also of being unable to make up his mind what he wanted. Evidently, since Hazledine's meeting with the committee, he and Clark had had a correspondence about the strength of the bridge. Hazledine had been so concerned that he had arranged to meet Clark at the latter's home in Hammersmith in February, but had waited two days and Clark had failed to show up. The nub of Hazledine's argument was that ironwork for the current design was dangerously inadequate. As evidence for this he listed not only the Montrose Bridge, but also bridges at Morpeth, Middleham (Yorkshire), Cambridge and Manchester that had 'all fallen down within about 8 months'.

In response to this criticism Clark dithered and continued to lay the blame on Hazledine. Hazledine wanted an assurance than in the event of disaster it would be Clark, not himself, who would be held responsible. As the stalemate dragged on over the summer the committee became increasingly irritated. One member, Sir George Nugent, even threatened to resign, writing that,

> I more than suspect that our architect has so many irons in the fire of greater advantage to him than our bridge, he will not be made to attend to our concern without a most serious remonstrance from the committee.

Perhaps as a result, Clark began to give way, first allowing the bars of circular cross section to be replaced with rectangular ones. Even in this letter he criticises Hazledine, who, he says, 'very ingeniously wishes to transfer his own want of attention to the want of strength in the original dimensions.'

Young was again despatched to Shrewsbury to check on progress. In the end Hazledine took matters in his own hands, deciding by the end of July to make the bars to his own measurements. Clark's reply was, in effect, "if you insist on doing that, you must sign a new contract which expressly states that you now carry the legal responsibility." Hazledine, via his solicitors, refused. Clark was furious, writing to the committee,

> the sooner the contract [with Hazledine] is put an end to the better... Any further correspondence with Hazledine will be as bad as a chancery suit.

True to his word, Clark travelled to Staffordshire in early October 1831 and made a provisional agreement with the Gospel Oak Ironworks in Brierley Hill to complete the ironwork in the event of Hazledine failing to do so. Perhaps he hoped that this would put pressure on Hazledine, though he recognised that the logistics of two different suppliers working on the same job were probably insurmountable. Clark then travelled on to Shrewsbury for what the two men probably expected to be a very frosty meeting. In the event it appears that both sides were willing to accept a compromise. Clark was pleasantly surprised to see how far advanced the production of the ironwork was, much of which was ready to be loaded on barges for delivery.

Hazledine also promised that machinery to erect the work would go with it, followed soon after by his foreman (probably William Stuttle Junior). For his part, Clark was willing to strike a pen through the clause in the new contract that made Hazledine responsible for any failure in the ironwork due to the alterations he had made.

From this point things moved quickly. Clark's hope that the ironwork would be finished and delivered by January 1st 1832 was always going to be unrealistic, but both Young, who had remained in Shrewsbury, and Hazledine were able to report that much of the iron had already been shipped by the end of 1831. It went initially to Gloucester on the River Severn; from there it was probably sent via the Kennet and Avon Canal to the Thames. Young left Shrewsbury late in January, reporting that the last load of iron had been sent off, accompanied by a man who would ensure that there was no delay during the shipping. At the same time, Hazledine's men left Shrewsbury for Marlow to begin the erection of the ironwork on the last Monday in January. The fabrication and erection of the bridge seems to have proceeded smoothly over the following months, and by May 1832 the bridge was nearly finished. A nearby resident wrote,

> Our new bridge is now nearly completed, and a very pretty thing it is. It is very ingeniously and carefully constructed, and will be a great ornament to the neighbourhood.

The bridge was finally opened on 23rd September 1832, without any ceremony, perhaps a reflection of the discord and delay that had dogged the project. The local newspaper, however, was delighted, reporting that,

> This beautiful and convenient bridge is at length completed
> and opened to the public. Its execution is of the best kind and
> reflects the highest credit on the architect (Figure 40).[6]

The public was happy, but it seems that both the architect and the contractors were less so, as the magistrates of the two counties weren't keen to part with their money. Hazledine sent his first account at the end of January 1832, his bill for £3,200 14s 1½d being exactly the contract price. Despite being immediately approved by Clark, no payment was made. Hazledine wasn't coy about requesting what he was due, as he regularly reminded the magistrates! Eventually he received £1000 on 18.10.1832, but by then his final payment of £1277 was also due. Over the ensuing months he exerted all the pressure he could to get them to pay. He wrote on 15th November 1832,

> I am much in want of the money...having made engagements
> in the full expectation of receiving it.

He complained on 8th February 1833,

> Most assuredly I am not well used by delaying the payments,
> particularly considering the trouble and expense I was put to
> in doing a deal of the work twice over.

By July he started to add interest to the bill, and in September he threatened to come in person to collect it, but in the end it was settled on October 31st, but without the interest! The problem of late payment seems to have been partly due to the County having problems with their treasurer, whom they had had to sue, an action that cost them thousands of pounds. Hazledine's case was not exceptional, as all the contractors complained bitterly about the delay in being paid. Their problems were nothing, however, compared to Clark's. Though not as persistent as Hazledine, he was not slow to demand his money. The County wrote him a cheque in June 1835 for the balance of his account, but unfortunately it bounced, as the bank had gone bust in the meantime! As he had still not received his full payment by the following year he sued the County, and his bill was not finally paid until April 1838!

The modern plaque on the bridge (Figure 42) gives Clark all the credit for the design and erection of the bridge. But from what the archives tell us, perhaps the plaque should read, 'Original design by John Millington, alterations by William Tierney Clark, made safe by William Hazledine, and erected by Thomas Young and William Stuttle Junior'. All but Clark, though, have been written out of the official story, though it appears that Hazledine's role became a legend within the trade.

In 1884 Clark's Hammersmith Bridge was replaced. At that time, the Builders' Weekly Reporter carried an article that has confused later historians.[7] The reporter wrote that Clark and Hazledine had had an argument over the ironwork for the Hammersmith Bridge, but since there is no evidence Hazledine was ever involved with Hammersmith, this must refer to the building of Marlow Bridge. The reporter wrote,

> The contract for its erection was undertaken by the late Mr William Hazledine of Shrewsbury, the builder of other suspension bridges... After he signed the contract, Mr Hazledine did not at once proceed with his work, and legal proceedings were threatened. But that gentleman, having carefully perused the specification, found that the enormous weight of iron specified for in some parts of the structure would prove its own destruction, and declared that if the bridge were

built according to the engineer's design it would fall as soon as completed. This proved a serious stumbling-block, but Mr Hazledine – who was a thoroughly practical man, though not an engineer in the ordinary sense of the word – stipulated he would build a bridge according to the engineer's plan, but not in accordance with the specification, which he would guarantee to stand for more than 20 years.

In the event, the original Marlow Bridge lasted not just 20 but nearly 130 years without major maintenance. By the 1960s, however, the anchorages were giving serious cause for concern, and it was felt the bridge needed replacement. An initial plan to demolish it and build a modern replacement produced a storm of protest in the town, and it was decided to dismantle the bridge and rebuild it to exactly the same design, but using steel instead of wrought iron. When the wrought iron came to be dismantled, much of it was still safe and serviceable, a tribute to the original workmanship. When the chains came to be replaced,

> ...it was found advantageous to write a program for processing on an electronic computer [a novelty in 1966!] the calculation of the lengths of the eye-bar chain links, the geometry of the connector plates carrying the suspenders being somewhat complex.[8]

Hazledine didn't have such luxuries as computers in the 1820s – just experience and practical knowhow!

There is one more footnote to this story. The occasion when Hazledine visited Clark at Hammersmith and failed to find him in, was probably when Hazledine sat for the famous sculptor Sir Francis Chantrey at Twickenham.[9] There he had his portrait drawn (Figure 43), both from the front and in profile, and it was from these pictures that Chantrey sculpted the bust that is now in St Chad's

Church, Shrewsbury (Figure 4). One might well wonder how a rural ironmaster like Hazledine came to be sculpted by the foremost sculptor of his generation, who was a favourite of the royal family. It appears that it was through Lord Liverpool of Pitchford Hall that Chantrey met Hazledine. Quite why Hazledine commissioned the statue of himself at that time in his life is impossible to say, but Chantrey was evidently pleased with the result. When he visited Shrewsbury after Hazledine's death he remarked that,

> In his studio the bust of Mr Hazledine was used to be looked upon by him with pleasure, as the best effort of his chisel.[10]

Endnotes

1 D Smith, The works of William Tierney Clark 1783–1852, Civil Engineer of Hammersmith. *Trans Newcomen Soc* 1991, **17**:181-207, p.182.

2 Centre for Buckinghamshire Studies Q/AB/43/772a – 20.4.1828; most of the information in this chapter is from this collection. Detailed references are omitted for brevity.

3 Anon, Obituary of William Tierney Clark, 1783–1852, *Minutes of Proceedings of the Institution of Civil Engineers,* 1853 **12**:153-157.

4 H Wadsworth and A Waterhouse, Modern techniques and problems in the restoration of Marlow Suspension Bridge, *Proceedings of the Institution of Civil Engineers,* 1967, **37(2)**, pp.297-8.

5 B Mawson, Learning from bridge failure – in 1838, *Bridge Engineering,* 2009 **162(2)**:95-99. With hindsight, engineers realised that the main problem was that the decking was not stiff or heavy enough to withstand oscillations such as those produced by strong winds. Clark had made Hammersmith Bridge stronger in this way, but it is not clear if this was by accident or design.

6 Bucks Herald, 22.9.1832, p.3.

7 A copy of the article is in SA 901/1; it is undated.

8 Wadsworth and Waterhouse 1967, p.301.

9 Chantrey dated the portrait '28th to 31st Feb 1831' – presumably he meant January!

10 H Pidgeon, *Memorials of Shrewsbury,* 1851, p.60.

Chapter 11

Son of Shrewsbury

DESPITE having so many contracts in far-flung places, Hazledine also committed much time and energy to work within Shrewsbury. By the 1820s Hazledine was making good profits, much of which he invested in property. Most of this property he bought, while some he built himself. When some of his estate was sold after his death, fifty-one houses, some with stables, were advertised, along with a good deal of building land. This was in addition to the iron foundry, timber and brick yards and building sites.[1] (This was actually only a fraction of his property, as most of it was kept by his family as an investment). He specialised in buying at a knockdown price anything that looked a good investment, such as Coleham Brewery, sold in 1830 to Hazledine for 'a mere bagatelle', according to Charles Hulbert.[2] Much of his property was in and around Coleham, such as at the front of the Foundry, across the road along Longden Coleham, and between Longden Coleham and Belle Vue Road.

He also owned many properties in the town centre. This included Dogpole House, where he himself lived, Mountford's Carriage works opposite, small houses in Castle Hill, and, at the opposite end of the scale, Swan Hill House and a number of large properties adjacent to it on Swan Hill and on nearby Belmont. One property he had already sold was Bellstone, which he purchased privately in 1826 for £2,500 after it had failed to reach its reserve price at auction, 'in the general opinion much above its value', as Henry Pidgeon rather snootily noted in his diary.[3] Two years later, Pidgeon noted what happened next. Writing on June 17th 1829 he said,

> Mr Hazledine having modernised the exterior and interior of the ancient mansion in Barker Street called Bellstone, has been again the cause of the removal of the large stone from whence the house is supposed to have derived its name, and which is now placed on a small grass plot leading to the entrance. Mr Hazledine's alteration shows but little taste for the antique, and exhibits much incongruity of style.[4]

Despite these comments, it appears that he had no difficulty selling it later, no doubt at a handsome profit!

Another unusual project he had was a Museum, which was on Dogpole.[5] In 1838 this was leased to the newly formed Shropshire and North Wales Natural History and Antiquarian Society, and became the basis for the Town's Museum, which is now at the Music Hall.

As well as investing in his own property, Hazledine was keen to improve the town itself. When the Infirmary needed rebuilding in 1826 he proposed erecting an iron bridge where the Kingsland Bridge is now, and converting what was then the House of Industry (it is now Shrewsbury School) into the new Infirmary.[6] Despite his estimate that this would save £5000 on the building costs and offering £1000 of his own money to the scheme, the proposal was rejected on rather flimsy grounds. Perhaps his rejection was as much due to party politics as anything.

Hazledine's obituarist continues the story of his public philanthropy, writing,[7]

His want of success [in regard to the Infirmary] did not prevent him embarking largely in all other public-spirited improvements. He lent the aid of his head and his purse to the construction of the new Racecourse [opened in 1837]; he has done more for the improvement of the public streets, at his own cost, than the Street Act Committee, with their yearly revenue of £1500. He offered his services and his purse for the formation of a new Cattle Market at Kingsland [it was built in Smithfield instead]. He assisted liberally in lowering the hills on the Wyle Cop and Castle Gates.

What Hazledine seems to have realised, which his contemporaries didn't, was the need to move cherished institutions out of the crowded town centre, provided that proper bridges were built to ensure good communication. For example, building the cattle market on Smithfield Road resulted in over a century of mess and congestion, which would have been solved by having the site at Kingsland, with a new bridge to connect this with the town. It has only really been since the Second World War that this problem has been addressed.

The 1820s and 1830s were a time when Hazledine was very involved in politics. This was a period of great agitation for both parliamentary and local government reform, and Hazledine was one of the leaders of this movement in Shrewsbury. It appears that he had supported reform since the time of William Pitt, when the reform process had been abruptly terminated in 1793 by the fear of revolution. Speaking at a meeting in 1831[8], Hazledine commented that in regard to 'the means brought forward 38 years ago [i.e. 1793] ...in those days people were afraid of opening their mouths lest some of the great men of the land should jump down their throats'. By 1814 Hazledine was chairing a public meeting to support the adoption of Benjamin Benyon as the Whig candidate. This meeting passed a resolution,

That the freedom of election is a right, the inviolable exercise
of which is guaranteed in the Great Charters of English Liberty.[9]

The 'Great' Reform Bill became law in 1832, and Hazledine was
one of the most vociferous of the local supporters of the Reform
Society.[10] So he was prominent amongst those who celebrated the
passing of the Bill in June 1832. At the Shrewsbury Reform Festival
of that year it is recorded that,

> ….after parading the streets and suburbs, the procession halted
> in front of the Town Hall, where Mr Hazledine addressed a few
> words from his carriage to the immense crowd around him…[11]

To understand the feelings engendered by politics in this period it
is helpful to look at the career of Hazledine's younger friend
William James Clement (1802–70). Clement was a brilliant young
surgeon who returned to his native Shrewsbury in the 1820s to set
up in practice. So far so good, but, like Hazledine and many other
forward-thinking people, he had chosen a path of political
controversy, when it would have been much easier to avoid politics,
as did his older contemporary Dr Robert Darwin (Charles Darwin's
father).[12] The younger Clement had imbibed liberal political and
social views from his father, and he took them one step further by
aligning himself with the radical wing of the Whig party. Nationally
the Tories had been in power for a generation, and the same party
was able to dominate local politics because of the influence that
men of wealth and property exerted over the tiny number of men
eligible to vote at elections, and most Tories resisted reform by every
means they could.

After the passage of the 1832 Reform Bill, the Radicals
campaigned for reform of municipal corporations, many of which
had been unchanged since mediaeval times. In Shrewsbury public
meetings were held calling for reform, and at one Clement loudly

demanded 'a speedy reform to all rotten corporations'.[13] This echoed lines written by William Cowper 50 years before:

> Hence chartered boroughs are such public plagues;
> And burghers, men immaculate perhaps
> In all their private functions, once combin'd,
> Become a loathsome body, only fit
> For dissolution – hurtful to the main.[14]

This was just too much for members of the Tory-dominated 'rotten corporation'. Many years later Clement recounted what happened next.

> A meeting of my political opponents was called together, and a resolution was adopted pledging all persons then present never to employ me in my professional capacity. They thought proper to draw up a list, and when no one liked to head that list, the expedient that is called a 'round-robin' was resorted to. The circle was a very large one. It contained many names of influence, and the object of this ignoble and impotent attempt was to ostracise me from professional life.[15]

It appears that the outcome of this meeting was an 'open secret', and it was not long before it was put to the test.

In August 1835 Mr Humphreys, one of the surgeons at the Salop Infirmary, resigned. In those days the appointment of a new physician or surgeon at the Infirmary was a public affair. Candidates advertised themselves in the local paper, and all the several hundred Trustees of the institution were eligible to vote (provided their subscriptions were paid up). There were four candidates – Henry Higgins, who had been House Surgeon at the Infirmary for 10 years in the past, CT Hughes Clarke, a local surgeon, John Dickin, a more recent House Surgeon, and now partner of the retiring Mr

Humphreys, and William Clement.[16] On paper the result should have been a foregone conclusion – worthy as the other three gentlemen were, Clement's academic qualifications and practical experience should have counted heavily in his favour. But what about his politics?

On Friday September 18th 1835, knowing that this election was going to be far from routine, over 200 trustees assembled at the Infirmary to make their choice. The first news was that two of the candidates, Higgins and Clarke, had withdrawn – perhaps they sensed that they were about to be heavily defeated and so avoided that humiliation. After initial skirmishing as to who should be first to speak, it fell to Shropshire Tory MP William Ormsby-Gore to propose Mr Dickin. Pretending he didn't know what the real issue was, he blithely stated that,

> I think this election is to be decided on professional grounds alone, and not on any personal, far less political ground...[17]

He then stated that Mr Humphreys thoroughly recommended his protégé and now partner, and that the rumour that there had been a deal whereby Dickin would give Humphreys money if his election was secured was slanderous. Finally, he asserted that Dickin's candidacy was supported by three of the most eminent doctors at the hospital, Robert Darwin, Thomas Dugard and James Proud Johnson. Rev Cotton seconded Dickin, but there is no record that he added any new information.

Supporting William Clement were two of the 'biggest hitters' in the town. First to go was Samuel Butler, Clement's old head-master. Butler said he was profoundly grateful to the Clement family "for the skill and attention which they have shown for many years in their professional capacity while attending...my family." Regarding the younger Clement, he added that, "I have seen his medical skill exercised with a happy combination of promptitude and judgment on more than one critical occasion, where the result has been eminently successful [and] delay would have been ruinous. But for such decision, the issue must have been fatal." Butler then went on to emphasise Clement's excellent qualifications and experience.

Seconding the case for Clement was John Bather, Recorder of Shrewsbury, the most senior legal man in the town. He too had personal cause to be grateful to William Clement. "With what depth of feeling must I speak of him," he explained, "when to the successful exertion of those qualities, under God, I owe the life of my own son."

He then moved on to what the opposition had said concerning the endorsement of Mr Dickin by the senior doctors. All these eminent doctors had done, he explained, was that they had certified that Mr Dickin "properly attended his duties in his situation; and which certificate could equally be obtained by any young man who properly conducted himself." In other words, he had merely done his duty, and was a young man of promise, nothing else, whereas Clement had already proved himself.

Bather firmly rejected that the rumour of financial impropriety had anything to do with the Clement camp.

> Does [Mr Gore] think that any gentleman who knows honest
> Mr Humphreys would do such a dirty action, when every man
> who knows him must know it to be false?

Mr Bather contended to the cheering from his supporters. On a more serious note, Bather noted that 24 surgeons in the county had strongly supported Mr Clement's candidacy. He emphasised that,

> Throwing aside all professional jealousy (and they are but a
> jealous and waspish generation) [they] are unbounded in their
> admiration of his professional abilities.

And not only the local medical fraternity had recognised Clement's abilities, but his fame had even spread to the continent, with the translation of his 'Observations in Surgery' into French and German. He pointed out that,

> The French are a vain people, and they have translated it, the Germans are a cautious people, and they have translated it. Can higher testimonials be borne to Mr Clement than the united praises of the three greatest nations in Europe?

But he knew that the people voting in the election were not the French or Germans, or even local surgeons, but mostly Tories of the old school, so he finished with the key issue – politics. "When I hear Mr Gore say that no political considerations ought to bias your judgments this day…most cordially do I agree…" said a conciliatory Mr Bather. "I told Mr Clement that if I, a stiff-necked and a hard-hearted Tory, were to throw overboard my politics, I should expect like conduct from him. If we left our politics at the gate, he should not bring them into the house. Mr Clement pledged himself to forget his politics when they interfered with his duties in this Infirmary. We can, God wot [knows], have politics and political contests enough, without disfiguring our charities with them. Mr Clement, it is true, has taken upon himself, besides the care of our frail bodies, rather a large share of the political cares of this unhappy nation. But is there not room enough at our elections, will there not be room enough at our new Corporation contests for the explosion of all our political bitterness, without introducing them into this house of mercy?" he asked in conclusion.

At the end of the speeches an immediate show of hands suggested a considerable majority in favour of William Clement, but when a formal vote, including proxies, was taken the reverse was the case. The figures were – Mr Dickin, 221, Mr Clement, 168. When one considers that the rules only allowed proxies in the case of ladies, one wonders how many wives, mothers and daughters had been leaned on to vote according to the dictate of their male relatives?

The decision provoked outrage amongst many of the readers of the liberal-leaning Shrewsbury Chronicle. One local surgeon accused some of the Trustees of voting 'contrary to their conscience'.[18] Other correspondents were not so measured, one saying that it 'was really very disgraceful to the gentry of our county that party politics should thus warp their charity.' While another went even further, writing that 'through private interest, favouritism and intrigue' a 'nonentity' had been appointed, and the services of such a skilful practitioner had been lost to the hospital.[19]

Clement may have lost the battle of the Infirmary, but it was not long after that event that he won the first of many political battles. The same autumn of 1835, preparations were being made for the first borough elections under the new Municipal Corporations Act. This involved the dissolution of the old Corporation and the election of a complete set of new councillors with a much-increased electorate.

Needless to say, the Municipal Corporations Act, which would sweep away the old Corporations and replace them with councils elected on a wider franchise, was bitterly opposed by the Tory majority.[20] On the other hand, when the Act was struggling to get through the House of Lords, over 500 Freemen and other inhabitants of the town earnestly petitioned Parliament to pass the measure.[21]

The Act received the royal assent in September 1835, and the urgent process of registering all those entitled to vote was started. The first election of town councillors was fixed for Boxing Day 1835, so that the new Council would be able to start on January 1st 1836. William Hazledine stood as a Liberal candidate for Castle Ward (Within), but failed by four votes to be elected, although overall the Liberals triumphed by a majority of four.[22] The Shrewsbury

Chronicle reported many alleged cases of electoral fraud, and
overall that,

> The Liberals were triumphant wherever there was a numerous
> constituency and the Tories only where a contracted number
> gave them ready means of intimidation. The Liberals have
> chiefly very large majorities; the Tories crept in, in three cases,
> by one vote.

In this sort of poisonous atmosphere, the Liberals were in no mood
for compromise with regard to the position of mayor. Robert Burton
of Longner Hall, the Tory incumbent, who was only part way
through his period of office, was ousted.[23] The Liberals appointed
all ten aldermen from among their ranks, among whom was William
Hazledine, who was invited to become Mayor after the elder William
Clement had declined. Despite these inauspicious beginnings, it is
recorded that Hazledine 'passed through his mayoral year with
marked honour'.[24] He presented a red mayoral robe trimmed with
ermine to the new council, which he first used himself (Figure 1).

Such activities did not keep Hazledine from his work for long,
or from looking forward. One of his last public appearances a short
while before his death was at the committee of the Shrewsbury
Railway Company, 'where he expressed a hearty wish that his life
might be spared to see this great project carried into execution.'[25]
Perhaps his best epitaph is the following.

> A very short time before he was confined to bed by his last
> illness, a nobleman, equally distinguished by his literary and
> legal talents...arrived in the town at a little before seven in the
> morning, and inquired at the Lion [Hotel] if Mr Hazledine was
> likely to be up? "Oh, yes," was the reply. "He passed here an
> hour and a half ago, on his way to the foundry." "I regret that,"
> said his lordship, "for I wanted a few minutes' conversation with

him, which I cannot now have. But tell him from me, that Lord — [the newspaper did not divulge his name] inquired after him. My belief is," added his lordship, "that William Hazledine is the first [foremost] practical man in Europe."[26]

Endnotes

1 Sale Catalogue, SA 901/1.
2 Hulbert 1837, p.308, footnote; Hulbert went on, 'Mr Hazledine is also proprietor of a great portion of Coleham; many houses of consequence, and other premises in this town; his property in various parts of the county, and out of it, is beyond my description; and shares in public companies, etc almost immense'.
3 Henry Pidgeon, *Salopian Annals*, Vol. IV, 1826, p.37, SA 6001/3056.
4 SA 6001/3058.
5 SA 6001/134.
6 SC 22.9.1826.
7 SC 6.11.1840.
8 SJ 23.3.1831.
9 SC 6.5.1814; Benyon was not elected, but later went on to represent Stafford from 1818–26.
10 SJ 23.3.1831.
11 SC 26.10.1832.
12 A Pattison, *The Darwins of Shrewsbury*, History Press, 2009.
13 SC 6.2.1835.
14 William Cowper, *The Task, Book 4.*
15 SC 2.9.1870.
16 SC 28.8.1835.
17 SC, 25.9.1835 – all subsequent information about the meeting is from the same source.
18 Christopher Llewellyn, SC 2.10.1835.
19 SC 9.10.1835.
20 SC 25.6.1835.
21 SC 6.9.1835.
22 SC 1.1.1836 – further details from this source.
23 Robert Burton was later elected as Mayor in 1843 for a full term.
24 *Byegones*, Jan 6th 1875, p.173, SA C05.
25 SC 6.11.1840.
26 SC 30.10.1840.

Chapter 12

Postscript

WILLIAM HAZLEDINE left most of his property to his three surviving children, Mary, John and Anne. As for Coleham Foundry and his personal effects, one of the stipulations of his will was that these should not be sold till a year after his death. Quite why is not clear – perhaps he was hoping that by not rushing the process a buyer could be found to continue the work of the Foundry. So it was that in November of 1841 the family put the contents of Dogpole House, the Foundry and associated businesses, and 51 houses, plots of land etc. up for sale.[1] It appears that no buyer was found for the Foundry and it remained in the family, being managed by William Stuttle junior until it was taken over by William Lowcock in 1878.[2]

All three of William Hazledine's children were able to live lives of comfort and elegance because of the wealth they had inherited. Mary and Ann married well, the former to a 'gentleman'; the latter's husband was an attorney (solicitor). John (1793–1870), married his cousin Rhoda Brayne in 1827, and Hazledine senior built a large house in Coleham as a home for his son, which he named Moreton Villa, after Moreton Forge where he grew up. It appears that the original plan was that John Hazledine would follow his father into the iron trade. However, around 1830 the decision was made that he was not suited to this line of work, but that he would run his father's coal business instead.

Like his father, John Hazledine was active in local politics and his affiliation to the Liberal party was the same as his father. He, though, was of a very different character, being described as of a 'mild conciliatory nature'. Both father and son stood as Liberal candidates for the first election to the town council on Boxing Day 1835. John was a candidate for the constituency then known quaintly as 'Stone Ward (Without)', i.e. outside the walls. John Hazledine was one of the Liberals elected, coming top of the poll in his ward, and he retained his seat on the Council until his death, nearly 35 years later. He was elected Mayor for 1855/6 (Figure 44), and was also a magistrate, his main task being to officiate at the weekly 'police court', where those who had been arrested for minor offences, such as drunkenness, disturbing the peace, vagrancy and soliciting were quickly dealt with. John Hazledine seems to have fulfilled this role with firmness, but as much humanity as the law allowed. In 1864 he moved from Moreton Villa to the Woodlands, a new mansion he built opposite the Column.

John's elder son William had learning disabilities, but the younger son, also John (1844–91), had a legal career. After Rugby School he became a barrister and eventually moved to north Wales, where he was a law officer. After his early death, his wife married the owner of Boreatton Park, so the family grew up back in Shropshire, where there are still descendants, though the Hazledine name itself has died out.

So too did knowledge of William Hazledine and his achievements. The Tory-supporting Salopian Journal did not even publish an obituary, such was the antagonism that some Tories felt towards this upstart Liberal who had ousted their mayor just a few years before. The bust that he himself had commissioned was set up as directed in St Chad's, but its position behind a pillar in a dark corner was criticised by sculptor Sir Francis Chantrey (Figure 4).[3] Hazledine's diary, kept in meticulous detail year by year, appears to have been destroyed or lost, and so there are almost no personal letters and memorabilia.

Hazledine's world of cast-iron bridges, canals and stage coaches became obsolete with the coming of the railways and the development of new steelmaking processes in the decades after his death. Victorian engineers such as Stephenson and Brunel became household names, whereas the likes of Thomas Telford and William Hazledine were largely forgotten. What lists there were of Hazledine's works were inaccurate and incomplete, and non-specialists could not understand the technical originality and engineering achievement of these works. Perhaps a low point was the publication of the new edition of The Dictionary of National Biography in 2004 when Hazledine's name was spelled wrongly and he was given the wrong place of birth. Thomas Telford has now been largely rehabilitated, even to the extent of having a town named after him. For Hazledine, however, the process has just begun. No doubt there will be many more discoveries of the extent of his genius.

Endnotes

1   SA 901/1.
2   B Trinder, Beyond the Bridges, Phillimore, 2006, p.85.
3   SC 15.1.1841.

William Hazledine Timeline

	National/International events	Industrialisation	William Hazledine
1763	Treaty of Paris	Watt starts work on his engine	Born Shawbury, April 6th
1764			
1765		Watt invents steam engine with separate condenser	
1766	Pitt (Earl of Chatham) Prime Minister		
1767		Wright paints 'Experiment on a bird in an air pump'	Family moves to Moreton Forge
1768		Arkwright invents water-powered spinning machine	
1769		Watt patents steam engine	
1770	Increasing tension in America		
	Cook discovers Australia		
1771			
1772		James Brindley dies	
1773	'Boston tea party'		
1774	American declaration of independence	John Wilkinson patents cannon boring machine	
		Joseph Priestley discovers oxygen	
1775	American War of Independence starts	Boulton and Watt go into partnership	
1776			
1777	British lose battles in America		
1778	France and Holland join America		Begins apprenticeship to uncle, May 11th
	William Pitt dies (May 11th)		
1779	Spain joins the war	Samuel Crompton invents the spinning mule	

	National/International events	Industrialisation	William Hazledine
1780	Spanish navy defeated at Cape St Vincent		Does work at Upton Forge
	Gordon riots		
1781	Cornwallis surrenders in America	Rapid growth of cotton industry with new machines	Does work in South Wales
			The Iron Bridge opened (1st Jan)
1782	Preliminary end of American war	Watt invents double-acting rotary steam engine.	
		Josiah Wedgwood first to install steam engine in a factory	
1783	Treaty of Versailles – American independence	Henry Cort's first patent for producing iron by 'puddling'	
	William Pitt becomes Prime Minister	Arkwright first to install steam engine in cotton mill	
1784			
1785	First bill for parliamentary reform rejected	Edmund Cartwright invents the power loom	Ends apprenticeship, sets up as millwright
			? in Wyle Cop
1786		Economic boom begins with rapid industrialisation	
1787		John Wilkinson launches first iron boat	Thomas Telford moves to Shrewsbury
			? Iron foundry partnership with Robert Webster
1788	George III's first bout of insanity	Andrew Meikle invents threshing machine	Whitesmith business in Wyle Cop
1789	Outbreak of French Revolution	Abraham Darby III dies	Leases Pitchford Forge
			Builds first water mill in Staffordshire

	National/International events	Industrialisation	William Hazledine
1790		Crompton's mule harnessed to water power	John Simpson moves to Shrewsbury
		First steam rolling mill	Water mill in Nantwich
			Marries Eleanor Brayne (Jan); Mary born
1791	Birmingham riots against French Revolution	India rubber cloth patented	
1792	Tom Paine's Rights of Man published	Coal gas first used for lighting	Land drainage work in Wales
		John Smeaton dies	First recorded windmill design
			Ironwork for St Chad's churchyard
1793	War begins with France		Begins to build Coleham Foundry
	Economic depression		John born
1794	Habeas Corpus Act suspended	John Wilkinson patent for cupola for making cast iron	Vyrnwy Aqueduct (with Simpson)
	Howe defeats French fleet		Broadstone water corn mill; Fitz bone mill
			Elizabeth born
1795	Speenhamland poor relief system starts	Joseph Bramah invents hydraulic press	(Approx) Hawkstone windmill
	Hunger and high prices		
1796	Spain enters the war against Britain	Telford's Longdon-on-Tern Aqueduct	First mine lease at Plas Kynaston
	Jenner proves vaccination works	Telford's Buildwas Bridge	Longnor water corn mill rebuilt
1797	French landing and defeat in Wales	Shrewsbury Canal opens	Ironwork for Ditherington Flaxmill
	Spanish fleet defeated at Battle of Cape St Vincent		Ann born
1798	Irish Rebellion	Boulton-Watt rotary engine applied to spinning mule	Welsh lime works extended
	Nelson defeats French at Battle of the Nile		Telford's On Mills published

	National/International events	Industrialisation	William Hazledine
1799	Income tax introduced	Royal Institution founded	Leases whole Plas Kynaston estate
			Eleanor born (dies 1800)
1800	Poor harvests, high prices	Richard Trevithick – high pressure steam engine	(Approx) takes out lease on Upton Forge
	Malta captured	Henry Maudslay – precision screw-cutting lathe	Leases & converts Longnor Forge to paper
1801	Pitt resigns; another bad harvest	Richard Trevithick's steam carriage	Chirk Aqueduct opens
	First census; union of Britain and Ireland		Fanny born; Trentham Windmill
1802	Peace of Amiens – some economic recovery	Telford begins road building in Scotland	Abbey Foregate property; Buys and sells
	First Radical MPs elected	Billingsley Mines	
1803	French war restarts – invasion threatened	John Dalton introduces atomic theory	Queenbatch water corn mill built
	Mass Volunteer Movement	First wholly metal power loom	(Approx) Plas Kynaston foundry opens
		William Reynolds (ironmaster) dies	
1804	Pitt again Prime Minister; Spain declares war	Trevithick's steam locomotive for Penydafren Ironworks	Coleham foundry damaged by fire
			Welshpool Town Hall (with Simpson)
			Buys Jones Mansion (Wyle Cop)
1805	Victory at Trafalgar; defeat at Austerlitz		Pontcysyllte Aqueduct opened
1806	Deaths of Pitt and Fox	Gaslight installed in Lancashire cotton mill	
	'Continental system' causes economic hardship		
1807	Tories back in power	Geological Society of London founded	
	Slave trade abolished in British Empire		

	National/International events	Industrialisation	William Hazledine
1808	Peninsular War begins	John 'Iron-Mad' Wilkinson dies	
	Manchester weavers' strike		
1809	Defeat at Corunna – Wellington wins victories	Humphry Davy invents arc lamp	Severn Towpath engineer
		Charles Darwin born	Caynton Mills partnership dissolved
1810	Wellington wins victories in Spain		Relinquishes Pitchford Forge
			John Hazledine (brother) dies
1811	Prince Regent takes over permanently		Meole Brace Bridge
	Severe financial crisis; Luddite riots		
1812	Percival assassinated – Liverpool takes over		Long Mill and Cantlop Bridges
	Severe food shortages – more riots		Bonar Bridge
	Napoleon defeated at Moscow		
1813	Wellington invades France	Polarisation of light first described	
	Napoleon defeated at Leipzig		
1814	Napoleon abdicates	Stephenson builds first steam locomotive	Craigellachie Bridge
	Exceptional cold due to volcanic ash		? Rebuilds Hogstow water corn mill
1815	Congress of Vienna; Waterloo; Corn Laws	Davy's miners' safety lamp invented	John Simpson dies
1816	Economic depression and unemployment		Waterloo Bridge – Bettws-y-Coed
	Spa Fields riots – call for parliamentary reform		
1817	Widespread unrest; suspension of Habeas Corpus		Lease on Calcutt's ironworks
	Attempt to assassinate Prince Regent		
	Princess Charlotte dies		

	National/International events	Industrialisation	William Hazledine
1818	Habeas Corpus restored	Institute of Civil Engineers formed	Cound Bridge
		First iron ship built on the Clyde	Dolforgan Bridge, Kerry
1819	'Peterloo' massacre; large tax rises	Steamship 'Savannah' crosses the Atlantic	Work begins on Menai Bridge
	First factory act		
1820	Death of George III – George IV crowned	First iron steamship launched	Kington Tramway
	Cato Street conspiracy – hopes of moderate reform dashed	Samuel Brown's suspension bridge at Berwick-on-Tweed	Esk Bridge, near Carlisle
			Liverpool Docks swing bridges
1821	Agricultural distress	John Rennie dies	Fanny Hazledine dies
1822	Agricultural distress worsens		Work starts on links for Menai and
	Foreign Secretary Castlereagh commits suicide		Conway Bridges
		Dublin Custom House roof	
1823	Prison and criminal reform (Peel)	Chlorine liquefied (Faraday); calculator (Babbage)	Severe floods at Upton Forge
	First Mechanics Institute	waterproof fabric (Macintosh)	Plas Kynaston lease given up
			Elizabeth Austin (nee Hazledine) dies
1824	Loosening of anti-trade union laws	Portland cement patented	More floods at Upton Forge
	Economy overheats		Eaton Hall Bridge
1825	Commercial and financial crisis	Stockton to Darlington railway opens	Links for Menai and Conway finished
	Rothschild saves Bank of England	Benzene isolated (Faraday) and electromagnet invented	Helps finance lowering of Castle Street
			Gives up Longnor Paper Mill

	National/International events	Industrialisation	William Hazledine
1826	Many bankruptcies; weavers' riots	Royal Zoological Society founded	Menai and Conway Bridges opened
			Serious accident; Eleanor Hazledine dies
			Mythe Bridge (Tewkesbury); Boraton
			Bridge (Shropshire)
			Laira Bridge (Plymouth) erection started
1827	Lord Liverpool resigns	First friction matches	Laira Bridge finished – William Stuttle dies
			(October) Cleveland Bridge (Bath)
1828	Wellington Prime Minister; Corn Laws loosened		Holt Fleet Bridge (near Worcester)
	Dissenters obtain civil liberties		Buys the Armoury
1829	Catholic Emancipation debates; Metropolitan Police Act		Pulls down and redevelops Jones Mansion
1830	George IV dies – William IV succeeds	Opening of Liverpool and Manchester railway –	First ironwork for Marlow Bridge
	Agitation for Parliamentary reform –	William Huskisson killed	Buys Coleham Brewery; Salop Infirmary fence work
	Wellington replaced by Grey (Whig)		
1831	Rural (Swing) riots; riots over 1st rejection of Reform Bill	Darwin begins Beagle voyage	Contention over Marlow Bridge
		Faraday refines electro-magnetic induction	Swing bridges for London Docks
1832	Reform Bill passed	Major cholera epidemic	Marlow Bridge opens
			Meets Duchess of Kent and Princess Victoria
			Gives up lease on Calcutt's
			Elected Freeman of Shrewsbury

	National/International events	Industrialisation	William Hazledine
1833	Abolition of slavery in the Empire	Brunel's Great Western Railway begun	Remarries – Elizabeth Jane Dixon
	Factory inspection begun	Richard Trevithick dies	
1834	Poor Law amendment act	Thomas Telford dies (Sept 2nd)	Stretton Aqueduct
	Tolpuddle martyrs; Parliament damaged by fire		
1835	Municipal Corporations Act	Institute of British Architects founded	Shrewsbury Corporation abolished – bitter local election battle
1836	Chartist movement starts	Screw propeller invented	(Jan 1st) Becomes Lord Mayor, Tory ousted
1837	William IV dies – Victoria succeeds	Electric telegraph invented; Euston Station opened	Properties in Swan Hill
	Registration of births, marriages & deaths	British Museum opens	
	Severe commercial & financial crisis starts		
1838	Chartist agitation; Anti-Corn Law League	Regular steamship services to America begin	Helps to found Shrewsbury Racecourse
			Dogpole House museum
1839	County Police Act; Chartist riots	Photography and true bicycle invented	
1840	Marriage of Victoria and Albert; Penny Post	Incandescent light invented	Dies, October 26th – buried October 31st
1841			Sale of Dogpole House, Coleham Foundry

Index

By the same author

On Severn Shore - the story of the Drill Hall, Coleham, Shrewsbury,
Barnabas Community Church, Shrewsbury, 2004,
ISBN 978-1-904726-12-8

The Darwins of Shrewsbury,
History Press, 2009,
ISBN 978-0-75244867-1